Praise for Race in the Global Era

"Clarence Lusane's crisp and lucid essays are always ahead of the curve. He powerfully demonstrates the limits of nation-bound thinking and provides fresh insights into the politics of racism in the age of multinational capital. *Race in the Global Era* not only deserves the widest possible readership, but it ought to be translated into at least fifty languages."

—Robin D.G. Kelley, author of *Yo' Mama's DisFunktional!:*
Fighting the Culture Wars in Urban America

"There has been much commentary about the border less future, but little of it has the depth, clarity, and alacrity of Lusane's Race in the Global Era. Lusane takes conventional analysis and pushes its limits, using both his tools as a scholar and his passion as an activist to inform his arguments."

—Julianne Malveaux, author of *Sex, Lies, and Stereotypes:*
Perspectives of a Mad Economist

"Clarence Lusane is one of America's most thoughtful and critical thinkers on issues of race, class, and power."

—Manning Marable, author of *Black Liberation in*
Conservative America

"At a time when many black leaders and intellectuals are focusing narrowly on the plight of the black male, Clarence Lusane is to be commended for his sensitivity to the broader issue of gender, and the political concerns and contributions of black feminists."

—Barbara Ransby, activist and historian, Univ. of Illinois

CLARENCE LUSANE is an author, activist, scholar, lecturer, and free-lance journalist in Washington, D.C. For more than 25 years, he has been active in national black politics, U.S. foreign policy, and on domestic policy issues. Lusane has traveled to and lectured in Haiti, Panama, South Korea, East Germany, Zimbabwe, Cuba, Mexico, Jamaica, and England. Lusane also writes numerous articles for the *Black Scholar, Crossroads,* and *Z Magazine.*

RACE IN THE GLOBAL ERA

African Americans at the Millennium

CLARENCE LUSANE

Foreword by Julianne Malveaux

SOUTH END PRESS, Boston, MA

Library of Congress Cataloging-in-Publication Data
Race in the Global Era: African Americans at the Millennium/ by
Clarence Lusane.
   p. cm.
Includes bibliographical references and index.
ISBN 0-89608-573-2 (paper).—ISBN 0-89608-574-0 (cloth)
   1. United States—Race relations. 2. Racism—Political aspects—United States. 3. Afro-Americans—Politics and government.
4. Afro-Americans—Social conditions—1975– 5. Afro-Americans in
mass media. I. Title.
   E185.615.l93 1997
   305.896'073—dc21   97-31302
                                                              CIP

South End Press, 116 Saint Botolph Street, Boston, MA 02115
   02 01 00 99 98 97   1 2 3 4 5 6 7

Contents

Acknowledgments

I wish I could blame all my friends for my mistakes and misjudgments in this book and take credit for any insights, but alas the reverse is closer to the truth. No book emerges solely from the mind of one individual and, therefore, credit must always be given to the wide array of friends, acquaintances, associates, enemies, strangers, family, and "others" who contribute in countless ways to what eventually ends up on a bookshelf.

This list is, of course, desperately incomplete. Among the fabulous and brilliant people, *inter alia*, whose intellectual and political fingerprints are on this present work are Nikol G. Alexander, Karen Bass, Jean Carey Bond, Chris Booker, Sylvia Castillo, James Early, Amir el-Islam, Charles Green, Zahra Hamarani, Daryl Harris, Mark Harrison, Geoffrey Jacques, Keith Jennings, Charles Jones, Peniel Joseph, Robin D.G. Kelley, Melvin Lewis, Manning Marable, Rowena Martineau, Cheryl Mayia, Leith Mullings, Ridan Nytagodien, Basil Patterson, Barbara Ransby, Nathalie Richardson, Selina Roberts, Jocelyn Sargent, Karin Stanford, James Steele, Curtis Stokes, and Makani Themba. Through conversations, resources, and other means, they helped to stimulate and massage my thoughts on the many issues discussed in this book.

Over the last few years, I have had the great pleasure and honor to be associated with a number of African American research institutions that have provided me with immense material and non-material support including the Du Bois Bunche Center for Public Policy (Medgar Evers College), Institute for Research in African American Studies (Columbia University), Center for Drug Abuse Research (Howard University), and Ralph J. Bunche International Affairs Center (Howard University).

I also want to thank the Howard University faculty and students, who worked on the Million Man March survey including Lorenzo Morris, Joseph P. McCormick and Maurice Carney among others.

My thanks and appreciation to *The Progressive* magazine's Black Voices Media Project, and *Covert Action Quarterly* magazine who have generously published my work over the years and in which some of these essays have appeared in other forms.

Dionne Brooks, my editor, and South End Press have, as usual, been absolutely indispensable and disciplined in pushing this project forward.

Foreword

By Julianne Malveaux

Ever since President William Jefferson Clinton, biting at his lower lip, eyes misting over, suggested a race dialogue, there has been much race entertainment in the policy arena. Should the U.S. Congress apologize for slavery? An apology without remediation is an empty genuflection for our nation's terribly flawed past. Should O.J. Simpson's creditors be able to cash in and melt down his Heisman trophy? Whether we care or not, the O.J. question will get as much media attention as the more substantive one about slavery.

Myriad things get thrown into the mix of our race talk, whether it is analysis or entertainment. Talk of Ebonics may be covert talk about assimilation versus cultural integrity. Talk of welfare reform may be the real talk about family values. Whose families do we value, after all, those of corporate executives on the federal dole or those of mothers with two or more children who are trying to go back to school? How affirmative is our action? California's Proposition 209 passed, but millions of Californians, especially in cities like San Francisco and Los Angeles, say they prefer diversity to the narrow white occasion that 209 will produce. Is it an affirmative action to hanker for a segregated past? Or is it certainty that whenever there is economic insecurity whites will prevail? Is there something politically incorrect, even unpalatable, about these questions? Do they make you squirm? Unless we are uneasy, race talk becomes the talk of shadows and mirrors, of skewed stereotypes and misplaced emotion.

Where does race talk fit in a global future? Is it inevitable that national economies meld into an international market? The relationships that various populations have with a global economy has yet to be determined. There has been much commentary about the borderless future, but little of it has the depth, clarity, and alacrity of Clarence Lusane's *Race in the Global Era*. Lusane takes conventional analysis and pushes its limits, using both his tools as a scholar and his passion as an activist to inform his arguments. He weaves race talk, race entertainment, and race analysis into a sociopolitical framework that is all the more compelling for its unwillingness to cleave to popular clichés. This is race talk that is unexpectedly exciting, challenging, and uncharted. Lusane is all the more provocative because he looks at a set of issues through a kaleidoscope that has race, but not only race, as a critical lens. Unlike many of his peers, Lusane tackles class, gender, and nationalism as other factors in the determinants of an African American future in a global society.

Both frontally and subtly, Lusane addresses the role that the media plays in exporting a certain interpretation of "blackness" as an identifiable feature of U.S. culture. Why do people in Japan, Thailand, and Italy know Michael Jackson, Michael Jordan, and O.J. Simpson? Does the fact that these celebrities are all males say anything about the conclusions an international community might reach about African Americans? Does the fact that these men are tied with golden handcuffs to corporations that magnify their images raise any contradiction for those millions of minimum and sub-minimum wage workers who mortgage their futures to buy jeans, sneakers, and anything else that can be connected to a smiling, affable, African American face? Indeed, the face need not smile. Even the snarling postures of gangsta rappers are exportable for international entertainment. The "cool pose" of young black men whose poignant, painful poetry speaks to a chilling urban reality is repackaged as beat-driven boogie rhythm, angry, assaultive, misogynistic lyrics notwithstanding.

There is acceptance for the smiling black spokesperson, but less for the competitive business executive, and even less for those African Americans critical of the status quo. Lusane expertly captures the mixed acceptance of African American images, and the ways that all Americans interpret their space in a global society.

The ranks of race commentators are bloated with drive-by assessment and add-water-and-stir cogitation. Lusane distinguishes himself, though, with pointed, penetrating explorations, distinctive observations, and a comprehensive review of the state of race in a global era. Whether he is writing about the Million Man March, gangsta rap, the CIA-Contra drug connection, Ebonics, or the links between capitalism, race, and violence, Lusane's thinking is fresh and enlightened. This voice is rich, layered, and has a resonance that is powerful, incisive, and caring, unlike any other on the national scene. *Race in the Global Era* takes us past conventional 20th-century analysis and provides us with a prism through which we can view the challenges that African Americans, and the nation, face in the new millennium.

Julianne Malveaux
Washington, DC
September 1997

To all the children in my life

Introduction

As the countdown to the next millennium nears, we find ourselves in amazing times. Products and capabilities, such as cellular phones, video conferencing, and the Internet, that were barely imagined only a few years ago, if at all, have become part of our daily lives. The demise of the Cold War has given way to a new, uncharted political period latent with great opportunities and immense dangers. Virtually every point on the globe is instantly accessible from nearly every other point. Social, economic, cultural, and geographical barriers have fallen as new technologies bridge heretofore alienated relationships and connect groups from every corner of the earth. For the first time in history, as writer William Greider notes, "One World" is more than a metaphor.

As the year 2000 draws near, the entire globe waits in anticipation of a new century with the hope that the destruction and social devastation of the old will be addressed and eradicated. Even as that hope burns bright, regional and intranational conflicts abound, amassing waves of small wars and civil strife that are unrestrained even when international intervention occurs.

As the changes brought by new technologies and expanding global ties occur more rapidly than we can often comprehend, social relations are also being reconfigured. Race, gender, and class issues intersect and remold each other, constantly creating new relations that challenge all previous notions. Across the globe, the tension between racial groups appears to be growing. In post-Communist Europe, old enemies come together in NATO even as new civil strife brought by the rise of fascist and racist groups ripples through both the East and West. In England, police brutality and harassment and the rise of racially charged murders have marked the 1990s. Some British writers have joined the new eugenics movement and published so-called scholarly works that "scientifically" explain the inferiority of blacks and other people of color. In France, as elsewhere in the West, racial antagonism manifests itself in attacks on immigrants from Africa, Asia, and the Middle East. The Pasqua laws, passed in the early 1990s, gave French police extensive powers to stop, question, and detain those they perceived to be potential undocumented aliens. In post-Apartheid South Africa, black leadership struggles to bring justice and equality to a rigid system of economic division that has carried over from the Apartheid days. In post-dictatorship Latin America, new democracies are searching for ways of inclusion for all sectors of society even as a resurgent black consciousness movement grows in the region. From Uruguay and Brazil to Argentina and Peru, Afro-Latinos are organizing and mobilizing. In all these circumstances, race relations intersect with class, nationality, gender, ethnic, and religious issues, creating a complex arrangement of pressures and sources of conflicts.

In the United States, race relations and how they are conceived are in turmoil. A range of incidents in the 1990s alone have brought the deteriorating state of U.S. race relations to the public consciousness with the force of a lightening bolt. From the public responses to the O.J. Simpson trials, the Million Man March, black church burnings, street uprisings in Los Angeles, gangsta rap, and accusations such as Susan Smith's and others against the ghosts of black men to the public policy initiatives of Republicans and Democrats to race-tinged, citizen-driven ballot initiatives to the regular and regulated day-to-day racial disparities that exist, these are the worst of times.

The perception gap between people of color and whites—colored people are from Venus, white people are from Mars—regarding the significance of race expands as interpretations of the events and circumstances discussed above by academics, journalists, and politicians make concessions to a racial paradigm that leaves little room for an honest appraisal of the social dynamics of race in a postindustrial, capitalist society. Ideological conservatives blame liberals, cultural predispositions, and genetic makeup. Liberals, many of whom hold the same assumptions as conservatives, simply retreat and through their silence sanction the assaults, embrace the consequences, and render ideological differences between the two irrelevant.

It is one theme of this book that a change in how whites think about race, in general, and African Americans, in particular, from the early post-civil rights period to the present has occurred. This change has taken place on a global scale from South Africa to Brazil to England. It can be called, in a term used by political scientists, a mass "paradigm shift" on the issue of race—that is, a fundamental overthrow of the way race has been conceived since the heyday of the civil rights and Black Power eras. In the second half of the 20th century, the elimination of state-sanctioned legal racial segregation led to the spread of the ideology of color blindness, which is the central theme underpinning the myth of racial democracy.

A combination of factors have contributed to these shifts, including permanent transformation in the economic life of millions of whites, the rise of conservative political and religious demagogues, a pervasive media propagation of race that denies the existence of racism, and the influence of an intelligentsia—under the cover of "objective" and "nonpartisan" research—that unabashedly promotes racist theories, public policies, and stereotypes. Most critically, change has been driven by global political, economic, and cultural forces that generally are unacknowledged and unexplored. It has become impossible to understand contemporary race relations within a simple narrow national framework.

A State of Urgency

For our purposes, the most important discussion is the debate within the black community regarding the nature and causes of the crisis facing African Americans, and pathways toward solutions. From across the black political spectrum, there seems to be agreement that much of what can be called black life is in a desperate state. The essays in this book explore manifestations of contemporary racial politics or, more precisely, ways in which race crisscrosses and unites the span of society.

Race is only one of many prisms through which to analyze the political and social life of African Americans, and not necessarily always the most determinate one. In the United States (and elsewhere), it is a critical prism and one in which there has been insufficient interrogation of its contemporary dynamics. While issues of race are a daily source of news and entertainment, race is generally divorced from the more radioactive concern of racism, which is randomly lumped with other forms of discrimination and oppression. Racism is reduced to a relic of the past that only occasionally bursts onto the nation's conscious in the form of Klansman David Duke, rogue cop Mark Fuhrman, or, in a creative and distorted theoretical twist, through the newly created vehicle of the African-American racist.

Interrogation of the dominate U.S. racial paradigm is critical because it is exported to the rest of the world. An interactive dynamic exists at the nation-state level, where national leaders from England, Germany, France, and even South Africa have consulted with U.S. government and nongovernment leaders on how to handle racial issues. A similar interaction has occurred between community-based organizations in the United States and abroad. The interaction has been primarily in one direction. While the world has given rapt attention to the O.J. Simpson trials, the Million Man March, and the stories regarding CIA involvement in cocaine smuggling, few in the United States have given equal attention to issues of race in other nations.

Candid analyses of race and racism are urgently needed as the nation and world go through profound and unprecedented transformations. These changes are not necessarily racial or ethnic, but because they encounter societies as they are currently constructed, race and ethnicity filters their impact.

The Black Paradoxical Moment

Black America meets these changes at a crucial, if not decisive, moment in its history. Without question, there is a spirit of resistance that exists in the black community, even in the face of generally overwhelming and unrelenting odds. Yet there are few honest observers who would characterize the overall picture facing African Americans in this era as rosy and hopeful. Much of the consternation in the black community can be seen in these frustrating paradoxes:

- While black women have made great strides in countless fields—even as they continue to carry the disproportionate, multiple burdens and responsibilities of childrearing, homemaking, and socialization—they have become the demons of choice for New Democrat liberals, old-line conservatives, and prominent black nationalists.

- While the political growth of black elected officials has been remarkable—from less than 300 in 1965 to over 8,500 in 1995—African Americans have perhaps less public policy influence than at any point in the last four decades.

- While African Americans have achieved substantial positioning and influence at the very highest echelons of the Democratic Party—to the point where the party of old-time segregationists such as Lester Maddox and George Wallace selected the late Ron Brown, an African American, as chairperson—the Democratic Party under Bill Clinton has become more and more reactionary with each political season.

- While the black community has experienced the largest growth of a black middle class in U.S. history—estimated to be 40 percent by some analysts—the even larger growth of the black poor has proceeded unabated.

- While black intellectuals have achieved more popularity, have more resources at their disposal—and more access to the media than they have ever had—and due to white benefactors, funders, and supporters, they are also wealthier than ever—they exhibit a profound inability to produce socially and politically useful and accessible works.

- While black men are unrivaled in appreciation for their entertainment and athletic abilities—to the point where Michael Jackson and Michael Jordan are paid millions unrelated to their best-known skills to merely associate their name and likeness with a wide variety of commodities—the generalized view of black men as predatory, criminal, and in need of containment reflects itself in public policies whose impact (if not purpose) is to fill the jails and prisons of the nation in unprecedented numbers.

- While black unemployment figures rise—accompanied by the unprecedented social phenomena of tens of thousands of African Americans in their twenties and thirties never having had a full-time job—the demand for the elimination of affirmative action and other programs that economically benefit African Americans grows shriller.

- While progressive multinational, multiracial, multigender coalitions have historically been the vehicle of progress for black America—from the NAACP to the Mississippi Freedom Democratic Party, from Martin Luther King's "Coalition of Conscience" to the Children's Defense Fund and the National Rainbow Coalition—the rise of a conservative neonationalist movement in the black community, most dramatically manifested in the Million Man March, has defined much of mass black politics in the 1990s.

- While we live in an age where nearly unlimited information is available almost instantaneously—via the Internet, CD-ROMs, and dozens of 24-hour news programs—misinformation about black life, from perceptions about the actual number of African Americans in the United States to stereotypical views of blacks in terms of intelligence, welfare, and crime, is at an all-time high.

These paradoxes of black life give rise to some important strategic questions. Why has the growth in black elected and appointed officials not resulted in greater public policy favors for the African-American community? Why does it appear that the black wealthy have abandoned the black poor? Why have popular black academic intellectuals with so many resources produced so little of use to the black community and had so little impact? Why does traditional black leadership continue to give unquestioned loyalty and support to the Democratic Party even though the party has abandoned all pretense to a program of progressive racial inclusion? While it is wrong to indict all black leaders, intellectuals, elected officials, and other sectors of black life, many African Americans most in need feel a complete abandonment by the black elite despite the committed efforts of some.

Racism and the Rise of White Conservatism

Racism, whether unvarnished or polished, continues to be a central theme in U.S. social, economic, political, and cultural life. It was absolutely central to the assumption of conservative power in recent years, albeit with a new urgency and intensity. As the gross disproportionalities that African Americans suffer in health, criminal justice, education, and other areas became even more pronounced, implicit and often explicit code-wording strategies successfully launched many of the Republicans into power. Under the conservative leadership of Newt Gingrich, Rush Limbaugh, Bob Dole, Pat Buchanan, and Ralph Reed, these strategies have become open, naked assaults unconstrained by political or moral considerations on communities of color. Already, in the Gingrich era, Republicans brazenly call for female chain gangs and defend slavery. Although some of these extremists have been repudiated by conservative spokespersons, years ago they would not have had even the veneer of legitimacy. "States rights," once a rallying cry for opposition by civil rights leaders and liberals, has become the political objective of the 1990s by both parties, with little vocal or active challenge by Democratic black leadership.

Yet, it is on similar terrain that Clinton and the Democratic Leadership Council (DLC) came to power. Formed as a political counterweight to Jesse Jackson's progressive wing of the Democratic Party, Clinton and the DLC (which actually included a number of black members, such as Mike Espy and Bill Gray) adopted a strategy to win back white voters who had defected to the Republican Party in the 1970s and 1980s. This was in lieu of going after the millions of unregistered and unmobilized black, Latino, and even white voters who could have possibly been won to a liberal or even progressive program. In the end, the distinction (and the desire for distinction) between Ronald Reagan's Republicans and Clinton's Democrats disappears.

The "turning back," as scholar Stephen Steinberg frames it, in race policies and politics is not occurring at some random historic moment. The retreat is shaped by and, in turn, is shaping the redefined context in which the United States finds itself at the end of what has been called the "American century." Increased direct corporate authority and influence on public policy and policymakers, political parties, and governmental institutions are eroding even the symbols of democracy. With little real input into the decisions that determine the economic and social state of the nation, massive white frustration and disillusionment takes the form of blaming the traditional scapegoats: African Americans, Latinos, Asians, gays and lesbians, and the poor. This unwarranted blaming is encouraged and reinforced by the media, politicians, religious leaders, and intellectuals in hundreds of ways on a daily basis.

In the face of attacks and disintegration, as a significant degree of chaos reigns in national black politics, the liberal integrationist paradigm as a guide for black political agency has effectively come to an end. That is, the belief in the permanence of the welfare state and the lasting benevolence of the Democratic Party are shattered illusions embraced only as last ditch acts of desperation. Other modes of black politics are faring no better. Black nationalism has never disappeared as a resource in the black community and, at various historical points has dominated black politics. In this era, nationalism is driven by several factors, including the sanctioning and validation of institutional racism by conservative policymakers; racism manifested in every arena of popular culture; the devastating impact of globalized economies on white workers and their racialized response; and just lowdown, unashamed personal racism. Yet contemporary black nationalism demonstrates little capacity to theorize or intervene practically on the complexities of modern black life as it is affected by public policy, global politics, and gender issues. Black conservatives, perhaps even more rabidly than during the Reagan era, continue to be Trojan horses of white supremacy. Their solutions, encapsulated in warped constructions of "self-help" and "color blindness," amount to little more than genocide. Finally, radicalism has been marginalized and remains on the periphery of debate within the black community. Efforts at regroupment have begun, but the road back to becoming a significant influence in black politics appears to be a long one with many potholes.

Strategy Crisis

Despite the differences among black political activists, and with the exception of black conservatives, there is one reoccurring theme on which they unite: the Black Leadership Unity Fallacy (BLUF). Perhaps the most consistent strategic theme has been the notion that liberation, whatever the path, would require black leadership to be united. The repeated failure of attempts at black leadership unity has been attributed to the defects of individuals, attacks by the state and racists, and organizational ineptitude. While all of these have been important factors, at base is the flawed notion that black interests can be aggregated across class, gender, and ideological fault lines. This fallacy has led energies and resources to be spent on efforts that were doomed from the beginning and unable to address the pressing concerns of the most needy and desperate sectors of the black community. Rejection of the BLUF does not imply that consolidation of as broad a base as possible around particular campaigns and issues should not occur. Instead rejection signals a more sober and careful construction of coalitions in the black community built not just on race, but on a panorama of concerns and an ideological clarity on goals, objectives, and methods.

In the period ahead, the BLUF must be replaced with a strategy that constructs platforms and outlets for the silenced voices of black America. Black leadership in all forms, at best, continues to speak on behalf of the black dispossessed rather than with or behind them. The black poor, much ballyhooed in black leadership circles, must have expressive vehicles themselves that articulate and struggle for their interests, unfiltered by considerations external to their interests. The resources, skills, and experiences possessed by other sectors of the black community must be brought to bear on building these institutions and organs of mobilization and organization. As long as black politics is representational rather than organically driven, the crisis of the black poor will deepen, the alienation of the black middle class will continue, and the possibility of abatement of racism will remain illusive.

These essays interrogate black life at the end of an era. They also confront the pivotal and challenging questions facing African Americans as a new century dawns. An uneasiness pervades the black community as we search for answers and even the right questions to raise as a sense of collapse grows. Some seek conservative solutions in a call for a new morality, black self-help, and patriarchy. Others cry for economic development and an accommodation with capitalism. Still others demand more political power in the form of additional elected officials, more registered voters, and more seats at the table of the Democratic or Republican Parties. While all of these demands bear scrutiny and assessment, for the most part, they are besides the point. More fundamental is the recognition of a new historic juncture that completely reconfigures not only questions of race, but of every social, political, economic, and cultural issue facing the nation and, indeed, the international community.

It is not just that the new millennium is upon us. As a practical matter, the transition to the 21st century is mainly symbolic. Those who don't have jobs on December 31, 1999 won't have a job one day later on January 1, 2000. What is significant is that the chronological dawn of the new century coincides with an historic global transformation that now requires different modes of conceptualizing, socializing, and working. It also means the creation of new organizational forms and structures appropriate to the new period. All these concerns mean thinking and acting on old issues in new ways as well as identifying emerging ones. It is of paramount importance to recognize that 21st-century issues cannot be resolved with 20th-century paradigms. In the essays that follow, there are several themes:

Race matters and rules are in transition in profound and fundamental ways. It is insufficient to simply think of race in black-and-white terms. Race in the United States must be placed in a multilayered context in which issues of citizenship, class, gender, culture, and race are mixed into a pool of multiple Asian communities, multiple Latino communities, and significantly, multiple black communities.

There is a need to go beyond the political forms (i.e., political parties) of the 20th century. These forms, Left and Right, besides being undemocratic, are linear, static, and ill-equipped for the rapid adjustments and nuances that will characterize political participation in the future. Building and rebuilding coalitions and virtual political agency have already begun to supplant people's notion about political change.

Think globally, act locally and globally. In effect, the option to act locally has been disappearing rapidly over the last two decades. Now, every purchase is a global act and every business transaction is a step into the international community. Leisure activities are Internetted and hot-linked. Joining the local, national, regional, and global—what has been termed "globalization"—must be the beginning of political activism.

Institutions and economic and political systems critically determine the quality of and opportunities in people's lives. These essays reject all theories that blame African Americans, other people of color, women, and the poor for the multiple crises engulfing their communities. The thesis of personal responsibility is a fig leaf in social science that masks conservative reductionism regarding the role of the state and capital in shaping the life of society and the lives of citizens.

Finally, black intellectual life is also in transition. Contemporary black intellectualism, in general, suffers from a lack of purpose and is profoundly disconnected from the struggles and issues of the black community. The commodification of intellectual life has not escaped African Americans in academia and, indeed, is the inspiration of intellectual work in many cases. This situation is a break from historical patterns where black intellectuals were more involved in the daily concerns of black America. However, a new generation of black theorists have emerged today whose contributions are already challenging conventions and old-school black politics. This new generation, it should be noted, is significantly influenced by theoretically advanced critiques offered by black women thinkers on a broad array of issues, from postmodernism to feminism to social policy to black politics.

The issues addressed in these essays have sparked widespread concern and discourse among the elite and the masses of black people. This nexus is critical since it allows popular debates at a variety of levels. An examination of these issues allows us to overcome elite dismissals of popular issues, while at the same time, operating at a level of interrogation that is more substantive than generally pursued.

Chapter One examines at the impact of contemporary capitalist globalization on communities of color. It connects the current economic crisis of the black community with transformations both at national and global scales. Chapter Two reviews the contradictions between conservative attacks on welfare and welfare recipients and their support for corporate welfare. It analyzes how the collapse of the welfare state, through racializing and gendering the debate, becomes a vehicle for ideological assaults and capital accumulation. Chapter Three investigates racially charged issues, such as retreats on immigration and the elimination of affirmative action, that have occurred in recent years in California. These issues are markers for how the national debate and political struggles over them will take shape. Chapter Four looks at the controversy over Ebonics. It examines the ways the issue intersects with concerns around class, gender, and ideology, and the role of language struggles in this era of globalization. Chapter Five discusses the O.J. Simpson trials and phenomena. This case was a critical watershed in race and gender politics in the United States. Its global meanings and ramifications are also examined. Chapter Six interrogates the life, death, and meaning of the late rapper, Tupac Shakur. The chapter locates Shakur's life in the context of the issues facing black youth, cultural workers, and social theorists. Chapter Seven analyzes the ways in which the media projects the black image on a global scale. Blackness, particularly blackness as codified in the United States, has global signification that has increased dramatically in this period.

Chapter Eight examines the CIA-Contra-cocaine controversy. It argues that these links must be framed by global economic and political policies as well as the media's role in defending state and capital initiatives. Chapter Nine looks at the dominant paradigms on race that have evolved in the United States in the post-civil rights era. Chapter Ten analyzes the racial politics of the New South and contends that while important changes have occurred regarding southern racial politics, the ideology of a new South serves to hide ways in which racial hierarchy is reproduced and must be challenged. Chapter Eleven looks at the political significance and role of Nation of Islam leader, Minister Louis Farrakhan. The thesis is that, in many ways, Farrakhan embodies the long historical trend of blending black nationalism with conservatism. Farrakhan's militant rhetoric and targeting of genuine racial concerns obviates a more deep-seated conservatism that supports patriarchy, minimized state intervention, moralism, and capitalism. Chapter Twelve begins by analyzing the meaning of the Million Man March and what lies beyond it. The march is critiqued for its gender and political significance for black politics. The chapter next argues that African Americans must become part of the struggle, indeed, play a leading role, for a global civil society.

Globalization's Impact on Race Relations

"Our loyalties must transcend our race, our tribe, our class and our nation; and this means we must develop a world perspective."[1] —Martin Luther King, Jr.

Swoosh! That's the sound of a Michael Jordan basket as he defends his position as perhaps the greatest NBA player ever. It is also the symbol copyrighted by Nike that appears ubiquitously on its basketball shoes (including the Air Jordan line), caps, T-shirts, and other products. Jordan, the NBA, and Nike are global symbols that embody intersecting race, economic, and cultural discourses that define the current era. For many people around the world, the commodified image of Jordan is one of their few entreés into black America. Jordan represents more than just a media-constructed, popular-culture icon; he also manifests the connection between new global labor relations, global cultural production and promotion, and race. Nike pays Jordan about $20 million annually to promote their basketball shoes, which is more than the collective salaries of the Nike workers in the factories in Indonesia that produce the shoes.[2] The shoes, which cost Nike $5.60 a pair to produce, are sold in the United States for as much as $150 disproportionately to inner-city black youth who have (literally) bought into a commercialized notion of black authenticity that captures neither their reality nor their likely destiny.[3]

Meanwhile, Nike's Indonesian workers, overwhelmingly women, struggle for basic benefits and health care, and against sexual and physical abuse, low pay, and wages under $2.50 per day in a nation where the living wage begins at $4.25 a day.[4] Nike, Jordan, and other transnational athletic products, corporations, and black NBA superstars all deny culpability in this exploitation. Nike subcontracts its labor production thereby disallowing direct complicity in the exploitative working conditions that are endemic in such labor. Jordan and other NBA celebrities simply claim that their only involvement is the endorsement, making it clear where their alliances lie in the enduring struggle between capital and labor.

The NBA's own racial house is out of order. While African Americans constitute 80 percent of the league's players, they are virtually invisible in the management and ownership areas.[5] Yet, it was the star capabilities and marketing of certain black players in the 1980s and 1990s—including the "Dream Teams" that participated in the Olympics—furthering the cultural force of U.S. basketball, that brought the NBA from financial abyss and rebuilt it into a national and international economic powerhouse. As this sliver of globalization demonstrates, a complicated nexus of race, gender, economics, culture, and politics is defining the issues of our times. The new world disorder necessitates a critical rethinking by black leaders, scholars, and activists as we confront the new millennium.

This chapter focuses on the impact of globalization on the economic and social life of African Americans. I argue that there is an unbreakable interdependence between the local and domestic issues facing the U.S. black community and their intersection with international economic and social concerns. My thesis is that it has become impossible to discuss the advancement of the black community without theorizing about the location and relevance of African Americans in the global sphere, and that a progressive social and political program must weld together local, national, and international strategies that account for the new historic moment in which we find ourselves.

Racial Negotiation in the Globalization Era

"We have to look at discrimination not simply as a deviation from law in the U.S.A.; rather we must see it as part of a larger, international norm, and as consistent with a worldwide corporate culture that transcends national boundaries."[6] —Patricia J. Williams

The age of globalization is upon us. Here at the edge of the millennium, we live in a period and time when the world has shrunk considerably, and where economic and technological reach has brought together desperate nations, peoples, and cultures. The industrial age, to a great degree, has passed, and the digital-information era is shaping and defining all that we do and how we think.

Researcher Jerry Mander argues that "Economic globalization involves arguably the most fundamental redesign and centralization of the planet's political and economic arrangements since the Industrial Revolution."[7] Scholar Anthony Giddens defines globalization as "the intensification of worldwide social relations which link distant localities in such a way that local happenings are shaped by events occurring many miles away and vice versa."[8] Economist Robert Burnett writes that globalization refers to "the organization of production, distribution, and consumption of cultural goods on a world-scale market."[9] Where these various definitions of globalization find unity is in the view that economic, social, political, and cultural life is being reordered before our very eyes. This new stage of capitalism—postindustrial, post-Cold War, transitional, information, and high-technology-driven—and the new-found power of global corporations can be summed by economist Lester Thurow, "For the first time in human history, anything can be made anywhere and sold everywhere."[10]

The new capacities of global capitalism to produce and distribute virtually any commodity on a global scale has profoundly transformed the relation between labor and capital. Under these circumstances, labor's ability to bargain in its interests—that is, for increased wages, better benefits, greater safety guidelines, and more job protection—is severely undermined. For black workers, the impact of this transformation is compounded by racially discriminatory labor markets; lack of access to skills training; the disappearance of low-skill, mid-to-high-wage jobs; political peripherization in public policy and the major parties; and an ideological backlash that seeks to reverse the gains made by African Americans in the civil rights and Black Power periods.

In response to these developments, a large number of scholarly and popular studies have been written that are critical of the impact of globalization on labor, politics, the environment, and local cultures. This includes *Global Dreams*; *The Case Against Globalization*; *Jihad vs. McWorld*; *Lean and Mean*; *One World, Ready or Not*; *When Corporations Rule the World*; and *The Work of Nations*.[11] These works and others provide an outstanding critique of the social and human harm being wrought by an unchecked globalization process where there is little national or international authority. They highlight the necessity of a global response from below that can retard the debilitating impact of globalization from above. Although much attention has been paid to the importance of globalization on gender, class, cultural, and environmental issues, there is little discussion of the significance of these transformations on race relations. Economist Jeremy Rifkin's *The End of Work* is an exception. He dedicates an entire chapter to the historic impact of new technologies on African- American labor. For the black labor force, this is an old tale with a postindustrial twist. As Rifkin notes, "The story of automation's effect on African Americans is one of the least known yet most salient episodes in the social history of the twentieth century. The experience of the black community needs to be properly analyzed, for it provides a much needed historical backdrop for understanding the likely impact that re-engineering and the new automation technologies are going to have on the lives of working people around the world."[12] He demonstrates how technological changes in the past have had devastating economic consequences for black workers. Mechanization and technological innovations, among other factors, ended the sharecropping system, displacing millions of black farm laborers in the 1940s and 1950s. In 1949, only 6 percent of cotton harvesting was mechanical. By 1964, only 15 years later, that number had jumped to 78 percent and, by 1972, it was 100 percent.[13] Rifkin's insights echo that of analyst Sidney Wilhelm.

More than a quarter of a century ago, Wilhelm predicted that African Americans were being made obsolete as workers by new technologies. With keen insight, he wrote, "With the onset of automation, the Negro moves out of his historical state of oppression into one of uselessness. Increasingly, he is not so much economically exploited as he is irrelevant....[W]hite America, by a more perfect application of mechanization and a vigorous reliance upon automation, disposes of the Negro; consequently, the Negro transforms from an exploited labor force into an outcast."[14] Wilhelm also predicted the long-term costs of these changes. He writes, "An underestimation of the technological revolution can only lead to an underestimation of the concomitant racial revolution from exploitation to uselessness; to misjudge the present as but a continuation of industrialization rather than the dawn of a new technological era, assures an inability to anticipate the vastly different system of race relations awaiting the displaced Negro."[15] In making the link between race, automation, and the new international economic configurations, Rifkin and Wilhelm's observations are the exception among globalization scholars.

Beyond the economic ramifications, globalization and the new technologies are restructuring race relations, both domestically and internationally, in a wide variety of areas. All together, global race relations are being changed even as the consciousness of that transformation lags behind. In practical terms, however, these changes are already manifested in the daily lives of people. Three critical ways in which globalization is affecting race relations are:

- It undermines progressive economic integration of marginalized racial groups as it destroys jobs, fosters competition, depresses wages, cuts worker's benefits, and limits opportunities;

- It gives rise to new race-conscious political and social movements that attempt to resist racialized social assaults, policies of containment and imprisonment, and the elimination of the welfare state and;

- It has a negative cultural impact as manufactured racist and negative images of racial and ethnic groups are projected to the world, which has little or no alternative framework for assessing the lives and cultures of these communities.

Race, Work, and the Global Economy

The changing world economy is fundamentally remapping the way the world works and black workers are carrying a significant portion of the load. Access to jobs, already disproportionately tenuous for black workers, has become even more constricted in the current era. As scholar Holly Sklar notes, "While some workers have jobs with no future, others have futures with no jobs."[16] Responding to the jobs development crisis, President Clinton stated, "All the advanced nations are having difficulty creating new jobs, even when their economies are growing....We have to figure out how to unlock the doors for people who are left behind in this new global economy."[17] Chair of the Council of Economic Advisers Laura D'Andrea Tyson spoke similarly, "Globalization has depressed the wage growth of low-wage workers. It's been a reason for the increasing wage gap between high-wage and low-wage workers."[18] Despite this acknowledgment of the difficulties wrought by the new global economy, neither Clinton nor his administration nor Congress have adequately addressed the concerns of U.S. workers, but have instead, consistently acted in the interests of the transnational corporate elite.

In this era, job competition takes place on a global scale. Governments around the world, including the United States, have made it clear that they no longer have full employment as a goal. U.S. workers are not only competing with their next door neighbor for that potential new job, but with 700 million people around the world who are unemployed and beholden to the vicissitudes of capital.[19] As the International Forum on Globalization notes, "As many as one-third of U.S. workers are swimming in a global labor pool."[20] At any given moment, millions of U.S. workers are held hostage to the threat of replacement workers from lands thousands of miles away.

The International Labor Organization (ILO) reports that there are over 34 million people under/unemployed in the industrialized Organization for Economic Cooperation and Development (OECD) nations. In 1996, in Germany, France, Italy, and Sweden, unemployment was up 11.3 percent. In the United States and Great Britain, while unemployment stabilized or diminished , income disparities grew sharply.

In Latin America and the Caribbean, unemployment rose, particularly in urban areas. According to the ILO, the only developing nations that have seen significant growth in the last 20 years outside of Asia have been Chile, Jordan, and Mauritis. Depressingly, not a single African country has seen economic growth in the last two decades. ILO also reports that millions have shifted to laboring in informal sectors of the economy, including the illegal realm.[21]

Authors Richard Barnet and John Cavanagh note that the global economy can be divided into a pyramid of seven groups of nations. At the very top are about 24 nations located in North America, Western Europe, Japan, Australia, New Zealand, and South Africa. These economies generate about four-fifths of the world's economic activity. They are followed by the eight countries—Brazil, Mexico, Argentina, South Korea, Taiwan, Singapore, Hong Kong, and

India—who do large-scale manufacturing. A third group—including China, Thailand, Indonesia, and Malaysia—has reached the stage of limited industrialization. Developing rapidly with large inflows of Western capital, the former communist nations of Eastern Europe constitute a fourth group. More or less on economic par with the countries of Eastern Europe, the oil-producing countries of the Middle East make up a fifth block of economic power. The sixth group is composed of the poor nations in Asia, Latin America, and Africa whose prospects for development are dim making them vulnerable to exploitative investment and economic dependence. At the very bottom are the poorest of the poor nations, virtually all located in Africa with the notable exception of Haiti.[22]

Across the globe, economic woes and the social havoc that they generate have been racialized. In the United Kingdom, more than a million manufacturing jobs were lost between 1966 and 1976, and in Germany, "new technologies enabled manufacturers to eliminate more than 500,000 jobs in a single 12-month period between early 1992 and 1993."[23] Many of these jobs throughout Europe were held by black workers. Official employment and economic data from the United States, Canada, and England document that black unemployment is at least twice that of white unemployment. In Canada, a study by the Commission on Systemic Racism in the Ontario criminal justice system found that over an eight-year period black imprisonment grew 204 percent, while the white incarceration increase was 23 percent. The study also found that whites charged with drug crimes are released at twice the rate of blacks.[24]

The perception that globalization is having a racial impact has led to organized resistance at the regional and state levels. In Europe, efforts have unfolded that unite racial justice concerns with the economic issues facing the region. In 1990, the Standing Conference on Racial Equality in Europe (SCORE) was formed to address the economic, social, and racial impact of a unified Europe on blacks and other ethnic minorities. SCORE has chapters in all of the major European capitals and carefully monitors and assesses the European Union (EU) process. In 1994, they issued their "Black Manifesto for Europe." Among the demands of the manifesto were:

- Amend the Treaty of Rome to outlaw discrimination by race

- Adopt as a European Union Directive "The Starting Line," which promotes racial equality in law;
- Allow free movement for all EU residents, whether citizens or not;
- Ban incitement to racial harassment and eradicate racial violence;
- Create an anti-racist and anti-sexist immigration policy that is open to democratic scrutiny, in conjunction with the black, migrant, and minority communities who are most affected;
- Grant independent legal status to black, migrant, and minority women and promote the mainstreaming of their concerns in all areas of European work; and
- Give asylum seekers easy access to the EU and proper legal representation; they should not be detained, nor returned to countries where they could be in danger.

SCORE also outlined what it considers to be a racial bill of rights. It demanded that all black, migrant, and minority residents of the EU should have the right to vote in all elections; equal rights to housing; equal rights to education, including their own language, history and culture; equal rights to health and social services; and the right to family reunion.

In France, progressive groups are organizing against racial discrimination and economic attacks on workers. On May 1, 1997, May Day, thousands of workers marched in Paris to protest racism and unemployment. Organized by the French Communist Party *(PCF)* and the Socialist Party *(PS)*, the rally called for the creation of 700,000 youth jobs, reduction of work hours to 35 with full pay, and elimination of the racist anti-immigration Pasqua-Debre' laws. It was the first time in 14 years that *PCF* and *PS* had held joint actions. The crowd was estimated to be between 23,000 and 60,000, the largest in years. There were also provincial support marches in Marseilles, Toulouse, and Bordeaux. The French government, under former-President Jacques Chirac, made cuts in social programs and wanted to make more in pensions, unemployment insurance, and health care benefits. Unemployment in France is around 13 percent, one of the highest in all of Europe. Further evisceration of the French welfare state would be calamitous because 25 percent of the nation's workers are employed by the state.[25]

In Latin America, blacks in the region have come together under the auspices of the Organization of Africans in the Americas (OAA) and the Mundo Afro organization to counter the negative impact of the globalized economy. In December 1994, at their first symposium on racism and xenophobia in the region, OAA identified some common problems faced by blacks, including lack of access to political, financial, and educational institutions; human rights abuses; hunger; crime; murders of black people, black street children in particular, by death squads; and forced sterilization of women. According to Marta Moreno Vega, director of New York's Caribbean Cultural Center, who attended the meeting, "The most important thing to come out of the [1994 Mundo Afro] conference was an affirmation of the African presence in Latin America, which is often ignored throughout the globe. And the fact that organizations have developed and are continuing to develop, that are looking at the African experience as the center for political, economic, and social movement."[26]

Economic State of Black America

"Historically, discrimination was a powerful force in regimenting a disproportionate number of blacks to the secondary sector. Today, this segmentation continues even though more overt forms of racism have subsided".[27] —Thomas D. Boston.

In the 1980s, the loss of millions of manufacturing jobs due to plant closings, runaway shops, and the imposition of new technologies was central to the diminished fortunes of the working class in the United States and to increased national poverty. Between 1983–1988, 9.7 million U.S. workers lost jobs through plant closings and layoffs.[28] Companies that symbolized America's global corporate dominance in the past joined the exodus. General Electric, the company that hired superpatriot Ronald Reagan as its spokesperson, cut 25,000 domestic jobs while adding 30,000 foreign positions. RCA cut 14,000 domestic jobs while adding 19,000 globally.[29] It is estimated that in the United States during the 1970s, between 32 and 38 million jobs disappeared.[30] As Rachel Kamel notes, "Manufacturing employment in the U.S. fell by 1.4 million between 1978 and 1990 and the numbers out of work are increasing despite economic recovery."[31]

Deindustrialization had an injurious economic impact on black workers, who worked in large numbers in the factories of Detroit, St. Louis, Chicago, Pittsburgh, and other industrial cities. Driven by the desire for higher profits, close proximity to natural resources, access to local markets, and most critically, cheap labor, large-and medium-sized corporations fled North America and Europe as rapidly as they could. In 1950, one-third of all U.S. jobs were in manufacturing. By the mid-1980s, only 20 percent were employed in manufacturing, and by 1990 that had dropped off to 10-14 percent; it is projected that by 2005, the number will drop to between 2.5 and 5 percent.[32] Studies also show that blacks are paid less for the same positions.

The loss of manufacturing jobs have contributed to black job displacement. Those jobs have been replaced by low-wage work that generally offers fewer benefits and more exploitative working conditions, that is, no labor unions or collective bargaining. These often subminimal wage jobs include positions in areas such as retail sales, food service, janitorial, housekeeping, and low-level health delivery, jobs disproportionately held by African Americans. Between 1980–1987, half of all new jobs went to temporary and part-time workers.[33]

Black workers, already suffering from an unemployment rate that has historically been at least twice that of whites, are especially hard hit in this new era. In the 1970s, for example, "up to half of the huge employment declines for less-educated blacks might be explained by industrial shifts away from manufacturing toward other sectors."[34] This trend continued into the 1980s and 1990s. As the *Wall Street Journal* noted, referencing a General Accounting Office (GAO) report, African Americans suffered the worst in the recession of the early 1990s. According to the *Journal*, "Black wage earners made up nearly one-third of the 180,000 manufacturing jobs lost in 1990 and 1991," which translated into about 60,000 jobs lost at companies such as ITT, Bank of America, Sears, Coca Cola, Safeway, Campbell's Soup, Walt Disney, and General Electric.[35] Even more remarkable was the conclusion that "Blacks were the only racial group to suffer a net job loss during the 1990-91 economic downturn."[36] The GAO noted, "The high African American displacement rate was partially due to the impact of the recession on industries and occupations in which African Americans were disproportionately represented; however, differences still persisted after accounting for industrial and occupational affiliations, education levels, and worker age."[37]

Downsizing is happening at large firms as well as small ones because both are able to take advantage of the productivity that comes from employing the new technologies that make everything from telecommunications to transportation more efficient, faster, and profitable. Companies are now able to decrease their workforce while increasing their profit margin. In the past, increased productivity was qualitatively tied to a combination of new technologies and an expanded workforce. For the present and the foreseeable future, that is no longer the case. *The Nation* magazine reports that "the Fortune 500 firms shed 4.4 million jobs between 1980 and 1993, but during this same period, their sales increased 1.4 times, assets increased 2.3 times, and CEO compensation increased 6.1 times."[38] With these results, there is little incentive for companies to do anything but continue to downsize where possible. In 1995 alone, U.S. companies cut about 600,000 workers.[39]

In the 1990s, profits have grown for the top corporations. In 1992, profits jumped 19 percent, in 1993, they rose 20 percent, and in 1994, they shot up an amazing 40 percent.[40] In the United States, the richest 1 percent own as much as the bottom 95 percent.[41] They also own 46 percent of all corporate stock; while the richest 10 percent own 90 percent.[42] "Between 1980 and 1992, the nation's 500 biggest corporations more than doubled their assets from $1.18 to $2.68 trillion. In 12 years, the number of jobs at America's 500 largest corporations fell from 15.9 to 11.5 million."[43]

Between 1967-87, in many cities where African Americans comprise a significant proportion of the population, job losses in manufacturing have been severe. In Philadelphia, a 64 percent loss resulted in the disappearance of 160,000 jobs. In Chicago, it was 60 percent (326,000 jobs), in New York, 58 percent (520,000 jobs), and in Detroit, 51 percent (108,000 jobs).[44] African Americans in the South were also hurt by manufacturing downsizing. As economist Lester Henry observed, "Plant closings in the 1970s…were heaviest in the Northeast and in the old South, the two areas of the country where

African Americans are most populous."[45] The erosion of black middle- and blue-collar classes, due to job loss has exacerbated the economic crisis facing the black poor in these cities as localities struggle to compensate for the tax revenues that disappeared with jobs, middle-class flight, and declining federal and state financial support.

Even though there have been spots of reindustrialization, there is speculation that racial discrimination is also playing a role in this new era of fluid global investments. While evidence is scarce, the placement of new plants, and therefore jobs, outside of easy accessibility by inner-city residents can be seen as having a racial impact given the disproportionate inner-city residency of the black community. Even if premeditation is not present, the consequences of these site decisions exacerbate the job search crisis growing among the black poor. Political scientist Robert Smith writes, "A study of the location decisions of Japanese firms in the United States and of American auto companies found a fairly consistent pattern of location in rural and suburban areas about thirty miles from the nearest concentration of blacks, a distance that is thought to be about the limit of worker commuter time."[46] Henry notes, "The pattern of firms, both foreign and domestic, when choosing sites for opening new plants, has been away from predominantly nonwhite areas...The Japanese and other German firms have also show a similar preference for plant location in suburban and sunbelt areas where few nonwhites reside.[47]

One of the consequences of globalization is a severe reduction in the size of organized labor as a result of less manufacturing work. Union membership in the United Auto Workers fell during the 1980s by close to 500,000 workers—one-third of its peak total.[48] Steel unions were also especially hard hit by the loss of jobs in their fields. From 1974 to 1988, almost half of all jobs in the steel industry disappeared—a fall from 480,000 to 260,000.[49] Overall, labor union membership went from about 35 percent of all nonagricultural workers in 1960 to about 17 percent at present. If government employees are excluded, the number falls to about 13.4 percent.[50] Labor militancy has also declined in recent years. For example, strikes involving 1,000 workers or more averaged about 300 in the 1960s; in 1991, there were only 40.[51] Labor has lost control over job cuts, wage decreases, and work rules, and in some instances, has given back benefits won in the past. The give-backs are part of the necessary tactical moves by labor to hold on to jobs that are rapidly leaving the country. Labor's major weapon, the strike, has become impotent as capital is no longer held hostage to production shutdowns.

In the public sector as well, black job cuts have been disproportionate. According to the *San Jose Mercury News*, when the federal government downsized in 1992, it fired blacks at more than twice the rate of whites. An editorial noted, "Blacks who were 17 percent of the executive branch workforce in 1992, were 39 percent of those dismissed. Whites made up 72 percent of the workforce and only 48 percent of those fired."[52] The *Mercury News* stated, "It's not that they have less education, experience, or seniority. The difference has nothing to do with job performance....Blacks are fired more often because of their skin color....Rank didn't help. Black senior managers went out the door as often as black clerks. It gets worse. The deck is stacked against fired minority workers with legitimate grounds for reinstatement, the study shows. They win only one in every 100 appeals."[53] A General Accounting Office study found that blacks, more than whites or Latinos, "experience the longest spells of unemployment among displaced workers who eventually found jobs and showed the largest loss in wages in their new jobs."[54]

Other factors affecting black job loss are recent international trade agreements. In 1993, President Clinton forced through Congress the North American Free Trade Agreement (NAFTA), which had begun as a policy objective of the Bush administration. Although he did not explicitly say so, Clinton believed that NAFTA would provide economic progress and development gains for all thereby benefiting African Americans and other minorities. His "rising tide will lift all boats" view was a means of attacking racial divisions. This perspective mitigated against explicit race-oriented social programs in favor of general economic ones.

While not guaranteeing that even its economic components will work, this view completely fails to address racial discrimination in its broad political and social forms. The argument is also reductive in that it narrows racism down to economic disparities rather than a system of relationships of power that are not only economic, but social, political, and cultural. While economist Martin Carnoy contends that

Clinton's class approach to race may garner some economic benefits for African Americans that are more substantial than what occurred under Presidents Reagan and Bush, it

> ...does not solve the problems of wage discrimination and the lack of decent-paying jobs and upward mobility for those same people. It does not overcome the disintegration of the inner-city, or reduce the job discrimination and financial and educational difficulties faced by young blacks getting college educations. It falls far short of even a moderately aggressive use of federal agencies to reduce discrimination by enforcing civil rights legislation and of the kind of ideological reconstruction needed to push the electorate toward resolving racial inequality. It still consciously avoids putting the race issue explicitly on the table through either a return to solid enforcement of civil rights legislation or a thorough discussion of what must be done to begin to rebuild family and community in inner-cities. Hence, it not only avoids dealing with solutions to racial inequality, but runs the risk of failing even to address that (class) part of racial inequality associated with the disproportionate number of working blacks in lower-income groups."[55]

Many civil rights leaders, economists, and labor leaders testified before Congress that NAFTA would be most injurious to African Americans. Working-class African Americans engaged in fields of work, such as manufacturing, are most likely to be adversely affected. This perspective was shared by Thea Lee, an economist at the Economic Policy Institute. In her 1993 testimony before Congress, she stated that "African Americans, Hispanics, and Asian Americans hold a disproportionate share of the production jobs likely to be displaced by NAFTA."[56]

William Lucy, president of the Coalition of Black Trade Unionists (CBTU), argued a similar point. He wrote, "Black workers are more likely to be employed in those industries which will experience large job losses to Mexico including automobiles and trucks, apparel, household glassware, ceramics, major household appliances, and electronics....High-wage manufacturing jobs remain the only practical path of upward mobility for millions of black workers who do not have college degrees."[57] CBTU was one of the few black interest groups to take an early position against NAFTA, dating back to at least the 102nd Congress.

A statement issued by the Congressional Black Caucus captured a number of their arguments. It stated, in part:

> Our trade deficit with Mexico has already grown in many industries. Estimates of probable job losses due to NAFTA have reached as high as one million. State and local governments will lose tax revenues from businesses who relocate and individuals who become jobless. In those regions that suffer the most intense job losses, the corresponding loss of tax revenues will be substantial. NAFTA will have a negative impact on the generation of revenues in this country precisely at a time when entitlement benefits and services are under great peril. Also, an examination of the average hourly wages for production workers in those industries already affected reveals that the jobs being lost are high-wage, not only low-wage manufacturing jobs. Those who lose jobs because of import competition do not climb up the job ladder, but fall back to lower wages or fall off the job ladder into unemployment. There is little to support the claim of NAFTA proponents that free trade will create higher wage jobs for U.S. workers because Mexican workers will take jobs at the lower end of the skills ladder while American workers will move up to better paying jobs.
>
> There has not been sufficient progress made with Mexico related to environmental protection. NAFTA must preserve the rights of states and the federal government to set high individual standards for the environment, conservation, health and safety. NAFTA does not provide a secure, dedicated source of funding for border clean-up, environmental infrastructure, conservation initiatives, protection of communities and worker health. The treaty does not prevent the flight of industries which seek to take advantage of lax environmental, health and safety standards in other countries. Further, there are not sufficient opportunities for public participation in trade and environmental disputes and in investment and trade decisions affecting individual communities.
>
> ...The Minority Business Community has never been fully consulted or considered on NAFTA. There are no current proposals to provide technical, financial marketing or educational assis-

tance to small business in general, or to minority business in particular, interested in trade with or investment in Mexico. Remedies must be carefully explored and should accompany the NAFTA.

Preferential treatment for Mexico—especially in areas of sugar, citrus and apparel—could result in significant diversion of trade from the Caribbean. Such a diversion would stall economic growth, and dislocate productive activity in both the United States and the Caribbean. If NAFTA takes effect in January, U.S./Caribbean commerce could erode by next spring. Using the textile industry as an example, NAFTA calls for a progressive reduction of tariffs on Mexican textiles and apparel over the next decade.[58]

Some analysts have argued that African Americans and the working population in general should prepare for the 21st century by reeducating themselves in the areas of high technology and computer science.[59] Projections of job creation in the early years of the 21st century, however, demonstrate that most will come in areas of low-pay, low-skill work. In the 1996–1997 edition of the Department of Labor's *The Occupational Outlook Handbook,* 20 occupations are expected to grow over the next 10 years. The top 10 occupations and their projected growth are cashiers (562,000 jobs), janitors and cleaners (559,000), retail salespersons (532,000), waiters and waitresses (479,000), registered nurses (473,000), general managers and top executives (466,000), system analysts (445,000), home health aides (428,000), security guards (415,000), and nursing aides, orderlies, and attendants (387,000).[60] Other jobs in the top 20 included truck drivers, secretaries, childcare workers, and maintenance repairers.[61] With the notable exceptions of general managers/top executives and system analysts, and perhaps registered nurses, most of the new jobs will be at or near minimum wage, keeping a large segment of even full-time workers under the poverty line. These are also categories that disproportionately hire women at very low pay and with few benefits.

These projections are grim news for the African-American community. Even if African Americans can prepare themselves for the jobs that are going to be created, it will be difficult to build families and communities on the wages that will be available. For African-American men, in particular, the traditional entry-level laboring positions that for generations allowed them to still earn a living wage with low level education have vanished like the smoke from the long-gone, not-to-return factories.

Neither should the illusion that black businesses will solve the black employment crisis be fostered. In 1993, the *Black Enterprise* top 100 industrial and automotive companies collectively employed only 45,628 blacks.[62] While this is a 22 percent increase over the previous year, it accounts for only 1 percent of the current black labor force. And, like other capitalist businesses, those black businesses with the potential to grow are capital intensive (media and technology) rather than labor intensive (manufacturing). Black businesses, however, are not located in the capital-intensive expansive area of the economy. As economist Margaret Simms states, "Most minority-owned businesses are not well represented in the kinds of industries where international trade possibilities are strong."[63]

In 1992, based on the latest U.S. Census Bureau data available, out of a total 17 million U.S. businesses, there were roughly 620,000 black businesses, with receipts of $32.2 billion.[64] These businesses averaged receipts of $52,000 per year with black women averaging $31,000 compared to the average of black men of $69,000.[65] Significantly, 56 percent of the businesses earned less than $10,000 per year. Perhaps, the most salient statistic regarding the black employment possibilities is the fact that 94 percent of black businesses were sole proprietorships![66] In other words, only 6 percent of black businesses hired anyone at all, whether that employee was black or not. In virtually every black community, nonblacks own the majority of businesses. In Washington, D.C., although blacks are 65 percent of the population, they own less than 10 percent of the city's businesses. In Los Angeles, according to the last census, one of every 10 Koreans own their business; for blacks it's one out of every 67.[67]

For the black community, especially its youth, the racial disparities in the economy are mirrored in other areas, such as education. Marian Wright Edelman, president of the Children's Defense Fund, sadly points out that "A black high school graduate is nearly one and a half times more likely to be unemployed than a white high school dropout, and a black college graduate is more likely to be unemployed than a white high school graduate with no college."[68] Edelman also gives some sobering statistics on the opportunity differences between white and black children:

- 78 percent of white children live with both parents compared to 39 percent of black children;
- 63 percent of white children live with parents who own their home vs. 28 percent of black children;
- 23 percent of white children have a father that works full-time and a mother that is at home full-time contrasted to a mere 8 percent of black children;
- 30 percent of white children have a parent that has completed college, only 13 percent of black children;
- 71 percent of white children are covered by health insurance compared to only 44 percent of black children;
- 16 percent of white children compared to 41 percent of black children are poor;
- 19 percent of white children live in central cities vs. 41 percent black children.[69]

While the white infant mortality is 7 per 1,000, the figure of 16 per 1,000 for African-American children is more than double the white rate, which approaches that of many developing nations. For whites, the low birth rate is 6 percent; for African Americans, it is 13 percent.[70] The future for children in the United States, in general, is so grim that the country was given a rebuke by the United Nations. A UNICEF report noted, "the living conditions of poor American children are far worse than those of poor children in most other industrial countries....Only four other countries—Australia, Canada, Ireland and Israel—have child poverty rates of more than 10 percent."[71] According to the report, without government help, the poverty rate in the United States and France would be 25 percent, but with the difference in their individual welfare systems, France has reduced child poverty to 6.5 percent while the United States has only reduced it to 21 percent.[72]

Jobs, Race, and Globalization

On January 11, 1944, in an address to Congress, President Franklin D. Roosevelt called for a "Second Bill of Rights under which a new basis of security and prosperity can be established for all—regardless of station, race, or creed."[73] Attempting to speak not only the immediate crisis of war and work in which the nation was immersed, he also set forth an inclusive vision for the country:

> The right to a useful and remunerative job in the industries or shops or farms or mines of the nation; the right to earn enough to provide adequate food and clothing and recreation; the right of every farmer to raise and sell his products at a return which will give him and his family a decent living; the right of every businessman, large and small, to trade in an atmosphere of freedom from unfair competition and domination by monopolies at home and abroad; the right of every family to a decent home; the right to adequate medical care and the opportunity to achieve and enjoy good health; the right to adequate protection from the economic fears of old age, sickness, accident, and unemployment; the right to a good education.[74]

Representative Ron Dellums (D–CA) has fashioned and updated Roosevelt's bill of rights into H.R. 1050, "A Living Wage, Jobs For All Act." As Dellums writes, "The bill is particularly significant at this time in that more and more of our people feel that they are slipping rapidly into an increasingly limited job market, a condition of seemingly permanent low wages, and the loss of real prospects for improvement in their economic condition. As more companies merge, downsize, reduce, layoff, and dismiss their workers, it is clear that opportunities to work for adequate wages are shrinking. Increasingly, it seems that the private sector views its responsibility as only making a profit for the top investors and to provide opulent benefits for its chief executives."[75]

The purpose of the bill is captured in its full title, "To establish democratic overall planning for such living wage job opportunities as will help fulfill basic human rights and responsibilities, facilitate conversion from unneeded military programs to civilian activities that meet basic human needs, and strengthen democracy by reducing poverty, inequality, violence and the concentration of economic power." H.R. 1050 calls on the president to "implement the economic and social obligations of the Federal Government under the Employment Act of 1946, the Full Employment and Balanced Growth Act of 1978, the Charter of the United Nations, the Charter of the Organization of American States, the Universal Declaration of Human Rights, and the International Covenant on Civil and Political Rights."[76]

Dellums is specifically trying to address the job and employment crisis that has been ignored by other policymakers and the White House. He writes, "H.R. 1050 acknowledges the increasing reality of growing unemployment and takes the responsibility of creating jobs in sectors which need work to be done; in building housing, educating our young, protecting and cleaning up the environment, providing childcare, healthcare, expanding public transportation, and in other areas of need. It is unrealistic to expect that corporations, which are only market-oriented, will take the responsibility for a healthy, national economy. Only we, the people, through our common action, can accomplish this. We need to realize the power of our joint action and take responsibility for our future. This bill is a step in that direction."[77]

For the black community, Dellums' bill and his effort to popularize the struggle for genuine full employment is critical. While specific race-remedy programs, such as affirmative action and minority set-asides, are important to maintain a broad view is necessary that locates black job issues within the framework of global labor changes. The battle for a guaranteed living wage is being fought in nation after nation as adjustments to a period in which fewer jobs will be available for more workers than ever. In Canada, Denmark, Japan, the Netherlands, and other countries, various forms of state welfare programs to cushion the cost of downsizing have been won by the struggles of labor organizers, community activists, and progressive elected officials.[78] In the United States, African Americans in solidarity with other sectors of society have to rebuild and reenergize a movement that seeks as its goal nothing short of a redistribution of economic and political power downward that provides development, prosperity, and fairness.

2

If I Were a Rich Man: Race, Gender, and Poverty

"The plantation and the ghetto were created by those who had power both to confine those who had no power and to perpetuate their powerlessness. The problem of transforming the ghetto is, therefore, a problem of power."[1]—Martin Luther King, Jr.

Largesse for the poor from the modern welfare state has never been an act of generosity and charity, but in fact, has always been a response to the political mobilization and organization of the poor and their allies. The real issue confronting the poor has been about power. To the degree that the poor has been demobilized and out of contention for power, as in the current period, retraction has occurred. The modern welfare state—its stability and even existence—is a consequence of the enduring political power struggle between capital and the state, on the one hand, and labor and its most marginalized sectors, on the other.

The modern welfare state is also a gendered one. Efforts to curtail state commitment to the poor are often waged on the ideological grounds of patriarchy, where it is argued that the traditional family, ostensibly the stabilizing core of both modernity and postindustrial society, is threatened by welfare policies. Male power, actualized through institutional and systemic economic and political power relations, has been undermined by the empowerment brought by women liberating themselves from the traditional family structure by their incorporation into the economic base of society and their role in the political and ideological struggles in the superstructure. A diminished or dismissed welfare state reasserts male privilege.

The political and ideological questions surrounding poverty and gender intersect with those of race, quilting together a popular yet benefactors of the welfare state. This framework sees those black, poor, and female sectors of society as social pariahs and the most undeserving of even the meager wages of welfare that they receive. Within the black community, this framework serves to demonize black women, reify the family and traditional family roles, and (re)center black men. This agenda then finds a confluence of support from white reactionaries, black conservatives, neoliberals, and some prominent black nationalists.

In fundamental ways, this construct is being played out on a global scale. The welfare state, which has been a central feature of post-War War I advanced capitalist nations, is being eroded away. From France and Canada to Australia and England, social spending on the poor and the lower rungs of the working class has come under attack even as the needs of the poor have increased dramatically in these societies.

Thus, the battle over welfare in the United States merges with ongoing global issues and concerns. The thesis of this chapter is that the elimination of welfare for the poor in the United States is viewed by policymakers as a necessary concession to capital in the postindustrial era to create a more acceptable atmosphere for investment and capitalist economic development. In the United States, the ideological component of this task is the requisite racializing and gendering of the debate both in the larger public discourse as well as within the African-American community. The debate in the black community over welfare reform explicates the ideological tensions of this period between those who, either explicitly or covertly, adhere to a reworked and sometimes Afrocentrized version of the cultural pathology thesis, and those who target economic and political powerlessness as the root causes of poverty. The policy, political, and strategic implications of the two views are diametrically opposed. The former leads to advocacy for the elimination of welfare programs while the latter demands a strengthening and expansion of the state's responsibility to the poor. While the former targets the poor as the unit of change, the latter targets political mobilization of the poor as a necessary strategy leading to institutional and systemic transformation.

Modern U.S. Welfare State Emerges

The United States was one of the last industrialized nations to institute welfare programs aimed at the poor and disadvantaged. In Germany, sickness insurance was instituted in 1883 and health insurance in 1880. In the United Kingdom, sickness insurance came in 1911 and health insurance in 1948. In both nations, insurance was not income or age determined. In the 1930s, the Great Depression created a dual crisis of stability and legitimacy, and forced a state response to the spontaneous social movements, many of them infused with socialist and communist yearnings, that threatened the entire social construct of liberal democracy. Social movements led by workers, blacks, farmers, and others forced concessions that withstood the crises of the period and lasted until the most recent times.[2]

In the 1950s and 1960s, the civil rights and Black Power movements won even more gains from a state that again sought and could afford social pacification. It is critical to note, however, that it was not only the movement from below that sparked these changes, but also movement from above. Changes in the nature of the postwar capitalist economy, most profoundly the expansion of U.S. capital on a global scale and the necessity of an expanded labor force that would include African Americans, women, and others, meant that a "progressive" wing of corporate elites saw the value in supporting an end to racial segregation. Social integration facilitated economic integration, which was good for business.

Finally, the welfare state was enhanced by the emergence of a black, political, managerial class that found itself engaged in policy debates and, increasingly, policy decisions. The administrative and managerial seizure of the cities, left behind by a fleeing white middle class, created a tension in the political system that mitigated a full-blown retrenchment and social take-back by conservative and reactionary forces, at least until Reaganism.

Just as Thatcherism in England would attack the gains of the English working class, so too would Reaganism, with plentiful support from congressional Democrats, erode the decades-old victories won by the U.S. working class, including African Americans. The prism through which Reaganist salvos would travel was initially into areas that could be easily racialized and genderized. Essential to this effort was winning the public ideological fray over how welfare was defined and viewed.

Redefining the Welfare Discourse

A critical struggle in the welfare discourse is the need to change the terms of the debate and popularized definitions of welfare. For most, welfare is reduced to government transfer programs that are aimed at the inner-city poor, who are disproportionately women of color. There is a twofold problem with this conception of welfare. First, it obscures the class power that lies behind state decisions regarding the distribution of wealth in the United States. A reductive casting of welfare only acknowledges and designates government aid to the poor as "real" welfare, thereby disaggregating billions of dollars in transfers that are given to corporations, veterans, farmers, the elderly, and other sectors of society. Second, a reductive definition of welfare serves the ideological mission of codifying and popularizing racist and sexist assumptions about the poor and poverty that are not only in variance with the facts, but construct bigoted social theories on which social policy is built.

Welfare, in its broadest sense, should more appropriately be seen as the normal operation of the modern capitalist economy that requires both economic transfers to help maintain social peace and ideological loyalty. Economic transfers further the interests of the economic elite. The emergence of the welfare state in 1935 was not as much a surrender to the social movements that rapacious capitalism inspired, but an adjustment in the functioning of the modern industrial nation state.

Political scientist Mack Jones argues similarly when he writes, "The concept of the welfare state comprises all of the interventionist practices of governments,...which involve transferring publicly generated resources to private individuals and groups and the pattern of beliefs and social relationship emanating therefrom. This definition subsumes not only those transfer payment programs earmarked for the poor and referred to pejoratively as 'welfare,' but the whole array of payment programs including those targeted to other non-poor population groups...ranging from price stabilization programs of the agricultural department, export subsidy and trade adjustment programs of the commerce department to the development programs of HUD."[3]

The retreat from welfare for the poor reflects the balance of power in the contestation between the needy and the political and economic elites. Even in this disengagement, capital's true agenda is exposed. While policymakers decry the welfare system as hopelessly bloated, anti-work ethic, and counter to free enterprise, major corporations are lining up to seize the economic opportunities available as welfare devolution to the states occurs. Researcher Adam Fifield documents, for example, how Lockheed Martin Corporation in Los Angeles has secured a four-year, $50 million contract to manage major parts of child support in California, including tracking down fathers, holding hearings, and even administering blood tests.[4] Lockheed, according to Fifield, has contracts to perform some aspect of welfare services in 45 states. In 1997, in Texas, a bidding war took place between Lockheed, Anderson Consulting, and EDS—H. Ross Perot's computer company—for a $2 billion contract to integrate Medicaid, Food Stamps, and welfare services into one computer system.[5] Policymakers claim that the objectives of privatization are reduced welfare rolls, integrated services, recipients being put to work, and a downsized public sector. They fail to add that poverty is unalleviated, very few recipients find permanent full-time work, and an inefficacy expressed in "a pattern of incompetence, cost overruns, and broken promises" is created.[6]

What is Welfare for the Poor?

The nation's welfare system for the poor is not just one program, but actually a number of federal and state programs that constitute what is popularly known as "welfare." At the federal level, this includes Supplemental Security Income (6 million), Food Stamps (20–25 million), Medicare (36 million), Medicaid (25 million), and perhaps the best-known and most debated, the former Aid to Families with Dependent Children or AFDC (14 million), now restructured as Temporary Assistance to Needy Families (TANF) since 1996.[7] Prior to the most recent reforms, states worked with the federal government to administer the various programs. While there were federal guidelines that had to be followed, states had a great deal of flexibility in some areas of administration and were able to apply for exemptions to the rules to experiment with different approaches to welfare.

AFDC was first created by the Social Security Act of 1935 as part of the New Deal legislation initiated during the Depression by the Franklin D. Roosevelt administration. In addition to what was then called Aid to Dependent Children, the act established social security and unemployment insurance. AFDC, along with Food Stamps and other federal welfare programs, were entitlements, which meant that the federal government guaranteed states that funds would be available to meet their needs no matter how those needs might grow—for example, in periods of economic recession.

A family had to meet certain income tests to be eligible for AFDC. States established need standards indexed to the poverty line and state-measured calculations of basic income needs. While a family's gross income could not exceed 185 percent of the state's need standard for the relevant family size, a family's net income had to be below the state's payment standard, which in 35 states was lower than the needs standard.[8] In 1994, the median cash transfer for welfare recipients for a single, nonworking mother of two was $366 in cash and $295 in Food Stamps.[9] This came to about 69 percent of the poverty line, which, in 1993, was $14,764 for a family of four. AFDC was unavailable to single people who had no dependent children.[10] The program was dominated by single women with children, who made up about 90 percent of all recipients.[11] AFDC families, due to their low-income status, also qualified for Medicaid, the federal health insurance program for the nation's poor.

There was also a work component attached to AFDC in the form of the Job Opportunities and Basic Skills Training (JOBS) program. Once their youngest child reached the age of three, the parent had to participate up to 20 hours per week; when that child reached six, up to 40 hours per week.[12] States were technically responsible for child care, transportation, and other work-related costs. In 1992, most states were providing JOBS slots for only about 20 percent of their eligible population.[13]

In the debates concerning welfare, many myths have been perpetuated regarding recipients. These include the views that most welfare recipients are single teenage mothers; that welfare families are vastly larger than the average family in the nation; that most people stay on welfare for many years, if not a lifetime; that most welfare recipients are urban African-American women; that welfare to the poor is bankrupting the nation; that welfare recipients live well off their benefits; that welfare recipients do not want to work; and that welfare creates a culture of dependency. All of these views, carefully crafted fables that do not hold up to scrutiny, facilitate the attacks on welfare and its recipients.

Those who benefit the most from AFDC and other welfare programs are children. In 1992, the welfare caseload consisted of 9.2 million children and 4.4 million adults (virtually all of them mothers).[14] Indeed, most of the beneficiaries are young children. About half the children on welfare are under six years old and one-quarter of them are under three.[15] These children are being raised by a mother who is 25 years old or older, and either divorced or separated.[16] The mother is generally unemployed and has, at most, a high school education.[17]

Studies also demonstrate that welfare families are about the same size as the average family not on welfare in the United States. In 72.7 percent of AFDC families, there were two or fewer children.[18] In fact, the average AFDC family size has decreased from 4 to 2.9 persons since 1969.[19] Despite the calls for a "family cap," which would make ineligible for assistance any new child(ren) born into a family already receiving assistance, at least 10 major studies have demonstrated that there is no direct effect on childbearing and getting on welfare.[20] In other words, there is no conclusive evidence that women are having more children to get or increase their welfare benefits.

Some studies have shown a correlation between nonmarital births and welfare among some women, but not in the way that many would believe given the racialized manner in which welfare is discussed and presented. According to these studies, white women appear to be more likely to have children out-of-wedlock if they live in states where welfare benefits are higher. On the other hand, out-of-wedlock births by black and Latino women are not significantly correlated with higher welfare benefits.[21]

From the propaganda war against welfare, it would be easy to conclude that welfare recipients choose to stay on welfare endlessly.

But, welfare is not a way of life for most of its recipients. The majority leave the system permanently within four years; only 15 percent of recipients stayed on welfare continuously for five years or longer.[22] Studies showed that:

- 50 percent of recipients exit AFDC in the first year of welfare;
- 75 percent of recipients exit AFDC in the first two years of welfare;
- 40 percent of women who exit welfare through earned income remain poor;
- 42 percent of women return to welfare within two years of leaving it; and
- 75 percent of those reentering welfare exit again, and 50 percent of those do so within 12 months of return.[23]

Racially, whites constitute a substantial proportion of welfare recipients since poverty is fairly widespread. In the mid-1990s, African Americans and whites have both constituted somewhere between 38 and 39 percent with some going back and forth. Latinos were about 16 percent, and other groups about 7 percent, of those receiving AFDC.[24] This translated into 5.3 million whites, 5.5 million African Americans, and 2.2 million Latinos receiving AFDC assistance.

Unlike corporate wealthfare (discussed later), welfare for the poor accounts for a very tiny share of the federal budget.[25] In 1993, for example, AFDC costs were $22 billion, less than 1 percent of the entire federal budget. The states' share of the welfare costs was only about 2 percent of states' budgets.[26] Even when Food Stamps and other welfare programs are included, welfare still constituted less than 3 percent of the budget. In addition, administrative costs for AFDC, around $3 billion annually, have remained fairly constant between 1970 and 1993, and as a percentage of overall AFDC costs, have dropped from 19 percent in 1970 to 13 percent in 1993.[27] In 1993, adding in state costs, AFDC cost $22.3 billion, which accounted for about 0.35 percent of the nation's gross domestic product.[28] These numbers remained consistent throughout the mid-1990s.

Welfare benefits under AFDC were so low that even combined with Food Stamps families fell far below the poverty line. States with higher costs of living tended to pay more; New York, for instance, paid a maximum of $577 per month, a maximum of $6,924 a year. In other states—Mississippi for example—the maximum cash benefit was as low as $120 per month. On average, national annual cash benefits paid totaled about $4,392, only 36 percent of the federal poverty line of $12,320 for a family of three.[29]

The Politics of Welfare Reform

"The AFDC program could use reform, but not in the ways the new reformists suggest. Provide the very poor with access to health care, so they don't have to leave low-paying jobs that don't provide it when their children get sick. Allow recipients to go to school while receiving aid, so they can learn skills that better suit them to the labor market."[30] —Julianne Malveaux

Although President Reagan was famous for his false "Welfare Queen" statement, welfare was not a central issue in either his 1980 or 1984 campaigns nor in the presidential campaign of 1988 between George Bush and Michael Dukakis. The current battle over welfare reform can be traced to President Clinton's 1992 campaign pledge to "end welfare as we know it." In their book *Putting People First,* candidates Clinton and Al Gore wrote, "It's time to honor and reward people who work hard and play by the rules. That means ending welfare as we know it—not by punishing the poor or preaching to them, but by empowering Americans to take care of their children and improve their lives. No one who works full-time and has children at home should be poor anymore. No one who can work should be able to stay on welfare forever."[31]

Clinton propose that federal rules be changed so that able-bodied welfare recipients be required to go to work rather than have the option of not participating.[32] Once in office, Clinton made good on his promise to attempt to reform the welfare system. He established a Working Group on Welfare Reform and continued to raise the issue during his first year in office. Unfortunately for Clinton, the debate would move quickly beyond his office and become one of the most hotly contested issues of modern times. Clinton's Working Group proposed the unsuccessful "Work and Responsibility Act of 1994."

The bill's major provision was to create a two-year time limit on unrestricted cash assistance that would, in effect, restrict most AFDC recipients to a lifetime maximum of 24 months in the program. While this was similar to proposals being advocated by some conservatives, the Clinton administration included numerous exemptions, such as for mothers with disabilities, mothers caring for disabled children, and mothers of infants. Other provisions of Clinton's plan included the creation of a new program known as WORK, different from and in addition to JOBS. WORK would provide subsidized employment opportunities for recipients who were no longer eligible for cash assistance. One important change being proposed was that recipients would be forced to participate in the JOBS program after their child turned one, rather than three as in the current rules. The administration also called for tougher guidelines and penalties regarding collection of support payments from reluctant and absentee fathers.

While the Clinton plan was not as draconian as many conservative proposals, a number of sources criticized it harshly, particularly the WORK provision of the legislation. Critics from the Left charged that the plan seriously underestimated the economic picture that recipients would face and that its funding request was much too low to meet even its own minimum job creation objectives. The Congressional Black Caucus Foundation (CBCF) wrote that welfare recipients need marketable skills, and "will also need the creation of public sector positions, in which they can provide necessary and constructive services to society, in the event they are unable to find a position through traditional means in the private sector."[33] The bottom line, declared the CBCF, was that welfare reform must include "considerable job creation, meaningful job training, and more money."[34]

The Clinton plan died and several other proposals, such as Rep. Robert Matsui's (D–CA) "Family Self-Sufficiency Act of 1994" and Sen. Lauch Faircloth's (R–NC) "Welfare Reform Act of 1994," were introduced. By far, however, the bill that set the tone and tenor of the debate was the Republican's "Personal Responsibility Act of 1995," which grew out of the GOP's "Contract with America." The bill did not merely reform welfare, it destroyed the very principles that guided federal policy toward the poor for six decades.

On August 22, 1996, Clinton signed the Republican welfare bill that ended AFDC and created TANF. Although outrage among liberals and progressives was loud and steadfast, Clinton made an election-year decision that said he would rather throw perhaps more than a million children into deeper poverty than risk losing to Republican candidate Bob Dole on the grounds that he was soft on welfare and had broken one of his most noted 1992 campaign promises.

Draconian and oppressive in several ways, the bill got rid of a 60-year guarantee of commitment to the nation's poor, whether they are children, the elderly, or the disabled.. Welfare is no longer an entitlement from the federal government to the states to provide funding based on need. States now receive fixed block grants that once exhausted, despite the need, will not be replenished. Recipients are also restricted to a lifetime limit of 60 months of receiving TANF. States are also obligated to force a large percentage of recipients into workfare programs under the threat of losing funding. There are many more aspects of the new legislation that punish recipients, deny assistance to legal immigrants, and penalize teenage mothers, among other things. As Clinton sheepishly pledged to "fix" certain aspects of the legislation, he remained loudly quiet as another battle concerning welfare unfolded.

Expanding Wealthfare as We Know It

Corporate welfare—what some have appropriately called "wealthfare"—was virtually untouched by Congress and the White House in their frenzy to cut the "undeserving" poor from the government dole. Perhaps one of the biggest myths perpetrated regarding the U.S. economy is that it is a private system that operates with no assistance from the government. In fact, government handouts to corporations constitute a major source of operating capital for the business community. The Washington, D.C. watchdog group, Essential Information, states, "Federal government estimates on corporate welfare spending for 1994 total $104.3 billion, while spending for social welfare programs on the poor is estimated at only $75.1 billion."[35]

The hypocrisy of railing against welfare for the poor while sanctioning welfare for the rich has drawn even sectors usually supportive of congressional initiatives. The *Washington Post* noted, "The current vogue of welfare reform in Washington is curiously narrow. After all, 'ending welfare as we know it' means cutting off, not only the proverbial unwed mothers, but also those indolent corporations that have grown fat feeding at the public trough....This year, taxpayers will spend $51 billion in direct subsidies to business and lose another $53.3 billion in tax breaks for corporations, according to the Office of Management and Budget and the Joint Committee on Taxation. Those who want welfare recipients to work as a condition of public assistance should expand their efforts to cover corporations dependent on federal largesse."[36] Getting more specific, the *Washington Post* went on to say, "The most costly form of corporate welfare in 1994 will be subsidies for agribusiness, costing an estimated $29.2 billion. By contrast, the federal government will spend $25 billion on food stamps and $15 billion for Aid to Families With Dependent Children (AFDC), two of the programs most criticized by conservatives in the welfare reform debate. Ignoring the cost of corporate entitlements distorts the welfare debate and leaves most Americans with the false impression that poor people, rather than corporations or middle and upper income individuals, are straining the national budget."[37]

There are numerous additional examples that can be cited. Researchers Mark Zepezauer and Arthur Naiman list dozens of examples of welfare payments through government subsidies to various industries, including nuclear, aviation, mining, agricultural, and timber industries. They estimate that it costs taxpayers at least $448 billion a year in handouts to corporations and wealthy individuals compared to about $130 billion in welfare payments to the poor.[38] Further, they note that their figure for wealthfare leaves off numerous other payments, including state and local tax breaks for corporations.

The egregiousness of corporate welfare benefits has been so great that a coalition of conservatives, liberals, and progressives have joined together to attack the problem—albeit for different and often conflicting reasons. While the Left has argued against the hypocritical cruelty of cutting aid to the poor while throwing billions of dollars at the already rich, the Right, consistent with the slash-and-burn ideology of conservatism, wants to cut taxes and reduce the deficit. The Stop Corporate Welfare coalition, formed in August 1996, includes Republican tax terrorist Rep. John Kasich, chair of the House Budget

Committee and Americans for Tax Reform on the Right; the Cato Institute and the Progressive Policy Institute in the middle; and the Corporate Wealthfare Project, U.S. Public Interest Research Group, and Friends of the Earth. Out of the 12 wealthfare cuts that the coalition could find agreement on, it had victory on one: stopping legislation that would have doubled congressional funding for the Overseas Private Investment Corporation.[39]

In the 105th Congress, the Congressional Progressive Caucus (CPC) proposed H.R. 2534, "The Corporate Responsibility Act." The bill would make $800 billion in cuts in corporate welfare by getting rid of: funds to advertise and promote weapons ($500 million), depreciation ($32 billion), funds to 14 of the largest computer chip companies ($300 million), subsidies to millionaire farmers/ranchers ($40 million), use of federally owned lands by mineral companies ($200 million), advertisements for fast foods internationally ($110 million), and brand-name recognition promotion ($3.6 million). Overall, the CPC targeted 18 programs to be cut.[40]

The duplicity of attacking welfare payments to the poor while turning a blind eye to gifts to the rich raises critical issues regarding priorities and the political symbols used in shaping the welfare debate.[41] The issue of real need is obscured by a narrowing of the discourses about social policy for the poor. As Essential Information argues, "The problem is that corporate welfare has created a culture of dependency that has encouraged certain industries to live off the taxpayers. Year after year, these companies receive subsidies or handouts from the federal government and never learn to fend for themselves. And, unlike the vast majority of poor people who receive public assistance, most corporate welfare recipients are not particularly needy."[42]

Debate within the Black Community

To a significant degree, the debate in the black community has not focused on corporate welfare, the unjust nature of so-called welfare reform, or Clinton's betrayal of the black vote. Instead, much of the discussion has echoed the conservative jeremiads that welfare for the poor creates a culture of dependency. While black conservatives have been silent on the immorality of corporate welfare, they have been unrelenting in their attacks on welfare recipients and liberal black leaders who they view as welfare enablers. They promote a distorted perspective of the ideology of self-help and cultural pathology.

Black conservatives blame poverty and the issues that arise from being poor, such as family breakup, on welfare. Joseph Conti and Brad Stetson, both of the right-wing research group, the David Institute, state, "[W]elfarism contributes to family dissolution and ultimately hurts the people involved....Welfare programs and policies are a classic case of the iatrogenic nature of activist government policy: intending to help, it hurts."[43]

Arguments by black conservatives also tend toward patriarchy and recentering the role of men in the family. Brian Jones, president of the conservative Center for a New Black Leadership, writes, "To the extent that the incentives of the welfare system marginalize or even obviate the role of men as breadwinners and essential components of viable family units, it must be substantially reformed. As long as public policy undermines the economic rationale for marriage, communities will be powerless to confront very real impediments to socioeconomic mobility."[44]

Like their white counterparts, the black conservatives blame welfare for the economic condition of blacks. Black conservative Terry Lovelace notes, "[T]he current welfare state has helped destroy many black families by taking wage-earning fathers out of homes and replacing them with a monthly government check. Black Americans, though just 12 percent of the population, currently make up more than one-third of the entire welfare system in the United States."[45]

The conservative spin on welfare is often in sync with the views of some black nationalists. The plea for a ethos of self-help, long a common bond between black conservatives and black nationalists, means that welfare is seen as anathema to African-American self-determination. Minister Louis Farrakhan, leader of the black nationalist religious group, the Nation of Islam, while careful not to cast aspersions on the poor themselves, stated, "Welfare if you turn it around means farewell. It means bye to the spirit of self-determination. It means so long to the spirit that God gives to every human being and the duty that God gives to every human being to do something for self. It makes you a slave. Welfare, farewell."[46]

Not surprisingly, much of the defense of the rights and dignity of welfare recipients comes from black women scholars and activists. They identify not only the material harm and suffering brought by welfare reform, but also critique the ideological uses of welfare in promoting a white and male supremacist worldview. Scholar Wahneema Lubiano argues, "Read the newspapers, watch television, or simply listen to people talk: among other things, welfare queens are held responsible for the crack trade and crack babies. And they combine that with moral degeneracy within their families....She is [depicted as] the agent of destruction, the creator of the pathological, black, urban, poor family from which all ills flow; a monster creating crack dealers, addicts, muggers, and rapists—men who become those things because of being immersed in her culture of poverty....[Significantly, however,] the attacks on [welfare queens are] exercises of state power by means of invoking racist and sexist stereotypes passing themselves off as social-science-supported policy...."[47]

The particularizing of the attack on black women is not accidental. Black women become the supreme representation of the undeserving underclass in popular culture and imagery, thus doubling the predisposed prejudices that are readily available for the conservative project of eliminating the welfare state. According to historians Barbara Ransby and Tracye Matthews, "Regular attacks on our black women in the media, most often disguised as an attack on the admittedly inadequate welfare system, portray them as lazy, unfit mothers, members of a morally bankrupt underclass, who should be punished for their inability to sustain a middle-class family lifestyle on a sub-poverty income."[48]

Their words are again echoed by Lubiano, who writes, "The most immediately recognizable figure, the welfare queen, is omnipresent in the media—even when (and perhaps especially when) she is not explicitly named. Given a couple of centuries (and, in the corporate and/or mainstream press, an especially intense couple of decades) of seeing and hearing the behaviors and economic position of poor African Americans laid at the door of their 'problematic' family structure and/or culture, given the various ways in which every large urban newspaper and most small-town newspapers remind us of the 'blight' (political, social, and economic) of the cities, and given the ubiquity of political and community figures whose commentary focuses on attributing the 'decline of the nation' to the urban poor and the inappropriateness or inadequacy (take your pick) of state intervention against those problems, the welfare queen is omnipresent in discussions about 'America's' present or future even when unnamed."[49]

As perhaps the nation's most vocal advocates for poor children, the Children's Defense Fund (CDF) has produced numerous reports, fact sheets, briefing books, and other materials pointing out the harms that are likely to be a result of recent welfare reforms. As the CDF wrote in one strategy paper, these reforms "represent a fundamental shift in our nation's commitment to children. The federal government no longer will be the protector of last resort for hungry, disabled, poor, abused, and neglected boys and girls. It will pass the buck to 50 states with over 40 billion fewer dollars. And states are making no promises about how children will be protected."[50]

The Children's Defense Fund has also offered a number of conditions that they argue must be met if real welfare reform, beyond that passed by Clinton and Congress, and more importantly, the effort to end poverty are to be successful. This includes providing employment opportunities, childcare, education and training, job retention, health coverage, child support, family integrity, and work incentives. CDF calls for "substantial new investments" to achieve genuine reform and states that "If we merely impose a rigid new set of requirements on families receiving AFDC without providing more effective assistance to overcome their barriers to employment, we only add to the plight of our nation's poorest and most vulnerable children."[51]

The Joint Center for Political and Economic Studies (JCPES), a leading Washington, D.C.-based African-American think tank, has also weighed in on the debate. Similar to other liberal critiques, JCPES does not defend the welfare system, they note, "The welfare system is broken. Poor people who have to rely on Aid to Families with Dependent Children (AFDC), the program that provides cash assistance to families, know this better than anyone else. The current system does not reward initiative or hard work, and it discourages the formation and stability of two-parent families."[52] JCPES was deeply critical of the changes brought by the Clinton-signed bill. In their proposed agenda for reform, JCPES states that there are some important principles on which reform must be built:

- We must eliminate rules that make it difficult for two-parent families to receive help;
- Federal child support enforcement is the only effective way of ensuring that noncustodial parents who can pay support do so;
- Pro-work reform means encouraging all forms of work, including part-time work;
- Reforms must improve a parent's ability to support children by improving his or her skills and job prospects; and
- Finally, pro-work reforms must include job placement and job creation strategies.

In the aftermath of the 1994 Republican victories in Congress, the CBCF formed a working group of liberal and progressive lobby organizations to respond to the GOP's Contract with America. Among the groups and individuals involved were the Center on Budget and Policy Priorities, the Joint Center for Political and Economic Studies, the Institute for Policy Studies, the Democratic National Committee, congressional staffers, and other political activists. The CBCF's Working Group for a New Agenda for New Times (WGNANT) criticized the Republican Personal Responsibility Act and offered a number of suggestions for what would constitute meaningful welfare reform. Those proposals acknowledged the need to change the system as it existed, but offered to protect those most in need.[53]

The demands raised by the CDF, JCPES, CBCF, and other black groups generally went unheard. In the welfare reform that passed and was signed into law, few of the concerns about maintaining a cushion for the nation's poor were addressed. While lack of consensus was one factor, the overriding reason the black community was screwed was an unwarranted faith in the generosity and virtue of President Clinton rather than an effort to mobilize and organize the poor.[54]

Organizations Fighting Back

Discourses about welfare for the poor by conservatives, liberals, the major media, and academics tend to disregard the self-organization and resistance to marginalization by the poor themselves. This web of social science theorizing facilitates the erasure of the poor from the policy and political debates that have shaped welfare and welfare reform. While some progressive scholars—such as Frances Fox Piven, Richard Cloward, James Jennings, Mimi Abramovitz, Julianne Malveaux, Sanford F. Schram, to name a few—have noted the critical role that a mobilized poor has played in shaping welfare policies, in general, those movements have been whitewashed away, with important political consequences. As historian Robin D. G. Kelley notes, "The end result has been a failure to take into account opposition and human agency on the part of the poor. In particular, most social scientist overlook the role(s) of ideology and consciousness, the formation of oppositional movements among the inner-city poor, various forms of individual and collective resistance."[55] Scholar Marcia Bok sounds a similar concern when she writes that favorable policies for the poor will only come about as a result of "grassroots and mass movements in the United States."[56]

At the national level as well as the local, groups have organized to articulate and struggle for the rights and interests of the poor, involving the poor themselves in membership and leadership roles. The National Welfare Rights Union (a merger of the former National Welfare Rights Organization and several other groups) has perhaps been the most consistent and longest-fighting network of the poor across the nation. Also organizing on the national level are the Children's Defense Fund and Jobs With Peace. Significantly, all of these organizations are led by black women, although men are involved in a wide variety of roles.

Most activism regarding welfare rights, however, logically occurs at the local and state levels. Too often ignored as sites of contestation, the battles that are fought in these venues are much closer to the daily tribulations and struggles that welfare recipients experience. In *Under Attack, Fighting Back*, Mimi Abramovitz identifies a wide array of fight-back groups that have emerged in the 1990s to combat the punitive and ineffective welfare reforms coming from local and state officials as well as from the White House and Capitol Hill.[57] Among groups that she highlights are the Coalition for Basic Human Needs (Boston, MA), Parents for Justice (NH), Welfare Warriors (Milwaukee, WI), Welfare Warriors (Long Island, NY), Empower (Rochester, NY), the Reform Organization of Welfare (St. Louis, MO), Women for Economic Security (Chicago, IL), Women's Union (VT), Arise (Springfield, MA), Justice, Economic Development and Independence for Women (Salt Lake City, UT), and the Women's Economic Agenda (Oakland, CA).[58]

These groups and many more demonstrate the self-actualizing character of the poor and give lie to the popular notion that welfare recipients passively surrender to the assaults launched against them by policymakers. The material demands by these groups and poor individuals themselves for jobs, a living wage, educational opportunities, decent housing and fair rents, and accessible and adequate health care accompany the equally important demands for respect, dignity, and honor.

3

California Scheming

If there is any state in the nation that can be called global, it is California. It is the most racially and ethnically diverse state and is projected to become the first whose population is a majority of color. It is the home of the nation's technological revolution, sparking the global computer links that have transformed labor, pleasure, and social relations. These circumstances provided the political leadership of the state with the opportunity to guide the nation and perhaps the international community in addressing diversity concerns in this age of transition. Yet conservative elected leaders, the major political parties, and even academics have played anything but a progressive role on a number of critical race and ethnic issues.

In the 1990s, California became the font of racial conflict in the United States. From the Rodney King saga to the gestation of gangsta rap to the agonies of the O.J. Simpson adventure to legal fights over immigration to attacks on affirmative action to the struggle over Ebonics, the state has become the epicenter of the grand battle between those who would turn back the clock on racial progress and those who seek innovative and constructive ways to move forward. Therefore, it is useful and perhaps necessary to examine the meanings, myths, and movements concerning how California has waged struggles around immigration, affirmative action, and unequal education. These issues were codified in the campaigns over the passage of Proposition 187 in 1994, and Proposition 209 in 1996, and in response to the position taken by the Oakland Unified School District Board of Education regarding the role of black English vernacular (termed Ebonics) in the education process. All three of these issues generated elite and grassroots movements on the Right and the Left; forced responses from national political leaders, civil rights leaders, members of Congress, and the White House; and captured the attention of the world community.

These issues reflect the economic and political tensions and anxieties that increasingly define this age of transition. The shrunk and shrinking economy of the state—itself a consequence of defense cuts in a post-Cold War, post-Soviet world, and the subsequent loss of manufacturing jobs—shapes the mass response to the growth in immigration to California, the implementation of affirmative action, and the level of funding committed to public education. The fear of more job loss by whites to African Americans and Latinos, has helped to feed a racial backlash that has been exploited by conservatives across the state. From the conservative media to right-wing elected officials, whites are disingenuously told that affirmative action gives jobs to unqualified people of color and women; that Latinos and Asians are illegally entering the state, also taking jobs and state welfare resources; and that the poor, mainly people of color, are living luxuriously on the government dole at taxpayer's expense. While these issues have fed a resurgent, though weakened conservative crusade, they have also launched new multiracial mass movements and coalitions across the breadth and length of the state whose agendas now extend beyond the narrow issues that initially brought them together.

The growth of these movements is of high importance to the progressive movement as a whole since they indicate the resilience of people to resist even in situations where the balance of power is unfavorable. Although both propositions passed and the battleground shifted to the courts, and the controversy over Ebonics was diffused, the issues do not die and their political significance remains. More important, the issues consolidated several cores of activists who have vowed to continue to fight the conservative Right on a whole range of issues. These movements cannot be romanticized, however. They embodied the difficulties inherent in building coalitions with organizations that have conflicting interests and urgencies. Part of the problem is the tendency to reproduce organizational and political forms that reflect old styles of outreach, mass education, and political stances. Protest is a critical though limited form of struggle and is most effective in conjunction with other more sustaining strategies. Coalition forms, in some instances, are not conducive to the multiplicity of methods necessary to engage in contemporary struggles.

The issues raised in California remain at the center of the national political discourse on the nature and direction of race relations in the United States as the 20th century comes to a close. All indications are that, on the issue of race, the 20th century will end in ways very similar to the manner in which the 19th century ended: legitimation of proponents of eugenics; ideological and political campaigns against immigrants; creation of racist paramilitary groups; incessant attacks on the voting rights of African Americans; and growing economic inequality.

These concerns take on a global meaning. First, the issue of immigration necessarily raises international relationships and dynamics. The political and economic causes of immigration have often been obscured in the heat over the impact of immigration. Second, other nations and movements often look to the United States for guidance on resolving many of the racial and ethnic conflicts that they themselves are experiencing. The issues of immigration, affirmative action, and conflicting languages in education have been on the agenda of activists, administrators, and political leaders in England, France, South Africa, Nicaragua, and many other nations that have had to address the integration of marginalized communities into the broader society. Third, the downturns in the California economy are driven by changes in the global economy, the transformed role of the United States in the post-Cold War period, and by investment decisions made by transnational corporations over which state residents and leaders have little or no control.

Race, Class, and Politics in Contemporary California

California is the largest state in the nation. It has a population of nearly 30 million comprised of 58 percent whites, 25 percent Latinos, 10 percent Asians, and 7 percent African Americans. During the Reagan years, the state was one of the most prosperous in the nation due to the financial bonanza its large defense industry received as federal military spending exploded. As defense cuts went into effect in the late 1980s and 1990s, however, the economy took a sharp downturn.

In the new economic order, California has taken hard hits. A devastating recession, runaway shops, and downsizing in the military led to over 800,000 jobs leaving California between July 1, 1991 and July 30, 1992.[1] The end of the Cold War in the late 1980s reconfigured the global military role of the United States. Demands for cuts began to have an impact; some bases were closed, and the war industry was downsized significantly.

No longer the defense industry state, California has become the containment state. The state is building prisons at an alarming rate as it shifts its budget from schools and social programs to prison construction and criminal justice. The San Francisco-based Center on Juvenile and Criminal Justice's report, "From Class Rooms to Cell Blocks: The Effects of Prison Building on Higher Education and African American Enrollment," documents that in 1980–1981, 9.2 percent of California's general fund went to higher education and only 2.3 percent to corrections, but in 1996–97, corrections received 9.4 percent while higher education got only 8.7 percent. As the title of the study indicates, this shift has been particularly harmful to the prospects and opportunities facing African Americans in the state. In 1996, according to the report, California had twice as many African Americans in its prisons (45,000) as in its four-year public universities.[2] Broken down by gender, the study reports that between 1980 and 1995, the number of black men in prison increased more than 500 percent—from 8,139 to 41,434—while the number of black men in public higher education rose only 30 percent, from 8,066 to 10,479. By 2001, the ratio could be 7 to 1 if current trends continue.

The report, critical of the state's political leaders, especially the policies of Republican Governor Pete Wilson, states, "Since 1980, California has made policy and fiscal decisions that increasingly favor locking people up rather than providing them with higher education."[3] The study recommends a freeze on funding for prison construction, placing a cap on the state's prison population, creating more alternatives for nonviolent offenders, passing bond measures to renovate and expand the University of California (UC) and Cal State systems, and instituting aggressive efforts to promote minority enrollment in the state's universities. Finally, the report also notes that tuition increases at UC have far outpaced the growth in median household incomes. This has created a greater hardship on black families because while UC fees consume 35 percent of whites' median household earnings, they consume 57.5 percent of blacks'. Needless to say, Wilson and other officials in his administration have rejected the report.

California residents are going to jail and prison at such a fast rate that thousands are being let out due to overcrowding. It was reported in December 1996 that, for the first six months of that year, "an average 27,500 prisoners per month were released from jails due to overcrowding."[4] The situation is likely to worsen as unemployment increases, because more and more people will be forced to spend time in jail for minor crimes rather than pay even the small fines that they can no longer afford.

It is within this context that the backlash against the perceived advances of African Americans and Latinos have come under attack. Unwilling to focus their resentment on the policymakers and corporate executives in power, the poor, people of color, and women are scapegoated by those who fear further economic insecurity.

Saving "Our State" from Whom and for What

In California, "187" is the criminal justice code for murder. It is a popular term among gangbangers, gangsta rappers, and as it turns out, even state officials. In 1994, Californians voted in favor of Proposition 187, a ballot initiative that proposed cutting funding for public education and social services, including health care, to "illegal" immigrants and their children. The proposal was part of the national assault on immigration by the nation's conservative movement. Implementation of the law was projected to cost $10 billion in the first year.

The proposition was known by the name "Save Our State" (SOS), which raises questions as to what is being saved, who it is being saved for, who it is being saved from, and who is the "our"? For some, the message was an SOS for those who feared an imminent takeover of the state by so-called hordes of Spanish-speaking aliens streaming across the southern border. The 187 debate and immigration, in general, has never been about Canadians or Russians or Sweds coming to take "our" jobs. It was and remains tied to racial conceptions and notions. What is being saved are mythical views of job mobility and opportunities that were, and remain, controlled by financial elites and not poor immigrants.

The contemporary rising controversies over immigration are directly tied to the economic transformations wrought by globalization. In Latin America, Mexico in particular, labor is on the move as international corporations move in and remap the economies of the region. Linked with local financial elites, transnational corporations from Asia, Europe, Canada, and the United States have located operations in the region to take advantage of low wages, limited labor regulations, and governments willing to repress their own workforces.

Only four years after the contentious passage in 1993 of NAFTA, workers in Canada, the United States, and especially Mexico felt the deleterious effects of that legislation. According to the Washington, DC-based watchdog group, Public Citizen, 1,850,000 jobs have been lost in Mexico since NAFTA passed.[5] The percentage of Mexicans considered "extremely poor" grew from 31 percent in 1993 to 50 percent in 1996. The number of pesos to the dollar during this same period went from 3.1 to 1 to 7.88 to 1. While *Public Citizen* magazine noted that Mexico ranks fifth in the number of billionaires per country, 40 million of its 92 million citizens live on less than $5 a day.[6] The surprise is not how many Mexicans attempt to illegally come to the United States each year, but how many do not.

Although large numbers of illegal immigrants come to the United States annually—between 225,000 and 300,000, according to official statistics from the U.S. Census Bureau and the Immigration and Naturalization Service (INS)—these numbers are concentrated in a relatively few states.[7] About 40 percent go to California, 15 percent to New York, 11 percent to Florida, and 10 percent to Texas, states research by the Urban Institute. Illinois, New Jersey, and Arizona account for another 10 percent, while the rest are scattered in insignificant numbers around the country.[8]

Wilson's goals in defending Proposition 187 were completely political and had little to do with addressing the real impact of immigration on the state. Scholar Alejandro Ramos aptly demonstrated how Wilson and his charlatan economic advisers used bogus and faulty statistics to make a case for immigration reform. As Ramos noted, "the governor cites only those studies which conclude that immigrants receive more from the system than what they contribute overall."[9] For example, in estimating the number of undocumented aliens in the state, Wilson used the U.S. Census Bureau's higher unofficial estimate of 1.7 million rather than the more accurate INS estimate of 1.4 million.[10] The state also used studies that underestimated the amount of taxes collected from immigrants, off as much as 30 percent, and overestimated costs incurred by immigrants, according to Ramos. Wilson ignored at least 24 studies that conclude that immigrants are not economic burdens, including ones from the U.S. Department of Labor, U.S. Department of Justice, National Bureau of Economic Research, and the Urban Institute.

According to Proposition 187, schools must verify that every student in the school has legal status. In California, this would require interrogating about 10 million students on an ongoing basis. What this would mean is that students who look or sound "foreign" to a teacher might be subject to harassment on that criteria alone. For example, there are nearly 100,000 Puerto Ricans in the state. Puerto Ricans are U.S. citizens whose legal status is no different than that of any other U.S. citizen. Yet they become immediately suspect simply because they speak Spanish and are brown.[11]

The bill was coauthored by former Sacramento lobbyist Alan Nelson and former Western Regional Chief of the INS Harold Ezell. Nelson was a lobbyist for the Federation for American Immigration Reform (FAIR), one of the key groups fighting for the passage of SOS and pushing repressive immigration reform around the nation. FAIR calls for sealing the U.S. (southern) border. During the campaign, FAIR was exposed as having received more than $600,000, since 1988, from the ultra-conservative Pioneer Fund.[12] The latter is a group that has also sponsored research by various scientists, including the late William B. Shockley, who contended that blacks are inherently intellectually inferior to whites. In the Pioneer Fund's original charter, it called for "reproduction of individuals descended predominantly from white persons who settled in the original 13 states or from related stock." In 1985, in a move so hypocritical as to be laughable, the word "white" was removed.

Black leaders across the state, from Rep. Maxine Waters and then-Speaker of the Assembly Willie Brown to Rep. Ron Dellums and Los Angeles Police Department Chief Willie L. Williams, vehemently opposed the initiative. At the grassroots level, hundreds of black groups across the state spoke out against 187. Marches and demonstrations, some numbering as large as 70,000, and statewide coalitions were organized to defeat 187.

The battle over SOS inspired an historic turnout of Latino voters in the state of California. In 1990, 844,000 Latinos voted; in 1994, more than 1.1 million voted, an increase of 34 percent. Motivated and mobilized in opposition to SOS, 47.5 percent of eligible Latinos turned out to the polls.

Despite the heated opposition, Proposition 187 was approved by a wide margin of voters, 59 to 41 percent.[13] Although whites were the only racial/ethnic group to vote in majority supporting the initiative, it received strong support from every racial and ethnic group except Latinos. Whites supported 187 by a margin of 63 to 37 percent, while it was rejected by blacks (47 to 53 percent), Asians (47 to 53 percent), and Latinos (23 to 77 percent). The strength of black support for 187, as *Oakland Tribune* columnist Brenda Payton noted, was based on a growing economic insecurity that blames Latinos for taking (menial) jobs that were once held by African Americans.[14]

Within days of the vote, the bill was challenged in court and an injunction was imposed on its implementation. Jan Adams, writing in *Racefile,* summed up the Proposition 187 battle. Adams argued that 187 "so perfectly appealed to the racial anxieties of voting Californians that it is impossible to imagine an electoral strategy that could have defeated it."[15]

Proposition 209: Affirmative Reaction

"A society that has something special against the Negro for hundreds of years must now do something special for the Negro."[16] —Martin Luther King, Jr.

Two years after the passage of Proposition 187, voters in the state passed Proposition 209, known as the California Civil Rights Initiative (CCRI). Just as conservatives have done on other issues, their dishonest use of the term "civil rights" obscured that, in fact, the ballot initiative had the very opposite intent. CCRI's goal was simple: the complete elimination of state affirmative action programs in all applications. Affirmative action has served as a necessary though limited remedy to ongoing racial and gender inequities in U.S. society. The proposition prohibits any state government agency from implementing affirmative action programs, ends all minority or women set-aside programs, and ends all minority- or women-designated scholarships.

The attacks on affirmative action have escalated in this era. Pressures flowing from a more insecure global and national employment environment have fed the racially constructed myth that whites, especially white males, are losing jobs and educational opportunities due to government-ordered affirmative action programs that benefit women, African Americans, and Latinos.

The first blow in the campaign to rid the state of responsibility for affirmative action occurred on July 20, 1996 when the UC Board of Regents voted to end affirmative action in the UC system in admissions, faculty hiring, and business contracts. Protests by students, national civil rights leaders such as Jesse Jackson, and other supporters were to no avail, despite data demonstrating that a decline in black and Latino entrance into the system would occur. In February 1997, UC officials reported that, in fact, applications from African Americans and Latinos had declined. This decline occurred while the UC system was receiving a record number of applications (46,682) from California's high school seniors for the school year beginning in fall 1997 and as the number of black and Latino seniors in California also grew. At the same time, applications from out of state rose by 28.4 percent. Although the affirmative action decision would not take effect until the 1998 school year, some UC officials and others felt that a message had been sent to black and Latino students that they simply were not wanted.[17]

Leading the battle to end affirmative action in the UC system, and later the CCRI campaign, was Board of Regents member Ward Connerly, who is African American. Connerly, who achieved financial and career success through his years of friendship with Wilson, was used by a Republican and conservative cause that desperately needed a black face to be at the forefront of the attack on affirmative action. Like other black conservatives mainly sponsored by white conservatives, Connerly relished his puppet role in what used to be called the "Head Negro in Charge."

He mouthed the usual conservative babble about how African Americans "have become addicted" to government aid and affirmative action. He stated with no qualification, "I sense this yearning among white people just to really become color blind. They want black people to assimilate. And black people are fighting it with every fiber of their being."[18]

Connerly led the opposition to affirmative action on UC campuses, except when it came to himself and his friends. His company benefited through its designation as a minority-owned firm and, on at least one occasion, he intervened affirmatively on behalf of a community college student he knew with a mediocre 2.6 grade point average who was seeking admission to the state's premier public campus, UC Berkeley. Connerly pressed another regent to help that unqualified applicant get in, while thousands of better applicants were rejected.

Connerly's wishful notions about whites' sense of yearning has no basis. The fact that he and other affirmative action opponents deny is that broad race and gender inequities continue to exist. White males, who are 33 percent of the population, are:

- 88 percent of all tenured professors;
- 85 percent of partners in law firms;
- 95 percent of *Fortune 500* CEOs;
- 97 percent of school superintendents; and
- 99 percent of professional athletic team owners

What was the truth about affirmative action in California? Affirmative action in education was crucial in improving Latino access to the UC system. In 1980, Latinos comprised only 6 percent of the student body, but as a result of affirmative action that number had doubled to 12 percent by 1994. Over 35 percent of the state's college-age population, 18–24, is Latino. Even with affirmative action, black state workers in California still earn only 84 percent of what their white counterparts do. Latino workers earn even less. In 1995, according to the California Senate Office of Research, "White employees earn a median $40,313; black employees $33,774, and Latino employees $32,978."[19]

Studies have also found that women and people of color hired under affirmative action programs tend to be more than qualified rather than less, as affirmative action opponents charge. A study by two Michigan State University economists, Harry Holzner and David Neumark, found that those minorities and women who were hired, at least in part due to affirmative action, performed as well as or better than white men in comparable positions. The study examined employers in Atlanta, Boston, Detroit, and Los Angeles, and found, contrary to widespread opinion, that "African American women generally outperformed white males on the job according to job evaluations filled out by their supervisors."[20]

As in the case of Proposition 187, a number of statewide organizations were formed to fight CCRI. One of the largest was Californians for Justice, a grassroots political movement founded in May 1995 by the Center for Third World Organizing (Oakland), Coalition for Immigrant Rights (San Francisco), and Agenda (Los Angeles).[21]

In terms of coalitions, the largest was the Campaign to Defeat 209, which involved hundreds of groups around the state. Differences over strategies between some of the feminist and civil rights organizations within the group led to a split a month or so before the vote and a new group was formed called STOP Prop. 209, which included the state chapter of the National Organization for Women, the Feminist Majority, and the Rainbow Coalition. Since the split was not driven by race or gender issues, some women and civil rights organizations, such as the NAACP Legal Defense Fund and the San Francisco-based Lawyers Committee for Civil Rights, stayed with the main group. While the Campaign to Defeat 209 tended to focus on media ads and building a statewide operation of speakers and surrogates, STOP Prop. 209 organized large protest events and grassroots mobilizations. As the groups noted, the differences actually complemented rather than opposed each other, and the two worked together throughout the campaign. Media buys were coordinated.[22]

At the same time, the inability of progressive and liberal activists to hold together the original coalition reflected real tensions over strategies, goals, and perhaps ideologies. Proposition 209 passed by a vote of 54 to 46 percent. It was overwhelmingly supported by whites (63 to 37 percent) and men (61 to 39 percent). Conversely, other racial and ethnic groups solidly rejected the proposition, such as African Americans (26 to 74 percent), Latinos (24 to 76 percent), and Asians (39 to 61 percent). Somewhat surprisingly, only slightly more women voted against it than for it (48 to 52 percent). In terms of age groups, the older the voter, the more likely they were to support 209. Those 18–29 split their vote (50 to 50 percent), while those 30–44 (51 to 49 percent), 45–64 (58 to 42 percent), and 65 and older (60 to 40 percent) voted for the proposition.[23]

In terms of class, income level and level of education did not correlate. Lower- and moderate-income individuals making less than $40,000 rejected 209 (45 to 55 percent), while those making above $40,000 strongly supported it (60 to 40 percent). On the other hand, except at the lower end, the higher the level of education, the less support 209 received. Those with some college did support 209 (60 to 40 percent) and, to a lesser extent, so did those with a college degree or more (54 to 46 percent). Those with a postgraduate degree, however, rebuked 209 (48 to 52 percent), as did those voters with a high school degree or less (54 to 46 percent).[24]

Studies and polls demonstrate that the rejection of affirmative action in California reflects a national trend. According U.S. News and World Report, 51 percent of whites agreed with the statement, "Equal rights have been pushed too far."[25] This was the first time ever that a majority has done so. In a poll of 248,000 teenagers, 90 percent opposed affirmative action in hiring and college admissions.[26] Much of the opposition to affirmative action is based on the false notion of "reverse discrimination." A 1992 study by People for the American Way found that young, white Americans felt more oppressed by reverse racism than had sympathy for racial bias.[27] The reality, however, is that so-called reverse discrimination carries virtually no legal or evidentiary weight. The U.S. Labor Department found that out of more than 3,000 discrimination cases between 1990 and 1994, less than 100 were about reverse discrimination and only 6 of those were decided in favor of the plaintiff. Rebecca Gordon of Californians for Justice stated, "Affirmative action is not quotas or remedies for past discrimination. It's narrowly tailored conservative remedies for current discrimination."[28]

In the final days of the campaign, President Clinton publicly joined the fray. According to White House Press Secretary Mike McCurry, the president believes that affirmative action must "remain available as a tool to address persistent discrimination in our society."[29] Other state politicians came out against 209, including U.S. Senators Dianne Feinstein and Barbara Boxer.

In April 1997, a three-judge panel of the 9th U.S. Circuit Court unanimously lifted the injunction on 209 that opponents had won in the days following the vote. That injunction had been imposed on December 23, 1996 by U.S. Chief District Judge Thelton Henderson, who is black and had been appointed by President Jimmy Carter. The three conservative judges who overturned Henderson's ruling—Diarmuid F. O'Scannlain, Edward Leavy, and Andrew J. Kleinfield—were all appointed by either President Reagan (the first two) or President Bush (the latter). Movements to end affirmation action are gathering steam in Arizona, Colorado, Florida, Ohio, Michigan, and Washington State.

Conclusion

Very few people are California dreaming these days. The state that should be a beacon of diversity and racial progress has been led by reactionary politicians concerned with their own ambitions and willing to stifle and obstruct opportunities under the guise of color blindness. They were able to exploit a populace predisposed to think in racist frameworks about social policy and economic opportunity.

The recent experiences in California also demonstrate that people of color are not immune to backsliding on issues that become racialized and polarized. African Americans who supported attacks on immigrants because they bought into constructed tales of job thievery, or Hispanics and Asians who opposed affirmative action because of the black mask placed on it, underscored the necessity of an honest dialogue on race that is inclusive of all.

Finally, California's integration into the national and global economy means that the intersection of race, economics, and politics must be understood beyond its local roots and ramifications. Its coastal location, size, and demographics make it a bellwether of social relations in an era of globalization. Perhaps no other state, with the exception of New York, will have the influx of immigrants of all backgrounds and have to rapidly make the economic, political, and cultural adjustments and transformations that will need to occur. An eye on California is an eye on the future, a future that is quickly and inexorably approaching.

4

To Be or Not to Be?: Race, Class, and Ebonics

"It is not the black child's language that is despised. It is his experience. A child cannot be taught by anyone who despises him, and a child cannot afford to be fooled. A child cannot be taught by anyone whose demand, essentially, is that the child repudiate his experience, and all that gives him sustenance, and enter a limbo in which he will no longer be black and in which he knows that he can never become white. Black people have lost too many children that way."[1] —James Baldwin

In the movie *Airplane*, two well-dressed black men are on a plane. Whenever they talk, in what appears to be a foreign language, subtitles are displayed below for the audience. In fact, they are actually speaking what is called in the movie "jive," that is, a mixture of black dialect and black ghetto slang. What this scene signals, *inter alia*, is the recognition that even in popular culture, class notwithstanding black folks and white folks do not talk alike.

Language is about power. It is about national power. It is about class power. It is also about racial and ethnic power. In South Africa, in the mid-1970s, Apartheid was brought to its knees in the resistance by black South African youth to the imposition of the Afrikaner language in the school system. In Canada, the country verged on civil war as French-speaking Canadians fought the domination of English and the English-speaking majority. Across the globe, the ability to determine and designate the position of language(s) in society reflects broader power systems that embody class, race, ethnic, and nationality issues.

This chapter argues several points generated by the concerns and controversy over Ebonics. The first point is that the fight over Ebonics is about more than just a particular educational practice. It is a manifestation of a broader struggle reflecting political and racial consciousness and the effort to promote and protect African-American cultural autonomy. The second point is the link between Ebonics and the conservative political backlash of the current period. The attack on Ebonics is part of an agenda of reaction that must be challenged and exposed. Finally, this chapter briefly examines the English globalization project that embraces the material and ideological interests of capital. Unfortunately, the response by many black leaders to the Ebonics discourse ignored these critical intersections and, in some cases, fed into the most negative dynamics of the debate.

Black English and Black Power

The 1960s witnessed the emergence of a black consciousness cultural movement that penetrated every facet of U.S. cultural life, including language. Black Power adherents, with vast support from the black community, challenged the imposition of standard English and the notion that black English vernacular (BEV) was inferior. While black linguists demonstrated the technical language qualities of BEV and traced its history to African speech patterns, Black Power nationalists fought the political battle of having black English, as William Van Deburg notes, "recognized as the lingua franca of the black nation."[2] BEV was viewed as part of the counter-oppositional culture of African Americans. At the same time, black student activists fought to have African languages—such as Swahili, Yoruba, and Hausa—accepted as legitimate for the language requirements that most colleges and universities demand.

This political struggle, unlike many of the period, had a mass character to it because broad swatches of the black community were affected by its outcome. The legitimizing of the culture of the black masses, the verification of their humanity and dignity, helped build the political mobilization necessary to win policy and political battles concerning education inequity. For those middle-class African Americans who had become bilingual in standard English and BEV, this struggle bridged, to some degree, the class cleavages that were growing in the black community during this period. The social dismissal of BEV was read by race-conscious, middle-class African Americans as the erasure of a critical part of their history, cultural ties, and indeed, even family connections. Working-class African Americans gained as the black English battle was merged into the black education reform movement that initiated black history courses and black studies, but more importantly, placed the issue of relevance at the center of the discourse regarding schooling.

In the end, while BEV was never officially recognized by most whites or policymakers as a full-blown language, activists were able to win an ideological point that language is neither a neutral political site nor unrelated to policy decisions.[3] As many African Americans rose to become members of school boards and elected officials, the issue of equal educational funding and the controversy over BEV was never far from the surface or the field of battle. Partly in reaction to the BEV movement as well as the growth of similar challenges from other language minorities, a conservative reaction sprouted under the banner of English-only. Given the historical and racial heritage at the base of it, English-only had and has a double meaning.

English-only, Por Favor

The English-only movement in the United States is generally defended by its proponents as simply concerned with practicality and preserving a cultural heritage. This rationalization, however, dissolves in the face of the fact that a single-language society has never been the heritage or history of the United States. Even among European descendants, one language has never been the rule. Many of the nation's founding documents, such as the Articles of Confederation, were printed in German and English, and multilingual education has always existed. From the beginning of the nation, the languages of Native Americans and Africans have always been present even as they have integrated, developed, and remapped the English language itself. According to the U.S. Census Bureau, in the 1990s, more than 300 first or second languages are spoken in the nation, reflecting the international character and diversity of contemporary society. According to the National Education Association (NEA), more than 185 languages are spoken in New York City schools, 187 languages are heard in schools in Fairfax County, VA, and in just one school in Los Angeles, at least 60 languages are spoken in the homes of the schoolchildren.

The attacks on non-English or nonstandard English speakers are part of the larger conservative agenda that seeks a homogenized (read: whitened) U.S. society and has an intolerance for diversity. Quite often the politics of the English-only movement are explicitly racist, the anti-Hispanic rhetoric is overt, and many of the groups in the movement are directly linked to right-wing, anti-immigration organizations. English First, one of the major English-only groups, is part of the ultra-conservative Committee to Preserve the Family, which created the U.S. Border Control that aims to stop what it defines as "illegal" Mexican border crossings. U.S. English, another English-only group, is organizationally linked with the Federation for American Immigration Reform, whose major focus is passing (more) restrictive immigration laws.

The battle to promote English-only has also taken place at the policy level as conservatives have attempted to legislate a struggle that is being lost in the streets and homes of the nation. They desire a constitutional amendment that would make English the official language of the United States, strengthening their case that educational institutions only be conducted in English. This would further stigmatize those U.S. born who do not speak so-called standard English as well as immigrants from non-English speaking nations. In 1981, the English Language Amendment was first introduced in Congress and has been a pet project of several of the most conservative Congressmembers. Although it has never been voted on, it stands as a token of the possibility of English hegemony over the nation. Since a Constitutional amendment is being sought, it requires approval by two-thirds of the members of the U.S. House of Representatives and the U.S. Senate, and must then be ratified by three-fourths of the states (38). There have been other English-only bills as well, which have also not gotten very far.

Clearly, much of the resistance to passing the legislation comes from the fact that Congress is a diverse body (though not enough) of Congressmembers from a wide range of ethnic and racial backgrounds and heritages. This includes Asian, African-American, Caribbean, European, and Latin American ancestry.

At the state level, the English-only movement has had more success. In those states where language minorities have fewer political resources to bring to the fight, a number of laws have passed—although in some instances, they have later been overturned. According to the NEA, states that have instituted such legislation include Alabama, Arizona (the law was ruled unconstitutional in 1995), Arkansas, California, Colorado, Florida, Georgia, Hawaii (a bilingual state), Illinois (the law was repealed in 1991), Indiana, Kentucky, Mississippi, Montana, Nebraska, New Hampshire, North Carolina, North Dakota, South Carolina, South Dakota, Tennessee, and Virginia.

In some states, the laws prohibit state and local governments from providing bilingual services to residents even if those residents have limited proficiency in English. While some states have passed laws that prevent legislatures from ignoring "the role of English," other states maintain that English is the official state language. The ideology of English-only, of course, is incompatible with the politics of an assertive black English promotion.

The Struggle over Black English

The battle over the role of black English in education is not separate from the politics of the discourse regarding the English-only movement. As often happens in the United States, the political discourse on race obscures underlying issues of class, national power, and other systems of oppression. Nowhere has this been so clear as in the historic debates over the educational role that nonstandard black English or BEV plays.[4] In 1996, this battle (re)surfaced due to the decision made by the Oakland Unified School District (OUSD) Board of Education to radically address the issue of how the school system was responding to the language and educational needs of poor black schoolchildren.

On December 18, 1996, following the recommendations of the Task Force on the Education of African American Students, the board voted unanimously to use whatever instructional strategies, were appropriate to raise the level of English proficiency among all students in the system, but particularly the students who spoke, at least in part, BEV or what has been termed "Ebonics," a fusion of the words "ebony" and "phonics."[4] Ebonics is *not* a teaching method, as some have mistakenly thought, but the descriptive term used to identify distinct black speech styles. The task force had been created by the OUSD board and had met and researched the issue for six months. Based on the task force's report, the board passed a resolution approving the systemwide teaching of black English speaking styles to teachers and concerned parents as a means of helping Ebonics speakers learn standard English. Helping teachers recognize the language structure of Ebonics, it was argued, would better prepare them to help students bridge between Ebonics and standard English.

For example, Ebonics speakers, similar to many Asian or French speakers, attempt to approximate some English sounds that are not natural to their language structure. The "th" sound, which does not exist in most African languages or with Ebonics speakers, is usually replaced with a "d," resulting in "dem" instead of "them" or "dey" instead of "they." These substitutions, and other well-documented linguistic differences, should not be demonized, but rather, the understanding of their operations should serve as a learning tool by which the transition to standard English occurs. It means conceptualizing the distinct way in which tenses are grasped by different languages, such that the Ebonics speaker use of "be" as a verb—as in "he be coming over."—is what linguists term an "aspectual" system. This system is found in parts of the Caribbean and elsewhere.

The Ebonics controversy highlights the disconnection that has grown regarding society's concern about the quality of education for the inner cities, and black inner cities in particular—a popular though misinformed equation. Long before the controversy, programs to teach black English to teachers already existed. These "bridge" programs were in several cities in Texas, Michigan, and even parts of California. Oakland had programs to teach black English to teachers in 26 of its schools; Los Angeles had programs in 31 schools.[6] These efforts were part of initiatives by black education activists and scholars—including voucher programs, all-black-male schools, Afrocentric curriculum, school decentralization, and military-style academies—to raise the educational level of black children in an era when social abandonment was the norm.

The search for alternative methods to help Oakland's black students achieve more was driven by the abysmal educational crisis that the children were facing. While black students constitute 53 percent of the Oakland school district, they make up the overwhelming proportions of those in special education (71 percent), suffering suspensions (80 percent), accused of truancy (67 percent), and those held back a grade (64 percent). Almost 20 percent of black 12th graders did not graduate. Most dramatically, in a system where 4.0 is the highest grade point average that can be obtained, black students averaged a dreadful and unacceptable rate of 1.8.

The decision to teach black English to teachers ignited a firestorm of opinions and dissentions from both black and white racial spokespeople. Clearly, part of the response was to the term Ebonics, a word most had never heard, but which was suddenly and ubiquitously popping up on the news and in headlines in every major newspaper. It is likely that many, black and nonblack, thought it was some new black cultural agent, like rap music or dreadlocks, that was being imposed on an unsuspecting white populace.

Politically, although not a single penny had been officially or unofficially requested, the Clinton administration issued a preemptive rejection from the Department of Education stating that it had no intention of classifying Ebonics as a foreign language and no federal funding would be released for any program having to do with it. In fact, the OUSD did not seek new funds, but new ways to use the funding already available. It should be emphasized, however, that the demand for more funding is quite legitimate.

It was clear that many of the people who were criticizing the decision had displayed little concern for Oakland's black children before December 1996. The response to Ebonics is more insightful in assessing the nexus of race and class than any of the facile and misinformed critiques of the approach. An outcry bordering on hysteria mounted as news of the board's decision spread. Black and white commentators condemned the decision. Black opponents went across the political spectrum from the Right to the Left including conservatives and moderates such as Shelby Steele, Clarence Page, and Ward Connerly, to liberals, nationalists, and progressives such as Kweisi Mfume, Jesse Jackson, and Maya Angelou. Journalist Carl T. Rowan wrote, "Telling troubled youngsters that a slang called 'black English' (dressed up as 'Ebonics') is good enough for them is the foulest of 'gifts' this holiday season. It is guaranteeing failure for all youngsters who swallow this cop-out from hard work and study."[7] Political activist Rev. Al Sharpton, who was contemplating a run for New York's mayor's seat, stated, "If I'm elected mayor, my inaugural address will not be delivered in broken black English. It will be clear."[8]

Civil rights leader Rev. Jackson initially opposed the Oakland decision. He stated, "I understand the attempt to reach out to these children, but this is an unacceptable surrender borderlining on disgrace....It's teaching down to our children and it must never happen."[9] Soon after, Jackson went to Oakland and talked with the board (amidst dozens of cameras). After the meeting, Jackson appeared to everyone to change his position and he stated that the board had been misunderstood. He did not say that he was the one who had done the misunderstanding. He also did not support the teaching plan, saying only, "I endorse the intent to make our children proficient in standard American English."[10] Jackson said later, in Jesse-speak, that regarding Ebonics, teachers needed to "detect, redirect, and correct."[11] After an endless round of reports about how Jackson had retreated, he found it necessary to point out in his newsletter that "Reverend Jackson did *not* change his position on Ebonics; rather, the Oakland School Board refined their initial position at which point they reached common ground."[12]

Maya Angelou, who has built a career on her use of Ebonics in her novels and poems, claims that she was "incensed" by the decision and that "The very idea that the African American language is a language separate and apart is very threatening, because it can encourage young men and women not to learn standard English."[13] Angelou's logic is faulty here in that her first premise (Why is the idea of a distinct black language threatening and who is it threatening to?) does not lead to her second (Where has it been shown that speaking Spanish or French discourages learning standard English?). This is reminiscent of her logic in supporting Clarence Thomas during his 1991 Supreme Court nomination battle, when she reasoned that his being black would ultimately lead him to reject his conservative anti-black views. There, too, she drew a conclusion devoid of evidence and wisdom.

Though given little press, some experts supported the Oakland decision. For many in the media, it was more newsworthy to discuss the controversial nature of the decision and the conflict surrounding it than its merits. No less than the Linguistic Society of America declared their endorsement of the proposal to use Ebonics as a teaching tool. In January 1997, the Chicago-based organization passed a resolution that said, in part:

> The variety known as 'Ebonics,' 'African American Vernacular English' (AAVE), and 'Vernacular Black English' and by other names is systematic and rule-governed like all natural speech varieties....Characterizations of Ebonics as 'slang,' 'mutant,' 'lazy,' 'defective,' 'ungrammatical,' or 'broken English' are incorrect and demeaning....There is evidence from Sweden, the US, and other countries that speakers of other varieties can be aided in their learning of the standard variety by pedagogical approaches which recognize the legitimacy of the other varieties of a language. From this perspective, the Oakland School Board's decision to recognize the vernacular of African American students in teaching them Standard English is linguistically and pedagogically sound.[14]

In response to the storm of criticism, the board initially made a tactical retreat and revised the resolution considerably. For example, the sentence that originally read, "Whereas, these studies have also demonstrated that African Language Systems are genetically based and not a dialect of English," was changed to, "Whereas, these studies have also demonstrated that African Language Systems have origins in West (African) and Niger-Congo languages and are not merely dialects of English."[15]

The resolution was also changed to make it clear that Ebonics was not being taught to students. The original language stated, "The Superintendent...shall immediately devise and implement the best possible academic program for imparting instructions to African-American students in their primary language for the combined purposes of maintaining the legitimacy and richness of such language." The revised sentence read, "The Superintendent...shall immediately devise and implement the best possible academic program for the combined purposes of facilitating the acquisition and mastery of English language skills, while respecting and embracing the legitimacy and richness of the language patterns."[16]

Another passage was changed for the same reason. It went from "Whereas, the standardized tests and grade scores...will be remedied by application of a program featuring African Language Systems principles instructing African American children both in their primary language and in English," to, "Whereas, the standardized tests and grade scores...will be remedied by application of a program featuring African Language Systems principles to move students from the language patterns they bring to school to English proficiency."[17] By late spring 1997, the board issued a final report in which the term Ebonics was completely exercised.

In the flurry to reject and rebuke the Oakland decision, the critical issue of the consequences of young black students speaking nonstandard English and the impact that will have on their educational, academic, and work careers was lost. The most salient issue concerning the controversy is not just that the black students who most strongly and consistently speak nonstandard English are black, but that they are disproportionately, perhaps overwhelmingly, poor and lower-income working class. It is their continuing and expanding social and economic isolation that is determinant of the language skills they do or do not possess.

The motivation to learn standard English by non-English speakers is premised on the assumption of upward economic and social mobility. In other words, there is a belief that learning standard English will lead to a better life. Nonstandard English is promoted more as an issue of personal responsibility than the consequences of a history of social and economic isolation and abandonment. The issue is not whether black youth can learn standard English (or for that matter, computer programming, physics, or accounting), but whether the resources and opportunities will exist or be made available to facilitate such learning in a meaningful way. This question, of course, is broader than the black community and goes to the heart of the poverty issue in the United States.

On a cultural level, few raised the question of whether the promotion of a "standard English" is in itself a racist presumption. Built on the debatable notion that such a standard holds merit or could even functionally exist without the authority of social power over "others," the rule of English seeks to lighten those who speak the standard while it darkens those, including even nonstandard English-speaking whites from the South or Appalachia, who do not. The English standard is also typically American chauvinism. As the joke goes, those who speak three languages are called trilingual, those who speak two are called bilingual, and those who speak only one are called Americans. It is not only black English that is looked down on, but Spanish, Farsi, Japanese, and other languages spoken by millions of U.S. citizens. English itself, of course, is a hybrid constantly reforming as words and terms from dozens of other languages and dialects, including the lexicon of black English speakers, become popularized and internalized into the language.

An alternative to this language imperialism is the English Plus program advocated by the NEA, which values the extension and growth of English as it encounters an increasingly multilingual world. The NEA argues that many in the United States "speak native languages other than English" and that these linguistic resources should be conserved and developed; that the United States was "founded on a commitment to democratic principles and diversity"; that "multilingualism is a tremendous resource and helps in American competitiveness and diplomatic efforts"; that "multilingualism has helped national security including the use of Native American languages in the development of codes during World War II, the Korean War, and the Vietnam War"; and that "there is no threat to the status of English in the United States since it is spoken by 94 percent of U.S. residents."

On July 13, 1995, Rep. Jose Serrano (D–NY) introduced the "English Plus Resolution" into Congress. The resolution read:

> Whereas English is the primary language of the United States, and all members of the society recognize the importance of English to national life and individual accomplishment;
>
> Whereas many residents of the United States speak native languages other than English, including many languages indigenous to this country, and these linguistic resources should be conserved and developed;
>
> Whereas this Nation was founded on a commitment to democratic principles, and not on racial, ethnic, or religious homoge-

neity, and has drawn strength from a diversity of languages and cultures and from a respect for individual liberties;

Whereas multilingualism, or the ability to speak languages in addition to English, is a tremendous resource to the United States because such ability enhances American competitiveness in global markets by permitting improved communication and cross-cultural understanding between producers and suppliers, vendors and clients, retailers and consumers;

Whereas multilingualism improves United States diplomatic efforts by fostering enhanced communication and greater understanding between nations;

Whereas multilingualism has historically been an essential element of national security, including the use of Native American languages in the development of coded communications during World War II, the Korean War, and the Vietnam War;

Whereas multilingualism promotes greater cross-cultural understanding between different racial and ethnic groups in the United States;

Whereas there is no threat to the status of English in the United States, a language that is spoken by 94 percent of United States residents, according to the 1990 United States Census, and there is no need to designate any official United States language or to adopt similar restrictionist legislation;

Whereas "English-only" measures, or proposals to designate English as the sole official language of the United States, would violate traditions of cultural pluralism, divide communities along ethnic lines, jeopardize the provision of law enforcement, public health, education, and other vital services to those whose English is limited, impair government efficiency, and undercut the national interest by hindering language skills needed to enhance international competitiveness and conduct diplomacy; and

Whereas such "English-only" measures would represent an unwarranted Federal regulation of self-expression, abrogate constitutional rights to freedom of expression and equal protection of the laws, violate international human rights treaties to which the United States is a signatory, and contradict the spirit of the 1923 Supreme Court case Meyer v. Nebraska, wherein the Court declared that "The protection of the Constitution extends to all; to those who speak other languages as well as to those born with English on the tongue."

Now, therefore, be it Resolved by the House of Representatives (the Senate concurring), That the United States Government should pursue policies that

- encourage all residents of this country to become fully proficient in English by expanding educational opportunities;

- conserve and develop the Nation's linguistic resources by encouraging all residents of this country to learn or maintain skills in a language other than English;

- assist Native Americans, Native Alaskans, Native Hawaiians, and other peoples indigenous to the United States, in their efforts to prevent the extinction of their languages and cultures;

- continue to provide services in languages other than English as needed to facilitate access to essential functions of government, promote public health and safety, ensure due process, promote equal educational opportunity, and protect fundamental rights; and

- recognize the importance of multilingualism to vital American interests and individual rights, and oppose "English-only" measures and similar language restrictionist measures.

English around the Globe

More than ever, English has gone global. The power of U.S. cultural and media industries reaches every corner of the earth and it does so in one language: English. Whether it is CNN broadcasting the news to hotel lobbies in Zimbabwe, Panama, or Toyko, or Madonna bellowing popular songs on radios and walkmans in China, Israel, or Chile, or the NBA promoting Michael Jordan or Shaquille O'Neal in South Africa, England, or Spain, English remains the language of first choice.

Perhaps the globalization of English is nowhere more pervasive than on the Internet. Dominated by U.S. corporations and users, the international connections that are touted as bringing the world together in cyberspace are not as multilingual as one would hope. Although the challenge to the English-dominated Net will grow, the increasing concentration of ownership indicates that democratizing the Net's language will not be easy. Countries, such as France and China, have already attempted to institute guidelines that would contain the hegemony of English, but these acts of defiance are having little impact on the overall growth of English as the language of choice and necessity.

Mitigating English globalization is the ever-changing character of the language. In the United States, England, Canada, and other English-speaking nations, the growing multicultural nature of those societies, and the political and cultural movements embodied in them, infuses English with new dimensions and influences. The struggle for democracy includes language rights and respect for linguistic diversity.

Finally, in terms of the United States, English as spoken by the whitest of whites embodies a fusion of words from all over the world, including Africa. According to PBS's Robert MacNeil, that most American of words, "okay," actually comes from the West African word "wakey."[18] So as we listen to the debates around Ebonics and English-only, first and last, it is instructive to remember the words of James Baldwin, who wrote, "Now, I do not know what white Americans would sound like if there had never been any black people in the United States, but they would not sound the way they sound."[19]

5

O.J. and the Symbolic Uses of Racial Exceptions

In spring 1996, fulfilling my civic duty and unable to come up with an acceptable excuse, I found myself on jury duty in Washington, D.C. On the surface, it appeared to be a rather straightforward case. A middle-aged, homeless black man had been arrested (and held in jail for several months) for the illegal possession of a rifle. According to the prosecution, a motorcycle cop had asked him to stop loitering in front of a liquor store. As the man was moving away, he began to take a large green trash can with him. The cop stated in court that, at that point, a woman came up to him and told him that the man had a weapon inside the trash can. The officer stopped the man, looked inside the can and saw a rifle, and then arrested him.

As the testimony portion of the trial began, however, this story started to unravel fairly quickly. First, because of budget cuts in the District of Columbus, the Crime Scene Unit was unavailable to come out and gather evidence, being reserved for more serious crimes such as murder and rape. Also, somehow there were no fingerprints taken off the gun. Second, the arresting officer, who had a striking resemblance to the infamous Mark Fuhrman, had not bothered to get the name of the alleged woman who told him that there was a gun in the trash can. Therefore, nothing that she theoretically told him was admissible since it was unverifiable hearsay. Third, a second officer who arrived to take the homeless man to jail failed to identify him while on the witness stand. Instead, he identified the man's lawyer as the guilty party. While the defendant was fiftyish, balding, and dark-skinned, his lawyer was tall, with a full head of hair, and fair-skinned. To the amusement of the jury and judge, the lawyer stood up to announce that he had an alibi for the time of the crime.

The jury consisted of 11 African Americans and one white. When we retired to the jury room to deliberate, there was an atmosphere of "this will soon be over." We decided to take a quick vote on the charges to see where we stood. Everyone wrote down their verdict and passed them to the jury forewoman. As she began to read the slips of paper, it became obvious where the sentiment lay. She read out loud, "Juror number one, not guilty; juror number two, not guilty; juror number three, not guilty;" and so on. That is until she got to juror slip number 12, she read, "Juror number 12;" hesitated for a second, and then said, "guilty."

In complete unison, everyone turned and looked at the one white male juror. He stated sheepishly that he was the guilty party, so to speak. There was an excruciatingly loud silence at that point. Without prodding, the white man stated that perhaps he could see his way clear to reverse his position. In short fashion, a unanimous verdict was reached and we all went home. Race and the U.S. justice system maintained their rocky marriage for at least one more day.

The O.J. Spiral

For most people in the United States and around the globe these days, when they hear the words "O.J.," they are not thinking of orange juice. Since the horrific murders of his wife, Nicole Brown Simpson, and her friend, Ronald Goldman, the trials (in both senses of the word) of ex-football legend, corporate shill, and sometimes actor Orenthal James "O.J." Simpson have never been far from the mass media and tabloids' front pages and lead stories. The case and the controversies around it highlighted the race, class, and gender issues of the period, and in a critical sense, our understanding of these concerns were mediated through a growing concentration of global media empires that determine much of what the world hears and sees.

While hyper-exploitation of the tragedy has known no bounds, it remains critical to explain and understand the O.J. story. It is difficult to underestimate the pervasiveness of the O.J. saga on a array of concerns and the important transformations and debates that have arisen as a result of the tragedy. This includes popular and scholarly discourses regarding the media, race relations, legal precedents, gender relations, the image of black males, and questions of class privileges. What can be called the O.J.-ing of America and the world signals a turning point in the popularization of contemporary racial meanings in public and private sites. The case has become a racial reference point for most Americans who struggle to grasp the increasingly complex race dynamics of late capitalism.

The pillorying of O.J. reflects the limits and contradictions of the philosophy of racial exceptionism. This philosophy posits the generation of black public figures who are cited as beyond racial boundaries, that is, deniggerized individuals who never become white, but land in a place that is far and away from the "other." These individuals are thus created as "another," nonthreatening and removed from the jungle terror that afflicts so many others of their hue and history. The O.J. stories scuttle this notion. The deniggerization and then reniggerization of O.J. Simpson exposes the racist underbelly of "color blindness" and its ultimate inability to be blind to color.

Beyond all the hoopla and hatred, of course, is the question of whether O.J. did it or not. It is quite likely that a constellation of racial factors, *inter alia*, conspired to frame a guilty man. In his criminal trial, a California jury of nine blacks, two whites, and one Latino said the prosecution did not prove its case and Simpson was found not guilty. In the civil trial, the jury of nine whites, one Asian, one Latino, and one person of mixed black and Asian ancestry found Simpson guilty. In the courtroom of public opinion, several mixed verdicts also appeared. During the criminal trial and since, most whites continue to believe that Simpson is guilty. Little coverage or analysis, however, has been given to those whites who think Simpson is innocent, a much more intriguing and provocative inquiry. What drove upwards of 40 percent of whites, according to some polls, to buck the racially logical trend and pronounce their view that O.J. should have been let loose? How did this break down in terms of gender, class, educational level, and region?

The views of African Americans were equally complex. In many parts of the black community, O.J. was viewed as innocent and a victim of a grand conspiracy. O.J. was seen as the latest in a long and documented history of white legal terror against African Americans, black men in particular. This included the classic cases of the Scottsboro boys and Emmett Till as well as their modern carnations in Rodney King or the even more racially and gender entangled rape, sexual harassment, and drug cases of Mike Tyson, Mel Reynolds, and

Marion Barry. Given the drama inherent in binary racial dispositions about the case, including media-staged events of white anger and black jubilation, it is not surprising that little attention was given to those blacks who were unequivocally convinced that O.J. was guilty.

In a *USA Today* poll in October 1995, at the time of the criminal verdict, 49 percent of whites, thought that the verdict was wrong. Conversely, only 10 percent of blacks surveyed thought the decision was wrong, while 78 percent of blacks thought it was right. A year later, whites' views on Simpson had hardened. In October 1996, 64 percent of whites, a rise of 15 percent, felt that the decision was a mistake. The number of whites who thought the verdict was correct dropped to 20 percent.[2] For blacks, the number of those who thought the decision was wrong rose 3 percent, while the number who thought it was correct dropped by 16 points to 62 percent. More than anything, it appeared that there was a growing doubt about the verdict rather than complete disagreement. The percentage of those who said they did not know or had no opinion doubled from 12 to 25 percent.[3]

These disparate views were used by racial cynics to highlight the obvious: that whites and blacks see the criminal justice system and its treatment of African Americans, even wealthy and estranged ones like Simpson, through vastly different lenses. Given that on the issue of race and criminal justice, blacks and whites have historically had vastly different opinions, why would the Simpson case be different?

By the civil trial, which began in August 1996, only 58 percent of African Americans thought that the verdict of not guilty was right. Whites who still agreed with the decision fell two points to 18 percent.[4] The symbolic use of Simpson for racial purposes and agendas was not restricted to whites and their revolt with pollsters. Incredibly, Simpson, who despite his reniggerization found little motivation to articulate even a black conservative politic, found strong support from some black nationalist groups and individuals that argued that Simpson had learned his lesson, no longer wanted to be estranged from the black community, and should be welcomed as a hero. Nationalist activists in Washington, D.C. even sponsored a visit by Simpson to the nation's capital.

The Many Narratives of O.J.

Several narratives of O.J. have been constructed over time. The first was O.J.. the athlete-hero. In the mid-1960s and early 1970s, as a college and pro football player Simpson was elevated to sports star status. It is here that O.J. began his transformation toward becoming a symbol of racial exception. In 1968, Muhammad Ali, Kareem Abdul Jabbar (then Lew Alcindor), Tommie Smith, John Carlos, and other black athletes were speaking out and protesting against racism inside and outside of sports—what sports scholar and organizer Harry Edwards called the year of the "Revolt of the Black Athlete"—challenging college, professional, and Olympic authorities. Militant black athletes, most notably those who organized the Olympic Project for Human Rights, sought greater black participation in key positions regarding the 1968 Olympics, but also called for the exclusion of racist Rhodesia and South Africa.[5] Simpson, preparing for a career of accommodation, denounced the protests. Radical politics has never been an element of the athlete-hero myth and Simpson was not about to break that tradition. According to Edwards, in 1967, Simpson was worth about $500,000 annually to the University of Southern California sports program. He was already commodified and politically contained.[6]

The athlete-hero narrative, as expressed through O.J, Michael Jordan, and others, also masks the reality that thousands of young men, particularly young black men, never become football (or basketball) pros. They waste years in college, where they end up not graduating in record numbers. According to *Emerge* 1995 annual report, the graduation rate for black male football players was only 42 percent.[7] The critical point here is that graduation was never the goal in the first place.

Finally, the athlete-hero construction in its non-white form manufactures a racial harmony that exists only so far as white hegemony remains unchallenged. From Jackie Robinson and Muhammad Ali to Dennis Rodman and Tiger Woods, the super "other" becomes a target of reconfigured racism in which one's athletic exceptionalism becomes the barrier behind which liberal white supremacy hides. It took O.J. 25 years to discover what Woods found out in the early stages of his acclaim: the "inevitability" of their blackness in public life.[8]

Following his retirement from football, the world witnessed the construction of O.J. as pitchman for corporate America. Here Simpson's duties were simple: grin and sell it. The idea, of course, was to associate narrative one with narrative two. Celebrities market their fame and link it to products that they have little knowledge of and could care less about how those products are produced, the producers, or the social impact of the product. Simpson expressed no more concern about the working conditions, salaries, or racial and gender issues faced by Hertz workers than Michael Jordan, a generation later, does about the horrible working conditions experienced by the international network of workers who make Nike products. Nike capitalism serves to not only produce sneakers, but also ideology, for Jordan's silence says much. To be like Mike is to conciliate to the worse that contemporary global capitalism has to offer, all the while embracing dreams of riches and fame that will for only an infinitesimal few remain just that.

The comparison with Jordan is appropriate for many reasons. Like Jordan in the 1990s, Simpson in the 1970s was the national and global embodiment of a vast number of products and services. Hertz, General Motors, Royal Crown Cola, Schick, and other companies fell over themselves to have the person called "the most watchable man in the world" hawk their goods.[9] In 1977, *Advertising Age* would designate him as the top celebrity spokesperson in the United States.[10] Also similar to Jordan, Simpson was projected as nonracial, as "another," his blackness was irrelevant to his appeal, or perhaps more accurately, he was to be seen as transracial, that is, his blackness had to be erased and disconnected from the popular conceptions of black usually seen as the negative.

The third construction was Simpson the actor and sports announcer. Reproducing a common image of black men in Hollywood films as mostly clowns, Simpson grinned his way through a number of movies, always playing a buffoon of some sort. In the *Naked Gun* movie series, Simpson actually played a Los Angeles police officer, albeit one that was abused and clowned by his fellow officers and his own cognitive limits. He tried dramatic roles in a few films, but that was not the image of Simpson that America wanted or that he was prepared to sustain. His role in *Roots,* another brick in the construction of the "we have overcome" black upward mobility rap, was stereotype and vapid. As a so-so sportscaster, Simpson was distinguished by a black diction and presentation style, yet played the role of sidekick to his white male counterparts.

All of these roles made Simpson wealthy, famous, and loved by a white population that was increasingly supporting the targeting of other black men (and women) for containment and marginalization, a project with unlimited media reinforcement. These roles also did not prepare America and the world for the fourth and decidedly sinister narrative of Simpson as the psychotic wife-killer. The scope of the feelings of betrayal were measured exactly in the perception of how far the door had been opened to let "one of them" in. Despite the entertainment value that Simpson had provided for three decades and the millions he had made sports programs, professional football teams, and multinational corporations, he was quickly thrown back over the fence. Ironically, Simpson's banishment would open new channels of wealth accumulation.

Minting the O.J. Industry

The political and financial exploitation of tragedy is as old as capitalism itself. In the O.J. era, however, this perversion rose to new heights. Making money off O.J.—not an unusual occurrence—went from a small cottage industry to a multi-million dollar spread of enterprises involving everything from T-shirt sales to product placement in the courtroom by *Fortune 500* transnationals. Within the first 100 days of the criminal trial, by March 1996, the *Wall Street Journal* cynically calculated that the profiteering from the " O.J. industry" had easily surpassed the Gross National Product of Grenada.[11]

From the very beginning of the case, money began to flow. Simpson's famous highway ride was watched for hours by an estimated 95 million people. Those people, glued to their television, did not bother to stop and cook or go out for dinner; they ordered pizza. Domino's Pizza reported that during the Bronco ride, "...was the single greatest hour for pizza delivery in national pizza history."[12]

Even the furniture in the hotel room where Simpson was contacted and informed by police that his wife had been murdered was sold at a huge profit. Wasfi Tolaymat paid $4,000 to the hotel manager who sold him 31 pieces of furniture and fittings. Tolaymat, in turn, had received and rejected an offer of $300,000 for the furnishings.[13]

Mezzaluna Restaurant, where Goldman worked and the site of the last public outing of Nicole Simpson before their killings, became more popular than ever. Within months of the murders, the restaurant was serving 240 more meals a day to curious tourists and local fans. Its profit line was expected to grow by $1 million.[14]

During the first trial, IBM, Coca-Cola, and Sony all managed to get essentially free product placements as their logos showed up regularly. The presiding judge in the trial was Lance Ito, whose ever present IBM Think Pad laptop computer was visible for all to see. IBM was enterprising enough to make sure that the logo was inverted so that those watching would see it the right way. Ito also had a taste for Diet Coke, which was usually prominently displayed in front of him. Even the specially designed chair, which sold for $1,250, that Ito had brought in to ease his back troubles saw a rise in popularity and sales. On one of the prominent monitors in the court, the Sony logo nearly leaped off the screen it was so huge. For some television-addicted watchers, the trial was one long commercial.

Desperate for funds, Simpson used his renewed fame to exploit his football glory years. He signed off on the issuance of commemorative coins in gold and silver celebrating his record-breaking 1973 pro football season when he became the first runner in history to gain more than 2,000 yards in one season. The 1,000 gold coins sold for $69.95 a piece; the 5,000 silver ones for $34.95.[15] There were an official 21-inch bronze statutes of Simpson in his football uniform, which sold for $3,395 each. More than $5 million worth of these had been sold halfway through the first trial.[16] The manufacturer expected to eventually make $85 million.[17]

Simpson did not let a little thing like being locked-down prevent him from make money off his troubles. While in jail, Simpson "wrote" a book titled, *I Want to Tell You*, autographed trading cards to be sold for $500 each, and even operated a 1-900 number. More than 600,000 copies of his book were printed along with 250,000 audiocassette versions of it.[18]

Simpson, of course, was not the only one to write a book about the case. Ghostwriters had a booming business. Dozens of books were produced including ones by prosecutors, defense lawyers, dismissed jurors, jurors who endured, witnesses from both sides, family members, friends and acquaintances, journalists, detectives, and nearly anyone who had only peripherally been touched by the trial. Simpson attorney Johnnie Cochran's ex-wife and Simpson's mother both had books. Kato Kaelin, the nation's best-known houseboy, sold 800,000 copies of his book, *The Whole Truth,* which at $20 each was a potential gross of $16 million.[19]

The commodifying of the Simpson tragedy was carried on the context of exploiting the racial tensions, indeed, racial rage, already inherent in the public sphere. This rage found relief in the grand media-built and promoted narrative that cared little about seeking the truth, but a great deal about mining the multiple opportunities available for sensation in a case that involved celebrities, interracial relationships, wealth, two gruesome homicides, and gender conflicts. As Anne DuCille writes, "the Simpson scandal is good news precisely because it is good business."[20] It is hard to imagine a case more ripe for media exploitation.

Media Circus or Media Bonanza?

What appeared to be an exceptional media circus of the highest order was an icon of things to come. The O.J. trial and aftermath has been great for the media conglomerates. From the cable networks to the tabloids, they have seen their profiles and bottom lines grow and grow. Who really watched Court TV before the trial? The drive for profits means that O.J.-type trial coverage will become more the norm, given the technologies, competition, and increasingly desperate acts that define modern society. The construction of hyper-media hegemony that engulfs the public sphere and increasingly the private sphere, is well on its way.

The Simpson saga coincided with these changes and, in turn, became an opportunity for the growth and hegemonic objectives of media conglomerates. A true story involving a fallen hero, race, sex, Hollywood, and sports wrapped in a murder mystery with two brutal slayings could not have been better scripted by the best fiction writers. The revolution in media—new technologies and new global reaches—fostered an already predisposed national and international interest, an opening that the cable channels were more than prepared to meet. It was reported, during the height of the criminal trial in 1995, that for the first time ever more people watched cable channels in the first quarter of that year than watched the three major networks. This, of course, gave a massive boost to the ratings and profits of CNN and Court TV.[21] CNN charged $24,000 for a 30-second commercial slot and made more than $45 million on its coverage of the trial. Geraldo Rivera's cable show was about to be canceled prior to the Simpson criminal trial. By having his show become a platform for white anger and black defensiveness about the case, he turned his ratings around and prospered. Meanwhile, the networks took a beating as their daytime soap opera and game shows were little competition for the drama of Marcia Clark, Johnnie Cochran, and Judge Ito.

O.J. through the Prism of Race

Though discreetly avoided and deftly denied in the media and public discussions, race was at the center of the Simpson drama. He was not just a famous athlete suspected of killing his wife. Simpson was a hero, accepted into white society as a safe African American, who was now being accused of brutally and viciously murdering his young white wife and her Jewish friend. The contemplation of such betrayal was stunning. The nation has never been comfortable with interracial marriages and relations. Indeed, it was only a generation ago that such links were outlawed in many states. U.S. history is filled with the bodies of black men who have been accused of affronting white women, let alone marrying them.

Simpson's fondness for white women was well-known. His leaving his black wife for the young and blond Nicole was public knowledge and perhaps a critical part of the O.J. legend. It signaled to Simpson and others the completion of his transition from black sports figure to transracial American hero. Simpson was the racial exception embraced by white America, a black man who did not raise social or political issues, who was willing to market his fame to sell any product, who played golf, and who caused no one trouble but himself.

Many commentators only saw racism manifested in the trial when Los Angeles police officer Mark Fuhrman was exposed as a liar and racist. Ignored was years and years of black community-police tension in the Los Angeles area, so profound that any situation involving African Americans and the L.A. Police Department (LAPD) or Sheriff's Department was suspect from the beginning. Well-documented cases of police brutality, planted evidence, murders, and racist organizing found a black community predisposed to believe little and suspect all related to the prosecution's case. This was, after all, the city of Rodney King. The so-called race card was a whole deck dealt by the LAPD long before Fuhrman took the witness stand. Apologists sought to individualize racism in Fuhrman and not ascribe it to the police department that hired, promoted, and sent him to court repeatedly to "testi-lie," nor to the prosecutor's office that was aware of Fuhrman's racist proclivities, nor to local and state officials that aggressively resisted progressive reform of the police department.

Fuhrman's brand of racism was more than just an occasional racial epithet. Cochran's comparison of Fuhrman to Adolf Hitler, which brought Cochran condemnation, was entirely appropriate in that Fuhrman advocated black genocide. As it came out in court, Fuhrman stated that he wished "nothing more than to see all niggers gathered together and killed."[22] Replace the word "niggers" with Jews or Greeks or women or any other group and there is little doubt that Fuhrman would be seen and projected as the villain he is. But complete indictment of Fuhrman undermined the official story and, therefore, the indictment itself had to be undermined. So prosecutor Clark and others continued to defend Fuhrman, relegating his statements to little more than hyperbole and zeal. The legal system saw otherwise. Exactly one year after the first Simpson trial, Fuhrman pleaded no contest to perjury charges, was fined $200, and given three years probation.[23] Media coverage was limited.

The trial was potentially Simpson's passage back to blackness. This was not because Simpson was going to change due to his exposure to a racist criminal justice system experienced by so many other black men, or his drubbing in the media where infamy in this era is not necessarily a negative thing. Rather, the trial served as a transformation in white attitude, probably permanent, towards Simpson. He became a modern black outlaw, a Bigger Thomas, an Othello, a murderer of white women. And, whether he wanted to go that route or not, Simpson and his lawyers were forced into a defense that further polarized him from his betrayed and furious white fans. Symbolically, the sight of Simpson being protected by the Nation of Islam's Fruit of Islam security force enhanced the racial divide that the case turned into signaling that this was not the Simpson of earlier narratives. Leaving one point, however, does not necessarily get you to another, so Simpson's race consciousness was still elusive.

One further racial dimension that garnered little exploration was the public perception of Judge Ito. Asian Americans have often been portrayed as one of the in-between "races" in U.S. society—certainly not white, but also not black. But more than that, in the media and popular imagination, Asian Americans have been painted as the "model minority," i.e., an acquiescent community that does not aggressively struggle for equality, political power, or civil rights, preferring to quietly melt into the pot. This false picture belies decades of struggle by the Asian-American community for inclusion, an inclusion and equality that has been resisted at both the mass and state level. Ito, at one level, was the "model judge." Clearly, either a black or white judge would have only fanned the racial flames of the trial no matter what posture they took. Given the place that Asian Americans are constricted to in the popular racial hierarchies, Ito's role was seen by some as comic relief, a tension breaker, for the more stubborn and explosive black-white conflict. Racist parodies of Ito—Jay Leno's "dancing Itos" and Sen. Al D'Mato's sick Japanese accent impression—did exist and should have been criticized, but were relegated to sideshow status as the big event unfolded. More seriously, Ito was also given his share of the blame (along with the mostly black, mostly female jury) for the not guilty verdict feeding the argument that non-whites have little business being placed in charge of serious matters.[24] Clark's incompetence, unprofessionalism, and inebriation on a newly acquired celebrity status were dismissed as possible causes for the decision. Coincidentally, the judge in Simpson's civil trial was also an Asian American, Hiroshi Fujisaki.

O.J. through the Prism of Class

It was estimated by the Associated Press that Simpson spent between $3 and $6 million on his defense in the criminal trial (the prosecution spent $9 million).[25] Simpson's fortune guaranteed that he would not simply be railroaded as so many poor and working-class black men and women have been. Few, black or white, could afford the "Dream Team" of lawyers, researchers, and experts hired by Simpson for his defense. Although some were for show and their in-fighting became legendary, Simpson's assembly of legal power brought down the best that the state had to offer. Few, if any, of Cochran's critics would have turned down his talents should they have found themselves in a situation similar to Simpson's.

It was Simpson's wealth and fame that protected him in previous brushes with the law over his physical abuse of his wife. While male-controlled structures and ideologies reinforce the oppressions that women face domestically, class provides another cushion on which men escape responsibility and punishment for exploitative and violent treatment of women. To the degree that poor men face a judge on spousal abuse charges, they more often than not get something beyond just community service.

Though lambasted in the media, Simpson also enjoyed what could be called a celebrity credit card, where he was given the benefit of the doubt simply because he was famous and rich. Personal identification with Simpson, mediated through public relations and professional marketing, led many to accept his version of the story with little investigation or exploration into the contradictory evidence. Note the multiracial cheering that occurred on the bypasses and streets of Los Angeles as Simpson made his aborted freedom ride.

Even if Simpson had been convicted in the criminal trial, he was guaranteed an appeal virtually before the first witness took the stand. While thousands of his black and poor fans are falling victim to three-strikes provisions, the death penalty, and mandatory minimums, none of which Simpson has ever expressed an opinion regarding let alone done anything about—wealth and financial power make one thing clear: class matters. Despite the racial edges of the trial, Simpson's court experience was one of privilege and power.

O.J. through the Prism of Gender

The case, of course, also raised a number of issues related to gender inequality and oppression. Whether Simpson was guilty of killing Nicole and Goldman may never be truly known. There is little doubt, however, about his activities regarding spousal abuse. Pictures of a battered Nicole, the 911 tape of her screaming as O.J. attempts to break into her home, and other witnesses' claims that he physically mistreated her erased any allegations to piety that he might have. The grinning, affable O.J. known to millions was transformed into a battering monster before everyone's very eyes.

His brutal and brutalizing relationship with Nicole raised some perplexing and confounding questions related to the nexus of race, class, and gender. Was there a basis for black and white sisterhood on the issue of abuse even though that was not what the trial was about? Was the ferocity toward Simpson by many white feminists a response shaped by racism and the failure to entertain the thought that the whole case might have been a racist frame-up? How should progressives, even those who thought Simpson not guilty, respond to the demonizing of Nicole as a cocaine-abusing, money-grubbing whore, implying that she probably got what she deserved (although not from Simpson)? One also has to wonder how strong the white outcry would have been from the black and white communities had Nicole been black.

The Simpson trial, like the trials of Mike Tyson, Mel Reynolds, and Clarence Thomas, again provided a glimpse into the state of the debate on gender relations among African Americans. Those cases are distinct from O.J., however, in that they do not involve interraciality, that is, the accused and the victim were of the same race. Yet similar themes do appear, such as uncritical defense of the black male and the demonizing of the woman who is involved. Given the daily rapes, spousal beatings and murders, and general violence experienced by black women, their erasure from the mass and black media makes it clear that the popularity factor is also a strong motivation in deciding whose story gets told. As many black feminists have pointed out, only interracial rape (or charges thereof) mobilize, not the more ordinary and pervasive intraracial kind.

It is telling that the organizers of the Million Man March sought to have Simpson superlawyer Cochran appear at the event, in effect, as a way to celebrate the acquittal of a spouse abuser who had demonstrated little interest in the problems of the black community. They were turned down not because Cochran professed any outrage at the exclusion of women, but because it was exclusive of other racial and ethnic groups. Cochran has a lengthy history of speaking out on racial concerns and, in a sterling follow up to his Simpson case, managed to free imprisoned Black Panther Geronimo Pratt, who had been incarcerated for more than two decades on what many believe was a state frame-up.

Clearly missing, in any organized or relevant way, are the voices of black male feminists or even what scholar Joy James calls black women nationalist feminists in a debate that often seems to be only between black women feminists and male nationalists. Black feminists have been branded traitors by some nationalists and generally have been fighting an uphill battle to have black women's issues seen as of equal importance to these of black men.[26]

O.J. Forever

In 1997, Simpson lost the civil case brought against him by the families of Nicole and Goldman. O.J. was ordered by the court to pay $33.5 million to the families, a sum that he had little apparent ability to pay, according to his lawyers, and court appeals are in the works. Judge Fujisaki was criticized for making several huge legal mistakes, such as allowing into evidence a lie detector test by Simpson and the tape of a phone call to a battered women's shelter by someone claiming to be named Nicole (though not proven to be Nicole Simpson). In addition, a juror who was discovered to have lied about her ties to the prosecutor's office was dismissed after jury deliberation had begun, creating more grounds for an appeal. Finally, unlike the criminal case, the judge would not allow the testimony and behavior of racist cop Fuhrman to be discussed, a cornerstone of the defense in the first trial. Fuhrman was a central figure from the very beginning of police involvement in the case: Fuhrman found the bloody glove, discovered the knit cap, and was the first officer to enter the Simpson compound.

There are also more books, films, and inevitable Simpson-related scandals and news events on the way. The case made household names of previously unknown lawyers, sports figures, family members, and people who happened to be jurors, store clerks, forensic specialists, and so on. Whether we like it or not, these people will remain in our lives for a very long time to come.

More critically, the case brought into sharp relief the race, gender, and class tensions that refuse to go away and, in fact, are intensifying in this period. O.J. was a global sensation made available by new technologies and expanded media networks. Unlike other famous legal cases that found an international audience—such as the Scottsboro case in the 1930s, Angela Davis in the 1970s, and Mumia Abu Jamal in the 1990s —the politics of O.J. were not about an obvious injustice and, therefore, nothing approaching global support for Simpson emerged. Indeed, given the image of blackness, and black males in particular, that has been projected on the global scale, Simpson's demonization was simply one more incident in a long string of such.

O.J. the phenomena provides a platform, at an emotive level, for nearly everyone's anxieties about race, gender relations, violence, privilege, and postindustrial capitalism. What is liberating (and disturbing) about the Simpson case is that it allows for and encourages absolutes. Either you think Simpson is guilty or not. Either you think the criminal justice system is fair or not. The complexities of the intersection of race, gender, class, the criminal justice system, and the media demand much more rigorous analysis and attention than emerged around the Simpson case, even as that case set the tone and has become a reference point for those interactions for many years to come. The multiracial dimensions of U.S. society deserve and require a seriousness of analysis from intellectuals, policymakers, journalists, and activists that took a walk regarding O.J. and the tragic circumstances of his life. Yet more than anything, the Simpson case moves beyond Simpson the individual—who lived a life of luxury and isolation, privilege and wealth—to challenge the ideology of racial exception. In the end, he said it best in his suicide note, "Don't feel sorry for me, I've had a great life, great friends." Guilty or not, Simpson achieved in infamy what he was unwilling to do otherwise: expose the racist underbelly of the myth of color blindness and the limited value of racial exceptions.

6

Thug Life:
The Rap on Capitalism

How many brothas fell victim to tha streetz
Rest 'n peace young nigga
There's a Heaven for a 'G
Be a lie if I told ya that
I never thought of death. My niggas
We tha last ones left. But Life Goes on.[1] —Tupac Shakur

In the film *Juice,* rapper Tupac "2-Pac" Shakur's signature cinematic turn, his character Bishop cold-bloodedly guns down two people in less than five minutes, one of whom is his best friend. In that pivotal moment, Bishop obtains "juice," the street term for power. Having street juice, however, is a fluid circumstance, and not too long after, in the inevitable cycle of destruction brought on by a philosophy of take-no-prisoners, Bishop suffers a violent death and juice passes on to the next unlucky soul.

As a rapper and one of the most visible commodified global black male images, Tupac had juice.[2] As a leading signifier in the world of rap music, Tupac's controversial life provided a platform of debate for both the proponents and opponents of the genre. Posturing as an unrepentant thug, Tupac shamelessly celebrated and acted out as his generation's Stagolee—a national outlaw unrestrained by social conventions or rules, pointing a ring-adorned middle finger at both the streets that attracted him so strongly and the social system that (often successfully) sought to exploit and contain him. With an artist's irony, he relished the belief that he would die young, violently, and with street glory. In his song "Life Goes On," he discusses the death of his friend as well as his own death and funeral, a premonition that now appears as inevitable as it was chilling. His murder at the age of 25 also pushed buttons and graphically linked studio gangsta fantasies with lived ghetto realities.

By all accounts, Tupac was a gifted artist at a young age, and enjoyed acting, dancing, and writing poetry as a high school student at the Baltimore School for the Arts. Hope was alive and possibilities appeared limitless. But these were the Reagan years and crack was king. Tupac's mother, like countless others, became addicted to the drug, which made for an unstable home life. In response to this situation, Tupac took off for the West Coast, where he would eventually build his rap career. He would also become fascinated with black gangster culture. The child of a Panther, Tupac's rearticulated militancy found expression in his hard core raps and in the lifestyle of "don't give a fuck" that he embraced. Over the years, he gained gangsta rap credibility through his troubles outside the studio: a shoot-out with police in Atlanta; a shooting in Marin near San Francisco; his own robbery and shooting in New York; and most determinant, his conviction and imprisonment for his alleged part in a gang rape.

The fan-driven notion that gangsta rappers must be more than "studio" hoodlums has a disturbing quality to it. While few expect Arnold Schwarzenegger, Bruce Willis, or Jean-Claude Van Damme to act out their tough guy roles in daily encounters, quite the opposite is true in the rap game. To their legions of fans, the legitimacy of gangsta rappers is conditioned on the real troubles that they find themselves in. While actors can play prisoners convincingly without ever having been locked down, for too many rap fans, it is illegit to rap about prison if one has never been imprisoned. This is a perverse, and indeed racist, expectation that too many young rappers have adopted themselves.

It should be noted that this "authenticity anxiety" is not just felt by black youth wannabees, but has also been appropriated by a number of black intellectuals. In their desire to link with roots that many do not have—a charge often hurled at "studio" gangsta rappers—some scholars, such as Harvard University's Henry Louis Gates, have muted their criticism of the misogynist, self-destructive, and pro-capitalist character of certain subgenres of rap in their defense of rappers' first amendment rights and black essentialist proclivities.[3] This has been done at the expense of more politically critical rappers, who are increasingly finding little space or place for their music. The authenticity anxiety is also grounded in definitions of community and black life that segue into conservative notions of social and cultural pathology as the root cause of black strife. The black community is thus defined by its most destructive, dangerous, and debilitating elements.

At the same time, opposition to gangsta rap does not by definition signal a progressive turn. This is most vivid in the confluence of opportunism in the alliance concocted by civil rights activist and president of the National Political Congress of Black Women, C. Delores Tucker, and former Reagan official and national drug czar, William Bennett. While taking on the easy target of rap's most banal and base performers, they project a false community of interests between a civil rights agenda and conservative cause. Politics paraded as morality feeds an agenda that negates state responsibility for the crisis in the black community while promoting a cultural project that retards and restricts the resistance so needed in this period.

Is the inevitability of living a thug life dying a thug death? In many ways, Tupac mirrored his cinematic and audio bad boy image. On September 7, 1996, in a street scene scripted from dozens of gangster movies—*Scarface, Bonnie and Clyde, Goodfellas, The Godfather I, II,* and *III, Menace II Society, New Jack City,* and *King of the City*—Tupac was gunned down in a shower of bullets, his legacy rising almost immediately as a site for contestation over the intersection of rap, race, and reality. His shooting, and subsequent death one week later, once again raised questions and queries about the importance and significance of black marginalized cultural styles on everyday life. As this chapter argues, in the saga of Tupac Shakur are embodied the unresolved dilemmas of community, gender, and commodified relations that haunt the black community.

Black Cultural Challenge

Contemporary black oppositional popular cultures express the complexities of race matters. Neither wholly liberating nor unmitigatingly depraved, rap music challenges and embraces bourgeoisie notions. Rap music and hip hop life-styles and practitioners continue to challenge prevailing orthodoxies even as they succumb to the corporate and conservative tendencies inherent in popular culture.

Tupac's dramatic death elevated the pivotal question: exactly what and who is the hip hop generation and where does its authenticity lie? How much of contemporary black popular culture is driven by market dynamics over which the black community has virtually no control? What is the relationship between hip hop culture and the criminalization of black youth? How is hip hop gendered and what are the implications of that? The answers to these questions gain new urgency every day as scores of black youth, in the words of Bone, Thugs, and Harmony's *Crossroads*, "keep passing away" in orgies of violence and retribution.

Scholar Mark Naison argues that the "outlaw culture" running rabid in black neighborhoods represents a new phenomena in black life. He writes:

> an 'outlaw culture' has emerged among low-income black youth that has rejected African American communal norms in favor of the predatory individualism of the capitalist marketplace. These youngsters living in neighborhoods bereft of resources and hope, have embraced a doctrine of 'might makes right' that converts everyone into a potential victim.[4]

These dynamics, increasingly mirrored in other communities, preoccupy much of the thrust of social activism in the 1990s. In some sense, Naison's thesis compares with Cornel West's concern about the increasing "nihilism" engulfing the black community. Although West greatly overstates his case and many criticize the cultural determinist character of his thesis, he raises a significant point when he writes that the "loss of hope and absence of meaning" for so many is the breeding ground for self- and community-directed destruction.[5] This loss of hope and absence of meaning must be grounded in the durability of racism and the broader state and corporate assaults on dispossessed communities.

Naison does not say that every young black person is engaged in gangsterish and destructive behavior. What he does argue, however, is that predatory styles are increasingly dominant and perhaps soon will have a hegemonic edge in far too many communities. There are some serious implications here. One is that the contestation for the moral soul of black youth, including many of those in the middle class, is being won by the streets despite the heroic efforts of parents and others. Lumpen street culture, with its masculinist dimensions on full throttle, criss-crosses the black community at a number of class and social levels. From the high school dropout to the college senior, contemporary black street culture weaves in and out of the lives of young blacks. Most important, however, this battle is not primarily or simply over behavior. It is the fight to recapture and reposition a value system and world outlook that emancipates rather than oppresses, that values service over materialism.

Outlaw culture is not the defining character of inner-city black neighborhoods. For every shooting that occurs, there is a teenage mother going back to school to finish her education. For every crack sale, there is a black couple taking in a foster child. For every drive-by, there are thousands of black workers who get up and go to work every day, to church on Sundays, and volunteer when possible.

Unfortunately, it is true that a small, relatively organized minority can terrorize a disarmed and ill-prepared majority. Many black neighborhoods are entrenched in fear, all too ready to surrender civil liberties and political rights because there are, indeed, drive-bys, crack sales, and brazen shootings. Among some black youth, the fusion of lumpen street culture with prison culture has created a new and spreading subculture that is passionately violent and without social or moral restraints.

The high unemployment rate for black youth, which is generally triple the official rate for white youth, exacerbates and feeds the economic desperation felt by so many. College opportunities for the poor and lower income of all races have been severely reduced since the Reagan era, with little prospects for a change. Even service in the military, once a way out, if not up, for many young black men is no longer the option it used to be in these downsized days when criminal records and low educational attainment become means for military rejection. Finally, the virtual absence of a vibrant black leadership contributes to a crisis of direction for the black community as a whole and youth in particular. Out-of-style civil rights leaders carry little leadership weight and black conservatives even less. The Nation of Islam is perhaps closest in the imagination of many black youth to a legacy of resistance, as evidenced in the closeness and even membership of some rappers in the group. Yet the Nation finds it difficult to sell—to an impatient black youth—the group's high demands for discipline, piety, and rectitude, and ultimately its conservative social and political agenda.

The dominance narratives existent in rap, which celebrate patriarchy, consumerism, and thuggery, do not emerge simply from the creative and misguided genius of black youth nor just the imperative of corporate profit and its exploitation of social depravities. These dynamics intersect and constantly reform their relationship, nurtured by the external demands of capital and the internal exigencies of black social and cultural life. Furthermore, the music reflects and generates broader discourses about power and capitalism filtered through race, gender, and class fulcrums. Shakur's music and life personified these debates and the struggle to resolve the conflictual tendencies of hope and struggle with despair and surrender.

Commodified

What role and responsibility do rap and rap artists like Tupac have to this set of circumstances? Popular music, including rap, plays a pedagogical role in the socializing of society. Rappers, particularly gangsta rappers, claim that they are only telling the truth when they describe the black community as a war zone where only the strong survive, a place where no one is to be trusted and where it is all about the love of money. In the rapper-constructed world, everyone is a commodity to be exploited and then discarded when used up. Women are "hos," commodified sex objects devoid of humanity, or bitches, too willing to confront males on heretofore sacred grounds, or mommas, nurturers whose priority is male protection and security. Those who work every day are suckers and prey for getting "jacked," that is, robbed and victimized.

This notion of community, however, must be rigorously interrogated because it manifests a narrow and, indeed, racist perspective that reduces black life to the worst pathologies of modern society. As an imagined and real community defined by historically and socially derived identities, African Americans reflect a broad array of class, gender, ideological, political, and social differences. Bourgeois blacks are as much a product of the racial history of the West as are working-class blacks and the black lumpen. To limit black authenticity to predatory life-styles remains a conservative vision that unites black rappers with white conservatives in an unholy alliance.

If the world created by rappers is a construct, the questions that need to be answered are who is doing the construction and for whose consumption? The near monopolization and concentration of the production and distribution of cultural commodities by forces far removed from the black community or its authority means that a small, unaccountable, and generally white elite is making decisions about the content of the music and where it will ultimately end up.

The most critical market for rap music is, of course, the hip hop niche—one that is studied by cultural theorists, sociologists, and market analysts alike. According to a study by public relations firm Yankelovich Partners, Inc., hip hoppers watch more game shows, award shows, music video shows, and late night entertainment, and fewer dramas and sitcoms, than the rest of society. In general, hip hoppers are loosely and popularly defined as those inner-city black youth aged 15 to 19. This group, however, comprises only 1.4 million—or 8 percent of all U.S. teens. In addition, it is disproportionately lower income with relatively little disposal income. Even if inner-city African Americans between 20 and 24 are added, they constitute only another 1.6 million. A potential market that maxes out at about three million at most is too small—and in reality much, much smaller—to be economically feasible in this era of global economies, which move billions of dollars and millions of commodities per hour.

The power over the development, production, and distribution of popular music is supremely concentrated. Six transnational corporations—Time Warner, Sony, Philips, Bertelsmann, Thorn-EMI, and Matsushita—account for more than 90 percent of all albums, cassettes, music videos, and compact discs sold in the world.[6] Their international aspirations are captured in their marketing slogans—Time Warner's "The World is Our Audience," Sony's "Think Globally-Act Locally," or Thorn-EMI's "A Truly Global Organization"—as well as in market shares.[7] Critics are painfully naive to think that these transnationals's target audience is black youth.

The real target is the market niche that seeks to bond and appropriate hip hop's constructed black inner-city authenticity. As one analyst noted, the apparent appeal to black youth is really a stepping stone to white youth who search for their own identity in the popular-ized cultural images of the inner city. These images are symbolized in material expressions that are easily reproduced and, most pivotally, sold in the form of baseball caps, designer sneakers, oversized, off-the-butt jeans, and compact discs. While nonmaterial signifiers, such as a walk or a snarl, cannot be sold, their link to real commodities can. All of this is done to the rhythms of rap, particularly gangsta rap. MTV's *Yo! MTV Raps* is a critical cog in the national and global mar-keting machine. The cunning genius of MTV is that it is a network made up entirely of promotional commercials for music successfully masquerading as entertainment and even news.

In 1993, MTV was beamed to 210 million households in 71 na-tions. On the air 24 hours a day, MTV through its *Yo! MTV Raps* pro-gram has sent videos of black rappers to the far corners of the earth. For many around the world, this constitutes their sole contact with black youth other than that perceived in feature films. The globaliza-tion of American culture also means the globalization of American racial and racist images.[8] Those images are in no small part images of gangsta rappers.

Gangsta rappers do not challenge the horror that many black communities face; indeed, they revel in and exploit it and, more often than not, advocate greater exploitation. They only resemble—in the words of Public Enemy's Chuck D's famous quip—a "black CNN" to the degree that they reproduce a media distortion that is normative. It is the media and corporate construction of ghetto and poverty myths that is more in line with the pedagogic value of most gangsta rap songs than the liberation ethos of the freedom songs of the past.

Capitalist mass media has always been receptive to outlaws. Af-ter all, since the days of Jesse James, Al Capone, and John Cotti, the "bad man" icon has fascinated and repulsed millions of viewers worldwide of Hollywood westerns and gangsta movies at one and the same time. Clint Eastwood's 1992 *Unforgiven* was designated best movie of the year with a message that essentially advocated that out-laws must challenge a corrupt and savage state apparatus, particularly one that sanctions the oppression and brutality of women and African Americans. While Eastwood should not be seen as a progressive or even a liberal, his film embodies a politics that celebrates individual initiative against perceived social injustice, albeit an initiative that promotes violence as the first and last weapon of choice. Gangsta rappers, with their rhetoric of lawlessness, anti-police themes, and espousal of violence, make connections with this legacy in many ways.

Naison also argues that contemporary black outlaw culture embraces many of the symbols of black nationalism of the 1960s combined with that period's glorification of the lumpen proletariat.[9] He contends that black activists and writers glorified criminal behavior, giving it a revolutionary character that it clearly did not deserve. The Black Panther Party is cited by Naison and others as being guilty of expressing these tendencies even as it attempted, in some cases, to eliminate or control such behavior. Ironically, Tupac was born into this Panther-lumpen nexus.

Tupac's mother is Afeni Shakur, a former New York City Panther and member of the infamous Panther 21, a group accused of conspiring to blow up stores in the New York area. She was acquitted of those charges. Afeni and Tupac had close ties with a few famous black political prisoners, including Mutulu Shakur (no relation), Assata Shakur (no relation), and Elmer "Geronimo" Pratt. Mutulu functioned as Tupac's stepfather and political mentor, Assata was close enough to be seen as a play "aunt," and Pratt is Tupac's godfather. Unfortunately, while many ex-Panthers are vigorously involved in various productive and progressive activities, for Tupac, by the time he came of age, most of the Panthers in his life were either in prison, in exile, or in the case of his mother, strung out on drugs and alcohol, unable to realistically pass on the urgency and commitment to struggle that had shaped their youth.

The Panther legacy and relationships haunted Tupac all his life as it carried unresolved political and personal issues that he played out in family relations and through his music. The lack of a popularized theoretical and political closure on the significance of the Black Panther Party for black politics was not Tupac's cross to bear alone, but that of the broader scholarly and political black community. It is only now, three decades after the founding of the Panthers, that serious, nonautobiographical scholarship has begun to emerge.[10] It is too late for Tupac, but not for a generation of black youth looking to the past for political guidance for the present. Unless a compelling summation is offered and struggled with, the mistakes of the past will be revisited time and time again.

Contained

It ain't a secret, don't conceal tha fact
Tha penitentiary is packed and it's filled with blacks
I wake up in tha morning and I ask myself
is life worth liven, should I blast myself?
I'm tired of being poor, and even worse I'm black
My stomach hurts, so I'm looking for a bud sack.[11]
—Tupac Shakur

So what is the agenda for black youth if their roles as producers and consumers are limited and dissolving? In a word: containment. In the last quarter of the 20th century, the United States has become a nation of prisons. Most significantly, as the country's jail population has tripled since 1980, that population has also become darker. This intersection is neither incidental nor accidental. It is a systemic response from above and below to social transformations that are rapidly creating a growing surplus labor force determined to survive by any means necessary. African-American males, particularly young ones, are going into the criminal justice system in unprecedented numbers. As of 1996, the Sentencing Project concluded that 32.2 percent of all young African-American males between 20 and 29 (827,440) are either incarcerated, on parole, or on probation nationwide. According to their report, in the period between 1989 and 1994, the number of black women in that situation increased 78 percent. Much of that increase had to do with changes in state and federal drug laws that had the impact of disproportionately hurting African Americans. According to federal records, while African Americans make up 13 percent of all illegal drug users, they constitute 35 percent of all drug arrests, 55 percent of all drug convictions, and 74 percent of all those who go to prison on drug convictions. Between 1986 and 1991, the number of black women incarcerated for drug offenses in state prisons increased by 828 percent. According to the Justice Department, at the end of 1994, there were 992,000 men and women prisoners in state and federal prisons; 94 percent men, 6 percent women, 47 percent white, and 51 percent black.[12]

Tupac not only rapped about going to jail and prison life, but had these experiences himself. His encounters the criminal justice system became part of his living legend. From his involvement in a shooting in Marin County in northern California that left a young black child dead to an altercation with police in Atlanta to his conviction and jailing on rape charges in New York, Tupac embodied a thug-life ethos. His street reputation, and perhaps the beginning of the inevitability of a violent end, grew considerably when he was shot five times and robbed and still survived during the middle of his rape trial. He was bailed out of prison, for about $1 million, by Marion "Suge" Knight, the CEO of Death Row records. Moving to southern California where Death Row is located and where it enjoys its own hoodlum reputation for being linked to some of the area's notorious street gangs, Tupac completed his transition to full-time outlaw.

Death Row is the record label started by Andre "Dr. Dre" Young (who is no longer with the company), the most creative mind and influential producer in gangsta rap. It is home to Snoop Doggy Dog, gangsta rap's one other true superstar. Dr. Dre, Snoop, and other Death Row artists have all had high-profile criminal trials in the short history of the company. The notoriety, however, only built the company's fame and infamy, allowing it to sell millions of records. In 1996, Death Row revenues came to $75 million.[13]

Despite its entrepreneurial success, Death Row has fallen on hard times since Tupac's murder. Suge Knight went to jail in October 1996 for parole violation and was sentenced to nine years in February 1997. More critically, the company is under ongoing federal and state investigations to determine if it is what the government calls a "criminal enterprise" dealing in drugs, money laundering, extortion, gunrunning, murder, and gangbanging. While Surge Knight and Dr. Dre received millions in financing from Sony, Time Warner, MCA, and Interscope Records to start Death Row in 1992, some investigators are alleging that the seed money, at least in part, came from drug dealers associated with Knight.[14]

On March 9, 1997, gangsta rap suffered another traumatic event with the drive-by slaying of Biggie Smalls (aka the Notorious B.I.G.) in Los Angeles six months after Tupac's killing. Smalls, 24, whose real name is Christopher Wallace, had once been close to Tupac, but later had a bitter falling out and was accused by Tupac of being involved in his earlier shooting in New York. A former drug dealer, Wallace also rapped about using women, thugging on the streets, and dying young. His first album is titled *Ready to Die,* while his last, released after his murder, is titled, *Life After Death... 'Til Death Do Us Part.* Both Tupac and Wallace's murders occurred amid street rumors and actual incidents of a "war" between East and West Coast gangsta rappers, more specifically, those affiliated with Death Row in the West and those affiliated with New York's Bad Boy records and its owner Sean "Puffy" Combs in the East. Although rap emerged first on the East Coast in New York City, by the late 1980s, hard-core gangsta rap from Los Angeles, Oakland, and Houston not only challenged the East Coast in popularity, but also in bravado. Initial insults traded in studios turned into ugly confrontations at music concerts, awards ceremonies, and in the streets. These feuds were fed by fans and rap media, as well as reputation-seeking rappers themselves.

Whether real or not, the "beef" between East and West Coast rappers—proclaimed and promoted in rap and mainstream media despite acclamations to the contrary—helps to sell long-sought hoodlum reputations, which helps to sell products. Incarceration is not a badge of dishonor but a rite of passage to the higher echelons of the gangsta rap financial ladder. Containment, thus, on a grand scale functions as a marketing device that pushes the "other" further from the mainstream which then serves to make even more attractive and abstract the commodified black identification politics of white youth. This interpretation is held by music corporate executives and authenticity-seeking homeboys and homegirls alike. Its ultimate social and human costs are simply bottomed-lined away.

Conclusion

The collaboration between some of the largest transnational corporations in the world and inner-city black youth is not as strange as it may appear. The creation of global market niches in this era is a driving force in the contemporary exploitation of black American cultural forms. The marketing of the "other" as entertainment, an opportunity to experience the dangerously exotic, even if only abstractly, motivates both corporate producer and nonblack consumer. In the middle are "declassed" poor black youth—that is, those who are marginalized perhaps permanently out of the labor force—whose efforts to avoid what are clearly unpleasant destinies generate innovative ways to prosper and survive. Those ways have become new modes of capital accumulation.

Rap has reached a crossroads. Far removed from its roots as principally a cultural expression of urban resistance and political rebellion, it is now in the possession of global corporations whose interest is market expansion and profit maximization. It was the genius and curse of Tupac and other rappers that they could merge their creative impulses with the imperatives of capital, and as a by-product, become global articulators of the plight and predicament of black youth, perhaps youth the world over. At the same time, a harsh judgment must be rendered on the project as a whole. Neither Tupac nor other gangsta rappers joined the struggle against the powers that exploit, oppress, jail, and otherwise marginalize African Americans, other people of color, and working and poor people in the United States and beyond. Indeed, their commitment to individual glory and success may have helped those processes along. Ultimately, as Tupac discovered, the commodification of thug life fails to resolve the underlying causes reproducing it in the first place and creates just one more arena of necessary struggle for African Americans to engage in against hegemonic corporate and state powers.

> I'll never die
> Thug niggas multiply.[15]
> —Tupac Shakur,

7

Globalizing the Black Image

"Monopoly is a terrible thing until you have it.[1]*"*
—Rupert Murdoch

Only a few short years ago, when the Internet was an infant, an attorney couple sent out a message over the Net advertising their law firm. Within a matter of hours, they were flooded with messages by outraged Internet users who felt that the "nonprofit" character and ethos of the Net had been violated. In a massive protest rarely seen in or out of cyberspace, they received so many E-mails that they were forced to give up their account and go underground, never to be heard from again. Millions celebrated what appeared to be a complete and vindicating victory against the commercialization of the Net. That incident now seems almost mythical.

The electronic revolution that has combined media, telecommunications, and computers—generally referred to as information technologies (IT)—has forever changed how information will be generated, distributed, and consumed. Some have heralded this era as an "information age" that will witness unparalleled democracy, shared prosperity, and harmonized social relations. For some this will be true. In many ways, however, far from challenging the status quo, the electronic revolution is a central component in the growth of an increasingly unfettered global capitalism. Information technologies open up new markets and new marketing opportunities. In ways unimagined by even the most free-minded free market thinkers, the century is ending with corporate power and control expanding into nearly every facet of life.

Economic globalization has led to the depression of wages, the permanent elimination of millions of jobs, the curtailment and erosion of the welfare state, extensive government deregulation, and unlimited access to markets worldwide. New technologies, robotics, computers, satellite technologies, and information technologies, such as the Internet and the World Wide Web, have transformed our path to the future. They have fed a process popularly known as globalization that is changing the economic, political, and cultural life of humankind.

All the while, working and nonworking people in the United States and the world over are being misinformed about the real relations of power underlying these changes by corporate-mediated news and by entertainment diversions from corporate-owned cultural industries. On the cultural front, what is being exported is more than just capital and industry. In particular, racist images of a media-constructed, African-American life, unmonitored and uncontrolled by that very same community, are transmitted around the world through a wide range of mediums. From rap videos to Hollywood gangsta films to television entertainment and news programs, the black image as corporate construction has been globalized. The ideological character of these images reflects dominate racial paradigms that convey a popular though flawed narrative where African Americans are their own worst enemies; racism exists only in the individualized expressions of white and black extremists, and black cultural pathologies and biological "limits" are normative. At the same time, the pervasiveness of blackness in U.S. popular culture—Michael Jordan and the Dream Team, *The Bill Cosby Show,* film stars Denzel Washington and Eddie Murphy, etc.—also falsely signals an integration and success that has little currency in the real world, but allows for broad denial that racism still exists in the United States.

Who owns and controls these media monopolies? What role do they play in globalization? How will they impact democratic participation? How do they affect race relations on a global scale? Understanding and seeking answers to these questions are critical for progressives involved in contemporary social movements.

The argument of this chapter is that the global media, dominated by U.S.-based firms, assumes a critical, if not decisive, role in the construction of contemporary images of race. The internationalization of the black image, filtered through conservative ideological fulcrums, has been facilitated rather than challenged by new media technologies and expanded media markets. While the popular images of whites in the United States reflect a broad diversity of characters, black images are stereotypical. As scholar Polly McLean notes, "Despite various restrictions imposed by some countries, the United States continues to be the major player in the international cultural marketplace. Therefore, it is important to examine the stereotypes prevalent in media culture that have helped shape the construction of social reality on both the domestic and the international fronts."[2] What gives these concerns new urgency is the speed, breadth, and pervasiveness of distribution in this period, which is unlike any in the past.

All the News that's Fit to Be Owned

Concentration in the media and entertainment industry has meant that a few people control most of the airwaves and other channels of communication. Those in control are primarily white males. One study has concluded that 8 individuals, families, and foundations control 91 television stations and networks, 71 radio stations and networks, 145 daily newspapers, and several dozen magazines, book distributors, film production businesses, and record production companies.[3] This includes the three major networks, ABC, CBS, and NBC, as well as the major newspapers such as the *Wall Street Journal* and *Washington Post*. These media conglomerates form interlocking boards of directors with multinational oil, banking, and industrial corporations, including Chase Manhattan, Coca-Cola, Chemical Bank, Xerox Corporation, AT&T, IBM, and American Express.

All of these corporations also have interlocking directorships with high-powered policy organizations, such as the Trilateral Commission, Business Roundtable, Business Council, Council on Foreign Relations, and Committee for Economic Development. The networks shamelessly flaunt their government links, raising serious questions about their "objective" reporting standards. For example, ex-President Ronald Reagan served as chief spokesperson for General Electric which owns NBC; deceased CIA Director William Casey was a major stockholder in Capital Cities, which owns ABC; and former Secretary of State Henry Kissinger sits on the board of CBS.

The mid-1990s saw a merger mania, where huge transnational corporations gobbled up media conglomerates. Mass media increasingly came to resemble an octopus with a few heads and many, many arms. In a brief one-year period, ABC, NBC, and CBS all underwent radical ownership changes as they were either bought or merged with even larger corporate powers. In the cutthroat world of corporate takeovers, even the biggest media operations are fish food for larger, imperial-minded enterprises. In 1995, in a pivotal two-day period, the Walt Disney Company acquired Capital Cities/ABC Inc, the number one television network, for a record $19 billion, while less than 24 hours later, CBS agreed to be bought out by Westinghouse Electric Corporation for $5.4 billion. It was only a decade ago that ABC was bought by Capital Cities. This further concentration of media power into a smaller number of hands continues the trend of placing much of the world's popular cultural agenda into the claws of corporate barons and executives.

The range of control of media that is held by only few hands is nothing short of astounding. In 1996, *The Nation* published a map of what it appropriately termed "The National Entertainment State" showing the various links of media ownership and control involving the three big networks.[4] General Electric, which was ranked number one with General Motors on the Forbes 500 list, along with its ownership of NBC controls a large number of television stations, news programs *(The Today Show, Meet the Press, Dateline NBC)*, and cable shows and networks (*Court TV*, which it shares with Time Warner, which now owns Turner Broadcasting, American Movie Classics, Bravo, and A&E, which it shares with Disney and Hearst). Westinghouse, already a powerful multilayered, multinational nuclear corporation, by taking control of CBS gained authority over its news division *(60 Minutes, Face the Nation, 48 Hours,* and *CBS Morning News)*, television stations, CBS Radio (21 FM and 18 AM stations), and cable outlets (Home Team Sports, The Nashville Network, and Country Music Television). Disney, a corporate media behemoth itself, in acquiring ABC, got ABC Radio (21 stations), ABC Network News *(Good Morning America, Nightline, 20/20,* and *Prime Time Live)*, and nearly 20 television stations.

This assessment does not even include Time Warner, the largest media conglomerate, or Rupert Murdoch, who owns the Fox network and sprawling international media outlets. By bringing Ted Turner's Turner Broadcasting under its wing, Time Warner gained control over CNN, which is increasingly the world's most dominant news machine, replacing local news from Austria to Zimbabwe. Murdoch's empire continues to grow, linking communication outlets of many types from New York to New Zealand. News Corporation, Murdoch's parent company in which he owns about 30 percent of the stock, controls or owns, *inter alia,* HarperCollins and Basic Books (publishing); the *New York Post,* the (London) *Times,* and the (London) *Sun* (newspapers); *Premiere, TV Guide,* and *The Weekly Standard* (magazines); the Fox Network and Twentieth Century Fox Television, which produces *The X-Files* and *Chicago Hope* (television); and Fox Sports Net, Fox Sports International, FX, and Fox News Channel (cable). In addition, Murdoch owns 22 television stations in the United States and the film studio Twentieth Century Fox. In 1995, News Corp brought home $9 billion in revenues.[5]

The power of Murdoch and others is not just about a growing concentration of economic power. It also highlights the dangerous trend of information control in a few hands shaping the social and political consciousness of tens of millions. As longtime media critic Herbert Schiller notes, "Packaged consciousness—a one-dimensional, smooth-edged cultural product—is made by the ever-expanding goliaths of the message and image business. Gigantic entertainment-information complexes exercise a near-seamless and unified private corporate control over what we think and think about."[6]

Black ownership of broadcast facilities is minuscule, resulting in little and limited ability by African Americans to shape national debates regarding race and other concerns. In 1995, according to the Department of Commerce, African Americans owned 2 percent of 4,929 AM stations, 1.4 percent of 5,044 radio stations, and 1.7 percent of 1,155 television stations.[7]

In the past, the news media and entertainment industry have often been criticized for being on the wrong side of issues facing people of color, the poor, and working people. In fact, it is increasingly clear that the mass media is not as much on the wrong side as they *are* wrong side. Tighter corporate control and concentration of the media—interlocked with the industrial, financial, and telecommunication industries—means that the news is being delivered by the same forces whose interests more and more diverge from that of the majority of working people.

Entertainment Concentration

Along with the concentration of the news into a few corporate hands, the entertainment and cultural industries are also increasingly controlled by a small economic elite. As entertainment has grown to become a multi-billion dollar industry, globalization has also penetrated the cultural sphere. In the United States, entertainment provided the third largest trade surplus in 1989, with sales of $8 billion, behind only food and aerospace products. Internationally, entertainment sales were about $150 billion. In every major area of popular culture, capital has gone global.

According to researcher Robert W. McChesney, there are five global entertainment giants: News Corporation, Disney, Time Warner, Viacom, and TCI. These five vertically integrate their ownership of film, television, cable, music, newspaper, radio, and advertising firms into one seamless, global operation such that the whole is indeed greater than what are already substantive parts.[8] There are perhaps a dozen more whose global reach is unrelenting. In every field, from music to films to video, the presence of transnational corporations is pervasive and they are encroaching on local cultures with brutal dominance.

In the 1990s, there were six major record companies that determine much of the world's music choices: Sony, Bertelsmann, Thorn-EMI, Polygram, MCA, and Time Warner. While only Time Warner is still a U.S.-based operation, U.S. popular music dominates, marketed on a global scale that takes full advantage of technical advances. In 1990, the world recording industry had sales of over $20 billion, including $6.5 billion in the United States, $8 billion in Europe, and $3 billion in Japan. Contrary to the popular image, it is not just the earphone-wearing, boom box-carrying ghetto youth who is tranquilized by the music. More than 100 million walkmans have been sold around the world and more than a million are still produced monthly.

Hollywood, of course, has also gone international. Of the seven major Hollywood studios, two are owned by Japanese (Columbia and Universal), one by Australians (Twentieth Century), and one by Italians (MGM-UA). Only Warner Brothers, Walt Disney Studios, and Paramount can lay claim to U.S. citizenship. Hollywood films have become dependent on the global market because only 20 percent earn back their initial investment on domestic sales.[9] American violence, and increasingly, American inner-city, black violence, is a universal language that sells well in both the developed and developing worlds. Black-oriented films such as *New Jack City, Malcolm X,* and *Boyz 'N the Hood* can be seen in countries as diverse as Guadeloupe, Chile, and the Peoples Republic of China. Black films, which almost always return a profit because they are so cheaply produced, do even better outside the United States, where they share longer runs with minimal advertisement and promotion costs.

The bulk of Hollywood's profits on these films are from non-blacks. Global and domestic film (and television) sales total about $137 billion annually.[10] In 1993, Hollywood films by black directors sold 29 million tickets.[11] This included *Hollywood Shuffle,* directed by Robert Townsend, which cost $100,000 to produce, but made at least $10 million in return.

MTV, which functions as one long 24-hour commercial for the record industry, is owned by Sumner Redstone. In 1993, MTV was beamed to 210 million households in 71 nations. In addition to MTV, Redstone also owns Viacom as well as VH-1, the Comedy Cannel, USA Network, Lifetime, Showtime, The Movie Channel, Nickelodian, and UPN. Redstone owns Simon & Schuster publishing house, Blockbuster video rental chain, controlling interest in Paramount (*Forrest Gump, Primal Fear,* and *Mission Impossible*) plus 5 television stations and 12 radio stations. In 1995, Viacom had revenues of $11.7 billion, employed 80,000, and had operations in over 100 nations. Viacom's motto is "Exceptional Content, Global Reach.

MTV is not just exporting videos, it is also exporting images that convey particular messages and stereotypes. Through its *Yo! MTV Raps* program, MTV has sent videos of black rappers to the far corners of the earth. For many around the world, this constitutes their sole contact with black youth other than that perceived in feature films. In effect, in the United States, Redstone impacts how black and Latino youth dress, their musical tastes, their views on gender relations, their political ideas, and even their language, the lexicon by which they articulate their worldview; globally, it shapes the world's views of African Americans and youth culture, while imposing those views on dozens and dozens of nations.

Entertainment consumption is high in the black community. According to a recent report, compared to whites, blacks watch television "90 percent more in late night, 59 percent more in daytime, and 55 percent more in early morning."[12] The average U.S. household has the television on 50.1 hours a week. In black households, the average is 77.3 hours a week.[13]

Although the corporate boardrooms and executive suites of the multinational multi-media are filled with mostly white males, some blacks have penetrated these enclaves of financial and cultural power. In 1994, for example, Time Warner—the world's largest producer of music in the world and the largest magazine publisher in the United States—named Richard Parsons company president.[14] Parsons sat on the board of directors before his appointment. Other blacks that have made it big in the mainstream cultural industry include Lamont Boles, Epic Records senior vice president of black music; Tony Anderson, Arista Records vice president of black promotion; Benny Medina, senior vice president and general manager of black music; Sylvia Rhone, Elektra/EastWest Records chairperson and CEO; Michael Moye, writer and *Married With Children* executive producer; and Kim Fleary, ABC Entertainment vice president of comedy series development.[15]

Overall, people of color constitute a smaller fraction of employment in the entertainment industry than in the workforce in general. While blacks, Latinos, and Asians are 22.6 percent of the nation's labor force, they are 16.1 percent of the high-level jobs in broadcasting and 13.2 percent in the cable television industry.[16] Complaints of biased images by African Americans, other people of color, and women are understandable when it is revealed that white males are 95 percent of all writers for television and that only a half dozen black directors can find consistent work.[17]

Several black entrepreneurs have benefited from the growth in black cultural commodities. A number of blacks have formed film production companies. These include Jackson/McHenry Entertainment, which produced *New Jack City* and *House Party II*; Denzel Washington's Mundy Lane Entertainment; and, of course, Spike

Lee's 40 Acres and a Mule. The most visible and successful beneficiary has been Oprah Winfrey. As a result of the financial success of her show and her film and television production company, Harpo Productions, Winfrey has earned well over $100 million annually for a number of years.

Other notable successes include Black Entertainment Television (BET) (cable television and music videos), Rush Communications (rap music), DPC, Inc. (hats), and Threads for Life (clothing). Robert Johnson, founder of BET, has big dreams. His hope is that the BET empire "become the focal point of black entertainment in this country" and internationally.[18] Already, the company has branches outside of the United States: BET International, which coordinates and develops programs for global consumption, and Identity Television, its London-based cable service that targets blacks in England. Currently, the BET business network includes: Black Entertainment Television, which reaches 39.7 million homes and accounts for 86 percent of the parent company's (BET Holdings, Inc.) $72 million in sales; Action Pay-Per-View, a cable network that has 7 million subscribers; the black monthly magazines *YSB* (Young Sisters & Brothers) and *Emerge*; a cable network that focuses on jazz; and United Image Entertainment, a joint effort with actor Tim Reid to produce black-oriented television programs.[19]

Future BET plans include building a sports arena in Washington, D.C., and launching several feature film production and distribution companies.[20] BET is looking to form its home shopping venture with the leader in the field, Home Shopping Network (HSN). The program would feature clothes, appliances, cosmetics, and other consumer items with a black emphasis to them. According to one study, black women spend $1.2 billion on beauty aids. This is the market that BET and HSN want to tap into. HSN brings in about $1 billion annually.[21]

Johnson began BET in 1979 with $15,000 of his own money and $500,000 from Tele-Communications Inc. (TCI). He owns 55 percent of BET's public stock, which is reported to be worth $130 million. TCI owns 21 percent and Time Warner owns 18 percent of the stock.[22] In 1991, BET had sales of $50 million and, in 1992, sales rose to over $60 million.

Much of BET's cable programming is dominated by music videos. These programs are cheap to produce and highly profitable. Similar to MTV's *Yo! MTV Raps,* BET's *Rap City* is very popular among young black viewers. These videos tend to be high in abuse and degradation of women and unnecessarily violent. According to one researcher, there is an average of 18 violent acts per hour in music videos.[23] Although BET and some other networks that broadcast rap videos have created policies to prohibit videos that show violence, profanity, or weapons, there has been no censoring of the portrayal women as whores or the glorification of gangster lifestyles.

No one better symbolizes the contradictory aspirations of the rappers than Russell Simmons and his phenomenal achievements with Rush Communications and its rap label, Def Jam. By any estimation, Rush Communications is huge. Home to legendary rap groups such as Public Enemy, Run DMC, and Big Daddy Kane, and producer of the highly-rated, hip hopish cable comedy series *Def Comedy Jam* on HBO, Simmons has transformed what was essentially a small basement operation into a $34 million conglomerate.[24] Rap artists at Rush have earned, at least, 10 gold records, 6 platinum records, and 2 multiplatinum records. Plans are afoot to expand the conglomerate into film production and even sell public stock. In 1994, Rush Communications was the 32nd largest black-owned business in the United States and the 2nd largest black-owned entertainment company, and is likely to grow larger due to a distribution deal signed with PolyGram in 1994.[25]

As CEO, Simmons earns about $5 million annually.[26] Usually attired in sneakers, a sweatsuit and a baseball cap, Simmons is a major driving force behind the music and in often attacking the racist structures of the popular music business that have historically reduced the role of African Americans to that of powerless entertainers. Simmons' success and efforts are as laudable as they are remarkable. They do not, however, represent a break from the economic system that is responsible for the misery that forms the substance of the music that Rush produces. The commodification of black resistance is not the same as resistance to a society built on commodification. Rap artists, even those who obtain some economic power and independence, are still slaves to a market system that requires an economic elite and mass deprivation.

There are other players in the television image game. Since the demise of the racially sugarcoated *The Cosby Show* in the early 1990s on NBC, the major networks have gotten out of the black sitcom business. In fact, they have gotten out of the black shows business altogether. The void was initially filled by Rupert Murdoch's Fox Network. The upstart network put a steady stream of black sitcoms on the air, including *In Living Color, Living Single,* and *Martin,* among others. The Fox strategy was to corner the inner-city, urban market that is disproportionately young, consumer-oriented, and black. The approach was highly successful as Fox's black programs shot to the top of the list for black viewers.

In the mid-1990s, Fox shifted its strategy. Having established itself, the network was now ready to take on the big three networks on their own turf. Murdoch paid $1.6 billion for the rights to broadcast National Football League games and $575 million for professional baseball.[27] In 1996, in a decisive move away from black-oriented programs, Fox attempted to emulate the success of shows like *Seinfeld* and *Friends,* popular sitcoms with no black characters. Yet Fox shows like *Party Girl, Lush Life,* and others bombed completely and were quickly withdrawn. Fox had more success, phenomenal success in fact, with cynical dramas like *The X-Files,* and *Millennium.*

Picking up the slack on black programs have been the syndicated networks Warner Brothers and UPN. Virtually overnight, these two networks captured the black market with shows like *Moesha, Homeboys in Outer Space, In the House, Parent 'Hood, Jamie Foxx, Steve Harvey, Sister, Sister,* and *Wayan Brothers.* Despite differences in tone and level of silliness, these shows have several factors in common. Aimed at a black hip-hop audience, they are all comedies that send a deceptive message: essentially, the conditions facing African Americans are humorous and always good for a laugh. Black men are buffoonish, roguish, immature, and always in trouble. Black women are loud, domineering, oversexed, and always taking care of black men. The black elderly and black children are never without quirks and behave abnormally. On the surface, these shows advocate nonviolence, tolerance, the Protestant work ethic, what are popularly perceived to be middle-class values, and a love-thy-neighbor ethos. Underneath, however, lies an ideological order that dismisses alternative, radical political action, sanctions corporate authority, promotes consumerism and materialism, and reinforces status quo social relations.

The comedies developed by Fox, Warner Brothers, and UPN have a global audience. *Martin* is produced by HBO which in turn is owned by media Hercules Time Warner. *Sister, Sister, Jamie Foxx,* and *Wayan Brothers* are all on the Warner Brothers network which is also owned by Time Warner. From London to Cape Town to Port-au-Prince to Mexico City, these programs are watched by millions. MTV's black thugs and the other networks' black jesters are two sides of the same coin. The complexities and multidimensional character of black life rarely appear on television. The few sitcoms that miraculously make it to the air and attempt a more genuine reflection of the dynamics of the black community, such as *Roc* or *Frank's Place,* do not last long.

The global market is key and transnational entertainment corporations are spending billions to reach consumers the world over. In 1995, global advertising was $335 billion. It is projected to be $2 trillion by 2020.[28] Time Warner receives at least 25 percent of its revenues outside the United States.[29]

Does the Net Work?

The Internet has increasingly become one of our most important means of communications and research. In a few short years, it has gone from obscurity to addiction for many. Some have called it electronic heroin. Even more have hailed it as the next stage in democracy. Whatever the Internet and the World Wide Web represent, they do not represent democracy. This can be seen not only in the history of the Internet, but in its growing commercialization.

The Internet was initially designed by the U.S. Department of Defense—not exactly what most would call a democratic institution. In 1969, the Pentagon's Advanced Research Projects Agency (ARPA) created ARPANET, essentially the first network of computers that could talk to each other. ARPANET was turned over to the Defense Communications Agency in 1975. In the 1980s, academic networks tied to military and defense-related research began to develop nodes (networks) under the auspices of the National Science Foundation. The NSFNET replaced ARPANET in 1990. By the early 1990s, nearly every college and university was connected to the Internet as well as most government agencies and departments. Although the Internet still functioned as a system used primarily by the economically and educationally privileged, it was overwhelmingly for nonprofit purposes.

The invention and spread of the World Wide Web, which allows easy use of the Internet, as well as audio and video enhancements, popularized the Net to millions. The Web was started in 1989 at the European Center for Particle Research, a military-connected institute, but did not emerge to be the force that it has become until the invention of Web browsers that allowed any user to easily access and surf the Web. With the popularity of the Web came the hyper-commercialization. In 1993, only 4.6 percent of the Web sites had extensions that ended in "com," the signature designating a commercial site. By 1995, "com" far outnumbered all the "edu" and "gov" sites combined.[30] Many studies have shown that anywhere from 60 to 80 percent of what is on the Internet is controlled by major corporations, and that percentage is growing. It has been predicted that by the year 2000, the Internet will account for at least $1 trillion in commercial transactions.[31] The *Playboy* magazine Web site, which was receiving over three million visits or "hits" a day, was charging and getting $100,000 for businesses to have a link on their Web screen.[32]

Rather than becoming the new engine for democratic input naively hoped for by progressives and others, the Internet has increasingly become a new vehicle for capital accumulation. As *Monthly Review* notes, "Although the Internet clearly has opened up important space for progressive and democratic communication, the notion that the Internet will permit humanity to leapfrog over capitalism and corporate communications seems dubious unless public policy forcefully restricts the present capitalist colonization of cyberspace."[33] In a similar vein, the American Libraries Association depressingly predicts that, in spite of its democratic potential, the Internet "will be owned, controlled, and dominated by unregulated media giants that are driven by profits, not the hope for cultural understanding, greater democracy, the decrease of poverty, or educational enhancement."[34]

The black presence on the World Wide Web has grown substantially in the last few years. Web sites, such as "The Black World Today," "Black America On-Line," and dozens of others, provide critical news and information regarding black life. There are thousands of personal, business, community organizations and professional black home pages. In other words, the opportunity to get accurate and extensive information about African Americans exists.

There are also numerous sites on the Web regarding Africa as well as the Caribbean, Latin America, and other parts of the African diaspora. Clearly, a strength of the Internet is the ease and speed with which it unites distant activists, scholars, and researchers, rapidly creating new bodies of information and new channels of exchange. The images and discourses found on the black Internet flow are counternarratives to the dominant portrayals expressed in other mediums, where black input is limited or nonexistent.

At the same time, racist propaganda and advocacy have a growing presence on the Internet. A long list of right-wing militias, fascists, white nationalists, skinheads, neo-Nazis, Ku Klux Klan, white supremacists, and racists of all sorts are spreading their messages and building their networks through the use of Web pages, E-mail networks, list servers, and news groups. The racist right has had a presence on the Internet for a number of years, dating back to at least the late 1980s. Hate groups have also engaged in sabotage over the Internet, attacking progressive and black sites in a number of cases by rewriting code and posting racist messages. Some black sites have been inundated with racist jokes while others have had pictures of African Americans being lynched or killed sent to them from somewhere on the Internet. While conservatives and censors from the White House to the Republicans and Democrats in Congress have taken on the issue of pornography on the Internet, they have been loudly silent on the issue of cyberhate. Conservatives are stressed that children may see nude pictures or read profanity, but are quite relaxed that those same children may first learn the word "nigger" from the Internet or be told that African Americans and Latinos are less intelligent than whites.

The fight-back against cyberhate has grown, however. At the forefront has been Atlanta's Center for Democratic Renewal,

Montgomery, Alabama's Klanwatch, Los Angeles' Simon Wiesenthal Center, the National Bar Association, and New York's Anti-Defamation League. There are also a number of World Wibe Web sites that are dedicated to exposing racism and fascism on the Internet. Unfortunately, most civil rights organizations have ignored this arena of struggle. In part, it has to do with the lack of technological skills, computer accessibility, efficiency, and orientation by these groups. It also has to do with not taking seriously enough the threat posed by cyberhate.

More than ever, there is a need for public intervention in the development of the Internet. Left to the free market, the Internet will soon disappear into simply an instrument of commercials and entertainment, only occasionally interrupted by relevant information and news. At a minimum, there needs to be a federally sponsored "Corporation for Public Networking" that ensures diversity, access, and an alternative to corporate networking. Public television and radio, as weak as they may be on issues of diversity of content and management control, were created to counter the corporate and exclusionary nature of those commercial mediums.

Activism in the Globalization Age

This era is being defined by the globalization of corporate power concentrated in fewer and fewer hands. A 1996 study by the Institute for Policy Studies found that global corporations now constitute 51 of the world's largest 100 economies.[35] The combined revenues of the top 200 corporations, according to the study, are larger than the combined economies of 182 countries; all but the top nine.[36]

This growth in power by the transnational corporations has paradoxically not translated into global job expansion. The top 200 corporations employed only 18.8 million globally, less than one-third of one one-hundredth of one percent of the world's labor force.[37] Today, the world economy is being driven by only a few transnationals. The 300 richest corporations in the world account for 70 percent of all foreign investments and 25 percent of the world's capital assets.[38] Left out of this phenomenal growth and prosperity are large regions of the world that are being sacrificed and marginalized. Here at the millennium, about one billion people live in absolute poverty around the world.

When it comes to real-world equality, unlike the much celebrated "virtual equality," the World Wide Web is not so worldly. The electronic and information revolutions have failed to make much of a progressive impact on many, if not most, parts of the developing world, especially Africa. More than 90 percent of the world does not have telephones.[39] Two-thirds of the globe's televisions and radios are owned and controlled in Europe and North America though these two regions constitute only 20 percent of the world's population.[40] Sub-Saharan Africa, which has 12.1 percent of the world's population, has only 3.7 percent of the world's televisions and 1.3 percent of its radios.[41] North America has 798 televisions per 1,000 residents; Africa has only 37 per 1,000.[42] South Africa, the most developed nation in Africa, has 60 telephones per 100 white residents, but only 1 per 100 black residents.[43] Assessing the Internet and advanced telecommunications technologies reaching the masses of African people, South African Deputy President Thabo Mbeki states, "The reality is that there are more telephone lines in Manhattan, New York than in Sub-Saharan Africa."[44]

In the United States, economic inequity has also increased and is starker than it has ever been. According to the U.S. Census Bureau, 94 percent of all financial wealth in the United States is owned by the top 20 percent of the population, while the top 1 percent owns 48 percent. The top 200 U.S. manufacturing corporations own 60 percent of all manufacturing assets in this country, with the top 710 owning 80 percent.

This economic power has led to powerful and growing corporate influence over public policy, particularly that related to corporate interests. American corporations won significant victories with the passage of NAFTA in 1993, the General Agreement on Tariffs and Trade (GATT) in 1994, and the Telecommunications Act of 1996. These legislative wins smashed all illusions that control of the globalization process and corporate development of cyberspace would be ceded to democratic input without a battle. Computer nerds, academics, political activists, undergraduates, and those looking for dates notwithstanding, the struggle to accentuate the democratic potential of the Internet will be fierce and long term.

One of the most critical concerns of this period is that of governance. In an era where international economic, political, ecological, and cultural relations increasingly dominate the national and local, there is an urgent need for international political bodies with the authority to manage those relations.

All of these issues must be taken up by progressives and others fighting for a more democratic world. The technical revolution in information production, distribution, and consumption must be accompanied by a social revolution to increase democratic participation and control unchecked corporate power. Movement organizers must address the contradiction that people need to be informed in order to fight back against the consequences of media concentration and economic globalization, but that the means by which most people are informed are by those very media corporations in the first place.

All progressive organizations, including women's groups, civil rights organizations, environmental organizations, and labor unions, have critical roles to play in these struggles. Trade unions, in particular, with their broad base, economic interests, and experience, hold a potentially strong leadership role in this new era. As University of Wisconsin journalism professor Robert McChesney wrote, "Organized labor has a crucial role to play. It is uniquely situated with the resources and the perspective to battle the media and communication status quo....Labor needs to devote significant resources to the policy battles against profit-driven communication and for public broadcasting. It needs to subsidize a healthy independent non-commercial journalism and media. It needs to learn the conventions of mainstream journalism well enough to improve the amount and quality of its coverage. In sum, the labor movement needs to learn from its enemies and take ideological warfare as seriously as economic warfare."[45]

Fighting the power means fighting racist images. Working-class unity, national and global, has consistently shattered on the grounds of racial equality and opportunity. One step in breaking with that tragic past is the construction of new ideologies that challenge assumptions and prejudices. The Internet and other mediums can be used to foster this development or retard it.

If the problem of capitalism has shifted from how to manufacture goods to how to distribute and market them, then the roles of the new information technologies and media concentration become strategic, in different ways, both for capital and labor. For some, such as Bill Gates, who wrote, "The information highway will be able to sort consumers according to much finer individual distinctions, and to deliver to each a different stream of advertising," the era is only the latest stage in capitalism.[46] For the billions around the world, however, who seek development, employment, and democracy, this new era must be break with the past and truly build a world unified for peace and prosperity for all.

8

How Cracked is the CIA-Contra Drug Connection?

As the debate raged over who introduced crack cocaine into the U.S. black community, the super-addictive drug was discovering new global markets. From Soweto to Brixton to the city of Bluefields in Nicaragua, black communities are being inundated with rocks of concentrated cocaine as drug cartels solidify international channels of production and distribution. Crack cocaine is a perfect symbol of the new commodities of the global era. Cocaine capitalism involves international channels of production, distribution, and consumption, unregulated and disrespectful of national borders. While the drug trade has always been international in scope, the expansion of the Colombian cartel operations has given it the power and reach of transnational corporations.[1] The cartels, along with the Italian Mafia, the Russian gangs, the Japanese *Yakuza,* and the Chinese triads, have developed networks of economic interests that rival the capacities and drive of the traditional corporate world. Increasingly, these organizations collaborate as they, too, take advantage of the new technologies and opportunities opened up by economic globalization.

In writing about the global drug trade, French journalist Roger Faligot noted, "The Colombian cartels produce the cocaine, the Chinese take it in exchange for heroin that can then be smuggled into the U.S. The triads bring cocaine to Japan and distribute it with the help of the Yakuzas. Then the Asian mafiosi launder their drug money in Europe."[2] The market focus of the global drug networks are, first and foremost, those communities most economically and politically vulnerable. In this context, drug concerns intersect with those of race and class. For the drug moguls, in the words of the 1970s' rock group War, "the world is a ghetto."

U.S. drug policies and problems have reverberated to the rest of the world and black communities are being the most devastated. Drug profits from U.S. consumers built the international drug conglomerates that are opening new markets in poor black communities in South Africa, Nicaragua, England, France, and elsewhere. In sensational fashion, crack cocaine has come to South Africa. Freed from decades of apartheid segregation, the people of South Africa, particularly those in the black townships, face a new enemy and find that their budding democracy is now threatened by the politics of a drug war that has quickly gotten out of control.

In August 1996, the very public burning and shooting of a drug dealer in the Cape Town area dramatized that South Africa had arrived in the modern era. Confronted by a 500-car caravan, drug dealer Rashaad Staggie, leader of the notorious Hard Living drug gang, was killed by members of the anti-drug group People Against Gangsterism and Drugs (PAGAD). The entire incident, broadcast live, divided a nation already frustrated by growing street crime and insecurity. While many condemn the vigilantism of PAGAD, its take-no-prisoner tactic also has wide support, particularly among Indians. A political and racial division has transpired as the black government finds itself on the defensive regarding the drug issue. One consequence of the Staggie killing was the emergence of a united front of drug dealers. About a week after Staggie's death, 150 drug gangs from the western Cape met and formed an umbrella group called "The Firm," which, in a surreal move, issued a press statement that it would fight back against PAGAD. A few days later, a shoot-out happened between PAGAD and The Firm.

The rise in drug trafficking in South Africa is driven by the gruesome economic and social conditions facing millions of black South Africans. The unemployment rate for black South Africans, for example, is officially about 48 percent. These dire economic times coincide with a dramatic rise in cocaine imports into the country. In 1992, authorities seized 24 pounds of cocaine; in 1995, that number rose to 411 pounds. It is no wonder that the *Washington Post* called South Africa "one of the hottest new transshipment points and domestic markets in the world."

In Nicaragua, crack is devastating the black and Indian populations of the Atlantic coast. The bags of cocaine that routinely wash up on shore, dumped by planes and boats along the trafficking routes that go from South America to the United States, are 90 to 95 percent pure. But since at least 1993, that cocaine has been processed into crack and sold for less than $1 per rock, which is starting to result in growing overdose deaths. One Miskito Indian community estimates that as many as half their young men may be addicted to the drug. In 1997, in Bluefields, a largely black community, police conservatively estimate that there are over 100 crack houses in a city with a population of only 50,000.[3] In the region, unemployment runs as high as 90 percent in most areas.

The intersection of race, politics, and drugs has been most salient in the United States. For a number of years, black activists and leaders have charged that the federal war on drugs has been a war on communities of color and the poor. It would take the controversy of one reporter's dogged determination, however, before these concerns would reach a popular level.

Spies, Lies, and Ghetto Ties

The politics of drug trafficking reached banner headlines in the United States in fall 1996 when a relatively unknown regional newspaper decided that the lead story on the inauguration of its Web site would be a tale of the links between Los Angeles' black street gangs, drug trafficking counter-revolutionaries, and one of the United States' most surreptitious agencies. Few media stories in recent years have generated as much response from the black community as the *San Jose Mercury News*'s investigative series published on the CIA-backed Contras' involvement in crack cocaine trafficking.[4] Written by investigative reporter Gary Webb, the series makes several allegations concerning the relationship between drug dealers tied to the CIA-backed Contras and the spread of crack cocaine in the black community of Los Angeles. Webb asserts that U.S.-backed Contras and Contra supporters imported cocaine into the United States; that the cocaine was sold to at least one major Los Angeles' black drug dealer with ties or membership in the Crips street gang; and that the

CIA was aware of the Contra drug activities and choose to either ignore them or protect the traffickers.

The response to the series has been phenomenal and is an instruction in the power of the intersection of race, new technologies, and foreign policy politics. Internet access to the series meant that a rapid and national, indeed global, exposure of the stories occurred and spread like wildfire. Reprints of the story have been put together and are being sold on the streets of Harlem, Washington, D.C., and other U.S. cities as well as Cape Town, Kingston, and Paris. Forums and meetings along with demonstrations and other protests have also taken place. Calls for investigative hearings have come from Congressmembers and black leaders.

Major broadcast media responded to the series by either ignoring its existence or, as in the cases of the *Los Angeles Times, New York Times,* and *Washington Post,* doing stories imputing Webb's motives and research skills. The Department of Justice, the CIA, and other U.S. agencies also denied the validity of Webb's allegations, and promised internal investigations. The backlash was so strong that even Webb's editors at the *Mercury News* began to speak with some hesitancy in their support for his work and even launched their own investigation of Webb's charges.[5]

This is a complicated story with many layers and serious implications for African Americans, the nation, and the global community. It would be a grave mistake to simply reduce the issue of the CIA's role in drug trafficking to conspiratorial legend or to the excessive activities of some of its operatives or the groups that it has employed over the decades. While all of these things are true, a much larger concern exists. Only by framing the discussion in the context of a critique of the political and economic foreign policy objectives of Congress and U.S. presidents since the mid-1940s can a genuine appreciation of the link between international affairs, racism, and illegal drugs be grasped. This framework can only be discussed briefly here, but it is a necessary discourse for sorting through the media and policy defenders of the status quo and assumptions of legitimacy that are accorded the CIA and government officials in general.

Under the cover of anti-communism, every U.S. administration from Truman to Bush justified global covert operations that directly led to the opening and expansion of trafficking routes for illegal narcotics, whose trafficking was then either ignored or even supported by operatives associated with U.S. intelligence agencies.[6] The role of U.S. intelligence agencies in narcotics trafficking has been a direct function of U.S. foreign policy both during and after the Cold War.

These policies were not race neutral. People of color in both the United States and the developing world have been the victims. The consequences of drug trafficking to and in the black community, and the subsequent growth in substance addiction, have been devastating. In this light, the black community has a deep vested interest in uncovering the truth behind the forces of drug trafficking as well as demanding that appropriate remedies and policies be instituted to rectify the problems created by the drug crisis.

Further, the growth and harvesting of cocoa leaves, opium, hashish and other crops essential to illegal drug production are also driven by global capitalist economics that have relegated developing nations to producing, under profoundly inequitable circumstances, for the developed world. Trade policies, such as NAFTA and GATT, also facilitate the spread of drugs. These policies have made not only the movement of money more efficient and faster, but have also made importation and distribution easier as inspection barriers have been relaxed. Since NAFTA was implemented in 1993, 70 percent of the cocaine that comes into the United States and one-half of the marijuana comes through Mexico. Government experts attribute this growth to a vast increase in trucking traffic from Mexico and limited inspections, both derived from NAFTA implementation.[7] The "NAFTA Accountability Act," H.R. 978, was introduced in the U.S. Congress in 1997 in an effort to address this problem.

Virtually all of the media stories, including the *Mercury News* series, have ignored the economic imperative driving the production of illegal drugs in the developing world and retail trafficking in the United States. In conjunction with whatever role the CIA and other intelligence agencies have played in narcotics trafficking, the corporate-driven international policies of the U.S. government are central to the economic woes of the masses of workers and peasants in the developing world and in the inner city and rural poverty belts of the United States.

What the *Mercury News* Articles Say and Don't Say

Webb asserts that U.S.-backed Contras and Contra supporters imported cocaine into the United States and sold that cocaine to black street gangs in Los Angeles. The Contra drug dealers, according to the *Mercury News,* "met with CIA agents both before and during the time they were selling the drugs in L.A."[8]

More specifically, Webb's investigation states that from 1982 until 1986, L.A. cocaine trafficker Danilo Blandon and his San Francisco-based supplier Norwin Meneses sold hundreds of kilos of cocaine to "Freeway" Rick Ross, a then 22-year-old, black street dealer with ties to the Crips gang in Los Angeles.[9] Ross, according to Webb, turned the cocaine that he received from Blandon and Meneses into crack. Ross grew to be a major dealer and, therefore, had broad influence over the spread of crack in Los Angeles because he was able to receive kilos from Blandon and Meneses at prices well below normal.

The millions in profits made from the drugs sold to Ross, according to court records obtained by the *Mercury News,* were "then used to buy weapons and equipment for a guerrilla army" created by the CIA to overthrow the Sandinista government in Nicaragua.[10] The Nicaraguan Democratic Force (FDN), a coalition of several groups waging war against the Sandinistas, was created in mid-1981, and authorized by the Reagan administration in its fight against communism.

Although the CIA and Contra leaders now state that Meneses was a key player in the Contra war and that they are surprised to find out that he was involved in drug trafficking, those disclaimers don't ring true. Meneses says that, for at least five years, he raised funds for the Contras, visited Contra camps, and sent people to Honduras to work for the Contras.[11] Although Adolfo Calero, the U.S.-based political leader of the FDN, downplays Meneses and says that he was unaware of his drug trafficking, Meneses and Calero were photographed together at a Contra fund-raiser in San Francisco and Calero concedes that Meneses visited Contra camps numerous times during the 1980s.[12] Also, Calero's denial of knowledge about Meneses' trafficking activities is not credible. The *Los Angeles Times* noted earlier linkages had been reported between Meneses' drug trafficking and his Contra connections.[13] Not only was Meneses well-known in the

United States as a large dealer, as the *Mercury News* pointed out, but he was heralded in Nicaraguan newspapers as "Rey de la Droga" (King of Drugs).[14]

Webb writes that the cocaine sold to Ross and later turned into crack created "the first mass market in America" for the drug with which the black community is all too familiar.[15] It is generally agreed that the eruption and broad growth of crack in Los Angeles occurred around this time. While Webb perhaps over enthusiastically writes at one point that Ross was "the Johnny Appleseed of crack in California," which led the *Washington Post* to charge in its attack on the articles that Webb claimed that Ross was the key to the crack epidemic, Webb never states that Ross was solely responsible for the spread of crack.

The series does not state, as some in the media have accused, that the CIA, Blandon, or Ross initiated or invented crack. Webb clearly states that crack existed before the Blandon-Ross relationship. As one of the *Mercury News* articles notes, Blandon's entry into cocaine trafficking coincided with a time period in which "street-level drug users were figuring out how to make cocaine affordable...by changing the pricey white powder into powerful little nuggets that could be smoked—crack."[16]

The series also does not say that the CIA as an agency or any identifiable employees of the CIA directly sold drugs in the United States or specifically targeted the black community. These charges have been made by both critics and proponents of the series.

The series raises two key questions that the black community has long sought answers for: did the CIA and other officials of the United States authorize and participate in the marketing and distribution of crack cocaine to the black community as a matter of policy or strategy?; and has the CIA and other U.S. intelligence agencies through their covert operations and other activities facilitated the flow of drugs into the United States, generating the greater narcotics trafficking that has resulted in increased drug use and sales in the black community?

On the first question, neither the series nor other reports and studies provide evidence of such high-level authorization or a targeting of the black community. While there are examples of U.S. officials being arrested and convicted of illegal narcotics trafficking, no conspiratorial network of top officials inside the CIA has ever been identified. This is not to clean the moral or political slate of the CIA, however. The record shows that high CIA officials did nothing to stop, and often protected, traffickers. No official sanctions or authorities were necessary for the events being charged to have happened.

On the second question, there is plenty of evidence and a long, documented history of CIA involvement in the facilitation of illegal narcotics trafficking. In addition to the CIA, the FBI, National Security Agency, State Department, Justice Department, Military Intelligence, and other agencies have also been shown to be aware of narcotics trafficking on the part of operatives and agents employed and used by these entities. This knowledge went all the way to the top of these agencies, and many believe, to the White House and the presidents.

Jack Blum, chief investigator for the Senate Subcommitete on Terrorism, Narcotics, and International Operations, told the *Los Angeles Times,* "If you ask: In the process of fighting a war against the Sandinistas, did people connected with the U.S. government open channels which allowed drug traffickers to move drugs to the United States, did they know the drug traffickers were doing it, and did they protect them from law enforcement? The answer to all those questions is yes."[17]

A Long History of Involvement

Official collaboration between U.S. government entities and known drug traffickers dates back to at least the World War II era. The Office of Strategic Services (OSS), the predecessor to the CIA, made deals with the Corsican heroin traffickers as well as with gangster Lucky Luciano in the U.S. effort to prevent communists from gaining a political foothold in postwar France and Italy. Luciano had dealt heroin in the United States since 1915.[18] The OSS's Operation Underworld would negotiate a deal that would eventually free Luciano from prison in 1946 in exchange for his role in helping to secure the docks of New York from Nazi sabotage and using his mob contacts in Sicily to attack the Italian Communist Party.[19]

From 1924 to 1944, the U.S. heroin addict population dropped from 200,000 to about 20,000.[20] These numbers would begin to grow again after the war and after Luciano established a worldwide network of traffickers, distributors, and retailers for heroin.[21] The U.S. government, "through the CIA and its wartime predecessor, the Office of Strategic Services, created a situation that made it possible for the Sicilian-American Mafia and the Corsican underworld to revive the international narcotics traffic."[22]

Similar alliances led to similar consequences in Southeast Asia. In Laos, beginning around 1960, the CIA created a secret army of 30,000 Hmong people to fight the communist in charge of the nation. Hmong Gen. Vang Pao was allowed to use the CIA's Air America planes to traffic opium, the Hmong's major cash crop. This heroin would not only be used to addict thousands of U.S. soldiers fighting in Vietnam, including a disproportionate number of African Americans, but it would eventually comprise about one-third of all heroin in the United States by the end of the war in the mid-1970s.[23] By 1989, 73 percent of the world's heroin was being produced in Southeast Asia.[24]

Beginning in the late 1970s, in Southwest Asia, in the area known as the Golden Crescent where Afghanistan, Pakistan, and Iran come together, the United States supported the anti-communist Mujahedeen guerrillas fighting to overthrow their Soviet-backed government. The covert activities of the CIA would create trafficking lines that did not previously exist. A tremendous spurt in heroin production occurred that would have a direct impact on heroin use in the United States. As researcher Alfred McCoy notes, "As heroin from Afghanistan and Pakistan poured into America throughout 1979...the number of drug-related deaths in New York City rose by 77 percent."[25]

The trafficking surge would also directly impact the black community. Although heroin in Harlem had traditionally come from Southeast Asia, by the early 1980s, as a result of trafficking routes opened by U.S. intelligence operations in Afghanistan and Pakistan, about 42 percent of Harlem's heroin was now coming from southern Asia.[26] As McCoy notes, by late 1980, heroin from the region "had captured 60 percent of the U.S. market."[27] Between 1982 and 1985, covering the first Reagan term, the number of cocaine users grew to 5.8 million, a 38 percent rise.[28]

The pattern of exploding narcotics trafficking would be repeated when the Reagan administration made the decision to support anti-communist rebels in Central America. From Honduras to Costa Rica to Panama to Nicaragua, the CIA and other agencies would employ numerous drug traffickers to assist their covert wars against the Sandinistas in Nicaragua and guerrillas fighting to overthrow military and political dictatorships in El Salvador and Guatemala. The rationale for these unsavory alliances is captured by Gen. Paul F. Gorman, former head of the U.S. Southern Command, who said, "The fact is, if you want to go into the subversion business, collect intelligence, and move arms, you deal with drug movers."[29]

It is critical to note that it was not just the CIA but the entire U.S. foreign policy apparatus that was brought into play in implementing the covert war. This included all branches of the military, the National Security Agency, and the U.S. State Department. All of these activities and connections would be revealed in the investigations and hearings held by Senator John Kerry (D-MA) in the late 1980s. The report issued by the Subcommittee on Terrorism, Narcotics, and International Operations of the Committee on Foreign Relations in the U.S. Senate stated, for example, that "The U.S. State Department paid four contractors $806,401.20 to supply humanitarian aid to the Contra forces in Central America. All four of these companies were owned by known drug traffickers."[30] It went on to say that the U.S. State Department made "payments to drug traffickers...for humanitarian assistance to the Contras, in some cases after the traffickers had been indicted...on drug charges."[31]

Although the *Washington Post* attempted to imply that the Kerry report was ambiguous, a careful read reveals fairly clear conclusions. It states, for instance, that "on the basis of this evidence, it is clear that....elements of the contras....knowingly received financial and material assistance from drug traffickers....In each case, one or another agency of the United States government had information about the involvement."[32]

The Kerry report also concluded, "The logic of having drug money pay for the pressing needs of the contras appealed to a number of people who became involved in the covert war. Indeed, senior U.S. policymakers were not immune to the idea that drug money was a perfect solution to the contras' funding problems."[33]

The increased influx of drugs into the United States, whether Contra carried or otherwise, had a devastating impact on the black community. The harmful effects of drug trafficking and growing substance abuse would be compounded by Reagan, Bush, and Clinton's war on drugs, which has disproportionately been aimed at African Americans.

Racism and the War on Drugs

Historically, U.S. wars on drugs have without exception singled out and accused communities of color of being the main traffickers and users of drugs. Although this has never been the case, since the mid-1960s, drug use by African Americans has grown as heroin, cocaine, and other illegal narcotics have flooded the inner cities.

In the 1980s and into the 1990s, the black community has been ravaged by a drug crisis of historic proportions. The drug crisis among African Americans has resulted in "crack" babies, record drug overdoses, unprecedented numbers of black male youth incarcerations, a rise in AIDS cases, and numerous other harms. In Los Angeles County alone, according to the *Mercury News,* there are more than 70,000 children in foster care for drug-related reasons[34] In Washington, D.C., of the thousands of neglected and abused children that had to be removed from homes, 90 percent of those cases have involved crack mothers.[35]

The war on drugs has exacerbated the drug crisis in the black community. As scholar Michael Tonry writes, "The war on drugs foreseeably and unnecessarily blighted the lives of hundreds of thousands of young, disadvantaged Americans, especially black Americans, and undetermined decades of efforts to improve the life chances of members of the urban black underclass."[36] One aspect of the racialized drug war that has received the most attention is the sentencing discrepancy between the laws regarding crack cocaine as opposed to the ones regarding cocaine powder. Under the Omnibus Anti-Drug Abuse Act of 1988, possession of five grams of crack cocaine nets a mandatory sentence of five years. For an equal amount of cocaine powder, there is no minimum sentence and, indeed, many offenders receive probation. It takes trafficking of 500 grams of cocaine powder to receive a sentence of five years.[37]

According to the U.S. Sentencing Commission, there are three times as many users of powder cocaine as crack cocaine. Meanwhile, there are far more prosecutions for crack than for powder. Although 91 percent of those who use cocaine snort it, 31 percent smoke it, and 10 percent swallow it, most of the law enforcement focus is on the 31 percent who smoke the substance, according to the 1992 National Household Survey on Drug Abuse.[38] In 1992, of those arrested for federal crack cocaine offenses, 92.6 percent were black. According to one sampling by the U.S. Sentencing Commission, of the defendants charged with simple possession of crack cocaine in the second quarter of 1992, all were black.[39] The disproportionate targeting of African Americans for drug crimes is fostered by a mass media perspective that demonizes and racializes crack users while steadfastly refusing to conduct serious investigation into the genesis of drug importation into black communities or the connections between U.S. foreign economic and political policies and global trafficking.

Media Misinformation

The thunder of response to the *Mercury News* articles forced other major newspapers to reluctantly address the issue and do their own investigations. The big three newspapers—the *Washington Post, Los Angeles Times,* and *New York Times*—all did stories about the series and how other news outlets were covering the controversy. The outrage in the black community—manifest in black newspapers, black talk radio, cable programs, and C-SPAN-broadcasted forums—became too strong to ignore and left the big three with little choice but to put their own spin on a story that the upstart *Mercury News* had scooped them on.

At one level, it is not surprising that the major media organizations would not report about an issue in 1996 that they were given information about in 1986. Despite Senate hearings and the work of the former Christic Institute to bring the stories of Contra drug trafficking to light, major media outlets dismissed the accusations and gave scant attention to these issues.

In their coverage of the story, the major papers—most notably the *Washington Post, New York Times,* and *Los Angeles Times*—had a number of objectives. First, they sought to prove that Ross was not a major dealer and, thus, not the catalyst for the spread of crack. Second, they argued that the Nicaraguans who were involved were marginally, if at all, tied to the Contras. Third, they contended that the amount of cocaine trafficked by the Contras was relatively minuscule. Finally, without questioning the veracity of the CIA, they supported the view that CIA officials had no knowledge of and gave no support to those Contras who were involved in drug trafficking. All of these objectives were in sharp variance with the facts and even these newspapers' own histories of reporting.

As *The Nation* discovered, the *Los Angeles Times* published stories critiquing the *Mercury News* series that contradicted other reports that had appeared in their own paper. In an effort to rebut the *Mercury News* assertions that Ross was the central figure in the distribution of crack cocaine in the Los Angeles area, *Los Angeles Times* reporter Jesse Katz attempted to downplay Ross' role. He quoted a source that stated, "Even on the best day Ricky Ross had, there was way more crack cocaine out there than he could ever control."[40] In fact, this is a rather sensible statement and it is doubtful that Webb or anyone else would disagree with it. Yet, in 1994, in grand hyperbole, Katz wrote in the *Los Angeles Times,* "If there was an eye to the storm, if there was a criminal mastermind behind crack's decade-long reign, if there was one outlaw capitalist most responsible for flooding Los Angeles' streets with mass-marketed cocaine, his name was Freeway Rick."[41] Katz went on to write, "[Ross] was a favorite son of the Colombian cartels, South-Central's first millionaire crack lord."[42]

The purpose of the attacks on the *Mercury News* series by the majors was to refocus the debate away from the more general charge of U.S. government complicity in what many consider the nation's most pressing social problem to a concentration on trivial details and the questionable character of the drug dealers and street operatives that Webb interviewed.

The *Washington Post* asserts that the CIA's role in illegal narcotics smuggling is only alleged and not proven. The *Post* fails, however, to cite any reference to research by academics and journalists that challenge that position.[43] As shown earlier, there is ample evidence of a long history. The *Post* and other papers not only failed to expose the illegal activities of the Contras, but served as a cheerleader for Reagan's wars in Central America and Bush's drug war on the black community. In fact, the reporting was so slanted that the newspaper's ombudsperson, Geneva Overholser, wrote a pointed criticism of the coverage: "The *Post* (and the others) showed more passion for sniffing out the flaws in *San Jose* [*Mercury News*]'s answer than for sniffing out a better answer themselves....Overall, the *Post*'s focus seems to have been misplaced. A principal responsibility of the press is to protect the people from government excesses. The *Post* (among others) showed more energy for protecting the CIA from someone else's journalistic excesses."[44]

The media has diverted attention from the main point of the allegations: the Contras were involved in drug trafficking. Even if the Contras, created by U.S. intelligence agencies and paid for by tax dollars, only dealt one rock of crack, and that had the tacit approval of U.S. officials, then serious policy and ethical problems must be raised (not to mention legal ones) that cannot easily be dismissed because there were other larger drug dealers operating.

Finally, the approach of the major media regarding the black community's response has been to chalk it up to "black paranoia."[45] While noting that a long history of government-sponsored activities against the black community have justified suspicion, the majors have categorized those suspicions as baseless theories about government conspiracies not that different from the rantings about UFOs and tales that the earth is flat.

Policy Implications and Ramifications

Outrage characterized the black community's response to the series. Given the devastation that crack trafficking and addiction has wrecked on the African-American community, it is more than understandable that the discovery that U.S. officials were involved at any level in the spread of crack would initiate a fury that flows from centuries of memories of transgressions.

As a consequence, a mass movement emerged to distribute the *Mercury News* series as widely as possible and to force investigations into the validity of the allegations. Black political leaders and activists called for hearings and investigations. Representative Maxine Waters (D-CA) in a letter to Attorney General Janet Reno wrote:

> In addition to the stress caused by crack cocaine use, I am also terribly disturbed by the heavy-handed, arbitrary, and discriminatory mandatory minimum sentences which politicians have attached to crack cocaine use and possession. These sentences have the effect of severely punishing small-time users, and are prosecuted in a discriminatory way which disproportionately impacts African American males....I would like to request a full and complete investigation into the connection between law enforcement agencies, most particularly the CIA, and the early 1980s importation of crack cocaine. In addition, I would like to know what actions may have allowed these drug shipments to continue. I would also like to know the status of any efforts to investigate, punish, or prosecute those involved in this matter.[46]

Letters were also written by Senators Barbara Boxer (D-CA) and Dianne Feinstein (D-CA) to the Justice Department.[47] San Francisco Mayor Willie Brown and Los Angeles Mayor Richard Riordan expressed outrage over the series allegations and sent letters to President Clinton and other U.S. officials asking for a federal investigation.

Outside of Congress, Rev. Jesse Jackson and other black leaders demanded that Clinton order a complete and independent investigation into the issue by his Intelligence Oversight Board. Jackson also called for the release of all classified documents on the CIA's involvement in the Contra war, all Drug Enforcement Agency (DEA) records related to the Contras, and all DEA files on Meneses and Blandon.[48]

What catalyzed the movement was grassroots activism and black talk radio. Other activists have been arrested in acts of civil disobedience. Longtime civil rights organizer Dick Gregory, radio host Joe Madison, activist Mark Thompson, and Rev. Joe Lowery, president of the Southern Christian Leadership Conference, were arrested for demonstrating at the CIA headquarters in Langley, Virginia and at the Justice Department. Gregory and Madison also went on hunger strikes. From Washington, D.C. to California, there were protests, rallies, and forums. Howard University law students held a march and rally on the U.S. Capitol steps.[49] More than 1,500 people showed up at a Congressional Black Caucus forum on the issue.[50] In Los Angeles, 1,000 people turned out for a forum held by a local coalition that included Waters and city leaders, while 1,500 more waited outside.[51] In many cities, ongoing multiracial coalitions formed to distribute updates on the story and hold community meetings to link the issues raised in the *Mercury News* series with other local, national, and even international concerns.

Madison, through his syndicated radio show, and other black radio personalities from Washington, D.C. and New York to Oakland and Houston, not only kept the black community informed and updated on the ever-unfolding story, but also provided a platform for a counter-oppositional dialogue where the black community could voice its views. Just as black talk radio became the medium through which a popular black voice could offer alternative narratives regarding the O.J. Simpson case, the Clarence Thomas nomination, the Rodney King beating, and the Million Man March, so too did it become the megaphone of opposition to the institutional and mass media denials and attacks.

Conclusion

On October 23, 1996, at a U.S. Senate hearing, CIA Inspector General Frederick P. Hitz testified that, based on their investigation, there was "no credible information" to support the *Mercury News* stories.[52] That pretty much sums up the position that the agency, other government bodies, the major media, and most white lawmakers embraced and continue to stand behind.

Incredibly, that also became the position that Webb's editors at the *Mercury News* would take. On May 11, 1997, *Mercury News* Executive Editor Jerry Ceppos published an editorial directed to the readers of the Webb series. He wrote, after months of criticism and internal evaluation, that "the series did not meet our standards" and that the paper was, in effect, disowning the reportage.[53] Ceppos contended that Webb and *Mercury News* editors exaggerated Webb's findings and, "Through imprecise language and graphics, we created impressions that were open to misinterpretation."[54] He also wrote that the series was often one-sided and that many of those accused of being involved with Contra drug trafficking were not given an opportunity to present their side of the story. Ceppos wrote, for example, "We also did not include CIA comment about our findings, and I think we should have."[55]

The rebuking of Webb, indeed, of the very paper itself, was widely applauded by the major papers. Newspapers that were initially reluctant to cover the story at all, within days of Ceppos' retreat, published editorials essentially celebrating their journalistic victory over the now-humbled *Mercury News*. Among the editorial headlines that appeared after Ceppos' statements were: "Editorial: A newspaper says 'mea culpa'" (*Chicago Tribune*, 14 May 1997); "Editorial: A destructive newspaper series," (Scripps Howard News Service, 14 May 1997); "Editorial: The *Mercury News* comes clean" (*New York Times*, 14 May 1997); "Expose on Crack Was Flawed, Paper Says" (*New York Times*, 13 May 1997); and "CIA Series 'Fell Short,' Editor Says" (*Washington Post*, 13 May 1997). None of these editorials mentioned that even as Ceppos was apologizing, he noted in the same editorial, "Our series solidly documented disturbing information: A drug ring associated with the Contras sold large quantities of cocaine in inner-city Los Angeles in the 1980s at the time of the crack explosion there. Some of the drug profits from those sales went to the Contras."[56] The real journalistic failure here is not the recantation on the part of the *Mercury News*, but the complete disregard by the major papers to pursue the answers to the questions raised by the series as they focused more on battering their upstart competitor.

The *Mercury News*'s turnaround was more than just on the paper's editorial page. In June 1997, Webb was transferred from the paper's office in Sacramento, the state capital, to Cupertino. This obvious demotion was preceded by months of rancor inside the paper, with many staffers and other reporters calling for Webb's dismissal. Apparently, many reporters and editors felt that their careers were jeopardized by Webb's continued tenure with the *Mercury News*.[57]

Despite Ceppos' statement, the Department of Justice and the CIA pledged that their investigations would continue. This had less to do with the search for truth by these government officials than the ongoing pressure from the Congressional Black Caucus, and grassroots activists, as well as continuing media attention to the issue. Few believe that these investigations will result in anything close to the truth, let alone indictments.

The controversy around this issue underscores the necessity of black community awareness and involvement in U.S. foreign policy. The creation of the Contras was a policy initiative that emanated from a Republican White House and was supported by both Democratic and Republican policymakers. It is more disturbing that the CIA-Contra activities were not rogue operations, but, in fact, sanctioned and sustained by the highest U.S. officials.

Black leaders must move beyond merely criticizing the possible role that the Contras had in drug trafficking to questioning a foreign policy that shows little regard for democratic processes or the interests of poor and working people in the developing world. It is not enough that those involved in Contra narcotics trafficking be brought to justice—an unlikely prospect at this point—but that a larger critique be advanced that calls for an overhaul of the mission and practices of U.S. intelligence agencies.

It is also timely for black leaders to renew the call for major reform of the nation's drug laws. Numerous studies have demonstrated that the current laws and policing practices are racially discriminatory in regards to arrest patterns, sentencing, imposition of mandatory minimums, the aforementioned crack-powder sentencing discrepancy, and the punitive character of laws such as the "three strikes you're out" provisions in a number of state and federal statutes. It is also important to reiterate the demand that treatment access be given a higher priority in the federal drug budget. Under Reagan and Bush, 70 percent of the drug budget was aimed at law enforcement, while only 30 percent was focused on education, prevention, and treatment. Under Clinton, two-thirds of the budget is still focused on law enforcement. If the concerns raised by the *Mercury News* series and the U.S. war on drugs in general are to be seriously addressed, major reforms in U.S. drug policies and their links to domestic and foreign political and economic concerns are a necessary beginning.

9

The Souls of White Folk

In *White Man's Burden*, a film in which race *and* class roles in the contemporary United States are reversed, a subtle but sophisticated point is underscored: race and class are shown to be inexorably connected in a system of discrimination that is institutionalized, socialized, and systematic. It becomes impossible, in other words, to portray even a mythologized white oppression without constructing a profound and pervasive class oppression.

In the film, the dominant positive images on television are those of African Americans except for the news coverage, where the criminals are white. Cops beat up on white people for no apparent reason other than harassment. In one scene, a charity fashion show is held in which all the models are black and the money raised goes to help poor, inner-city white children. Racial privilege, petty and broad, is reversed. Even more intriguing, the film struggles to identify the racist mind. Racism is not only a way of acting and benefiting, but of thinking and imaging. It is what African Americans think about whites in the movie that is most compelling, and perhaps most chilling, to watch. Whites are without redemption for most blacks in the film; doomed to a ghetto existence without reprieve, whites are forever shackled by their own limits and irresponsible behavior. These moments, played to great dramatic effects, tease out the multilevel dimensions of racism. Racist attitudes become a material force generating frustration and even hatred among its recipients.

What really drives the point of white oppression home, however, are the class images that pervade the film: all the servants are white, the unemployment office is overwhelmingly filled with whites, and blacks drink expensive wine while pontificating on the genetic and cultural limits of whites. It is African Americans who do the hiring and, often on a whim or an irrational fear, the firing. The filmmakers even create a predatory white underclass that plays loud and irritating music.

Despite the fact that, in the end, it degenerates into classic liberalism of the "can't we all just get along" kind, the richness of the movie is that it overthrows the categories of race and class as they are articulated in popular culture, thereby exposing a necessary link between what is often projected as unrelated identities. In the rhetoric of intolerance that passes for mainstream political discourse today, the individualizing of race and class relations weakens the social response while perpetuating the notion that all discrimination is personal.

What makes the film science "faction" is the reality that there are poor, working-class whites who do suffer from class oppression, albeit a class oppression that travels through the funnel of race. In that funnel, a great transference happens. The concrete material reality of class power is replaced by the abstract threat of racial and ethnic social groups. These perceived threats become hardened views that are easily and repeatedly reinforced.

One issue avoided in the film is the role of those who are perceived to be neither black nor white. In this sense, the film embraces a politically outdated paradigm that whitens or blackens all others. While the social construction of race varies incredibly from nation to nation, the United States has perhaps been the most stubborn in adhering to a simplistic white/black bipolar racial scheme even when the obvious social participation of Native Americans, Asian Americans, and Latinos has always existed. This framework is even more problematic and complicated when one considers the notion of a multiblack African-American community that incorporates the distinctiveness of blacks whose ancestry of the last few hundred years is located in the United States and blacks who have most recently migrated from the Caribbean, or from the many nations of Africa.

The Whiteness of the Ideology of Color Blindness

In the 1990s, the ideology of officialized segregation has been superseded by the ideology of color blindness, which brands racial categories as inherently without merit and relics of the past. It asserts boldly that society is not organized into social groups, but rather individuals with individual strengths and weaknesses, individual talents and limits, and individual value systems and cultural behaviors. Color blindness also jettisons the ramifications of a long history of racial oppression marked not only by the oppression of people of color, but significantly, by substantial white privilege. The view that race is not biological or essentialist—that is, the recognition that racial categories are social and ideological constructs—appears at first blush as progressive, but in fact, color blindness as advocated in the mainstream attempts to neutralize rather than explain the social power of race.

The ideology of color blindness is a smoke screen for a more dangerous and disturbing mission, however, than just to make race neutral. Within the framework of color blindness, all colors of value become white. As legal theorist Kimberlé Williams Crenshaw notes, "Neutral functions here as a euphemism for white."[1] Underneath the progressive notion that race is a social construct and should not matter is an insistence that race will not matter even in circumstances where racial inequities prevail, that is, color blindness becomes racial blindness. In the post-civil rights era where open defense of racial privilege is impolitic, both sides of the ideological spectrum succumb to this theoretical non sequitur. While liberals and some progressives defend color blindness and selectively blind themselves to real racial issues, contemporary conservatives use the rhetoric of color blindness to justify the elimination of social programs and policies deemed to remedy problems that disproportionately affect racial minorities. The conservative appropriation of a term historically associated with progressive politics is rooted in the current dislocation and marginalization of the Left, the lack of a popular radical discourse that argues that the eradication of racism is a social responsibility, and leftist concessions to theories of pathology and personal responsibility.

Despite appropriation of the term and its dominance in popular debate by some well-known conservatives, there is a growing conservative critique of the ideology of color blindness. Theorists, such as Charles Murray, Dinesh D'Souza, and their national and international counterparts, argue that there are determinant cultural and even biological differences between the "races."[2] Their view is that race does, indeed, matter. They offer models, of course, that give supremacy to whiteness. While they claim objectivity and scholarly investigation, their project is thoroughly political in nature and their goal is to influence public policy. It is not social inequities that they seek to eradicate, but rather the societal responsibility and white sacrifice required to do so. Murray and D'Souza get to the same spot via different roads. Initially wedded to the idea that black cultural behavior and social pathology are the causes of black problems, Murray subsequently migrated to building his case on neoeugenics in *The Bell Curve.* D'Souza, who when convenient lays claims to third worldness, argues against multiculturalism, in defense of slavery, and for the abolishment of all government programs that foster "dependency" and perpetuate "victim mentalities."

Race at the Millennium

What are white folks thinking about in these days of great transitions when they think about race? If national opinion polls, academic papers and books, the pabulum of the mass media, and the rhetoric of elected officials are any indication, then they are thinking some pretty appalling, disturbing, and wrong ideas. Recent polls show that not only are whites (and other groups) factually misinformed on a wide range of questions related to race and perceptions of the "other," but that those views shape attitudes and beliefs that rationalize and support racial discrimination.

Media-derived views of race, for example, have led many to believe that African Americans constitute a larger percentage of society than they really do. According to a survey done by the *Washington Post,* whites believe that they are being swamped by a dark plague. Most whites, Hispanics, Asian Americans, and even African Americans said they believe the black population, which is officially about 12 percent, to be twice that size.[3]

More important than just incorrectly guessing the percentage of African Americans in the United States, are views by a majority of white Americans that blacks have made it economically and are doing equal to or better than whites when it comes to employment and education opportunities. The survey found that most whites believed that blacks have reached parity. About 58 percent of whites said African Americans had jobs that were equal to (46 percent), a little better (6 percent), or a substantially better (6 percent) than those held by whites. Only 41 percent said that black jobs were either a little worse (26 percent) or a lot worse (15 percent) than white jobs.[4]

Ignorance was pretty evenly distributed. As the *Washington Post* noted, "White men were as misinformed as white women, wealthy whites were only slightly more informed than lower-income whites and white Republicans surveyed were slightly more informed than white Democrats."

Not surprisingly, African Americans had different views on whether parity had been reached. A vast majority of blacks, 68 percent, stated that racism is alive and kicking and remains "a big problem in our society today." African Americans surveyed believe that not only was racism real, but that it also was a major cause for the deteriorating economic and social conditions faced by millions of blacks. Only 38 percent of whites felt that racism was significant.

The view that blacks have reached parity or equality with whites has far-reaching implications. First, it means that there is little reason to feel sympathy with or special concern for the plight of poor blacks. If inequality and discrimination are not the cause of black poverty, then the problem is clearly African Americans themselves, the reasoning goes. Sure, there was discrimination in the past, but those days are gone. Whether whites' views were generated by images culled from the mass media, nativist fears of a black plague, overgeneralized personal experiences, or ideological predisposition and affinity, the bottom line is that historically derived and socially perpetuated black subjugation is no longer canon.

A second implication of these views, which propelled conservative Republicans into control of Congress in 1994, is that government can not and should not attempt to intervene and address the problems of blacks. According to the survey, "two-thirds of whites interviewed said the federal government had no responsibility to make certain minorities have jobs and incomes equal to whites." The message here, of course, is that programs like affirmative action and minority set-asides are no longer needed.

Significantly, both blacks and whites expressed deep fear and anxiety about the future. Economic dislocations—sparked by runaway shops, depressed wages, downsizing, new technologies that replace workers, and other factors—have people searching for answers and solutions. Although sharing the same fears, the survey shows that whites and blacks have opposing perspectives on what to do. A majority of whites conclude that efforts such as affirmative action and government welfare programs, as well as the growth in immigrants of color, have all contributed to diminishing their quality of life and should be abolished or halted. On the other hand, an overwhelmingly number of blacks who felt concern about the future favor programs like affirmative action and felt that government has a role and responsibility to intervene where possible to alleviate economic and social problems.

In 1997, a poll by the Gallup Organization on race drew major media attention. The poll, conducted between January 4 and February 28, interviewed 1,680 whites and 1,269 African Americans, a significant number given the usual underrepresentation of blacks even in surveys that are about race. The 1997 poll traced the opinions of blacks and whites on issues of race that compared with previous polls. What is important to note about the poll is that it reflects the subjective perspectives of those interviewed rather than the reality of race relations. Gallup notes in the executive summary:

> Whites are more positive than blacks on a variety of perceptual measures of how well blacks are faring in our society, and how they are treated in the local community....Whites also tend to view themselves as having very little personal prejudice against blacks, but perceive that "other" whites in their area have much higher levels of prejudice against blacks. Blacks also ascribe to whites significantly higher levels of racial prejudice than whites give themselves. Blacks claim that they have little prejudice against whites.

On issues of personal relations between blacks and whites, the poll found evidence of a significant decline regarding some racial prejudices held by whites, such as living and working with blacks or sending their children to school with blacks. It also documented amazing changes in whites' attitudes toward interracial marriages and their expressed support for voting for a black candidate for president. In 1958, only 4 percent of whites approved of interracial marriages; in 1994, the number had risen to 45 percent, and in the 1997 poll, the number was 61 percent.[5] Similarly, in 1958, 35 percent of whites said they would vote for a black presidential candidate; in 1987, the number was 77 percent, and in the 1997 poll, 93 percent.[6]

These numbers are not coterminous with the reality of race relations. Residential and school segregation is strong and growing. And, while the number of interracial marriages has grown, many couples still face discrimination and individual prejudice. There is also little evidence that whites will actually vote for a black presidential candidate when given the chance as opposed to being asked an abstract question. Studies have shown, for example, that the responses of people in surveys often reflect what appears to be the right thing to say rather than what they really believe or how they will actually behave. That people believe that the right thing to say is not to express open prejudice can be seen as progress and a result of the influence of the movement against racism.

Even with the popular hesitation to be seen as prejudiced, whites had little trouble in stating their opposition to programs such as affirmative action. There were also big gaps in the perception of how much race relations have advanced. More than three-quarters of whites, 76 percent, say that blacks are treated equally in local communities, while only 49 percent of blacks felt the same way. While 59 percent of blacks felt that "government should make every effort to improve conditions of blacks and minorities," only 34 percent of whites thought so. Overall, a majority of blacks, 56 percent of those without a college degree and 76 percent of those with one, felt that racism would always be a problem in the United States. Fifty-five percent of whites felt the same way.

The differences in perception about race between whites and blacks grows out of the distinct realities that the two communities face. Those differences are also fostered by the wide dissemination of conservative and racist views on race, in the form of books, films, news programs, television shows, and other popular outlets. Much of this work comes from those ensconced in academia.

Writing Racism

The disparate views of whites and blacks are, in part, massaged by contemporary academic discourses regarding the nature and function of race as a determinant of social and cultural outcomes. Conservative academics have increasingly taken on the role of creating racial scapegoats and providing "scholarly" cover to justify social attacks on people of color and the poor. In the United States in the 1990s, under the guise of scholarly inquiry, racism has taken on an academic veneer in books such as *The Bell Curve* and *The End of Racism* that have dramatically helped to shift the popular debate on race (and racism) to a debate on genetics and personal responsibility. Funded by conservative and right-wing think tanks, these works have political agendas that have been ignored by the mass media as it legitimizes them as works worthy of intellectual debate. Other academics who engage in what one writer called "scientific pornography" include City College of New York's Michael Levin, Johns Hopkins University's Robert Gordon, University of California at Santa Barbara's Garrett Hardin, University of Delaware's Linda Gottfredson, University of Pennsylvania's Daniel Vining Jr., University of California at Berkeley's retired Arthur Jensen, and University of Georgia's R. Travis Osborne.[7]

Views, ostensibly scientific in nature, about the intellectual inferiority of African Americans (and other blacks in the diaspora) are not limited to the United States. A global backlash has emerged as marginalized and oppressed communities have contested social status quos in all the major industrialized nations. As in the United States, rationalizing state cutbacks and a reduced welfare state on the backs of people of color and ethnic minorities is a task that has been embraced by some academics, which serves the purpose of diverting critical focus by the majority population on genuine power centers while allowing racialized targeting to occur unchallenged.

Social scientists, in particular, have rushed to meet this task. Canada, which has become increasingly multicultural due to large immigrant populations from the Caribbean, Africa, and India, has produced a number of racial theorists in *The Bell Curve* mode. Canadian psychologist J. Phillipe Rushton has long been notorious for his crackpot studies on the relationship between race and intelligence. In his *Race, Intelligence, and Behavior,* he echoes a long history of scientific rationales for racist views about blacks as well as the intellectual and even physical superiority of whites.

In 1996, in England, a similar controversy about race and intelligence arose around the book *The G Factor: General Intelligence and Its Implications*, written by a little-known psychology professor at Edinburgh University named Christopher Brand. At a press conference to promote the book, Brand boldly stated that "I am perfectly proud to be a racist in the scientific sense. It is a scientific fact that black Americans are less intelligent than white Americans." That Brand would cite African Americans as his racial target of choice is significant in two ways. First, it reflects the globalized perception of the racial struggle in the United States. Second, it denotes the media power—unaccountable, unmitigated, and discursive—underlying global articulations of race. After broad outrage, John Wiley & Sons, the publisher of the book, withdrew it from circulation, stating belatedly that they recognized that the book was "making assertions we find repellent."[8] Brand also suffered the indignity of students boycotting his lectures and organizing rallies demanding his ouster.

The eugenics argument is old, very old, and not worth dignifying as an intellectual function. Stephen Gould's *The Mismeasure of Man*, Barry Mehler's *The New Eugenics Movement in the United States*, Daniel Kevles' *In the Name of Eugenics*, and other books have thoroughly repudiated the argument. The question that really has to be raised, as Harvard scholar Henry Louis Gates and *Harper* editor Michael Lind both noted in a special issue of *The New Republic* that published critiques of *The Bell Curve*, why are these works being published now and given such widespread exposure? The agenda of these writers and the foundations that fund them is social and political, not academic. It is not about "ending racism," it is about ending welfare and other distributive economic programs. It is not about issues of intelligence; it is about reform that punishes legal immigrants of color and attacks those who are undocumented. It is not about "less qualified" blacks and Latinos taking white jobs; it is about less aid to the cities and abolishing all social programs.

A clear message is being sent to whites, blacks, Latinos, Native Americans, Asians, and other sectors of society. Whites are being told not to feel guilty about being less sympathetic to the plight of the poor, especially the poor of color. First, it is their own fault, due to their social and cultural predispositions, and perhaps even their genes.

Second, government would do better to reallocate funds for social spending to other projects since "those people" cannot be helped anyway. The message to groups of color is that you are on your own, and that you need to accept your intellectual and social limits and remain as isolated from the rest of society as you can.

White Politicians and the "Constant Curse"

In 1997, Representative Tony Hall and a number of other white Congressmembers proposed that the government apologize to African Americans for slavery. The apology would involve no reparations or any programs that would compensate African Americans for not only the experience of slavery, but the legacy that has crippled the economic and social life of the black community up to this very day. The response of Harvard Law Professor and former Clinton aide Christopher Edley to the proposed apology was appropriate. He stated, "Our problem is the lingering ideology of racial difference and caste along with the inherited economic disadvantages of slavery and segregation. So long as that subtle legacy of slavery remains, an apology would be superficial, not reflective of the moral change truly required of America."[9] The idea was rejected by House Speaker Newt Gingrich and other Republican Congressmembers as unnecessary since, in effect, racism was no longer a problem in the United States. Meanwhile, Clinton was constructing an intervention of his own.

President Clinton has given a number of speeches related to race since he has been in office and two stand out: his second inaugural speech on January 20, 1996, and his June 14, 1997 speech launching a national race relations initiative. These speeches were markers of Clinton's views on race and the legacy he seeks to leave behind. They were attended by well-known civil rights leaders and black elected officials, and received broad media coverage. Neither speech was a breakthrough regarding policy, but both capture Clinton's struggle to balance his stated desire to bridge the nation's great racial divide with his centrist political sensibilities that proffer unnecessary concessions to the rhetoric of personal responsibility and equal culpability.

Clinton's celebration of his second inauguration was planned to occur on Martin Luther King Jr.'s birthday holiday. Appropriately, in his remarks, Clinton spoke about racial divisiveness in the United

States. He stated, "The divide of race has been America's constant curse. Each new wave of immigrants gives new targets to old prejudices." He also referred to race when he said, "We cannot—we will not—succumb to the dark impulses that lurk in the far regions of the soul, everywhere."[10] Like most liberal interpretations of King that seek to de-radicalize him, Clinton's references that day to the slain civil rights leader focused on his "I Have a Dream" speech from 1963. He said of King, "Like a prophet of old, he told of his dream that one day America would rise up and treat all its citizens as equals before the law and in the heart. Martin Luther King's dream was the American dream. His quest is our quest—the ceaseless striving to live out our true creed."

It is likely that King would have appreciated having a president, from the South no less, acknowledge that racial discrimination is still a problem in the United States *and* that the government has some responsibility to intervene to end that discrimination where necessary and possible. King also would have likely seen the value of the diversity of men and women of all races and backgrounds—entertainers, civil rights leaders, business leaders, and elected officials—standing with Clinton.

In spite of those acknowledgments, it seems highly probable that, based on Clinton's policies and politics, King would not have been found anywhere near Washington on inauguration day. Just as he challenged Presidents Dwight Eisenhower, John Kennedy, and Lyndon Johnson, and other white moderates, I seriously doubt if he would have given Clinton any easier time. Given that Clinton has taken positions that, at best, could be called moderate Republicanism—such as welfare and crime, whose impact on millions of African Americans, Latinos, and the poor is nothing short of long-term disaster—if King's record is any indication, he would have consistently called for resistance. While many black leaders today have found accommodation with Clinton, preferring to grouse about his duplicitous politics and then return to the fold, King operated in a period where strong black leftist and nationalist trends helped to radicalize otherwise moderate civil rights leaders, forcing them to strongly challenge presidential initiatives deemed harmful to African Americans.

This is speculation, of course. No one knows where King would be today if he had lived. Indeed, as the Discovery Channel showed on its historically hypothetical program *What If?* King might have even become president of the United States, given the right historical configurations. In any case, we do have King's own words as guidelines to where he stood on issues of race, poverty, democracy, and equality. In the last years and days of his life, King was passionately devoted to ending the nation's shameful poverty as well as racial discrimination against African Americans, two interlinked but distinct social concerns. He died before the term "affirmative action" came into vogue, but he made it clear that he did support special government programs to remedy the centuries of oppression of African Americans. King wrote, "Whenever the issue of compensatory treatment for the Negro is raised, some of our friends recoil in horror. The Negro should be granted equality, they agree; but he should ask nothing more. On the surface, this appears reasonable, but it is not realistic." King, who did not merely dream about a "color-blind" society, argued that something aggressive had to be done to actualize it. He stated, "A society that has done something special against the Negro for hundreds of years must now do something special for the Negro"[11] if competition on a just and equal basis is ever to occur. King also did not bifurcate radical politics from the struggle for equality. Those who would evoke King's words in the name of a conservative or neoliberal agenda, as Clinton did, profoundly misread King's revolutionary vision of a society reconstituted and reconstructed along the lines of radical social democracy.

The de-liberalizing of Clinton's cabinet in his second term demonstrates the hypocrisy embedded in evoking King while moving to implement a political agenda that countered all that King stood for. Behind the symbolism of having a cabinet that "looked like America," was the reality of a cabinet that thought like big business. By all appearances and, indeed, in preinaugural rhetoric, Clinton seemed all too ready to accommodate the Republican Congress on a wide range of issues. Clinton's notion of a "vital center," his explanation of the core politics of the Democratic Party, is significantly to the Right of the liberal Democratic politics of most of the last 30 years. Vital centers do not make radical change. Clinton's political equivocations underscore that a leadership of vision and audacity—exemplified by King—is sorely missing on the national political scene from politicians of all races.

On the issue of race, King would have sadly witnessed over the years, by both Republican and Democratic political leaders, including Clinton, the twisting of his notion of a color-blind society to mean a society in which history is erased, group experiences are meaningless, and the burden of addressing concerns of ongoing institutional and systemic discrimination are placed on the individual. King's vision of a society where people are not judged on the basis of the color of their skin or the shape of their eyes or the familiarity of their tongue presumed the *a priori* existence of equality, justice, and opportunity.

In his speech, Clinton talked mainly in generalities when he addressed issues of race and he proposed no programs or initiatives to address America's racial divide. By not speaking to the wide range of racial incidents that have occurred during his tenure in the White House, from the exposure of corporate racism to the militias to attacks on affirmative action, he left the impression that responsibility for the racial divide is evenly tasked out between whites and people of color. This fits into the conservative bromide that African Americans can be just as racist as whites, dismissing the fact that racist violence is overwhelmingly targeted at African Americans, Asians, and Latinos; that the perpetrators of these acts are almost universally white; and that institutional and systemic racism are still relevant and critical factors. Clinton also did not discuss the urgent crisis facing America's cities that disproportionately inflict injuries on the African-American and Latino poor. In his first term, Clinton avoided serious discussion of the cities, growing economic disparities, and public school abandonment. Finally, in the speech, he also avoided any criticism of the real sources of racist power that reside in the social institutions, political structures, economic configurations, and popular media of this society.

In June 1997, Clinton launched his "Race Initiative" project, which has five goals: "to articulate the President's vision of racial reconciliation"; "to help educate the nation about facts surrounding the issue of race"; "to promote a constructive dialogue" about race; "to recruit and encourage leadership...to help bridge racial divides";

and "to find, develop, and implement solutions" in the area of race relations. To achieve these goals, an Advisory Board was created to "assist the President in outreach efforts," such as holding town hall meetings and other efforts. The Advisory Board is headed up by imminent scholar and historian John Hope Franklin, who is African American. He is joined by Linda Chavez-Thompson, an executive vice president with the AFL-CIO; Rev. Suzan D. Johnson Cook of New York's Bronx Christian Fellowship Church; Thomas H. Kean, former Republican governor of New Jersey; Los Angeles attorney Angela E. Oh; Robert Thomas, CEO of Nissan Motor Corporation; and William Winter, former Democratic governor of Mississippi. Chavez-Thompson is Latino, Oh is Asian American, Kean, Thomas, and Winter are white, and Cook is black. Clinton's former adviser on affirmative action policies Christopher Edley, who is black, will serve as consultant to the board.

After weeks of buildup, where the White House fed the press numerous stories about Clinton's sincerity and life experiences regarding race relations, Clinton delivered a commencement speech at the University of California at San Diego where he talked about race and his proposal to generate a national dialogue on the issue. Attending the speech were a large number of African Americans from Congress and Clinton's administration, including Labor Secretary Alexis Herman, Transportation Secretary Rodney Slater, Veteran Affairs Secretary Jesse Brown, Congressional Black Caucus Chairperson Representative Maxine Waters (D-CA), Representative Jim Clyburn (D-SC), Representative John Lewis (D-GA), and Representative Juanita Millender-McDonald (D-CA).

Overall, Clinton's speech revisits common ground. It came at a pivotal time in the nation's angst over race, creating a rare opportunity for leadership and vision, neither of which Clinton was able to furnish. Never straying from the center, Clinton moderates the excesses of the Right while keeping an arm's length from even the liberals in his own party. His remarks, thus, continue the evasion and denial of responsibility for the nation's race problems that must be assumed, at least in part, by policymakers and politicians. The speech begins with a candid acknowledgment of the sordid and murderous racist history of the United States, tracing a spring of incidents and themes from the slave sanctions ensconced in the Constitution up to the present era. Clinton declared, "We were born with a Declaration of Independence which asserted that we were all created equal and a Constitution that enshrined slavery....We pushed Native Americans off their land....Japanese Americans...were herded into internment camps....Though minorities have more opportunities than ever today, we still see evidence of bigotry—from the desecration of houses of worship, whether they be churches, synagogues or mosques, to demeaning talk in corporate suites."[12] Significantly, the word "racism" is never mentioned in connection with these events. Euphemisms, acting in the interests of Clinton's color blindness perspective, are employed—such as "discrimination," "demeaning talk," or "disturbing tendency"—underscoring Kimberlé Williams Crenshaw's insight that the "triumph of the ideology of colorblindness has effectively rendered explicit racist discourse entirely unsuitable within mainstream political debate."[13] Clinton stays on safe and acceptable turf and, as further described below, never lets himself be put in the position of seeming to unduly blame whites for the nation's problems regarding race.

He next asks the rhetorical question, "Can we become one America in the 21st century?" It is a question complicated not so much by the growing diversity of the nation, as hyped in the mass media, academia, and political circles, but by the policies of the state and the unchecked power of corporate America. It is easier to fret and rant over what conservatives and many whites view as an invasion of nonwhites than identify and address straightforwardly the ideological and power foundations on which inequality stand in the United States. Clinton then explains why diversity should be seen as in the interests of the nation. He states, "We understand the benefits of our racial, linguistic, and cultural diversity in a global society, where networks of commerce and communications draw us closer and bring rich rewards to those who truly understand life beyond their nation's borders." Here, again, Clinton equivocates the differences in interests from the majority of working people, who are not benefiting necessarily from globalization, and the transnationals, which truly do receive benefits "beyond the nation's borders."

Clinton defends his record on race and again underlines his theme of personal responsibility by stating, "For four and a half years now, I have worked to prepare America for the 21st century with a strategy of opportunity for all, responsibility from all, and an American community of all our citizens." He then addresses what many view as his most controversial and certainly enduring decision regarding concerns about race and poverty: welfare reform. To the cheers of the mostly white crowd, he stated, "We must press forward to move millions from poverty and welfare to work."[14] This is Clinton at his sophistic best. Analyst after analyst has shown that welfare reform, as fashioned by Clinton and the Republican Congress, will move millions, including perhaps a million children, from welfare to poverty. Welfare reform is doing more to create a class of sub-minimum wage workers who are forced to endure menial work, with virtually no opportunities for obtaining skills or advancing their educational level, than any other legislative reform in the last 50 years. The fact that the momentum behind the reform was built, to a great degree, by racializing conceptions of welfare recipients only makes Clinton's signature on the bill and ongoing rationalizations even that more hypocritical.

Even in his support for affirmative action in the speech, he selected moderation. He first choose to not sharply criticize the 1996 vote in California to eliminate affirmative action by stating that Californians who voted for the repeal possess no "ill motive." He then goes on to say that for "those who oppose affirmative action, I ask you to come up with an alternative. I would embrace it if I could find a better way." Here, Clinton is signaling that he feels trapped by the present policy, that perhaps it does harm whites, and that he does not really have a deep commitment to the policy. This is a message to both conservatives and neoliberals that he is about realpolitiks and not necessarily won over to a program of racial remediation. He implores those who support affirmative action to reach out to those who disagree with it and to point out the *practical impact* of the policy. A moral imperative to racial justice, as far as Clinton is concerned, has no place in this debate.

There are several schools of thought as to why Clinton created his Race Initiative. One belief is that he sincerely wants to improve race relations in the nation. Certainly no president since Lyndon

Johnson has spoken so publicly and often on the subject of race. Unfortunately, sincerity has little to do with the development of public policy or the urgency of personal political agendas. A second view is that Clinton is responding to the polls and surveys that demonstrate that race relations in the United States are strained and that presidential leadership is wanting. A third view is that Clinton is concerned about what the historical record will show about his presidency in the years ahead. As he faces his legacy, despite his bombast to the contrary, Clinton must recognize that his record on race is mixed at best and that little that he has done has mitigated the nation's racial discord. While his policies on civil rights and other racial matters can arguably be seen as better than those of Reagan and Bush, few black or Latino leaders are ready to cheer the work that he has done thus far and many see little difference. The list of issues in which he has adopted policies and positions inimical to the black community is long, including: his treatment of Haitian refugees, the Lani Guinier nomination, his jettisoning of Joycelyn Elders, his refusal to end the crack cocaine/cocaine powder sentencing disparity, his support for draconian Republican budget cuts, his back and forth on affirmative action, his signing of NAFTA and the 1994 Crime Bill, his support for the death penalty, and the bungling of the Henry Foster surgeon general nomination. Above all, as previously noted, Clinton's signature on a Republican welfare reform bill, which wiped out 60 years of guaranteed assistance to the nation's poor, who are disproportionately black, potentially sending millions into destitution, has consolidated for many African Americans a negative appraisal of his terms in office. Whether Clinton's Race Initiative can partially rescue what may ultimately be seen as a poor, perhaps even disastrous record on race—from the president who promised to be a leader on the issue—remains to be seen.

It is doubtful. The Race Initiative is much too little, much too late. Clinton made clear in his remarks before and after the speech that he was not going to initiate any new programs or address any of the concerns that civil rights leaders and others have been proposing for years. As he noted, the Race Initiative was primarily about dialogue, an exchange of ideas. When pushed against the wall, he simply would not go any further than the moderate program that had characterized his whole presidency. Clinton's White House was long on symbolism and short on substance when it came to race relations actions. As even Harvard University Law Professor Randall Kennedy, who has fashioned a career on wringing his hands about the overemphasis on race, noted, "The tribute to Jackie Robinson, the medals for the long-ignored black heroes of World War II, the apology for the Tuskegee experiment, and the condemnation of racially motivated violence were all politically safe gestures rendered according to wholly conventional formulas."[15]

Ideologically, even as Clinton noted the long history of brutality against African Americans, Latinos, Asian Americans, and Native Americans, and a continuing disparity on a wide range of measurements, he fell back on the conservative mantra of "personal responsibility." He stated in the speech, "Beyond opportunity, we must demand responsibility from every American. Our strength as a society depends upon both—upon people taking responsibility for themselves and their families, teaching their children good values, working hard and obeying the law, and giving back to those around us."[16] Note that Clinton lays down no challenge to the corporate powers that determine much of who works, where they work, how they work, and the nature and viability of communities from coast to coast. The devolution of the welfare state under Clinton's watch has continued with little trouble. Conservative policymakers and the transnational corporations have had a friend in the Clinton White House that has supported virtually every demand that has arisen from the global economic powers based in the United States.

Following the speech, the Advisory Board had hardly begun its work when internal division arose. A public and embarrassing debate emerged among board members over how the race question in the United States should be framed and addressed. Asian-American board member Angela Oh argued that the discussion and the project should move beyond what she calls the traditional "black-white paradigm." She contended that the United States has become too racially and ethnically complex to define the race issue in dichotomous black-and-white terms. The two African-American members of the board Franklin and Cook, countered that the foundation of racial conflict in the United States and its legacy arise from slavery and the experiences of blacks. The dialogue, argued Franklin, must begin and be framed by coming to terms with the historical racism against African Americans.

In a number of ways, the debate misses the point. Franklin and Cook would certainly agree that the race issue in the United States has never been simply black and white. To believe that would mean erasure of the memories of the murderous land grab against Native Americans and Latinos. It would also mean obscuring the history of brutality perpetrated against Asian Americans, as manifested by the internment camps for Japanese Americans during World War II. These are concerns that Franklin has himself written about and is more than capable of discussing. At the same time, Oh should have been astute enough to recognize that the pervasive racist images associated with issues such as crime, welfare, and affirmative action are overwhelmingly, if not exclusively, black, and this is not accidental or incidental. The complicated configurations of race relations in the United States, where ethnicity and skin color find multiple and overlapping representations in how race is conceived have not diminished, in the minds of most, the notion that the conflicts between blacks and whites are the most intense, persistent, and immediate. Full integration of African Americans into mainstream society has stalled in many areas even as it has opened up for Latinos and Asian Americans in some ways. Indeed, a conservative retrenchment against African Americans is in process, and, in the end, that retrenchment hurts all people of color.

There are other factors that color the debate on race in the United States that the Advisory Board did not seem to identify. The changing racial demographics of the nation have been noted, but important subtleties have been overlooked. While it is true that Latinos will become the largest group of color in the decades ahead, public perception of that growth will be affected by Latinos disproportionate concentration in certain states, such as California, Texas, and New York. For the most part, African Americans will continue to have significantly disproportionate and often decisive influence in most of the nation's major cities by virtue of not only their numbers, but also their history, political experience, and demographics. This particular configuration will mean that both African Americans and Latinos must engage in coalitions if both groups are to progress. At the same time, it must be recognized that the differences between African Americans, Latinos, Asian Americans, and Native Americans have not disappeared. None of these groups are excluded from the racial socializing process that occurs through the media, education system, and other institutions that instruct us on how to think about race.

It is interesting to note that neither side of this debate raised the issue of Native-American participation on the Advisory Board. If there is any group in the United States that has been marginalized and dispossessed, it has been Native Americans. As Clinton even noted in his remarks, the native population was robbed of its land through the most brutal program of genocide in the nation's history. Yet, when he put together his board, representation from the Native-American community was overlooked. Perhaps that oversight alone is more telling about the ultimate worth of the Race Initiative than its stated concern of racial reconciliation. African-American leaders, scholars, and policymakers must go beyond Clinton in finding white leaders who are prepared to honestly poise and answer the hard questions of race that the nation faces.

On January 11, 1996, a different kind of speech was given by former Senator Bill Bradley at a gathering in Los Angeles. Titled "Race Relations in America: The Best and Worst of Times," Bradley located the nation's racial problems in both its past and future. He stated, "Slavery was America's original sin, and race remains its unresolved dilemma."[17] Unlike Clinton and others, Bradley did not avoid the touchy subject whose consequences resonate down to the present era. He does not claim that slavery is an irrelevant relic; rather, he sees it as a central part of the nation's history and a shaper of its development.

Bradley also talked about the racial tensions of the current era and what is driving those tensions. He stated, "So what is the state of black-white relations in America? Both black and white America is caught in a traumatic economic transformation in which millions of Americans feel insecure about their future for good reason."[18]

He called for a new racial paradigm and for whites to reconceptualize how they think about race relations in the United States. In his challenge to whites he said, "We have to recognize that the flip side of racial discrimination is racial privilege, which consists of all those things that come to white Americans in the normal course of living; all the things they take for granted that a black person must never take for granted....As long as white America believes that the race problem is primarily a black problem of meeting white standards to gain admittance to white society, things will never stabilize and endure."[19]

In the end, Bradley called for a new political vision for the nation. Implicit in his words was a critique of the current configuration of political leadership. By most measures, neither party has played a progressive role in race politics in recent years. He stated:

Above all it will take a new biracial political vision that acts....A new political vision requires people to engage each other, endure the pain of candor, learn from each other's history, absorb each other's humanity and move on to higher ground. Such is the task of racial healing. It won't happen overnight nor will one person bring it however illustrative his career, nor will one person destroy it, however heinous his crime or poisonous his rhetoric.[20]

Old Stories from the New South

More than 13 decades after the end of the Civil War, the South still holds a peculiar fascination in the imagination of the people of the United States. Following the destruction of the first Reconstruction, the South led the nation in the creation of an encompassing segregation. It took 70 years between the 1895 *Plessey* decision and the 1965 Voting Rights Act for a second Reconstruction to occur. In this reincarnation, the mythology of a New South was constructed that argued that the old way of doing things and the old way of thinking were in the past. In this New South, whites no longer defend Jim Crow and African Americans have unprecedented opportunities.

The South has risen again, at least in terms of national politics. In a remarkable political flip, white southerners have switched in increasing numbers to the party that defeated them in the Civil War. If that was not notable enough, add the Republican takeover of Congress in 1994, the growth in the number of Republican mayors and governors, and the southernization of the White House.

Among the southern national leaders are President Bill Clinton (former Arkansas governor), Vice President Al Gore (former Tennessee senator), Speaker of the House Newt Gingrich (Georgia), House Majority leader Dick Armey (Texas), and Senate Majority Leader Trent Lott (Louisiana). In the 104th and 105th Congresses, southerners also chaired critical committees: Jesse Helms (North Carolina), Senate Foreign Relations; Strom Thurmond (South Carolina), Senate Armed Services; John Warner (Virginia), Senate Rules and Administration; Robert Livingston (Louisiana), House Appropriations; Thomas Bliley (Virginia), House Commerce; Larry Combest (Texas), House Intelligence; Floyd Spence (South Carolina), House National Security; and Bill Archer (Texas), House Ways and Means.

For African Americans, where the South has historically been the bane of racial progress, the southernization of American politics has significant and worrisome meaning. Polls and surveys consistently show that the South remains the most politically conservative region in the nation. It is no surprise, therefore, that as the Democratic Party moves to the Right, it moves South.

Not coincidentally, the South is also the poorest region in the country. It boasts the highest unemployment and poverty levels, and the lowest incomes. Southern states are very stingy when it comes to income transfers to the poor. Combined state welfare benefits and Food Stamps in many states—Alabama (46 percent), Louisiana (49 percent), Mississippi (42 percent), Tennessee (48 percent), and Texas (48 percent)—do not bring recipients up to even half the official poverty line.[1] The southern economy is also being battered by NAFTA. As researchers Sarah Anderson and Karen Harris write, "Layoffs related to the trade pact are accelerating throughout rural America, especially in the South. Rural workers comprise only 21 percent of the U.S. workforce, yet they have suffered 46 percent of NAFTA-related job losses. Of the rural layoffs, 42 percent occurred in the South."[2]

Seeking new opportunities, African Americans in the 1990s are returning to the South in record numbers. In places such as the suburbs of Atlanta, Montgomery County, Alabama, and the small city of Petersburg, Virginia, the black population is growing. A number of factors are contributing to this return, including African Americans in the army who have relocated, and a flow of immigrants from the Caribbean and Latin America to agricultural regions in Florida and other southern states.

Yet economic progress has been elusive for most African Americans in the South. Take the case of black farmers. As John Zippert, director of program operations for the Federation of Southern Cooperatives, writes, "For black farmers in the rural South, there has been a 'continuing crisis' for this entire century. Black farmers have faced not only the general decline in the farm economy, but also fraud, neglect, racial discrimination and economic exploitation."[3]

Although the wealthiest black middle class in U.S. history exists in the 1990s, the height of black landownership goes back to near the turn of the century. In 1910, the U.S. Census of Agriculture found that African Americans owned 15 million acres of land. Since that time, black landownership has declined. In 1960, African Americans owned only 6 million acres and, by 1987, that had dropped to 2.4 million acres. By the mid-1990s, African Americans were losing land at a rate of 1,000 acres per day. According to one low calculation, this costs the black community over $262 million a year in the early 1980s.[4] Almost a decade later, the House Committee on Government Operations reported, "The sad truth is that little has changed since the 1982 publication of the U.S. Civil Rights Commission report....[T]he Committee finds that ironically, FmHA [the Farmers Home Administration] has been a catalyst in the decline of minority farming."[5]

As the *Washington Post* reported, "Black farmers wait far longer for loan decisions, and are more likely to be rejected for loans, than their white counterparts....USDA investigators said that white farmers...typically waited 84 days for loan decisions while black farmers had to wait an average 222 days. Investigators also found that 84 percent of the white applicants had their loan applications approved, while only 56 percent of black applicants were granted loans." It went on to state,

> Government studies show that minority farmers are underrepresented on the local committees that make loan decisions, particularly in the South. One internal USDA probe found that local officials were "rude and insensitive to black farmers," that their projected crop yields were calculated differently from those of white farmers and that blacks were sometimes rejected because of "computation errors."

The 1982 U.S. Civil Rights Commission report, ominously predicted that if land loss trends continued, "there will be no more black farmers by the year 2000."[6] From 1982 to 1992, the number of black farmers dropped from 33,250 to 18,816.[7]

Leading the fight to save black land and black farmers, as well as to address farm issues more generally, is the Federation of Southern Cooperatives. It has worked in coalition with a number of other groups, including the Rural Coalition, Indian Tribal Agriculture Council, North Carolina Land Loss Project, Rural Advancement Fund, Arkansas Land and Farm Development Corporation, Rural Development Leadership Network, National Family Farm Coalition, and National Council of La Raza.

It would be unfair, of course, not to acknowledge the progressive movement in the South, which consists of activists of all colors. From progressive elected officials, such as Rep. Cynthia McKinney (D–GA) and Alabama State Senator Hank Sanders, to longtime anti-racist activists, such as Anne Braden and Gwen Patton, the southern progressive movement is alive and strong. In addition to the traditional civil rights groups, such as the NAACP and SCLC, organizations like the Federation of Southern Cooperatives, Institute for Southern Studies, Southern Poverty Law Center, Center for Democratic Renewal, and others have been on the frontline challenging racist and class attacks on working people in the region.

The fact remains, however, that the region continues to be the center of national racial strife. The illusion of a reconstituted South is continually shattered by the reality of inequities, discriminatory public policies, and the predicates of a conservative cultural resurgence. As the century ends, in the South, churches are burning, Confederate flags are still flying, chain gangs are breaking rocks, and the South has reemerged in the imagination of the nation.

Race Governs

On June 27, 1981, out for a good time on a hot summer night, 17-year-old Susie Deer and several friends went joyriding through the small town of Hot Springs. The car full of drunken white teenagers made the fateful decision to go to the black section of town. It was about 4 a.m.

Driving through the neighborhood, the teens threw beer cans and yelled racist epithets at the few folks who were out at the time. Billy Ray Washington and his wife were walking home from a late-night bar and restaurant when someone in the car chucked a beer can at Washington and called him a "motherfucking nigger." In response to these provocations, Washington picked up a slab of concrete and threw it at the car, where it went through a window and smashed Deer in the face.

Bleeding profusely from the mouth and nose, Deer was rushed to the emergency room at Ouachita Memorial Hospital. Since the injury was not considered life-threatening, she was not even brought into the operating room, where the doctors were to perform plastic surgery to repair her teeth, nose, and jaw, until about 9 a.m.

The operation proceeded well for a while, with no apparent concerns. About three hours into it, however, a serious problem arose. The doctors asked the nurse-anesthetist to move the oxygen tubes that were in Deer's nose to her throat, a common procedure known as re-intubation, so that they could perform the nose surgery. At first, no one noticed that the nurse was having trouble moving the tubes and, by the time they did, Deer had stopped breathing. One of the doctors, James Griffin, finally had to do the task. For more than an hour, the doctors worked to get Deer breathing again, with no success. At 1:13 p.m., Deer was pronounced dead.

As it turned out, this particular nurse had a history of problems in the operating room. Records showed that she often read racing forms or filed her fingernails while administering anesthesia to patients. Even more disturbing, at the time of Deer's death, this nurse was being sued for negligence by the family of Laura Lee Slayton, who had died at Ouachita Memorial the year before. In that case, minor elective surgery turned into tragedy when the nurse had trouble getting oxygen to the patient. The case was eventually settled in the family's favor.

Given the circumstances under which Deer died, the case was turned over to the state's medical examiner, Dr. Fahamy Malak. Under Arkansas law, Malak had sole authority for determining how to rule on Deer's official cause of death. The circumstances of the case and the written summations by the doctors involved in the operation would lead one to believe that Malak would conclude that the hospital and nurse bore responsibility for Deer's untimely demise. But this was Arkansas. Malak ruled that Deer had been murdered. Billy Ray Washington was arrested, charged with negligent homicide, and spent several months in jail.

Now this is where our story becomes interesting. Malak had a long history of professional incompetence. He once ruled that a man who had been shot five times in the chest had committed suicide. Pathologists from around the country would routinely come to Arkansas and give counter-testimony to Malak on the witness stand. His rulings were so notorious and frequently wrong that a citizens' group was formed specifically to have him ousted from office. The group was named VOMIT—Victims of Malak's Incompetent Testimony.

Malak had been appointed by Clinton during his first term as governor (1979–1980). The Deer-Washington incident occurred during the two-year period (1981–1982) when Clinton was out of office, but Malak still retained his position as the state's medical examiner. Clinton was returned to office in 1982 and held the position until he ran for president in 1992. For most of the period of his second coming, Clinton refused to fire or punish Malak. In 1991, just three weeks before he announced his presidential candidacy, Clinton fired Malak, but only after Joycelyn Elders had found him a $70,000 position as an official at a state hospital.

The nurse in this drama was Virginia Dwere Kelley, Clinton's mother. No one accused Clinton of aiding either his mother or his appointee Malak. They certainly couldn't accuse him of helping Washington.

Traveling Down Nigger Road

"Nigger" still has the power to emote. For blacks and whites, the term initiates a strong reaction. As researcher Geraldine Wilson writes, "For black people the word *nigger* symbolizes almost four hundred years of anti-African racism and cultural repression" [emphasis added].[9]

"Nigger" was quite a public term at the turn of the century. It was regularly uttered from the lips of the nation's leaders in public venues. The word also adorned many symbols of popular culture. With in-your-face boldness, numerous products were sold that brazenly used the term "nigger" as a selling and marketing point. Among them were Nigger Head Brand canned fruits and vegetables, Nigger Head stove polish, Nigger Head teas, Nigger Head tobacco, and Nigger Head oysters.[10]

In the aftermath of the civil rights and Black Power movements, few public figures would dare use the term, as it became a sign of political retrogression. Though doubtless used with great abandon in private, to be caught using the term in public now challenges the official story of color blindness and racial progress and is the kiss of political death.

The term saw a public resurgence in the 1980s and 1990s. Employing what cultural theorist Richard Merelman has termed "black cultural projection," rappers and the hip hop generation have attempted to seize the term and construct counter-narratives and a different reading of the word. Merelman defines black cultural projection as "the conscious or unconscious effort by a social group and its allies to place new images of itself before other social groups, and before the general public."[11] Rappers boastfully see themselves as "niggers with attitude," where nigger is a badge of authenticity. It is not only being a nigger that is key, but accepting the term as a definition of one's self. In the hands of rappers, the term also embodies notions of masculinity and male bonding. Women are or can be niggers to the degree that they reflect images of black maleness, images that are more often than not media-created stereotypes of violence-prone, predatory, destructive behavior.

Despite these tortured efforts by black youth (and white youth who called themselves "wiggers"), the term still retains oppressive power. Few African Americans, if any, accept the term in any form from whites—not as a slur, not as a term of endearment, and very suspect even in academic settings. Fighting words.

Though hurled from coast to coast, in the minds of many, it is the sound of nigger with a southern drawl that most symbolically and viscerally evokes racism and days long thought forgotten. Visions of lynchings, beatings, castrations, and brutal death echo in the resonance of southern tones, be they aristocrat or redneck. To hear the word "nigger" in the South generally means the initiation of a chain of events that do not have a happy ending.

Given this context, it remains disturbing and significant that after hundreds of years of struggle, the defense of the word "nigger" by some whites in the South has resurfaced. The *New York Times* reported in November 1996 that in eastern Kentucky a battle has ensued in Magoffin, Rockcastle, Knox, and other counties between local residents and county officials, on the one side, and civil rights groups and the state Human Rights Commission, on the other. As part of the effort to bring these areas out of their social backwardness, a number of changes have been initiated, including putting up road signs where none previously existed. The commission, however, has adamantly refused to use the local popular names for the roads. Local whites there have resisted the removal and changing of road names that are racist and offensive.[12]

In those counties, there are a number of well-traveled roads with names such as Nigger Fork, Little Negro Creek, Negro Town Hill Road, and Negro Creek. Residents have told county officials, who have responded to complaints from the local NAACP and other civil rights groups in the area, that they will continue to use the old names. One resident, Betty McCarty, offered up the folktale that Nigger Fork was named in honor of a deceased black midwife from the area. She added that this midwife was buried in an unmarked grave.

The Fires this Time

I vividly remember the moment, as a child of 10, when I found out that four young girls had been killed in the bombing of a black church in Alabama. On September 15, 1963, only 18 days after Martin Luther King Jr. had delivered his famous "I Have a Dream" speech in the nation's capital, a bomb ripped through the 16th Street Baptist Church in Birmingham on Youth Sunday. I can recall my own fear and confusion, rage and bewilderment as the minister in our church in Detroit told a weeping congregation about the event and then asked everyone to go home and pray. Those four girls—Addie Mae Collins (14), Denise McNair (11), Carole Robertson (14), and Cynthia Wesley (14)—were the victims of an atmosphere of racial hatred, made even more evil and depraved by choosing a site of worship and religious sanctuary for the base act.

In the 1990s, echoes of that incident arose as a spate of church burnings spread across the South. According to the Center for Democratic Renewal, there were 33 church arsons from January 1990 to December 1994. In 1995, there were 41 church arsons; in 1996, that number rose to 288.[13] In every southern state, from Alabama to Virginia, there were arsons, vandalism, and fire bombings. From churches in tiny towns, such as Hatley, Mississippi's St. Paul A.M.E. and Hemingway, South Carolina's Sandhill's Frewill Baptist Church, to places of worship in the big cities, such as Apostolic Faith Assembly in Louisville, Kentucky or Inner City in Knoxville, Tennessee, the fires raged.[14]

Throughout history, the black church has served as the last haven of security for African Americans, the final gathering ground against the storm of racism. To attack the church is to attack the soul of black people. On a daily level, the black church, rural and urban, North and South, carries on programs of assistance to the black poor that cannot be found anywhere else. This includes housing, child care, job training, medical services, and other programs that bond them to large parts of the black community. The black church is also a central point of communication for African Americans as well as a source of information and potential mobilization. It was the black church, of course, that served as a basis for the efforts of Martin Luther King and the civil rights movement, and 20 years later, for the historic presidential campaigns of Rev. Jesse Jackson in 1984 and 1988. As a number of observers have noted, the financial independence of black ministers, in many cases, allows for a freedom of expression and resistance that has historically thrown up black ministers as leaders.

As voices from the black community identified the growth of church attacks, those voices became a movement demanding local and federal investigations of these crimes. History led many to believe that these burnings were not simply spontaneous, but may indeed be part of a larger, coordinated effort. It became hard to know what was more frightening—a conspiracy involving organized racists who were systematically assaulting black churches, or instead, widespread, random hatred that may be even more difficult to stop.

After much protest, the Clinton administration established the National Church Arson Task Force. In its investigation, it found that 331 church arsons, bombings, and attempted bombings had occurred. About 150 suspects had been arrested for their involvement in over 100 cases. More than 30 of these cases resulted in prosecutions. Millions of dollars were raised through federal and volunteer efforts. The Bureau of Alcohol, Tobacco and Firearms received $24 million to continue their investigation, while the Department of Housing and Urban Development received $10 million to assist some of the churches in their rebuilding.[16]

The movement to stop the church attacks served as a vehicle for black church mobilization. Not only did churches in the South come together, but they also found solidarity with black church activists in the North. The National Council of Churches became one of the national leaders in the effort to expose the situation and to push the administration to respond. The movement also embarrassed white church leaders, even including the Christian Coalition, which has been spearheading and promoting conservative policies and politicians across the country. The Christian Coalition offered a $25,000 reward for information on who was attacking the black churches. Many of the black ministers, however, saw this for the hypocrisy that it was. As Rev. Joseph Lowery of the SCLC noted, "We'd be glad to join with any members of the community of faith to fight injustice, to fight poverty. But they're not going to absolve themselves by exploiting these fires."

Long Live the Confederacy

Oh I wish I was in the land of cotton, good times there are not forgotten. Look away, look away, look away, Dixieland.

According to Republican leader Pat Buchanan, the Confederate flag is a symbol of courage and honor. He also stated that singing "Dixie" was the equivalent of African Americans singing "We Shall Overcome." His views have been echoed in a number of incidents in recent years that show that, for some, the Civil War is still being fought. For many white (and black) journalists, academics, and politicians, it is easy to dismiss the Buchanans of the world as dinosaurs whose little brains will eventually lead to their extinction. Why get upset over a few silly symbols and even sillier defenders of those symbols?

At one level, they simply miss the critical point that if the victims of these symbols do not raise a challenge to these politics, then who will? While many whites might feel offense at the Confederate flag, few have bothered to take an activist stand against it. At another level, these symbols are mobilizing forces in the support and perpetuation of racist ideologies. They are not neutral elements devoid of concrete historical and social capital, but instead function as socializing forces in an overarching ideological system of white supremacy and black oppression.

Needless to say, there are those who do vigorously defend the flag. In 1996, a new controversy arose in Maryland when the state issued 78 special license plates emblazoned with the Confederate flag. Protests led the Maryland Motor Vehicle Administration (MVA) to recall the plates, which they had issued on behalf of the 25,000-member Sons of Confederate Veterans (SCV). The group is comprised of people who can prove that they had an ancestor who fought as a Confederate soldier. SCV member Charles Goolsbie claims that blacks participate in their events and "are not bothered by the flag." But at the time, no African Americans came to their defense. MVA spokesperson Ronald Freeland acknowledged, "As a state agency, the MVA must be sensitive to symbols that may be offensive or otherwise objectionable to members of the general public."

In January 1997, clearly in response to the criticisms and controversy from the license plate incident, SCV got its first black member, Anthony Cohen. At the ceremony inducting Cohen, the Confederate flag was raised and the gathering sang "Dixie." Cohen, who is of mixed black and white heritage, stated, "I came to join the Sons of Confederate Veterans to honor my family history and to honor American history."[17] More ironically, Cohen is an historian. He did not say which family history he was honoring. Was it the African American side of his family, who one would presume were slaves and unlikely defenders of that one great southern tradition known as slavery? Or was it the heritage of his white family, which fought to maintain their right to own human beings? The picture of Cohen standing under the Confederate flag and bellowing out "Dixie" with the good ole boys must surely have warmed the hearts of people like David Duke and Mark Furhman.

Cohen claims he is writing a book on the Underground Railroad. It is difficult to see how he can reconcile anything positive about the Underground Railroad—whose goal was to help blacks escape from slavery—with his membership in the SC, whose purpose, in effect, is to honor the slaveholding tradition.

SCV has taken the role of incorporating a black defense of the Confederacy even further. They are promoting the work of Dr. Edward Smith, who they note is a *black* professor and dean of American Studies at American University. In the *Black Confederate Heritage*, Smith notes that "tens of thousands served the Confederacy" and goes on to describe a number of "black" Confederate war heroes (see http://www.scv.org). While acknowledgment of and scholarship on the role of blacks during the Civil War is legitimate and worthy, the SCV operates with a more disturbing agenda, which is to rationalize a conservative analysis of the racial politics of the war and the United States more generally. Academics, such as Smith, naively play into this project, at best, and at worst, collaborate in celebrating racist interpretations of the Civil War and the ongoing effort by conservatives to deny the fallacy of the melting pot thesis.

Meanwhile, in Alabama, the debate over flying the Confederate flag took on an even more bizarre character. Charles Davidson, a white candidate for the state senate, argued that not only was black slavery justified, but that the source of justification was the Bible. In a speech he was to give in an upcoming senate debate over the flag, he wrote, "People who are bitter and hateful about slavery are obviously bitter and hateful against God and his word, because they reject what God says and embrace what mere humans say concerning slavery.... The incidence of abuse, rape, broken homes and murder are 100 times greater today in the housing projects than they ever were on the slave plantations in the old South. The truth is that nowhere on the face of the earth, in all of time, were servants better treated or better loved than they were in the old South by white, black, Hispanic, and Indian slave owners."[18]

Davidson's rationale for defending the flag was extreme, to say the least, but his stated purpose was well within the logic of those who link the flag to the honor of the South. He argued, "The issue is not race. It's southern heritage. I'm on a one-man leadership crusade to get the truth out about what our southern heritage is all about." There is not a single word or intent there that is different from the more "acceptable" Republican leaders, from Buchanan and Reagan to Bob Dole, George Bush, and Gingrich.

The state and national Republican Party tried to create some distance from Davidson. State GOP National Committee member Martha Foy moaned, "I've never heard anything like all this. It's shocking to me." Yet there is no reason to be shocked. The GOP has created and fostered an atmosphere that not only allows, but encourages racism and white supremacist tendencies. Davidson mercifully lost.

"Dixie" is not the only song playing on the southern conservatives' top ten hits. In most states in the South, the official state songs are unsubtle praise for the slave period. In Virginia, the battle over "Carry Me Back to Old Virginny" rages on. The song was written in the 1870s by James Black, a black New York minstrel who had never been a slave himself. Phrases in the song refer lovingly to "old massa" and yearn for a return to the slave fields with lyrics like "Dat's where dis old darkey's heart am long to go." To his credit and as a reality check on his power, L. Douglas Wilder unsuccessfully agitated against the song for most of his public life, beginning back around 1970 through his tenure as governor and to the present. Although the Virginia House of Delegates had voted to kill the song's status as the state's official song (established in 1950), it was not until 1997 that a compromise was reached in which a majority in the Virginia Senate voted to retire the song as emeritus.[19]

Defenders of the Confederacy argue that there is a moral equivalency in the South's role in the Civil War that others miss. They contend that southerners' defense of slavery was rooted in the great American and southern traditions of states' rights, private property protection, and individual freedom. Of course, there is little discussion that the rights that are being defended involved the bartering, brutalizing, and murdering of human beings; that the private property being protected was African Americans in bondage; and individual freedoms stopped at the door of white skin.

"It's the Sound of the Men ..."

Chain gangs have returned to the nation with a vengeance. In 1995, espousing the get-tough-on-criminals line that has come to dominate contemporary approaches to criminal justice, Alabama reinstituted the notorious chain gang system.

On May 3, 1995, under the rule of Republican Governor Fob James and Ron Jones, the commissioner of the Alabama State Department of Corrections, Alabama became the first state to reinstitute the chain gangs after their disappearance more than 30 years ago. Films like *Cool Hand Luke* and recent documentaries on southern chain gangs led to national repulsion at the cruelty and inhumanity of that particular prison custom.

But this is the 1990s, and traditional values are back in favor. Alabama's Limestone Correctional Facility became the test site for the modern day chain gang. Inmates from the prison are chained together in groups of five in leg irons and put out on the state's highways and back roads. They wear uniforms with the words "Chain Gang" stitched in large letters on the backs. Generally, they work 12 hours a day.

Initially, the inmates cleaned up highways, painted fences, and dug ditches. Jones apparently felt that this was coddling and soon the prisoners found themselves breaking rocks into gravel. "The rock breaking programme is our way of finding something meaningful for these inmates to do," Jones stated.

As if busting rocks was not difficult enough, chained inmates also face unique dangers and embarrassments. Truck and car drivers, many distracted by a sight that they had only seen in the movies, zoom by at high speeds, guaranteeing multiple victims if there is an accident of any kind. Given that it is the Alabama countryside, poisonous snakes are also a constant threat, exacerbated by the inability to flee in any useful manner. Inmates also remain chained when they have to relieve themselves into a chamber pot, which is carried with them during their work.

Some prisoners refused to go on the chain gangs, complaining of the dangers and inhumanity of the experience. Instead, they ended up with a visit to the "hitching post," a metal bar where prisoners are handcuffed with their arms above their head and kept for up to 10 hours in the sun and without food.

In his first year in office in 1995, Jones followed the lead of recent federal crime legislation and abolished such inmate "privileges" as television (black and white as well as color) and weight rooms. He went even further, however, than those on Capitol Hill. He took away inmates' access to orange juice and coffee. Jones had other innovative ideas concerning prison reform. According to *The Nation,* Jones also proposed:

- housing prisoners in tents;

- calling black prisoners "niggers";
- an electric fence around one prison for a "lethal shock";
- destroying vegetable plants tended by inmates with AIDS;
- caning inmates; and
- making prisoners who masturbate in front of women wear pink prison suits.[20]

Jones' tenure was cut short when he went one step too far. Happy with his work with male prisoners, he also proposed putting women prisoners on chain gangs. Whether Governor James actually supported the idea or not, the embarrassment to the state forced him to publicly criticize Jones, who was ultimately made to resign.

Despite being a brutal throwback, the chain gangs are popular. As can be imagined, blacks and whites see things differently. A poll taken by the *Mobile Register* and the University of South Alabama found that while 77 percent of whites favored chain gangs, only 43 percent of blacks did. Although the chain gangs are racially mixed, they are disproportionately black and the image that has been popularly conveyed is that of African-American prisoners.

Unfortunately, Jones' views are in vogue in Congress and there are a number of bills that would nationalize these policies. Rep. Dick Zimmer (R–NJ) has proposed H.R. 663—the "No-Frills Prison Act. This bill would restrict federal funds for prison construction only to those states that abolish smoking, weightlifting, and family visits for prisoners. On the Senate side, Alabama Republican Richard Shelby has proposed a bill forcing states to work prisoners a minimum of 48 hours a week plus another 16 hours of mandatory study as requirements for inmates to enjoy the very few privileges they have left. Like the Zimmer bill, federal dollars are to be withheld if states do not comply.

Alabama may have been the first, but it is not the last. Florida and Arizona have also instituted chain gangs. Wisconsin and several other states, at this writing, were debating the issue. The southernization of the nation continues.

Of Louis Farrakhan and Others

At the turn of the century, Booker T. Washington was the most influential black leader of his time, or perhaps even in U.S. history. From 1895, when he delivered his infamous "Atlanta Compromise" speech, to his death in 1915, he single-handedly wielded influence over vast areas of black life, including presidential appointments, jobs in business and education, and funding from foundations and philanthropists. In that speech, Washington stated that African Americans are "the most patient, faithful, law-abiding, and unresentful people that the world has seen....In all things that are purely social we can be as separate as the fingers, yet one as the hand in all things essential to mutual progress....The wisest among my race understand that the agitation of questions of social equality is the extremist folly."[1] In his words, he essentially declared that he would lead the muting of black resistance to racism and side with the racists who were aggressively instituting official American apartheid. Under his leadership, he would implore African Americans to make no political demands on the government, separate themselves from the mainstreams of social life and power, and ignore the increasing racism of the period.

Thus, when W.E.B. Du Bois chose in 1903 in his book *The Souls of Black Folk* to challenge Washington's position as the preeminent black leader of his era, Du Bois' entire career, livelihood, and standing in the black community were on the line.[2] Yet his integrity and sense of principles would not keep him silent and he courageously took on the Washington machine. The historic burden of moving the black community forward fell on the shoulders of Du Bois and the radical activists around him. Their critique of the conservative and race-limited views of Washington, and later Marcus Garvey, would usher in a new era of black radical thought and practice.

Du Bois' sense of urgency was driven by important changes in the racial climate of the period: the persistence of lynchings and other forms of racial violence, decreasing access to the ballot, a virtual end to black elected officials at the federal and local levels, and the codification of segregation in nearly every institution of public life.[3] Du Bois believed that neither black conservatives nor black nationalists could provide the leadership so desperately needed by the black community in the face of the advancing technology, rising racist violence, expanding global relations, and emerging capitalist social vision that had all come into being early in the century. Even though he was sharply critical of the racism and white reaction of the times, he nevertheless argued that a radical united front between African Americans and others was not only possible, but necessary. This view conflicted sharply with that of Washington and his white supporters.

In the 1990s, a new world order and a rapidly approaching future requires that black leadership move beyond the limits of the conservatism, nationalism, and liberalism ideologies. Of the four political trends that have historically existed in black politics—conservatism, liberalism, nationalism, and radicalism—the latter holds the most promise for advancing the cause of black liberation. Black radicalism stands at a unique juncture on the scale of black political agency. On the one hand, only the radicals and liberals, in general, see the necessity and benefit of multiracial organizing and solidarity. On the other hand, only the radicals and the nationalists, in general, see the necessity of systemic transformation. In other words, in terms of arguing for a multiracial assault on capital and racism, and the social destruction they have wrought, black radicals stand alone.

In this last decade of the 20th century, Minister Louis Farrakhan, leader of the Nation of Islam (NOI), has risen to the top of the black leadership totem pole. Leading up to and following the success of the Million Man March (MMM), his popularity and renown within the black community seem boundless. Many of those in the black community who had written him off as too extremist, anti-white, anti-Semitic, homophobic, a defender of patriarchy, and theologically suspect were clamoring to be on his stage on October 16, 1995 when he stood before over one million black men (and women) with tens of millions more watching around the nation and the world. Unlike

Washington, Farrakhan is loathed by many whites and, until the post-march period, was persona non grata in mainstream white political circles. Yet he appears ubiquitous in the white media and news programs. He has appeared solo on *Donahue, Nightline,* and *Meet the Press,* among other shows, and he has been the subject of numerous debates on these programs and others. The NOI has also been the subject of debate in Congress, having the distinction of being the *only* group in the history of the United States to be rebuked by a congressional resolution for a speech deemed racist by one of its members, Khalid Muhammad. The obsession by the white media and political elite with Farrakhan and the NOI is premised on the belief that his leadership in the black community, whether desired by the mainstream black political class or not, is significant enough to require a consistent monitoring of his words and deeds.

Farrakhan and the NOI are also international in their reach and popularity. Distinct from most African-American leader, Farrakhan is a global figure. Before and after the march, the NOI has spread its organizational wings with affiliations and influence among blacks throughout the diaspora. The NOI has chapters in Jamaica, Canada, and England, as well as supporters in many nations on the African continent. In 1990, it opened a mission in Accra, Ghana.[4] From October 5 to 9, 1994, the NOI held International Savior's Day in Ghana, an event that was opened by Ghanian President Jerry Rawlings and drew about 30,000, including 2,000 African Americans.[5] Farrakhan's 20-nation "World Friendship Tour," following the MMM, also gave him a global stage on which to build his popularity and spread his gospel. Nationally and internationally, Farrakhan's time has come.

To offer a harsh critique of Farrakhan's politics, framed by the nexus of black nationalism, patriarchy, and conservatism, which this chapter tries to do, is no idle undertaking and is presented with the utmost seriousness and calculation. It is also humbly understood that a single examination, no matter how sincere or well-argued, will have minimum impact on an individual and institution of Farrakhan's stature, power, and reach. Criticism of Farrakhan and the NOI, in particular, has resulted in accusations of being a race traitor, to put it mildly. Journalist Salim Muwakkil notes, "Many of those with serious criticisms of the Nation of Islam's authoritarian methods are reluctant to speak on the record."[6] More generally, one's position on Farrakhan has become, as political scientist Adolph Reed explains, a litmus test for whites and blacks.[7] A black leader's entrance to or continual residence in the mainstream is contingent upon a public rejection of Farrakhan. This racist criteria has been visited upon Rev. Jesse Jackson, Rev. Al Sharpton, NAACP chief Kweisi Mfume, and other contemporary black leaders. In the black community, often in response to the racism of the white predisposition to determine black leadership, "the more he is attacked, the greater his authenticity and the more emphatically he must be defended."[8] For blacks, as has often been the case in the past, criticisms of black leaders, even from a Left perspective, are seen as an attack on the whole black community and frequently dismissed out-of-hand. Yet, from my vantage, there is no more urgent task in black politics than a rigorous, principled, and unyielding self-critique of the state of black leadership as we edge into the next millennium, and that means that Farrakhan as well as other contemporary black leaders must be fairly, but sharply assessed.

For many, with the success of the MMM, Farrakhan has achieved the Holy Grail of black nationalist objectives: the mobilization of millions of African Americans along the lines of race-based unity. That such an effort was constructed on the basis of a conservative and anti-feminist program underscores the criticality of an analysis that attempts to negotiate the seemingly conflictual politics of a militant, even radical rhetoric and a moderate, even reactionary agenda. It is with this nationalist agenda, with its complex history and multiple varieties and expressions, that we begin our interrogation.

Calling our BLUF

Black nationalism, as social perspective and praxis, is as old as the black presence in the United States. Theoretically, black nationalism is less an ideology than a framework through which views along the political spectrum are expressed. In other words, conservative and radical perspectives have been acted out on the stage of black nationalism, which comes in many modes, including religious, cultural, political, territorial, and economic expressions.

At the core of black nationalist thought is the notion that a single—that is, mobilizable—black interest exists among African

Americans, an interest that can be operationalized through the unity of black leaders. That paradigm, which I call the Black Leadership Unity Fallacy (BLUF), has resulted in both progress for African Americans in their struggle against white supremacy and racism, and immense limitations as it has obscured real differences and conflicting interests that arise from the diversity of the black community.

The BLUF argues that, first, despite ideological, political, class, and gender differences among African Americans, a basis for a united front against racism exists. Indeed, these other identities, regardless of their saliency, intensity, and intersectionality, are flattened and subsumed under the category of race. The black united front against racism, the organizational expression of the BLUF, takes the form of a coalition of black leadership in which all parties should have an equal voice. Efforts to build such a front have occurred throughout black history, including, *inter alia,* the National Negro Convention Movement, National Negro Congress, Congress of African People, National Black Political Assembly, National Black United Front, National Black Independent Political Party, National Black United Front, and National African American Leadership Summit. Black nationalism essentializes blackness, that is, the experience of being black is read as a bonding character for all African Americans in spite of other identities, experiences, or worldviews. That other identities mitigate, inform, and filter the race dynamic is theoretically avoided and politically disallowed.

Black nationalists have also sought different objectives. While some have advocated a separate territory for African Americans within the boundaries of the United States, others have longed and organized for a mass return to Africa.[9] Many nationalists seek cultural separation, generally asserted through some form of claiming an African identity, theology, cosmology, ethos, or system of values. This often results in the selection of an African name, the wearing of African garb, eschewing relations with whites as much as possible, and a worldview bordering on eugenics. Viewing these identifications as more than just symbolic, black cultural nationalism, in the form of Pan-Africanism or Afrocentrism, seeks a rupture with the African-American present by embracing a (mythologized) African past.

The Rise of the Nation of Islam

The NOI, however, emerges out of a different nationalist tradition. While advocating racial separation, it dispenses with African cultural manifestations. Instead it locates its place in the dual and intersecting historiographies of African Americans and Islam. According to researcher Allan Austin, African Muslims were found in the New World prior to Columbus.[10] Estevanico, a black Muslim, was the first non-Indian to enter the lands that would become New Mexico and Arizona and is said to have planted the first wheat crop in the Americas. Most of the African Muslims who ended up in the United States were slaves, perhaps as much as 10 percent of the slave population.[11] By the time the NOI emerged in the 1930s as the creation of the mysterious Wallace D. Fard, who is viewed in NOI lore as the messenger of Allah (God), and his most loyal disciple Elijah Poole (later Elijah Muhammad), it stood on a long history of Islamic faith in the black community. The narrative constructed by Elijah Muhammad broke significantly from the traditions of Islam and created a black supremacist vision for black America in which whites were "blue-eyed" devils created by a mad scientist, Yacub, and were doomed to perish.[12] Throughout the 1940s and 1950s, advocating black self-help, moral rectitude, economic development, and an avoidance of political participation, the Honorable Elijah Muhammad, as he became known, built the NOI—on the hard work of inner-city, working-class blacks and prison recruits—from a small sect to the most visible black organization in most northern cities.

The politics of the NOI, despite its anti-white theology, were extremely conservative and much attention was given to what could be considered European values, dress, and standards of behavior. Men and women were trained in proper etiquette and dress, for instance, that evoked Victorian morality more than African or African-American norms. Women, in particular, were given very distinct and generally subservient roles in NOI theology and practice. Economically, the NOI advocated the building of black-owned small businesses in the black community. These businesses, it was argued, would lead to a form of black economic independence, a crucial element in the liberation model constructed by the NOI theology. While not specifically calling this endeavor black capitalism, the economic logic and practical applications of the effort were consistent with the general exploitation and limited development of small businesses under capitalism. Workers in NOI businesses, similar to workers in small businesses everywhere, were underpaid, overworked, had few real benefits, such as health care and retirement, and minimum opportunity for growth. From this economic program, the NOI found success and grew substantially.

During this period, the NOI gained two crucial recruits: Malcolm Little in New York, later known as Malcolm X, and Louis Eugene Walcott in Boston, later to become Louis Farrakhan Muhammad. Born on May 11, 1933, Farrakhan was born in the Bronx to a Jamaican father, Percival Clark, and his mother, Mae Clark, from St. Kitt. Farrakhan's father, whom he barely knew and who died when he was young, was extremely light-skinned and perhaps of Portuguese heritage. Indeed, Farrakhan has even speculated that his father's ancestors may have been "members of the Jewish community," a critical point given the antagonistic relationship that Farrakhan has had with Jews.[13]

A talented child who played the violin and sang, Farrakhan was one of the first blacks to appear on national television when he won on *Ted Mack Original Amateur Hour*.[14] Although he had a potentially successful career awaiting him as a singer and nightclub performer, he joined the NOI in 1955 in New York. His oratory and political skills quickly made him valuable and he became Malcolm X's assistant at Mosque Number 7 in Harlem. He was later sent to Boston, where he soon became the minister of that mosque. In 1964, after Malcolm X split from the NOI, Farrakhan returned to New York to take Malcolm's place as head minister at Mosque Number 7, later participating in the NOI campaign to silence and rebuke Malcolm X. At one point, Farrakhan wrote in *Muhammad Speaks,* "Such a man as Malcolm is worthy of death."[15] Despite the animosity that many in Harlem and elsewhere felt toward the NOI after Malcolm's February 1965 assassination, Farrakhan and the mosque managed to survive and eventually thrive. Farrakhan's success would lead to him being appointed the national spokesperson for the NOI under the leadership of the Honorable Elijah Muhammad. Fortunes would change, however.

In 1975, on the February 25th death of Elijah Muhammad, the NOI was taken over by his seventh son, Wallace, who quickly began to make profound changes in the theology and operation of the NOI. White-skinned people were no longer seen as the devil and were allowed to join the NOI. More important, the group began to move closer to traditional Islamic teachings and to downplay the NOI's nationalistic rhetoric and teachings. Given his position under Elijah Muhammad, Farrakhan was viewed as a potential threat and was removed from the center of the organization. He was transferred to the West side of Chicago, which at the time was a backwater for the NOI. His speeches were monitored and, in general, he was pushed to the political periphery. In November 1976, the group's name was changed from the NOI to the World Community of al Islam in the West (WCIW) and, in April 1978, it would change again to the American Muslim Mission (AMM). The Fruit of Islam, the NOI's security force, was dissolved.

In should be noted that the U.S. government had a vested interest in who would succeed Elijah Muhammad. This was in keeping with the long history of infiltration and covert operations against the group by the FBI and local police forces. As early 1969, the FBI concluded that Wallace Muhammad was the only one who "could give proper guidance to the organization."[16] It wrote, "The NOI appears to be the personal fiefdom of Elijah Muhammad. When he dies a power struggle can be expected and the NOI could change direction. We should be prepared for this eventuality. We should plan how to change the philosophy of the NOI....The alternative to changing the philosophy of the NOI is the destruction of the organization. This might be accomplished through generating factionalism among the contenders for Elijah Muhammad's leadership or through legal action in probate court on his death."[17] Wallace Muhammad, as far as the FBI was concerned, was "the only son of Elijah Muhammad who would have the necessary qualities to guide the NOI in such a manner as would eliminate racist teachings."[18]

Farrakhan and the Revival of the NOI

Farrakhan (and others) grew more and more disenchanted with these new directions, and on November 8, 1977, he announced that he was leaving the WCIW and reestablishing the old Nation of Islam "on the platform of the Honorable Elijah Muhammad."[19] While holding onto much of the theology, ideas, and structure of the old NOI, such as reinstituting the Fruit of Islam and closing membership to whites, the NOI under Farrakhan's leadership made some significant adjustments. Its decision to become involved in Jackson's campaign and even run candidates for office was a critical break from the nonpolitical involvement that the earlier NOI preached and that frustrated Malcolm X. The NOI under Farrakhan also became more aggressive in seeking a seat at the table of black leadership. In a number of black coalition efforts, the NOI was involved, or created a controversy by its noninvolvement generally in situations where liberal black leaders sought to also involve leaders and organizations from the Jewish community.

For much of the late 1970s and early 1980s, Farrakhan and the NOI remained obscure to those outside the black community—except for the Jewish community, which had long identified Farrakhan as the nation's leading black anti-Semite—and was viewed as somewhat fringe by many black activists. Just as the AMM would begin to seek a more middle-class membership, so too would the new NOI. Although the NOI was still rooted in black working-class communities, black professionals were increasingly recruited and given visible positions in the group. Farrakhan's projection on the national mainstream political stage, however, would not be through the work of the NOI, but the racial dynamics of presidential politics. In 1984, Farrakhan's relative obscurity would change dramatically as a result of his involvement in the Jackson campaign for the Democratic nomination. As numerous scholars and journalists have documented, Farrakhan's threatening rhetoric toward the black *Washington Post* reporter, Milton Coleman, who exposed Jackson's anti-Semitic, off-the-cuff remarks brought him to the attention of the major media, black political leaders, and the nation as a whole.[20] Jackson's forced disavowal of Farrakhan raised the latter's profile even higher.

Farrakhan's support for Jackson highlights the inherent problems of the BLUF, exacerbated by the fact that the NOI's incursion into the electoral arena took place on the terrain of mainstream politics. The NOI backed Jackson despite basic and unresolvable contradictions in political line, style, and objectives between the two. While Jackson sought for himself a placemat at the table of the Democratic Party, which views racial politics in soley integrationist terms, and a more generous welfare state for his rainbow constituency, this profoundly contradicted the NOI's advocacy of self-help separatism, policy of no coalition with whites, and attitude that the Democratic Party was irredeemably racist. Yet accommodation could be found due to the belief that race rules and, perhaps, naïveté that Jackson would side with blacks when the inevitable and predictable racial controversy arose.

Since that time, Farrakhan has never been far from the news and was cautiously, but begrudgingly brought into the family of black leaders. The embrace of Farrakhan was so sensitive that the Congressional Black Caucus held secret meetings with him, clearly aware of the spark that could be ignited if it became known that they were gathering with him, let alone actually working with him and the NOI. The perceived political impotence of the caucus and other black leaders is also the groundwork on which the NOI rebuilt itself during the Reagan era. As civil rights leaders and black elected officials engaged in racial bargaining and polite compromise, Farrakhan slowly built a constituency outside of NOI adherents among working-class and middle-class blacks who had grown doubly frustrated by the social and economic attacks of the period and the absence of even a strong rhetorical response.

The NOI has been attractive to many African Americans for the work that the organization does in communities around issues such as drug trafficking, AIDS, youth gangs, and security at inner-city housing projects. While other black organizations have little visible presence at the street level in the black community, the highly visible NOI—with its distinct persona of clean-shaven, bow-tie wearing, and pressed dress suit-sporting men—is ubiquitous as it provides security services, operates small businesses, and sells its newspaper, *The Final Call*. The complete abandonment by the state of any responsibility for the wretched and oppressive life that poor African Americans struggle with on a daily basis is further reason for the often positive reception that the NOI receives from the black community. The religiosity of the black community is also a basis for acceptance in that it is believed, whether one embraces Islam or not, that a spiritual force is driving the work of the NOI, and their membership in an African-American ecumenical alliance—a subplot of the BLUF—is wanted and necessary.

Beyond their community work, in many circles in the black community and most outside, the NOI is viewed as a radical organization whose goal is nothing short of the overthrow of white power in the United States. The apocalyptic rhetoric of Farrakhan and spokespersons for the NOI have helped flame the fires of a racial divide that the NOI did not create, but has been able to exploit. They have threatened and predicted all types of calamities and devastation that will be visited on the United States for its treatment of African Americans and other people of color. This militancy has led many young African Americans, the so-called hip hop generation, to believe that Farrakhan is the only national black leader offering a consistent and even revolutionary challenge to racism. The NOI's outreach to black youth, particularly young black men and rappers, distinguishes the efforts of the NOI from most black organizations.

Conservatism and the NOI

These efforts, notwithstanding their positive aspects, obscure the broader conservative agenda and program that the NOI brings to black politics. Its small capitalism economic plan, its willful alliance with political conservatives and reactionaries, and its conservative cultural agenda, in which regressive gender politics is central, are much more significant for understanding the political role of Farrakhan and the NOI in black politics than the media-driven debates over his anti-Semitism. Underlying the thrust of the NOI's politics, and black nationalism in general, is the politics of patriarchy. As a number of black feminist scholars have argued, patriarchy and anti-feminism are organically theorized in black nationalism, creating an intraracial conflict that, in this period, is most embodied in the public posture of Farrakhan.

The essence of Farrakhan's politics can be seen in how he problematizes the crisis facing the most desperate sectors of black America. As he envisions it, the most fundamental issue facing African Americans, particularly poor blacks, is not economic exploitation, political disempowerment, or an anti-black social agenda. While he does not deny these factors, often incorporating them into his speeches, they remain secondary and peripheral to the philosophy, politics, and practices of the NOI. For Farrakhan, it is the mind-set, behavior, and cultural praxis of African Americans that must be corrected. It is this perspective that brings Farrakhan into the sphere of conservative politics occupied by Newt Gingrich, Pat Buchanan, Pat Moynihan, and Charles Murray.

In this sense, the politics of the NOI harken back to the ideological mode of Booker T. Washington. While Farrakhan does not indulge in "darkie" jokes or promote a "turn-the-other-cheek" response to attacks on the black community, as Washington did, Farrakhan does engage in chastising African Americans for the ills they suffer. It is the inadequacies of African Americans that animates Farrakhan's efforts, economic and political. He also melds with Washington on the issue of racial separatism. Although it could be argued that he has serious doubts that African Americans and whites can be "one as the hand in all things essential to mutual progress," at the same time, he would find little disagreement that "in all things that are purely social, we can be as separate as the fingers."

NOI's Black Capitalism Project

The NOI under Farrakhan, similar to the old NOI, preaches the gospel of bootstrap capitalism. The ideology of economic self-help has meant, at one level, a focus on small business creation by the group. NOI enterprises include the Salaam Restaurant chain, Shabazz Bakeries, Fashahnn Islamic Clothings, food markets, NOI Security Agency, *The Final Call* newspaper, Clean 'N Fresh skin and hair care products, and Abundant Life clinics, as well as involvement in real estate, fish markets, farmland, and book and tape production and distribution.[21] While it is impossible to know how profitable these businesses are, media reports, public tax records, and statements from the NOI itself indicate the struggles that have occurred to keep the business side afloat. In early 1995, the NOI proudly announced the opening of the $5 million Salaam Restaurant in Chicago. About six months later, the restaurant was in receivership. Reports in the *Detroit Free Press, Chicago Tribune, New York Times*, and *Washington Post* detail the management and administrative problems that the NOI has encountered in operating the sprawl of businesses that it has built.

The problem is not the failure of the NOI's business agenda; small businesses fail at alarming rates in the United States. What is problematic here is the lack of candor on the part of the NOI about the apparently serious rate of nonsuccess and severe indebtedness that NOI's businesses have suffered. The black community is repeatedly asked to support these enterprises with little accountability in return. This adherence to an economic model that is fundamentally flawed is pernicious in two ways. First, it diverts energy and attention from the economic issues that affect large numbers of African Americans, such as access to job training, health care benefits, retirement plans, and other concerns. Second, the bootstrap model facilitates the illusion that business in the United States is a private matter rather than the dynamic interrelationship between public policy and capitalist economic development. The only thing that is private about the so-called private economy is the news that it is not.

A very disturbing hypocrisy on the part of the NOI also exists regarding the ideology of self-help. A central theme of the organization is the need for the black community to practice self-help and stop demanding a handout from the government. At one level, the arrogance of the statement ignores a long, long history of nothing but self-help on the part of the black community. But what makes this view really disingenuous is that, according to their own documentation, the NOI has grossed millions of dollars in government contracts since the late 1980s. Through their security services at public housing sites, which initially began as volunteer activities, the NOI has secured Department of Housing contracts that may be as much as $10 million. These contracts have inspired vicious and racist attacks on the NOI from the reactionary Representative Peter King (R-NY), who in 1996 forced congressional hearings on the matter. King's racist agenda notwithstanding, the NOI has little right to demand of others what it clearly is not practicing itself. It appears that the growth in the number of middle-class members turned the NOI toward more sophisticated skills needed to reappropriate, via federal and local grants, tax dollars.

Face the Nation: The NOI's Right-Wing Alliance

"He sounds like us." [22]— Armstrong Williams

The link between the NOI and conservatives has come under increasing criticism from black progressives. In March 1997, a debate flared up among Republicans after Farrakhan attended and spoke at the 13th annual gathering of Republican Party executives and investors held by conservative economist Jude Wanniski in Boca Raton, Florida. According to conservative columnist Robert Novak, this was only the third time in Farrakhan's long career that he spoke to an all-white audience.[23] Novak, who has attempted to bring Farrakhan closer to the Republican Party fold before, noted that the speech was a cross between "the Christian Coalition and libertarianism" and that "Farrakhan's stress on self-help and moral values evoked the longest sustained applause I have seen from the rich, sophisticated listeners—several of them Jewish."[24] In Novak's estimation, "Farrakhan…is knocking on the door of the Republican Party—the first modern black popular leader to do so," and that is not only significant for the party, but for the nation as a whole because "Republican aspirations to be a true majority would be enhanced by a foothold among African-Americans. More significantly, the racial animosity in this country could be diminished."[25]

While the immediate reaction among Republicans and the white media was outrage bordering on hysteria, only a few observers in the black community appeared concerned with this budding alliance. According to scholar Manning Marable, "The cordial relationship between Minister Farrakhan and white conservatives like Jude Wanniski also illustrated that black nationalism could be just as conservative as Reagan Republicanism. Newt Gingrich and Farrakhan both agree on conservative patriarchal family values, racial self-help, supply-side economics, and both oppose lesbian and gay rights."[26] There is little hope that a full-blown collaboration politically will occur between the Republican Party and the NOI, in spite of their ideological affinity. Neither the base of the Republican Party nor of the

NOI can be won over to going beyond the racial rhetoric that serves both sides and yet limits them from addressing the more fundamental ideological interest they share.

Farrakhan's conservatism has gone further than just his tentative relations with the Republican Party. Increasingly, the NOI has aligned with one of the most notorious fascists in the country, Lyndon LaRouche. An extremist by any definition, LaRouche has a long, thoroughly documented history of promoting, defending, and expressing racist and fascist views. In the past, LaRouche's organizations have attempted to destroy, manipulate, and corrupt, for their own purposes, black organizations and black churches. Even though LaRouche has formed close working relationships with neo-Nazis, Ku Klux Klan leaders, and other racists, he has also aggressively tried to infiltrate black southern churches using various front groups and by seducing elder civil rights activists with promises of political support. In the 1970s, one of LaRouche's front groups physically assaulted a number of black organizations.

In a variety of public forums since the early 1980s, LaRouche's followers have spoken in solidarity with members of the NOI. The two groups have mutually praised each other and freely quote from each other's publications. One of LaRouche's obsessions has been the Federal Reserve. He has developed all kinds of crackpot theories about the illicit power of the Reserve and the secret cartels that control it. These views have wound up in *The Final Call* and in the public presentations of NOI representatives.

This alliance is stranger still because, in 1985, LaRouche's newspaper, *New Solidarity,* attacked Farrakhan and the NOI. It wrote, "Rev. Louis Farrakhan is building a Nazi-communist terrorist movement closely linked to the Greens and their backers in the United States."[27] Yet, by the end of the decade, members of both organizations were meeting together around a variety of issues. The Center for Democratic Renewal, the black-run, Atlanta-based research center that has played a leading role in exposing the growth of racist and fascist organizations in the United States, wrote that by 1990, representatives of the NOI were singing LaRouche's praises. The center reported that NOI spokesperson Dr. Abdul Alim Muhammad had stated at one LaRouche gathering, "To Mr. Lyndon LaRouche and his wife, and to those members of his organization, especially those who are the teachers and writers who put out the *New Federalist* newspaper and the *Executive Intelligence Review,* I want to say on behalf of Minister Louis Farrakhan and the entire Nation of Islam, how much we admire you and respect you for the great work that you are doing."[28]

LaRouche is also linked to the NOI through Rev. James Bevel, who played an increasingly visible role around the MMM and its subsequent activities. Bevel was a close associate of Martin Luther King during the early days of the civil rights period. Bevel fell out with the movement, accusing it of being taken over by the FBI, and spent a number of years out of the limelight on a farm in Maryland. He resurfaced in the 1980s associated with right-wing religious forces such as Rev. Sun Moon. In 1992, Bevel emerged as LaRouche's vice presidential running mate.

The role of Benjamin Chavis Muhammad, former NAACP executive director and presently director of the National African American Leadership Summit (NAALS), in all of this is perhaps most egregious because he cannot claim ignorance of LaRouche's reactionary and racist politics. In 1986, he wrote an article in the *New York Voice,* titled, "LaRouche Invades the Black Community." In the article, Chavis Muhammad dwells on how important it is for African Americans to not allow LaRouche and his supporters to gain a foothold into the black community because "the LaRouche organization is clearly racist, works closely with the Klan, and is a supporter of the South African government as well."[29] Yet, a decade later, Chavis Muhammad shares podium after podium with LaRouche's surrogate, Bevel, and in at least one known instance (described below), with the man himself. In early 1997, Chavis Muhammad, who was one of the leaders of the MMM, announced that he had joined the NOI.

While Chavis Muhammad can perhaps be considered just an opportunist, Farrakhan's politics fit snugly into LaRouche's niche. As Marable wrote on another occasion, "Similarly, Farrakhan's conservative social and economic agenda finds parallels with LaRouche's fascist program."[30] The politics of the NOI are similar to LaRouche's in more ways than one. Just as LaRouche did not hesitate to try intimidation tactics on his perceived enemies, an atmosphere of intolerance for opposing views emerged regarding those in the black community who voiced criticism of the march. The charge of racial traitor awaited anyone, no matter what their politics, who dared criticize Farrakhan, the NOI, or the politics of the MMM. Racial authenticity was measured by how strong one supported or did not support the march.

March leaders had promised to hold a national black political conference after the MMM that would be the equivalent of the historic 1972 National Black Political Assembly. After months and months of delay and loss of support from key activists, such as political activist Ron Daniels and political scientist Ron Walters, a gathering was held in St. Louis in September 1996 sponsored by the remnants of the march leadership and NAALS. It was most notable for who was not there and what was not accomplished. Unlike the march, no celebrities, prominent elected officials, or nationally known activists showed up. Beyond the well-known, also missing were labor groups, civil rights groups, and of course, black feminist groups. Noted Harvard University scholar Cornel West spoke at the event, continuing his association with the march leadership and representing a token Left presence.

One person who did show up was Lyndon LaRouche. Although Chavis Muhammad and Bevel were apparently going to allow him to speak, protests from those in the crowd who recognized him and from others who simply could not figure out why a white man was going to speak at a black nationalist event prevented that embarrassment from happening. The fact that there was even a debate over LaRouche's presence, however, reveals the depths to which the link between nationalism and conservatism can sink. Even the harshest critics of the MMM's leadership would not have predicted that such an overt concession to reactionism could occur. At least one activist who attended the gathering believes that LaRouche and his organization played a key role in financing the event.

Farrakhan's consorting with reactionaries has not been limited to the borders of the United States. In March 1996, Farrakhan went on a World Friendship Tour, or what some called a "World Dictatorship Tour," of 20 nations in Africa and the Middle East. Without exception, he chose to visit and honor dictators and repressive regimes in

Nigeria, Zaire, Iran, Libya, the Sudan, and elsewhere. In Nigeria, the brutal Abacha regime has killed peaceful dissenters and jailed hundreds unjustly. Farrakhan's response to charges regarding the regime's execution of world-renowned Nigerian writer Ken Saro-Wiwa was, "They said that you hanged one man. So what? Ask them, too, 'How many did you hang?'"[31] His reported remarks led Randall Robinson, president of the black lobbyist group TransAfrica, to comment, "His statements and the things that were said appear to make Minister Farrakhan an apologist for an authoritarian, corrupt, and repressive regime."[32] In the Sudan, despite denials by the Sundanese government, slavery and the slave trade continue in the country, as demonstrated by *Baltimore Sun* reporters Gregory Kane and Gilbert Lewthwaite in their investigative report from the Sudan following Farrakhan's trip.[33]

His defense of these visits boiled down to his declaration that he could go wherever he chose—a right never questioned by anyone in the black community, as far as I can tell. In some instances, he acknowledged that some of these regimes were far from democracies, but they could be excused, he argued, because they were relatively new nations and the United States, with its long history of slavery and imperialism, had little moral authority to criticize another nation. While the latter is true, it has little relevance to his unwarranted defense of murderers and slave traders. And it is doubtful that the masses of people suffering under these regimes cared little about Farrakhan's right to travel or the historic and contemporary human violations carried out by the United States.

Conclusion

Farrakhan has long been accused of sprouting reactionary views on everything from gender to homosexuality to Jews. His general response has been that much of what he has said has been taken out of context or are simply attacks on his leadership from racist whites or sell-out blacks. However, despite the truth of his assertion that he is under attack and that some of his words have been distorted, there is plenty of documentation of Farrakhan's statements, in *The Final Call* no less, and those statements have been the reason many black progressives have kept their distance. A black conservative agenda, albeit dressed in black nationalist clothing, will not free black America. Whether it comes from Clarence Thomas or Louis Farrakhan, it merely perpetuates the crisis that already exists for at least of a third of all African Americans and half of all black children.

Beyond Patriarchy and Conservative Nationalism

The plethora of statistics and data chronicling the spiraling and multiple crises affecting large parts of the black community is more than an accumulation of depressing social analysis. Collectively, this information captures the tragic and growing collapse of African-American civil society (AACS). The space in which the black community reproduces itself, its culture, social relations, language, and even imagination of itself has been undergoing a dual process of external aggression and self-destruction. The array of social issues contributing to the havoc and despair raging through the black community, particularly but not exclusively in the inner cities, should not be an excuse, however, to romantically harken back to the Jim Crow segregation era.

It has become popular in some parts of the black community to nostalgically look back on the segregation period through rose-colored glasses. Although African Americans were legally suffering brutal dehumanization under separate and unequal circumstances, some academics and most black leaders maintained and popularized the view that a cross-class, cross-gender harmonious unity existed that generated an environment that collectively raised children, saw limited drug abuse, had minimal crime, and promoted communal de-classed relationships.[1] This "back-when-we-were-colored" perspective dangerously erases the negative socially debilitating impact of segregation, the accompanying (and state-supported) racist violence of the period, the very real and sharp class divisions that have always existed in the black community, and the particularly vulnerable position that African-American women faced. Unsurprisingly, this mythology arises from the class-privileged sector of the black community. As writer Adolph Reed, Jr., notes, "Only middle-class children who were protected from its social and institutional realities—or those who didn't live it at all—could remember the segregated world so fondly, as a naïve, communitarian metaphor."[2]

The progressive impulse behind the thirst for this imagined community is the attempt to rescue a picture of daily life in which relations of cooperation overwhelm relations of exploitation. It was this need that was touched upon and exploited by the Million Man March movement and event. It affected who came out to the march, what they viewed as solutions to the problems facing the black community, and the subsequent follow-up issues that emerged in the march's wake. Yet the conservative politics of the march eliminated the possibility that it would be the tool to hammer into place a rebuilt AACS. The struggle to reconstruct AACS must be contextualized within the framework of the cultural logic of postindustrial capitalism: for African Americans, the commodification and commercialization of social relations, occurring in an era of labor downsizing and job elimination, profoundly transforms the arenas of contestation and struggle. Increasingly, for African Americans, the physical and virtual manifestations of black community life take place at a multitude of sites, including work, leisure, family, public spaces, political enclaves, prison, and habitats of the welfare state, such as unemployment or welfare offices, all of which are themselves undergoing dramatic restructuring.

This chapter not only identifies the problems inherent in using the MMM as a vehicle for the reconstruction of AACS, but looks beyond the march to a reconceptualization of what African Americans will confront in the years ahead and what societal transformations must happen if there is to be progress and development. In one sense, this is an ideological and political struggle over the definition of the black community. The perspective that there is a heterogeneous black community fosters narrow and flawed strategies that are unable to address the diversity of black interests that collectively can be seen as a "community." It can be argued that there are, in fact, several black communities, shaped and oriented through the prisms of ideology, politics, class, gender, and regional location—communities that have distinct and often even competing interests. Yet, within the nationalist context that framed the MMM, there was a concerted effort on the part of the march's leadership to mute and suppress these differences. That effort undermined the internal discourses and struggles necessary to forge the broadest possible progressive political movement inside the black community, while it also surrendered critical political ground to external anti-black forces.

Nationalism and the Million Man March

Historically, in periods of massive white backlash, such as the present era, black nationalism grows and challenges the ideological dominance of liberal integrationism within black politics. In this sense, black nationalism is not only an oppositional discourse to racism, but also to the dominant ideological strategy within black politics. Yet, in each period, black nationalism emerges in new forms and with new political directions and purposes defined by the leadership of the time, the historic options available, and the capabilities of other political forces to contend for hegemony. Thus, as scholar E. Frances White notes about Afrocentricity, it can be said that black nationalism as a "site of counterdiscourse is itself contested terrain."[3] While some contemporary expressions echo many of the traditional themes and politics of past nationalisms, other variations bear little more than symbolic resemblance to their predecessors. In the last period of strong nationalist sentiment three decades ago, progressive nationalists who called for a radical program of systemic economic and political transformation vastly overwhelmed their more politically conservative counterparts, who desired to focus mainly on cultural or social issues within the black community. This was true on both a domestic and global scale, where nationalist movements led to the overthrow of colonial regimes in Africa, Asia, and Latin America. In contemporary black politics, a conservatism that is barely distinct from right-wing Republicanism is the dominant manifestation of black nationalist expression. Conservative black nationalism reduces and imprisons the categories of gender, nation, class, and culture to the realm of race, thus obscuring other modes of interactive struggle that can and must take place.

In a time when a growing, rapacious corporate authority is creating more of a basis for African Americans to unite with broad sectors of society, a vocal core of black nationalists call for more isolation.

This is not to minimize the resistance by whites and even other people of color to such a unity. The point here is that the objective basis for unity has grown as a result of economic and social changes, even as the subjective character of race has worsened. It is within this paradox that the possibilities of cross-racial unity and alliance, if it is to happen at all, rests. The politics of black nationalism eviscerates that possibility completely. In a period of global transnational corporate development and concentrated economic power, some nationalists advocate a romanticized and doomed black capitalism. In an era when institutional and systemic power is consolidated around racist and anti-working-class public policies, a core of black nationalists are arguing that individual morality and lack of personal responsibility are the chief causes of mass suffering. At a time when the exploitation of women's labor and a concomitant attack on women's rights are expanding, black nationalist patriarchy advocates a diminished leadership role for black women and condemns their issues to the back burner of black and national politics. In the 1990s, in the internal ideological battle within black nationalist politics, progressive black nationalists have had little public voice or political agency.

This culmination of contemporary, conservative black nationalism is nowhere more visible than in the movement around and the incidence of the MMM. Without question, the October 16, 1995 event was the largest mobilization of African Americans in U.S. history. It was championed not only by black nationalists, but by black elected officials, black conservatives, and a wide range of civil rights leaders. More important, it received support from millions of men and women in the black community. Despite the fact that the event was conceived and organized by Minister Louis Farrakhan and Reverend Ben Chavis (now Ben Chavis Muhammad), both of whom have been controversial within and without the black community, many well-known progressives participated in, promoted, and defended the march. From Rev. Jesse Jackson and scholars Cornel West and Michael Eric Dyson to civil rights leader Dorothy Height and poet Maya Angelou to millions of black men and women from around the nation, involvement was strong and overwhelming.

In the aftermath of the event, many black publications became vehicles for the continuing celebration of the success of the day. *The*

Black Scholar, Emerge, and other black journals and magazines devoted numerous pages to essentially uncritical, celebratory pieces that rarely interrogated the core politics of the MMM and tended to focus on the *potential* benefits of black men feeling good about themselves and possibly taking on the family and community responsibilities that they had abandoned before the march occurred. And there were credible stories of grassroots organizing, increased black child adoptions, growth in memberships of black organizations, increased black male voter registration and turnout, and many more offshoots that were directly attributed to the consequences of the MMM. The MMM was so successful that even for those who have quietly expressed a wide array of criticisms of the event, its leaders, its politics, and the problems of follow-up, there has been a reluctance to speak out in public against the march. As journalist Salim Muwakkil notes, "Many of Farrakhan's would-be critics prefer to downplay their disagreements for the sake of African American unity." Subsequent events have led some earlier supporters of the MMM to publicly criticize Farrakhan and Chavis, though not necessarily to repudiate the march itself. This includes well-known scholars and activists, such as activist Ron Daniels, political scientist Ron Walters, historian Manning Marable, and nationalist Ron Karenga.

What still remains to be done, however, is to pursue a critical dialogue among black progressives that is not simply focused on the political foibles of Farrakhan and Chavis, but addresses the logic of the conservatism and gender politics of contemporary black nationalism . This means taking seriously the criticisms and analysis offered by scholars and activists critical of the MMM, such as Barbara Ransby, Nikol G. Alexander, Robin D.G. Kelley, Adolph Reed, Jr., James Steele, Julianne Malveaux, Mary Frances Berry, Angela Davis, and many others whose progressive voices were drowned out in the wave of exhilaration flowing from the march. This discourse was absent at the time of the march and has had very little exploration since. It means that scholars and activists must soberly assess the role of the MMM as a historic moment in black politics and the long-term implications of its legacy. Rather than an uncritical reading of the event or a knee-jerk rejection of its simply because of the controversial character of its leadership, a more rigorous interrogation needs to occur that raises the level of debate on the MMM and similar political events emanating out of the complexities of contemporary black politics. For black progressives, in particular, it is necessary to continue to project an alternative vision and strategy to the current political trends of conservatism, nationalism, and liberal integrationism that confronts state and corporate power and reconstructs AACS.

The MMM has become a marker in black politics and black life. It has become a point of reference for this generation and is unlikely to be paralleled in the lives of most participants and observers. It is critical, however, that an iconization of the gathering and its accoutrements be nullified and that it not become a symbol beyond reproach and analysis. Like all great events, the MMM is a site of contestation over meaning, significance, relevance, and purpose. For progressives who have been hesitant to criticize the widely heralded gathering, the broad based support for the MMM requires even more that a critical discernment and inquiry into its role in black politics be done.

In my view, at one level, the MMM was a conservative, patriarchal call for black male mobilization—based on the faulty and gendered thesis of black male endangerment and rampant African-American cultural pathology—whose meaning was code-switched by many, if not most, of those who attended the event to an alternative interpretation that dismissed Farrakhan's central role, saw the need and value for spiritual bonding among black men, and advocated more personal commitment to black advancement. The political and gender meanings underlying the themes of black male endangerment and African American cultural pathology have been most sharply analyzed by political scientist Nikol Alexander.[4] Underneath this framework, a more important ideological operation was occurring: the popularization and canonization of right-wing views and propositions that politically united conservative Republicans, new Democrats, civil rights leaders, nationalists, some black male progressives (ostensibly with feminist sensibilities), and a cross-section of black women eager for epiphanic transformations at the personal, community, and racial levels. That this mosaic of interests could be forged around an agenda that effectively surrendered the mantle of resistance that has defined black struggle historically, identifies the depth and force of the rupture of radical politics from African-American life.

Surveying the Marchers and their Views

If we are to extract the long-term meaning and impact of the march, it is necessary to investigate exactly who was and who was not mobilized. For the purposes of social analysis, it can not and should not be assumed that an undifferentiated black mass came to Washington that day. It is important to know, as much as possible, exactly what demographic cohort(s) came to the march, why they came, and what they believed on a range of political and social issues relative to the black community. The march was promoted as a vehicle to allow black men to bond in their effort to reclaim responsibility for their community. Who were the men that came to the event? What did they think? What were their politics?

There were two major surveys done of those who attended the October 16th march. One was a joint operation between some faculty and students of Howard University's Political Science Department and the New Jersey-based Wellington Group, a black marketing firm.[5] The other study was done by black researcher and pollster Ron Lester for the *Washington Post*. The two surveys, in important ways, reinforced the findings of each other on a number of demographic and research variables.

In the Howard survey, 1,070 marchers were interviewed, all male, at the event. The study found that the marchers were overwhelmingly middle-class in terms of income and level of education. A large number of the participants (41 percent) had household incomes above $50,000 a year. Another 20 percent had incomes between $35,000 and $49,000. In terms of educational level, 78 percent had some college or above. The average age of the marchers was 36. Most of the marchers, 79 percent, were employed full-time. Overall, the attendees were solidly middle-class and middle-aged, and did not represent descriptively that strata in the black community—the lower-income poor (often mistakenly referred to as "the underclass")—that was much of the focus of the issues that the march sought to address. There was, in other words, a critical disjuncture between those who attended the march and the target of what has popularly been seen as the "endangered black male." Given the broad outreach that occurred in the black community in building the march, the absence of the lower-income strata appears to be caused either by a lack of resources to attend or conscious disengagement. A survey of those who did not attend, which did not happen, would have been extremely interesting.

Politically, a majority of the marchers identified themselves as either liberal (31 percent) or moderate (22 percent). About 13 percent said they were conservative while another 10 percent called themselves nationalist, meaning that despite the nationalist leadership of the march, 90 percent of the attendees did not identify themselves as such. This probably indicates both the limited number of African Americans who actually do identify themselves as nationalists, assuming nearly every nationalist in the country made an attempt to be at the event, and at the same time, the saliency of nationalist ideas (albeit through conservative and progressive filters) in the black community, particularly for middle-class African Americans, where coming together as blacks is viewed as important and a source of authentication. In terms of party preference, 62 percent declared themselves as Democrats, 20 percent as independents, and 3 percent as Republican. These numbers were fairly consistent with poll numbers, which in general show the black community to be political. What was politically different, however ,was the number of attendees who stated that they were registered to vote: 86 percent. This number may have been inflated, given that nationally there are about eight million unregistered African Americans and that large numbers of black males are unable to vote due to being disenfranchised because of their criminal record. It is likely that at the MMM, it was simply unpopular to state one's nonregistered status.

Given his role in organizing the event, it was not surprising that a large number of the marchers (44 percent) viewed Farrakhan as one of the most important leader in the black community. He was followed by Johnnie Cochran (36 percent), Coretta Scott King (34 percent), Maxine Waters (33 percent), Ben Chavis Muhammad (32 percent), Colin Powell (30 percent), Jesse Jackson (29 percent), Mary Frances Berry (21 percent), Al Sharpton (18 percent), and Clarence Thomas (8 percent). It is important to note that respondents were given a list of names rather than asked to volunteer their own choices. To some degree, the list of suggested leaders reflected popularity and it was difficult to know, for example, how respondents defined leadership, what issues they used to measure leadership capabilities, and how even these particular leaders were viewed as affecting their lives and communities. These responses should be seen as snapshots of the popularity and exposure of these particular black leaders at the moment of the march. Cochran, for example, was virtually unknown outside of the Los Angeles area before the O.J. Simpson trial, and Simpson's acquittal in his criminal trial happened only a few days before the march.

Although the march won support from millions, including an untold number outside the black community, it was the cohort identified above that most represented the base of support for the themes and symbols of the event. This group signified a complicated array of liberal and conservative ideas that are in contestation in the black community over which way forward and under what political and ideological banner.

The Politics of the March

Analysis and criticism of the MMM falls into several categories: the overall politics and themes of the MMM; the issue of gender exclusion; the reactionary politics of key leaders of the march; and the response by those around the march to those who detracted from it. These arenas of criticism do not stand apart from each other. Gender exclusion, for instance, was consistent with the theme of black male endangerment and the solutions proffered by the march's leaders, and their response to criticisms surrounding how they handled the concerns of black women about the politics of the event.

The politics of the march were conservative, moralistic, and patriarchal. They were conservative in that the fundamental causes of the problems driving the crisis for so many in the African-American community were seen as black behavior and attitude issues. In this way, the original call could be seen as a black version of the Republican "Contract with America." The focus on personal responsibility, atonement, and reconciliation fit snugly into similar conservative themes that obviate real questions about power and the role of the government, policymakers, and transnational corporations in determining the conditions of black life. Placing the burden for the perpetuation of problems confronting the black community on African

Americans themselves also becomes the framework for the solution to those dilemmas. Thus, by overrepresenting the concern about the lack of personal responsibility and self-help strategies on the part of African Americans, the march became a vehicle for protesting the black community and its "pathologies." This then becomes the real politics of the march and not the controversy over Farrakhan, Chavis, or other figures associated with the event. The perverted genius of the march, its magical essence, was that many African Americans who sincerely sought to both support the march and distance themselves from Farrakhan, the NOI's conservatism, and patriarchy missed the critical and decisive point that whether Farrakhan and his central role were present or not, the politics that he advocated were. Many of those attending the march were vocal in declaring their opposition to Farrakhan and stated that their attendance was not a sign of support for Farrakhan or his politics. The fact that so many felt obligated to make it known that they did not agree with the NOI's views was itself a sign of the pivotal role that the NOI and Farrakhan had over the march. While most of those in attendance may disagree with much of what Farrakhan had to say, it was Farrakhan who held the stage and determined who else was on it. Even if many of his destractors were not clear what at least in part the MMM was about, Farrakhan surely was: the projection and elevation of his leadership in national black politics.

This point apparently confused a number of intellectuals. Harvard Political Scientist Martin Kilson presented one of the most bizarre reasons for supporting the march. It was apparently his fear and disagreement with the "extremism" of the NOI that compelled him to endorse the event and attempt from the inside to defeat the forces of Farrakhan. He wrote, "We who endorsed the march—challenged in this sometimes by our intellectual and political allies among some Jewish intellectuals—must now make sure that the goal of taming and purging xenophobic and extremist patterns among groups like Farrakhan's Nation of Islam organization does in fact take place."[6]

The call of the march was for a "Holy Day of Atonement and Reconciliation" on the part of African-American men. The view behind this call was that the irresponsibility of black men was primarily responsible for the myriad of problems facing black people. According to the march's organizers, Farrakhan in particular, decades of family abandonment and disregard for community had reduced black men to less than what they could or should be. As the mission statement noted, "Some of the most acute problems facing the black community within are those posed by black males who have not stood up."[7] While there was occasional mention of the oppressive role of outside forces on the black community, generally under the broad sweep of racism and white supremacy, the focus was overwhelmingly on the need for self-actualization and personal responsibility. This agenda does not call for an explicit political and public policy challenge, and even more, strongly mirrors the conservative ideas of Gingrich, Reagan, and other Republican rightwingers. It substitutes moral righteousness and a theocratic stance for a democratic assault on the institutions and systems of political power that dominate black life. It should be noted that a number of activists close to the march, such as New York's Ron Daniels, fought for a more politically explicit agenda, but were rebuffed for the most part.

The reactionary views of Farrakhan dominated the politics of the movement that built the march and the march itself. As radical political scientist Adolph Reed wrote, "Farrakhan embraces a deeply conservative, politically quietest agenda for black people. Like Marcus Garvey, Farrakhan has wed an anti-democratic, conformist and morally repressive program to a superficial race militancy that gives it the feel of populist radicalism. This is the kernel of fascism, and Farrakhan's view of the world is truly fascist. His vision for organization of black American life is racist, authoritarian, sexist, homophobic, and theocratic."[8] Reed's critique is harsh, but not inaccurate. Those politics logically lead to support from and strategic alliances with political forces that represent some of the most reactionary and racist views in the country.

In fact, a large number of conservatives enthusiastically embraced the politics of the march even as they denounced Farrakhan. Rejection of Farrakhan, in the past, was mostly limited to his anti-Semitic remarks more than anything else. Former Republican presidential candidate Jack Kemp called the NOI's self-help program "wonderful."

In the main, the march failed to make any demands on the state, a state that is profoundly responsible for the conditions facing millions of African Americans and working people across the country. This squandered opportunity is made even more tragic by the relentless attacks emanating from Congress on a daily basis, attacks that are racially coded and driven, but for the most part remain unaddressed by the march's leadership. Even as the marchers stood a million strong on the steps of the Capitol, inside conservative policymakers were attacking, through racial coding, welfare, affirmative action, education grants, funding for drug treatment, minority set-asides, and other programs that disproportionately benefit the black community.

Gender Exclusion

"When African American men are exhorted to 'be a man' and 'take control,' what does that mean for African American women?"[9] —Julianne Malveaux

As a gendered worldview that gives priority to racial unity above all else, black nationalism has found no common ground with feminism. Viewed as a white women's ideology, feminism has not only been rejected by black male nationalists, but also by many black women, nationalist and otherwise. While black feminist discourses have gained some territory within academia in recent years, they still remain abused stepchildren within black politics. This schism would surface in the context of the MMM.

Scholar Pauline Terrelonge argues that there are five reasons why feminist consciousness has had limited reception by so many black women:

- The view that feminist consciousness is a wedge that potentially generates conflict between black women and black men.

- A hesitation by black women to bond with white women given the ideology of racism that often appears alongside of feminism as expressed by white women.

- A perception that liberation of the black man is more critical than that of the black woman.

- The notion that black men must combat the development of black matriarchy, where feminism is seen as feeding and breeding.
- The role of the black church and a theology that supports gender inequality.[10]

Much of the opposition and outrage concerning the march in the black community had to do with the principle in the original call and in the buildup for the event regarding the exclusion of black women. Although women did much of the work of organizing the march—as has been the case historically in black politics—the march explicitly privileged the plight of the most serious issue facing African Americans, and women were asked to stay at home that day and educate the children. After months of unrelenting criticism, the march organizers changed their initial posture and let it be known that if women showed up they would not be harassed or asked to leave, and they allowed some women to speak at the event, including the late educator (and Malcolm X's widow) Dr. Betty Shabazz, Cora Masters Barry (wife of D.C. Mayor Marion Barry), civil rights legend Rosa Parks, and author Maya Angelou. Though successful and exemplary in their own right, none of these women could be viewed as strong feminists or threats to publicly challenge the sexism of the event.

The problem, however, was not just the proposed physical exclusion of women from the Mall, a position that could not realistically or legally be defended in any case. The problem, in a larger sense, was the political exclusion of black women's issues and concerns. While it makes little sense to oppose a single gender event on principle, in the context of the MMM, gender exclusion was not a progressive stance. The politics of the march's leaders essentially said that only issues facing black men were issues for the whole black community, while issues facing black women were not. The march was boldly stated as being about the reassertion of black men as leaders of the black community. This view was fallacious on several points. First, black women have always had to fight for leadership roles in every area of black politics and community life. The presumption that black men are not the dominant leadership force in black community politics and social life flies in the face of history and contemporary circumstances. Second, the issues facing black men confront black women as well because they are issues that affect the black family and its stability. Arguably, black women may be even more harmed by destabilized black communities given the multiple roles they play as domestic and workforce labor. Third, in many, many ways, black women are doing worse than black men. Black women earn less money, are going to prison at a greater rate, and must fight triple racial, class, and gender oppressions. Black women are also victims of rape and spousal abuse at alarming rates, issues that rarely reach a level of community outcry except in rare instances of interraciality.

Black women have been demonized more than any other group in U.S. society. In addition to being stereotyped along with all African Americans as disproportionately criminal, shiftless, and stupid, black women are attacked by white politicians, academics, and journalists as welfare queens, promiscuous vamps, and demented bitches, Saffires, Jemimas, and Jezebels. One only need note the recent portrayals of the controversies surrounding Sistah Souljah, Anita Hill, Lani Guinier, Joycelyn Elders, and other black women in the media as opposed to the men that were involved in those incidents. And, as witnessed by the vicious attacks on the mostly black female jury that found O.J. Simpson not guilty in his criminal trial, white feminists also have little hesitation in making broad sweeping stereotypical and racist statements about black women.

Add to this the voices of gangsta rappers who gleefully and incessantly call black women "hos", bitches, skeezers, cunts, teasers, and other derogatory and dehumanizing terms. Black women have to endure the black male view that they are emasculating, money grubbing, and domineering, and that much of the attacks on black (male) leaders come from the "traitorous" behavior of black women—views routinely echoed in NOI doctrine and rhetoric. Rather than criticize Supreme Court Justice Clarence Thomas, D.C. Mayor Marion Barry, former Congressperson Mel Reynolds, or boxer Michael Tyson for not taking responsibility for their personal behavior in scandals that they have been involved in. Farrakhan and others have accused the women in these incidents of bringing or attempting to bring down these men.

The MMM did little to challenge any of these views and, indeed, may have reinforced them. In patronizing and absurd fashion, Farrakhan and others offered the disingenuous notion that they had asked and received permission from black women to hold the march. Farrakhan stated, "We have asked our women if they would permit us as their men to finally take the point and make a stand for our women and children on behalf of our suffering communities in the name of our ancestors for justice."[11] The use of "our" is not inarticulate; it buttresses the underlying view that the black community and everyone in it is owned by black men. Barbara Arnwine, executive director of the National Lawyers' Committee for Civil Rights under Law, had an appropriate response. She said, "It's a throwback. The role African-American women are given in this march is to tend the bake sale, raise the money or stay at home and take care of the children. I think that it is awful." [12]

After spending a year declaring that this would be a men-only march, similar to the men-only meetings that Farrakhan had been holding, in an effort to beat back the criticism while denying that such criticism had any legitimacy or even existed, a new line developed that said, "Of course there is a role for black women regarding the march." That role, as it turned out, was to be the laborers where possible. At the same time, a number of black professional women were prominently displayed and given positions to logistically move the march forward. They had no role whatsoever in determining the political and ideological thrust of the event except to agree with it. Many of these women accepted the view that to raise gender issues was divisive and that, indeed, it was time for black men to stand up and take responsibility for leading the black community. That black women's concerns were erased was rationalized as a necessary sacrifice given the "endangered" status of black men.

One reason the patriarchal black nationalist view has gained a wider forum is due to the general absence of a popular black male feminist expression. Black male progressives who have viewed themselves as feminists and supportive of gender equality, for the most part, have failed to defend the hidden and not-so-hidden injuries of race-gender oppression and the attacks on black women or, as described below, have been equivocal as they have attempted to reconcile their feminism with black nationalism. From misogynist music lyrics to attacks by white politicians, black women have often been left alone to fend off those attacks. And, in some instances, when black men have joined the defense, it has been from a vantage point that is patronizing and sexist, or what writer bell hooks calls "benevolent patriarchy." A genuine cross-gender movement against sexism and for gender equity in the black community and the broader society has yet to come together. Until that happens, gender-divisive movements like the MMM will continue.

Not all black nationalists, it is important to note, support the march or its sexist overtones. One activist and writer that came out against the march, who has generally been viewed as a nationalist, was Kalamu Ya Salaam, best known as the former editor of *The Black Collegiate*. Although he had numerous disagreements with the politics of the march, he mainly focused on the way in which women were dismissed and disrespected. He wrote, "I didn't go mainly because I disagree with the exclusion (& diminishing) of women both explicit and inherent in the call....Black women who did openly criticize and/or oppose the march were an obvious and ostracized minority."[13] Salaam also stated, "I am unwilling to pretend that there is even one iota of salvation in this genuflecting to a patriarchal, genetically based struggle."[14]

The response by the black gay and lesbian community was generally to not endorse the march because of what many viewed as "its sexist and patriarchal tone and the homophobic comments made by some march organizers."[15] Some black gay and lesbian activists did advocate participation, however. The National Black Gay and Lesbian Leadership Forum (NBGALF), for example, refused to formally endorse the march but encouraged "all black gay and lesbian people, and particularly men, to participate openly and visibly in the March," stating that "We will no longer allow outsiders to dictate who is welcome at the black family table or to divide African Americans by sexual orientation or by gender." [16] According to NBGALF, "We believe the March provides a unique opportunity to empower black gay men and lesbians and black gay youth. Because black gay people are part of the black community, we will see positive images of open, courageous, proud, and diverse black gay people. Hundreds of black gay people participating openly in such an event will send a powerful message, one that will enable many black gays to abandon their masks of invisibility and assume or maintain their rightful place as citizens, mentors, and leaders of their communities."[17]

Black Progressive Responses

Many well-known black progressives capitulated to the march. Most notable were scholars and popular authors Dr. Rev. Cornel West and Dr. Rev. Michael Dyson, both of whom have written extensively against sexism and patriarchy. Although both voiced hesitation at supporting a gathering that (initially) formally asked women not to attend, focused exclusively on the issues facing black men, offered a conservative solution to the problems facing African Americans, and was led by someone that West and Dyson have both criticized as undemocratic, homophobic, anti-Semitic, and patriarchal, they endorsed and supported the march, even making appearances with Farrakhan on national television.

The march's call for atonement and reconciliation for the behavior of black men segued nicely into West's well-known motif of black "nihilism."[18] That Farrakhan's atonement and West's nihilism serve the interest of the conservative movement in constructing a view of the black community that blame it for the problems that the black community faces went generally unacknowledged. Scholar Peniel Joseph, however, did see the link between the two. He wrote, "Even as racism continues to provide the theoretical underpinnings for conservative and anti-black public policy the state has made blacks the racists and black men have accepted Farrakhan's public articulation of Cornel West's misguided notion of 'nihilism' rather than systems of domination, oppression, and racism as *the* reason behind continued black underdevelopment."[19] In a similar way, writer Stephen Steinberg asserts that "West's problem…is not that he discusses crime, violence, drugs, and the other notorious ills of ghetto life. Rather the problem is that he presents social breakdown and cultural disintegration as a problem sui generis, with an existence and momentum independent of the forces that gave rise to it in the first place."[20]

Dyson also found himself in a compromising position. He wrote that he "sympathizes with the many Jews, gays, women, lesbians, whites and blacks who were troubled by the March."[21] He noted, correctly, that "crucial elements of the language of responsibility, in which the moral aims of the march were couched, remain deeply problematic for women and for sexual minorities." [22] Again, on the theme of sexism, Dyson wrote, "It must be admitted...that the march did not entirely repudiate distorted notions of masculinity."[23] In spite of these reservations, Dyson decided to endorse the event. Needless to say, West and Dyson were not alone among black male progressive academics, activists, and journalists who decided to support the march. Was it the genius of Farrakhan or the misguided and confused politics of some black male progressives that could elicit harsh criticisms of the politics and gender issues of the march and yet provide their ringing and active endorsements?

There were a significant number of progressives, women and men, who did not support the march. Historian and longtime activist Barbara Ransby was one. She wrote, "Many of those who will be attending the march have good and noble motives. But I still cannot support this march. I have fundamental criticisms of the politics behind the march, and the leadership at the helm. The most obvious problem is the sexist and inexcusable exclusion of women. Women have worked behind the scenes, and a few will be allowed on the podium as speakers, but the majority of us—more than half the race—have been told to stay home, take care of the children, and leave the business of political leadership to the men."[24]

Progressive economist Julianne Malveaux, who was afraid that the march would end up as a "feel-good mistake," argued against the idea that women had taken over the lead from men in black political life.[25] She wrote, "The justification for this gender bifurcation was that women had shouldered the burden to date and now it was 'men's turn'....If the history of leadership of our nation's civil rights organizations were examined in even a cursory way, one would have to say it wasn't so."[26] Malveaux contended that not only have men led, but that it has been at the expense of black women's agency and participation: "From where I sit, it is disingenuous for people to ask that men have a turn when, in terms of visibility and leadership, it has always been men's turn—often to the detriment of women."[27]

Mary Frances Berry, chairperson of the U.S. Commission on Civil Rights, stated her repulsion at the leadership of Farrakhan and Chavis. She wrote in the *Washington Post,* "I have not endorsed the march because I do not support the leadership of Mr. Farrakhan and Benjamin Chavis. Mr. Farrakhan routinely expresses the most despicable, anti-Semitic, racist, sexist and homophobic attitudes imaginable. Mr. Chavis' role in practically destroying the NAACP makes any enterprise in which he is engaged suspect as far as I am concerned. African Americans as a community are in deep trouble at this hour. However, let me make it unmistakably clear: I do not trust Louis Farrakhan or Benjamin Chavis to lead us to the Promised Land."[28]

New York University historian and progressive scholar Robin D.G. Kelley also came out against the march. He was critical of both the conservative and patriarchal politics of the march's call and linked it to the popular conservative intonation about "family values." Kelley wrote, "In many ways, Farrakhan's call was not only a historical, but also a step backward, akin in some respects to the words of conservative 'family values' advocates who insist the root of black people's problems is lack of male-headed households....I think that the assumptions and rhetoric that drove the march were fundamentally sexist and conservative. For this reason alone, I could not attend the march."[29]

Most black Congressmembers, in the end, either supported the march or opposed it quietly. Both Representatives Kweisi Mfume and Donald Payne, respectively chairpersons of the Congressional Black Caucus for the 103rd and 104th Congresses, were present on stage and gave remarks. One black Congressmember who was vocally critical of the event was Representative Major Owens. He wrote, "I refuse to participate in Farrakhan's march because the agenda is purposefully shrouded in contradiction and conflicting messages. March leaders consistently have been autocratic, reckless, and divisive. As a leader and elected member of Congress, I can not support a group whose isolationist posture and separatist strategy pose a long-term threat to the survival of the African American community."[30]

While many criticisms of the march came from individuals, there was at least one effort to collectively come together. In New York, Agenda 2000 was formed, a group of black women and men who sought not just to focus on criticizing the march, but to use the opportunity to construct a progressive dialogue in the black community on gender relations. At a press conference held by the group, a number of the women shared their views on the march. Scholar and well-known activist Angela Davis read from the groups' statement, "Justice cannot be served by countering a distorted racist view of black manhood with a narrowly sexist vision of men standing 'a degree above women.'"[31] Davis was referring to statements that had appeared in the NOI's newspaper declaring that men were a degree above women. Another Agenda 2000 member, historian Paula Giddings, stated that the politics of Farrakhan and the march represent "19th-century solutions to 21st-century problems."[32]

The Post-March Movement

Events since the march have bore out many of the criticisms raised about the trustworthiness of Farrakhan, Chavis, and Bevel's leadership. On October 16, 1996, the one-year anniversary of the march, a rally was held outside the United Nations in New York City. Crowd estimates were about 50,000, according to a number of sources. Farrakhan, Chavis, and Bevel all spoke in addition to local black leaders such as Rev. Al Sharpton. In a bizarre episode, Winnie Mandela was flown in from South Africa to speak. When it came time for her to talk, Chavis told the crowd that the U.S. State Department would not allow her to give a presentation so her remarks had to be given through someone else. The State Department and the South African government both later denied that they had placed any such restrictions on her.

Farrakhan's speech was basically apocalyptic. In his remarks, he stated that we live in a time of "darkness and doom," and no political leaders could do anything to "avert the war of Armageddon."[33] The solution, of course, was to follow the spiritual leadership of Farrakhan and the NOI.

In early 1997, Chavis announced that he had joined the NOI and changed his name to Benjamin Chavis Muhammad. He stated that he had been contemplating joining for some time and had been studying the Koran for at least five years. Many suspected that he was giving into the reality that he had nowhere else to go or that he was attempting to position himself to inherit the leadership of the NOI after Farrakhan. For his part, Chavis Muhammad stated that his conversion was religious-based and that he now viewed his life's mission to convert African-American Christians to Islam. Within a very short time after his joining, resentment and criticism from within toward Chavis Muhammad began to emerge, indicating that his tenure within the group may be unpleasant and short-lived.[34]

By the end of 1996, many had jumped on the bandwagon of condemnation of the march leaders. The lack of follow-up, Farrakhan's "Grand Dictator" tour to Africa and the Middle East, the black convention fiasco in St. Louis, Chavis Muhammad's megalomaniac and inept leadership of NAALS, and the suffocating dominance of the NOI were all charges made in the pages of *Emerge, Jet,* and black newspaper columns. Some saw the source of the problems in the egos and individualism of Farrakhan and Chavis Muhammad. Activist Ron Daniels, who had been involved in the leadership of the march at various stages, attributes the decline of the movement around the MMM and NAALS to the failure of Farrakhan and Chavis to operate in a collective and consultative manner. [35]

While all of these reasons are accurate, they tend to avoid a more disturbing, but perhaps truer conclusion: that the politics of Farrakhan and Chavis have been consistent and that their behavior has been the logical outcome of those politics. Farrakhan's global tour was not a mistake or a consequence of his not talking to black foreign policy experts. He was absolutely clear on why he went where he did, even if some of his supporters were not. His soft critics were also naive if they thought that after years of struggling to obtain the position of leadership afforded him by the march, he was about to decentralize his authority, particularly since the NOI was providing the foot soldiers and critical funding for the movement. His alliance with LaRouche, just as the NOI of Elijah Muhammad had formed tentative alliances with the Ku Klux Klan and the American Nazi movement, was also not a mistake or casual encounter. It was an ideologically driven choice that has every basis to grow and continue.

Within black politics, the dialogue concerning gender equality remains combative. While the march could have been an opportunity to highlight the issues facing both black men and women, the failure to do so allowed the atmosphere that demonizes black women to go unchallenged. Less than a year after the march, Congress passed and

Clinton signed welfare reform legislation; the long-term impact will be devastating to the black community, black families and children in particular. The opportunity to raise at least one million black voices—very likely a once-in-a-lifetime chance—in defense of needed social programs came and went. Given who led the march, however, even if the issue of welfare had been addressed, it is doubtful that the views expressed would have been that different from those of Gingrich and Clinton.

It is understandable why many in the black community so strongly supported the march. There is a desperate yearning for leadership, mobilization, and unity. And the issues facing black men are real (as are those faced by women, who are the majority of the black community). These sentiments and circumstances were exploited by Farrakhan and Chavis. While these issues are larger than Farrakhan, the march and the movement around and subsequent to it all have the permanent imprimatur of Farrakhan. The urgency with which people deny Farrakhan's role only highlights it. More important, it is Farrakhan's politics that are present even when he is not.

A black conservative agenda, albeit dressed in black nationalist clothing, will not free black America. Whether it comes from Clarence Thomas or Louis Farrakhan, it merely perpetuates the crisis that already exists for at least of a third of all African Americans and half of all black children. It is a moralistic and capitalistic vision, reinforced, in Farrakhan's case, by an authoritarianism that seeks to crush all voices of dissent.

Finally, in relationship to (re)building AACS, the MMM failed in several respects. Its call for African Americans to join black organizations, while not a problem in itself, is consistent with the moderate ideology of self-help that obscures the relationship between civil society, the state, and the market economy. This view also misses the point that the growing needs of millions, exacerbated by a job-destroying globalized economy and a shrinking welfare state, far outstrip the capacities of volunteer organizations. Massive public policy intervention, eschewed by the march's leadership, is required if even a modicum of possibility of advancement is to happen.

A Call for Insurgency

"However deeply American Negroes are caught in the struggle to be at last at home in our homeland of the United States, we cannot ignore the larger world house in which we are also dwellers. Equality with whites will not solve the problems of either whites or Negroes if it means equality in a world society stricken by poverty and in a universe doomed to extinction by war. All inhabitants of the globe are now neighbors. This world-wide neighborhood has been brought into being largely as a result of the modern scientific and technological revolutions."[36] —Martin Luther King, Jr.

In this era, with its world-changing, globalized economies and communities, an insurgent and bold Black leadership is needed now more than ever. This is a leadership that must not be captive to any of the major political parties which have made it clear that racial equality is, at best, a rhetorical device to buffer black resistance, and at worst, no longer a social or political objective. This is a leadership that must address the problems and intractability of race, gender, class, age, and nation without being mired in the limits of those identities. This is a leadership that challenges the power of the state and the economic elite, targeting their pivotal role in the destabilizing of poor black communities, while avoiding diatribes that blame the victims of these assaults. This is a leadership that must struggle with the difficult transitions in racial forms in the United States and beyond that are reconfiguring the black-white dynamic that has driven much of the racial heritage of the nation. This is a leadership that must fight to reconstruct AACS from within and without against the odds and against forces with significantly more ideological and material resources. If African Americans are to advance in the 21st century, this is a leadership that must come into existence.

There has never been a time when the consolidation of black leadership into one single individual has ever benefited African Americans. Whether it was the white-anointed reign of Booker T. Washington or the black groundswell that bolstered Jesse Jackson, a diverse and wide-ranging leadership has been necessary. This will become even more true in the coming years, as the arenas of struggle expand and new venues of cultural, social, and political expressions, some created by innovative and revolutionary technologies, emerge. In the current and coming period, black activists of all types have an important role to play. Most important will be the creation of popular vehicles that foster and allow for the generation, expression, and validation of grassroots leadership on a broad scale. Too often, the black poor have been "represented" by civil rights leaders, nationalists, and even conservatives, rather than allowed to be their own voice and the creator of their own machines of resistance. The resources, skills, talents, insights, and experiences possessed by activists should be converged with similar and complementary attributes from the people whose interests are ostensibly being advocated. The power of the civil rights and Black Power eras was not in the national leaders and national organizations that gained fame for their heroic deeds, but the rising up of millions of ordinary, everyday people who created and joined groups that fought for inclusion and equality throughout AACS. What has characterized the post-1960s period has been the disappearance of massive organic involvement by African Americans of all classes and strata in structures of struggle.

This activism should not be seen as missionary work, where the community is rescued and saved by outsiders with the correct word and vision. Nor is it a call to romanticize the black community as a progressive stronghold that just needs a spark to ignite it. A complex and competing array of perspectives exist in the black community that, at any given time, can forge extremely conservative or harshly radical discourses and battlefronts. Black intellectuals, both inside and outside of academia, can play a critical role in the reconstruction of AACS. As intellectuals, those who are committed to sorting through the way in which ideas manifest and shape society, the creation of accessible and relevant intellectual work, *inter alia*, in the areas of economics, culture, politics, and sociology would link needed scholarship with social activism. On the one hand, such an effort would combat the anti-intellectualism that reigns not only in the black community, but in U.S. society at large. On the other hand, the highly correct black criticism of the uselessness of much of what is produced by black intellectuals could be abated. Perhaps it is most critical that black intellectuals do not view themselves as separate from the black community, but as one wing of it with specific responsibilities and skills to contribute.

African Americans and the Global Civil Society

Many of the issues and concerns being confronted by African Americans in the United States are also being struggled with by other communities around the globe. Job displacement, cuts in social programs, a shrunken and disappearing welfare state, and racial and ethnic assaults are endemic to this period. Although in the past the black community did not have the luxury to ignore its connection with the rest of the world, it is with even greater peril today that an isolationist view must be avoided. As argued throughout this book, the option to act locally has vanished and every decision, in today's world, is a step into the international arena.

African Americans have a long history of solidarity with the global community and with peoples who have struggled for justice and fairness. African Americans supported Cuba in its independence struggle, fought in the Spanish Civil War, actively opposed Apartheid in South Africa, gave support to the Palestinians, marched against the Vietnam War, and, in general, have been engaged in global struggles for centuries. The forging of the black community itself was an expression of the internationalization of commerce, politics, and ideology that launched the slave trade, slavery, and racism. Black leaders, from Ida B. Wells and W.E.B. Du Bois to Malcolm X, Angela Davis, and Martin L. King Jr. to Louis Farrakhan, Colin Powell, Jesse Jackson, and Dorothy Height, not only advocated but practiced international politics at the highest level. From conservative to progressive interventions, black leaders have seen the necessity to comment and participate in the global issues that defined their era. In essence, the black community has always been an active member of the global civil society.

In the period ahead, new opportunities and challenges to global participation abound. Technologies have made access to the global community relatively easy, fast, and efficient. Never before in history has it been so convenient to obtain information and data on the issues confronting people from Africa and Asia to Europe and the Caribbean. In every area of life, from the social and political to the economic and cultural, the world can be touched with a few keystrokes or a phone call. Global reach is not just available to the world's elite. Millions of people can now bypass governments, parties, and other intermediaries in order to directly connect with their counterparts and people of similar views and interests. This ease and efficiency of linkage opens up numerous possibilities for constructing a world community that can collectively address the issues of this age and facilitate the global civil society project.

This reach also carries dangers. Much of the ultimate control of the new technologies is in the hands of unaccountable, unregulated, and uncaring transnational corporations whose efforts at economic and technical domination are helped by policymakers, who, in vain attempt to maintain the nation-state, are willing to make unholy concessions. Many, if not most, of these elected officials, the world over, have been purchased by these transnational corporations and have long surrendered any pretense of acting in the interests of the majority of the people they were elected to represent. With this power also comes efforts at ideological dominance. Racist ideology, mainly though not exclusively from the American perspective, is increasingly finding wider and wider audiences as it is broadcast and otherwise distributed to the global community via films, cable television, music videos, the Internet, and other medium. In a similar way, issues of gender, class, and nation are narratives being told from the point of view of a global elite.

The resolution of the tension between opportunity for solidarity among the global masses, and expanded economic and ideological hegemony for the transnational corporations will determine the stability and strength of global civil society. The contributions that can be made to this project by African Americans are immense. Positioned in the center of where much of the key economic, political, and even technology battles have and will unfold—from NAFTA and GATT to the Internet—African Americans are uniquely situated to expose, confront, and otherwise disrupt the process of power that threatens the future of those in the United States and beyond. In unison with others engaged in similar struggles internationally, African Americans can be part of the global work crew that builds King's "world house."

Imaging an Alternative Black Future

"Racism is no mere American phenomenon. Its vicious grasp knows no geographical boundaries. In fact, racism and its perennial ally—economic exploitation—provide the key to understanding most of the international complications of this generation." [37] —Martin Luther King, Jr.

King's dream was a global one. Contrary to reductive efforts to limit King's hopes to notions of racial friendship and harmony, he projected a radical vision that demanded a fundamental restructuring of society and the global community. He did not just want an end to segregation, but called for an end to racism. He did not just want to help the poor, but called for an end to poverty. He did not just seek to question U.S. involvement in Vietnam, but called for an end to all wars and the exploitation that generates them.

In spite of his visionary insights, King was a product of his times. He did not place gender equity at the center of his political vision, although it is implied in his work more consistently than other black leaders of the period. Neither did he speak at great length about, and perhaps was not able to see, the changing racial structure of the United States with the growth of the Asian and Hispanic communities. Nor could King, or anyone else at the time, predict the fall of global communism and the end of the Cold War that had determined international politics, economics, and culture for more than six decades. King was born into and died during the Cold War era. Finally, he could not appreciate in full how new technologies and globalization would (and continue to) restructure the world and daily life in both progressive and deadly ways. Amazingly, King did see the impact of technologies on the workforce even back then when he wrote of his distress "at thousands of working people displaced from their jobs with reduced incomes as a result of automation while the profits of the employers remain intact."[38] That millions of people would be displaced and that this phenomena would become the dominant character in modern economic life was, of course, unforeseen.

Learning from those historically shaped limits, King's world house is still on the agenda. African Americans have a vested interest

in thinking globally and acting globally even as we address the immediate local and national issues that confront us. It is critical that we
appreciate the historic transformations that are occurring right before
our eyes in our neighborhoods, our cities, in the nation, and around
the world. Working-class black communities around the globe, from
Soweto to Brixton to Rio to Toronto, are hurting and disproportionately suffering from unemployment, economic downsizing, a retreat-
ing welfare state, drug trafficking, lack of educational opportunities,
and inadequate housing. At the same time, tremendous struggles are
being waged to fight those problems that manifest locally but are part
of a global system. Racism, in conjunction with sex, class, and national dynamics, are driving these conditions as well as shaping the
fight back. For African Americans, it is timely and appropriate to
unite and join other struggles and ours. The world house, however, is
larger than just the African disapora. Communities of the poor and
working class are engaged in struggles that are also of meaning and
importance to the black community. Winning battles against corporate power, to save a ravaged environment, and for cultural diversity
also require a global vision that is inclusive.

Central to the unfolding vision necessary to move forward is the
issue of gender equity and inclusion. The black community will not
and can not advance as long as patriarchal ideas shape its thinking
and practice. In this period, the black community must resist whole-
heartedly the dominant ideology, shared by many black male leaders,
that preaches that the problems facing African Americans are centered around the breakdown of the traditional family and the absence
of a male presence in the home. On virtually every indices, black
women are doing worse than black men, and increasingly so. This is
also true for women on a global scale, where women "do two-thirds
of the world's work, earn ten percent of the world's income, and own
less than one percent of the world's property."[39]

King's world house is still under construction. It is being built by
children in Harare who are logging onto the Internet and communi-
cating with children in Harlem. It is being built by the Zapatistas in
Mexico who are resisting the outrages of NAFTA, thereby fighting in
the interests of communities in Mexico, the United States, and Canada. It is being built by women farmhands in Indonesia who sit on

panels with women farmhands from Jamaica at a conference in England fighting globalization. It is being built by students in China, Brazil, and South Africa who are computer linked and exchanging ideas on any number of subjects. It is being built by African Americans in South Central Los Angeles who take Spanish lessons so they can better work with their neighbors. The global civil society that will inhabit King's world house must include the black community. This is the task indeed the mission that we must embrace in the days ahead.

Notes

1. Globalization's Impact on Race Relations

1. Quoted in Kevin Danaher, ed., *Corporations Are Gonna Get Your Mama: Globalization and Downsizing of the American Dream* (Monroe, ME: Common Courage Press, 1996), 204.

2. Medea Benjamin, "Nike's Exploited Workers," in *Corporations Are Gonna Get Your Mama*, 86. Also, see J.B. Strasser and Laurie Becklund, *Swoosh: The Unauthorized Story of Nike and the Men Who Played There* (New York: HarperBusiness, 1993). Michael Jordan's role as the highest-paid black athlete hawking sports products may be superseded by golf phenomenon Tiger Woods. In 1996–97, Woods signed endorsement contracts of $40 million with Nike, $20 million with Titleist, $20 million with American Express, and at least another $8 million for books and other products. See Tim Lacey, "Tiger, 21, Signs for Millions," *Washington Afro-American*, 24 May 1997, 1.

3. James Rinehart, "The Ideology of Competitiveness: Pitting Worker Against Worker," *Corporations Are Gonna Get Your Mama*, 90.

4. Benjamin, "Nike's Exploited Workers," 86.

5. John Hoberman, *Darwin's Athletes: How Sport Has Damaged Black America and Preserved the Myth of Race* (Boston: Houghton Mifflin Co., 1997), 34.

6. Patricia J. Williams, "Disorder in the House: The New World Order and the Socioeconomic Status of Women," in *Theorizing Black Feminisms: The Visionary Pragmatism of Black Women*, eds. Stanlie M. James and Abena A. Busia (New York: Routledge, 1993), 118.

7. Jerry Mander, "The Dark Side of Globalization," *The Nation*, 15-22 July 1996, 9.

8. Anthony Giddens, *The Consequences of Modernity* (Stanford, CA: Stanford University Press, 1990), 64.

9. Robert Burnett, *Global Jukebox: The International Music Industry* (New York: Routledge, 1996), 12.

10. Lester C. Thurow, *The Future of Capitalism: How Today's Economic Forces Shape Tomorrow's World* (New York: William Morrow and Co., 1996), 114.

11. See Richard Barnet and John Cavanagh, *Global Dreams: Imperial Corporations and the New World Order* (New York: Simon & Schuster, 1994); Jerry Mander and Edward Goldsmith, eds., *The Case Against Globalization: And for a Turn toward the Local* (San Francisco: Sierra Club Books, 1996); Benjamin R. Barber, *Jihad vs. McWorld: How the Planet is Both Falling Apart and Coming Together, and What This Means for Democracy* (Toronto: Times Books, 1995); Bennett Harrison, *Lean and Mean: The Changing Landscape of Corporate Power in the Age of Flexibility* (New York: Basic Books, 1994); William Greider, *One World,*

Ready or Not: The Manic Logic of Global Capitalism (New York: Simon & Schuster, 1997); David C. Korten, *When Corporations Rule the World* (West Hartford, CT: Kumarian Press, 1995); and Robert B. Reich, *The Work of Nations: Preparing Ourselves for 21st Century Capitalism* (New York: Vintage Books, 1992).

12. Jeremy Rifkin, *The End of Work: The Decline of the Global Labor Force and the Dawn of the Post-Market Era* (New York: Putnam Books, 1995), 68.

13. Ibid., 71.

14. Sidney Wilhelm, *Who Needs the Negro?* (Cambridge, MA: Schenkman, 1970), 163.

15. Ibid., 156–7.

16. Holly Sklar, "Persistent Impoverishment," *Ecologist*, July/August 1996, 188.

17. Jeremy Brecher and Tim Costello, *Global Village or Global Pillage?: Economic Reconstruction from the Bottom Up* (Boston: South End Press, 1994), 27.

18. Ibid., 28.

19. United Nations Development Program, *Human Development Report 1992* (New York: United Nations, 1992), 6.

20. "A Divided World," *North–South*, November 1995, 9.

21. See "Employment in the World, 1996/1997," International Labor Organization, United Nations, 1997.

22. Barnet and Cavanagh, *Global Dreams*, 286.

23. Nicholas Hildyard, Colin Hines, and Tim Lang, "Who Competes?: Changing Landscapes of Corporate Control," *Ecologist*, July/August 1996, 128.

24. Lori S. Robinson, "Canada's Justice," *Emerge*, April 1996, 16.

25. Ian Grant and Rafik Benale, "May Day Marchers Protest Racism and Unemployment in France," http://www.tbwt.com/views /feat/feat69.htm.

26. Lori S. Robinson, "Black Latin America," *Emerge*, April 1995, 14.

27. Thomas D. Boston, *Race, Class and Conservatism* (Cambridge, MA: Unwin Hyman, 1988), 48.

28. Rachel Kamel, *The Global Factory: Analysis and Action for a New Economic Era* (Philadelphia: American Friends Service Committee, 1990), 20.

29. Barnet and Cavanagh, *Global Dreams*, 275–6.

30. Ibid., 292.

31. Nicholas Hildyard, Colin Hines, and Tim Lang, "Who Competes?" 127.

32. Kamel, *The Global Factory*, 15.

33. Barnet and Cavanagh, *Global Dreams*, 293.

34. William Julius Wilson, *When Work Disappears: The World of the New Urban Poor* (New York: Alfred A. Knopf, 1996), 29.

35. Rochelle Sharpe, "In Last Recession, Only Blacks Suffered Net Employment Loss," *Wall Street Journal*, 4 September 1993.

36. Ibid.

37. "Displacement Rate, Unemployment Spells, and Reemployment Wages by Race," General Accounting Office, Washington, D.C., September 1994, 3

38. David C. Korten, "The Limits of the Earth," *The Nation,* 15-22 July 1996, 18.

39. Thurow, *The Future of Capitalism*, 26.

40. "Why Today's Big Profits Mean Big Trouble," *Too Much,* Fall 1995, 1.

41. Holly Sklar, "Scapegoating and Slander," *Ecologist*, July/August 1996, 185.

42. Ibid.

43. See *Too Much,* Fall 1995, 3.

44. Wilson, *When Work Disappears*, 29-30

45. Lester Henry, *NAFTA and GATT: World Trade Policy Impacts on African Americans* (New York: Du Bois Bunche Center for Public Policy, 1995), 11.

46. Robert C. Smith, *Racism in the Post-Civil Rights Era: Now You See It, Now You Don't* (Albany, NY: State University of New York, 1995), 134.

47. Henry, 28-29. See Julie Graham, "Multinational Corporations and the Internationalization of Production: An Industry Perspective," in *Creating a New World Economy,* eds. G. Epstein, J. Graham, and J. Newbhard (Philadelphia: Temple University Press), 221–41.

48. Barnet and Cavanagh, *Global Dreams*, 313.

49. Reich, *The Work of Nations*, 213.

50. Ibid., 212.

51. Barnet and Cavanagh, *Global Dreams*, 311.

52. Sklar, "Scapegoating and Slander," 190.

53. Ibid.

54. Ibid., 189–90.

55. Martin Carnoy, *Faded Dreams: The Politics and Economics of Race in America* (New York: University of Cambridge Press, 1994), 236–7.

56. Thea M. Lee, "The Likely Impact of NAFTA on Women and Minorities," testimony before the Employment, Housing and Aviation Subcommittee of the U.S. House Committee on Government Operations, U.S. House of Representatives, 10 November 1993, 1.

57. William Lucy, "The Price of NAFTA: Guaranteed Short-Term Pain With No Guaranteed Long-Term Benefits," *Third World Viewpoint*, Spring 1994, 16.

58. *Congressional Record,* 17 November 1993, H9957.

59. Reich, *The Work of Nations*, 225-40.

60. Donald L. Barlett and James B. Steele, *America: Who Stole the Dream* (Kansas City, MO: Andrews and McNeel, 1996), 140–1.

61. Ibid., 133.

62. Alfred Edmond, "Coming on Strong," *Black Enterprise*, June 1994, 78.

63. Lorrie Grant, "GATT Gains Ground for Minority-Owned Firms," *Emerge,* February 1995, 25.

64. U.S. Bureau of the Census, "New York Metro Area Leads List for Black-Owned Firms, Los Angeles Tops in Women-Owned Businesses, Census Bureau Reports," press release, 16 March 1996.

65. U.S. Bureau of the Census, "Black-Owned Businesses Up 46 Percent Over Five Years, Census Bureau Survey Shows," press release, 12 December 1995, and "Number of Minority-Owned Businesses and Revenues Increase Substantially between 1987 and 1992," press release, 18 November 1996.

66. Ibid.

67. Barnet and Cavanagh, *Global Dreams*, 302.

68. Marian Wright Edelman, "A Portrait of Inequality in America," *Washington Afro-American*, 26 April 1997, A5.

69. Ibid.

70. Ibid.

71. Robin Wright, "UNICEF Report Cites U.S. as Leader in Child Poverty," *San Jose Mercury News*, 12 June 1996.

72. Ibid.

73. Samuel I. Rosenman, *The Public Papers and Addresses of Franklin D. Roosevelt* (New York: Harper & Row, 1950), 41.

74. Ibid.

75. Ron Dellums, "Seven More Members of the House Join Original 16 Cosponsors of H.R. 1050, 'A Living Wage, Jobs For All Act,'" *News & Views From Ron Dellums of California*, 8 February 1996.

76. H.R. 1050.

77. Dellums, *News and Views*.

78. See *Corporate Power and the American Dream* (New York: Labor Institute, 1994), 119.

2. If I Were a Rich Man

1. Martin Luther King, Jr., "Where Do We Go From Here: Chaos or Community?" in *A Testament of Hope: The Essential Writings and Speeches of Martin Luther King, Jr.*, ed. James M. Washington (New York: HarperCollins, 1986), 617. 37. Ibid., 621.

2. See Michael Harrington, *The New American Poverty* (New York: Penguin, 1985).

3. Mack H. Jones, "The Political Thought of the New Black Conservatives: An Analysis, Explanation and Interpretation," in *Readings in Political Issues*, eds. Franklin Jones and Michael Adams, (Dubuque, IA: Kendall/Hunt Publishing Co., 1987).

4. Adam Fifield, "Corporate Caseworkers," *In These Times*, 16 June 1997,14.

5. Ibid.

6. Ibid., 15-16.

7. Data on the characteristics of welfare recipients, unless otherwise noted, is taken from the 1994 House Ways and Means Committee's *Green Book* on federal

entitlement programs. This data is available on CD-ROM from the Government Printing Office.

8. Ibid.

9. Ibid.

10. Ibid.

11. Ibid.

12. Ibid.

13. Ibid.

14. The Twentieth Century Fund, *Medical Reform: A Twentieth Century Fund Guide to the Issues,* (New York: Twentieth Century Fund Press, 1995).

15. Ibid.

16. Ibid.

17. Ibid.

18. Ibid.

19. Ibid.

20. Ibid.

21. Ibid.

22. Ibid.

23. Ibid.

24. 1994 House Ways and Means Committee *Green Book.*

25. Ibid.

26. Children's Defense Fund, *Welfare Reform Briefing Book* (Washington, DC: CDF, January 1995), 4.

27. 1994 House Ways and Means Committee *Green Book.*

28. Ibid.

29. Ibid., Children's Defense Fund, 4.

30. Julianne Malveaux, *Sex, Lies, and Stereotypes: Perspectives of a Mad Economist* (Los Angeles: Pines One Publishing, 1994), 36.

31. Bill Clinton and Al Gore, *Putting People First: How We Can All Change America* (New York: Times Books, 1992), 164.

32. Ibid., 165.

33. Ibid., 12.

34. Ibid., 11.

35. "Survey Finds Corporate Welfare Spending Exceeds Social Welfare: Nader Criticizes Clinton's Welfare 'Reform' for Ignoring Corporate Entitlements," press release, (Washington, DC: Essential Information).

36. James P. Donahue, "The Fact Cat Freeloaders: When American Big Business Bellys Up to the Trough," *The Washington Post,* 6 March 1994.

37. Ibid.

38. Mark Zepezauer and Arthur Naiman, *Take the Rich Off Welfare* (Tucson, AZ: Odonian Press, 1996), 6.

39. Janice C. Shields, "Strange Bedfellows," *In These Times,* 12 May 1997, 28-9, 36.

40. Ibid. See *Wealthfare Reform Organizing Kit,* (Boston: Share the Wealth).

41. Activists have created sites on the World Wide Web that provide insight and data regarding corporate welfare. See, for example, the Share the Wealth Project (http://www.stw.org/); Cato Institute's reports, "Ending Corporate Welfare as We KnowIt"and"How Corporate WelfareWon" (http://www.cato.org/pubs/pas/pa~254es.html); Essential Information (http://www.essential.org); Rachel's Corporate Welfare Information Center (http://ww.environlink.org/issues/corporate/welfare/index.html); and *Utne Reader's* Corporate Welfare Resources (http://www.utnereader.com:80/archive/lens01/exchange/1naderres.html).

42. "Survey Finds Corporate Welfare Spending Exceeds Social Welfare."

43. Joseph G. Conti and Brad Stetson, "Are You Really a Racist?: A Common-Sense Quiz," in *Black and Right: The Bold New Voice of Black Conservatives in America,* eds. Stan Faryna, Brad Stetson, and Joseph G. Conti (Westport, CT: Praeger, 1997), 71.

44. Brian W. Jones, "Two Visions of Black Leadership," in *Black and Right,* 41

45. Telly Lovelace, "No Need for a Government Handout," in *Black and Right,* 47.

46. Louis Farrakhan, "The Sickness of Envy," speech delivered at Muhammad University, Chicago, 7 March 1990, cited in Mattiass Gardell, *In the Name of Elijah Muhammad: Louis Farrakhan and the Nation of Islam* (Durham, NC: Duke University Press, 1996), 319.

47. Wahneema Lubiano, "Black Ladies, Welfare Queens, and State Minstrels: Ideological War by Narrative Means," in *Race-ing Justice, En-Gendering Power* ed. Toni Morrison (New York: Random House, 1992), 339.

48. Barbara Ransby and Tracye Matthews, "Black Popular Culture and Transcendence of Patriarchal Illusions," in *Words of Fire: An Anthology of African-American Feminist Thought,* Beverly Guy-Sheftall (New York: The New Press, 1995), 526.

49. Lubiano, "Black Ladies," 332.

50. Children's Defense Fund, "Strategies to Protect the Safety Net for Children, Families, and Average Americans," (Washington, DC: CDF), 1.

51. Ibid., 38.

52. "Making Welfare Work: An Outline for Constructive Welfare Reform," (Washington, DC: Joint Center for Political and Economic Studies, 1995), 1.

53. The WGNANT recommendations were: (1) Job stimulus based on private-sector inducements for job creation for both poor men and women, supplemented where necessary by public-sector investments; (2) Education and job training—especially on-the-job training, two of the most important factors proven to help people move from welfare to work; (3) Adequate rewards for work—for example, expanding the Earned Income Tax Credit and raising the minimum wage in order

to make work pay; (4) Time limits that take differences among welfare recipients into consideration—for instance, shorter limits for those job-ready and longer ones for those who are not; (5) Labor law reforms—for example, expanding the unemployment insurance program to include contingency workers, and encouragement of collective bargaining in the low-wage sector; (6) Family-friendly policies—including eliminating disincentives in AFDC for two-parent families, increasing asset limits, raising earning disregards, increasing standards of need to fill the gap, budgeting, encouraging extended and step-parent families, strengthening voluntary paternity establishment procedures, providing nourishing homes for teen parents—including voluntary enrollment in group homes where necessary, providing support for single parents to combine work and family, and establishing required parenting classes for all adolescents in public schools; (7) Children-friendly reforms—for example, promoting early childhood development through more quality child care institutions, child support assurance for all children, building public-private partnerships to provide additional or alternative role models for children in single-parent families, providing the same range and quality of reproductive services for the poor that affluent people enjoy, and building a public campaign not only against unwed motherhood, but also toward valuing all children, regardless of the marital status of their parents, and; (8) Equal opportunity and anti-discrimination provisions to govern all aspects of welfare reform and level the playing field—including full civil liberties, civil rights, minimum wage protections, equal pay for equal work, and rights to earn seniority in jobs.

54. For a critique of Clinton's role in the welfare debacle, see Peter Edelman, "The Worst Thing Bill Clinton Has Done," *Atlantic Monthly,* April 1997.

55. Robin D. G. Kelley, "The Black Poor and the Politics of Oppression in a New South City, 1929-1970," in *The Underclass Debate: Views from History,* ed. Michael B. Katz (Princeton, NJ: Princeton University Press, 1993), 294.

56. Marcia Bok, *Civil Rights and the Social Programs of the 1960s* (Westport, CT: Prager, 1992), 150.

57. See Mimi Abramovitz, *Under Attack, Fighting Back: Women and Welfare in the United States* (New York: Monthly Review Press, 1996).

58. James Jennings also writes about several advocacy groups, including the Massachusetts Human Services Coalition, the Coalition for Basic Human Needs, Up and Out of Poverty Now (Detroit), and Congress for a Working America (Milwaukee). See James Jennings, *Understanding the Nature of Poverty in Urban America* (Westport, CT: London, 1994), 143.

3. California Scheming

1. John Wildermuth, "Immigrants Boost State Population to 31.3 Million," *San Francisco Chronicle,* 16 February 1993.

2. Elaine Woo, "Prison Spending Hurts Schools and Black Students, Report Says; Government: Study Says State Has Shifted Its Priority from Education to Incarceration. Spokesman for Governor Calls Conclusions 'Mindless Drivel,'" *Los Angeles Times,* 23 October 1996.

3. Ibid.

4. Mary Ellen Leary, "California Runs out of Jail Space as Voters Worry More about Schools than Crime," *Pacific News,* 11 December 1996.

5. Chris McGinn, "NAFTA Index: Three Years of NAFTA Facts," *Public Citizen,* Washington, D.C., 14 January 1997, 1.

6. Ibid., 3.

7. Brad Edmondson, "Life without Illegal Immigrants," *American Demographics,* May 1996.

8. Ibid.

9. Alejandro Ramos, "The Use and Abuse of Statistics: The Case of Proposition 187," http://www.aad.berkeley.edu/95journal/alejandroramos.html.

10. Ibid.

11. Alejandro Alonso, University of Southern California, http://www-bcf.use.edu/%7eaalonso/academic/187.html.

12. Haya El Nasser and Gale Holland, "187 Awakes 'A Sleeping Giant': Opponents Promise to Be 'A Force,'" *USA Today,* 10 November 1994.

13. Deeann Glamser, "California's Ballot Vote Now Spreading Fear 'Far and Wide,'" *USA Today,* 16 November 1994.

14. Brenda Payton, "Black Vote for 187 No Surprise," *Oakland Tribune,* 11 November 1994.

15. Jan Adams, "Pro 187—What's to Be Learned?" *Racefile,* January-February 1995, 20.

16. Martin Luther King, Jr., *Where Do We Go From Here:Chaos or Community?* (Boston, MA: Beacon Press, 1968).

17. Pamela Burdman, "Minority Applications Slip for 2nd Year at UC," *San Francisco Chronicle,* 5 February 1997.

18. George Skelton, "After 209, What's Next for Connerly?" *Los Angeles Times,* 18 November 1996.

19. California Senate Office of Research, "Taking a Look at Affirmative Action," 19 January 1995, 5.

20. Richard Morin, "Affirming Affirmative Action Hires," *Washington Post,* 12 January 1997.

21. See http://www.igc.apc.org/cfg/whoiscfj.html.

22. Bettina Boxall, "California Elections/Proposition 209; Opponents Go Their Separate Ways; Two Women's Groups and Civil Rights Organizations Leave Coalition. Some Call It a Rift, Others Say It Is a Division of Labor," *Los Angeles Times,* 11 October 1996.

23. "Elections '96; State Propositions: A Snapshot of Voters," *Los Angeles Times,* 7 November 1996.

24. Ibid.

25. Mortimer B. Zuckerman, "Black America's Mirror Image," *U.S. News and World Report*, 6 May 1996, 76.

26. Malik Miah, "Why the Leadership Vacuum?" *Against the Current,* July/August 1996, 13.

27. Farai Chideya, "Affirmative Action—Beyond Black and White: Equality? I'm Still Waiting," *New York Times*, 11 March 1995.

28. See http://www.qsanfrancisco.com/qsf/95fall/aff-action.html.

29. David G. Savage, "White House Joins Attack on Prop 209," *Los Angeles Times,* 21 December 1996.

4. To Be or Not to Be

1. James Baldwin, "If Black English Isn't a Language, Then Tell Me What Is?" *The Price of a Ticket: Collected Nonfiction, 1948-1985* (New York: St. Martin's/Marek, 1985), 652.

2. William L. Van Deburg, *New Day in Babylon: The Black Power Movement and American Culture, 1965-1975* (Chicago: University of Chicago Press, 1993), 222.

3. Some critical works on BEV that came out of the period were: J. L. Dillard, *Black English: Its History and Usage in the United States* (New York: Vintage, 1973); William Labov, *Language in the Inner City: Studies in the Black English Vernacular* (Philadelphia: University of Pennsylvania Press, 1972); Paul Stoller, ed., *Black American English: Its Background and Its Usage in the Schools and Literature* (New York: Dell, 1975); and Robert L. Williams, ed., *Ebonics: The True Language of Black Folks* (St. Louis: Institute of Black Studies, 1975).

4. Many linguists argue that BEV has its own syntax structure, pronunciations, and slang. For example, there is often no "s" at the end of third, person-singular verbs; the "k" at the end of words is translated to "x" ("ask" = "ax"); the "r" on the end of certain words is dropped ("for"="fo"), and many words ending in "th" are changed to end in "f" ("with"="wif").

5. See Robert L. Williams, *Ebonics: The True Language of Black Folks* (St. Louis: Institute of Black Studies, 1975).

6. Steve Holmes, "Black English Debate: No Standard Assumptions," *New York Times,* December 30, 1996.

7. "Who Said What about Ebonics, " *University Faculty Voice*, February 1997, 6.

8. Ibid.

9. "Jackson Assails Recognition of Black English," *Washington Post,* 23 December 1996.

10. Ros Davidson, "Jackson Shifts Stance on Black English Effort," *Washington Post,* 31 December 1996.

11. "Ebonics: Q & A," *Jax Fax,* 2 January 1997.

12. *JaxFax,* 23 January 1997.

13. *Sacramento Bee*, 23 December 1996.

14. Linguistic Society Resolution on "Ebonics," http://www.lsa.umich.edu:80/ling/jlawler/ebonics.html.

15. Lori Olszewski and Rick DelVecchio, "Ebonics Plan Toned Down in Oakland," *San Francisco Chronicle,* 13 January 1997.

16. Ibid.

17. Ibid.

18. Karen DeWitt, "Not So Separate: Ebonics, Language of Richard Nixon," *New York Times,* 29 December 1996.

19. Baldwin, *The Price of a Ticket,* 650.

5. O.J. and the Symbolic Uses of Racial Exceptions

1. Jonathan T. Lovitt, "Poll: More Now Believe O.J. is Guilty," *USA Today,* 4 October 1996.

2. Ibid.

3. Howard Goldberg, "Poll: Black-White O.J. Gap Narrows," *Associated Press,* 22 January 1997.

4. See Harry Edwards, *The Revolt of the Black Athlete* (New York: The Free Press, 1969); and David K. Wiggins, "Critical Events Affecting Racism in Athletics," in *Racism in College Athletics: The African American Athlete's Experience* eds. Dana Brooks and Ronald Althouse (Morgantown, WV: Fitness Information Technology, Inc., 1993), 23-49.

5. Edwards, *The Revolt of the Black Athlete,* 76.

6. Betsy Peoples, "Graduation Blitz," *Emerge,* November 1995, 56.

7. See Anne DuCille, *Skin Trade* (Cambridge: Harvard University Press, 1996). Also see, John Hoberman, *Darwin's Athletes: How Sport Has Damaged Black America and Preserved the Myth of Race* (Boston: Houghton Mifflin Company, 1997).

8. Leola Johnson and David Roediger, "'Hertz, Don't It?': Becoming Colorless and Staying Black in the Crossover of O.J. Simpson," in *Birth of a Nation 'hood,* eds. Toni Morrison and Claudia Brodsky Lacour (New York: Pantheon, 1997), 202.

9. Ibid.

10. Edward Helmore, "Making a Mint out of Murder," *The Independent,* 18 June 1995.

11. Garth Alexander, "America turns Simpson trial into big bucks," *Sunday Times,* 30 April 1995.

12. Ibid.

13. Ibid.

14. Ibid.

15. Helmore, "Making a Mint."

16. Alexander, "America turns Simpson."

17. Helmore, "Making a Mint."

18. Alexander, "America turns Simpson."

19. Helmore, "Making a Mint."

20. DuCille, *Skin Trade*, 161.

21. Alexander, "America turns Simpson."

22. A. Leon Higginbotham, Jr., Aderson Bellegarde Francois, and Linda Y. Yuch, "The O.J. Simpson Trial: Who Was Improperly 'Playing the Race Card?'" in *Birth of a Nation 'hood,* eds. Toni Morrison and Claudia Brodsky Lacour (New York: Pantheon, 1997), 40.

23. Ibid., 53.

24. Nikol G. Alexander and Drucilla Cornell, "Dismissed or Banished? A Testament to the Reasonableness of the Simpson Jury" in *Birth of a Nation 'hood: Gaze, Script and Spectacle in the O.J. Simpson Case* eds. Toni Morrison and Claudia Brodsky Lacour (New York: Pantheon, 1997), 57-96.

25. "Simpson Trials by the Numbers," Associated Press, January 18, 1997.

26. See Beverly Guy-Sheftall, ed., *Words of Fire: An Anthology of African-American Feminist Thought* (New York: The New Press, 1995).

6. Thug Life

1. "Life Goes On," *All Eyes on Me* (Death Row Records, 1995).

2. Others on this list include Mike Tyson and Michael Jackson. While some political figures, such as Rev. Jesse Jackson and Min. Louis Farrakhan, also enjoy international fame, global American blackness is reified in athletes and entertainers.

3. Luther Campbell and John R. Miller, *As Nasty As They Wanna Be: The Uncensored Story of Luther Campbell of 2 Live Crew* (Fort Lee, NJ: Barricade Books, 1992), 151-61.

4. Mark Naison, "Outlaw Culture," *Reconstruction*, Vol. 1. No . 4, 128.

5. Cornel West, *Race Matters* (Boston, MA: Beacon Press, 1993), 15.

6. Robert Burnett, *Global Jukebox: The International Music Industry* (New York: Routledge, 1996), 3.

7. Ibid., 8.

8. MTV is owned by media mogul Sumner Redstone, who also owns Viacom, VH-1, Lifetime, Showtime, The Movie Channel, and Nickelodeon, and has controlling interest in Paramount. He also has five television stations and 12 radio stations.

9. Naison, *Outlaw Culture*, 129-30.

10. See Charles Jones, ed., *The Black Panther Party Reconsidered* (Baltimore: Black Classic Press, 1997).

11. "I Wonder if Heaven's gota Ghetto," *2 Pac* (Death Row Records, 1994).

12. "Correctional Populations in the United States, 1994," *Bureau of Justice Statistics Executive Summary,* U.S. Department of Justice, Office of Justice Programs, 1.

13. Connie Bruck, "The Takedown of Tupac," *The New Yorker*, 7 July 1997, 46.

14. Chuck Phillips and Alan Abrahadson, "Government Probing Whether Rap Label is a Criminal Enterprise," *Washington Post,* 31 December 1996.

15. "Outlaw," *2 Pac* (Death Row Records, 1993).

7. Globalizing the Media

1. Lawrence Grossman, *The Electronic Republic* (New York: Viking, 1995), 173-74.

2. Polly E. McLean, "Mass Communications, Popular Culture, and Racism," in *Racism and Anti-Racism in World Perspectve,* ed. Benjamin Bower (Thousand Oaks, CA: Sage Publications, 1995), 84.

3. Devin Walker, "The Media Lords: The Great Deceivers of the Earth," *The Kermit Report,* August-September 1991, 2.

4. "The National Entertainment State," *The Nation,* 3 June 1996.

5. See http://www.thenation.com/extra/publish/map1.html.

6. Herbert Schiller, "On that Chart," *The Nation,* 3 June 1996, 16.

7. Ernest Holsendolph, "Who Owns What," *Emerge,* May 1995, 21.

8. Robert W. McChesney, "The Global Struggle for Democratic Communication," *Monthly Review,* July-August 1996, 2.

9. Barnet and Cavanagh, *Global Dreams,* 156.

10. Gracian Mack, "How to Spot Hot Entertainment Stocks," *Black Enterprise,* June 1994, 269.

11. Mark Lowery and Nadirah Z. Sabir, "The Making of 'Hollyhood,'" *Black Enterprise,* December 1994, 112.

12. I.R., "African Americans' Viewing Habits on the Rise," *TV Guide,* 26 March 1994, 36.

13. Barnet and Cavanagh, *Global Dreams,* 156.

14. David Lieberman, "Time Warner Picks Parsons as President," *USA Today,* 1 November 1994; Gary Hoover, Alta Campbell, and Patrick J. Spain, eds., *Hoover's Handbook of American Business, 1994* (Austin, TX: The Reference Press, 1993), 1036.

15. Matthew S. Scott and Tariq K. Muhammad, "The Top 50 Black Power Brokers in Entertainment," *Black Enterprise,* December 1994, 59-80.

16. Carolyn M. Brown, "Fighting for Air Time," *Black Enterprise,* December 1994, 96.

17. Ibid. 96-7.

18. Paul Farhi, "Johnson's Dream of a Team," *Washington Post,* 22 August 1994.

19. Ibid.

20. Ibid.

21. Mike Mills, "Going Shopping for a Black Audience," *Washington Post,* 20 July 1994.

22. Ibid., 16.

23. Barnet and Cavanagh, *Global Dreams,* 157.

24. Christopher Vaughn, "Simmons' Rush for Profits," *Black Enterprise*, December 1992, 67.

25. Ibid.

26. Ibid.

27. Paul Farhi, "Is Murdock Getting the Most for His Money," *Washington Post*, 1 September 1996.

28. McChesney, "The Global Struggle," 3.

29. Ibid.

30. The "edu" and "gov" signatures denote educational and governmental sites.

31. Paul Taylor, "Internet Users 'Likely to Reach 500m By 2000,'" *Financial Times*, 13 May 1996, 4.

32. Peter Golding, "World Wide Wedge: Division and Contradiction in the Global Information Infrastructure," *Monthly Review*, July-August 1996, 76.

33. McChesney, "The Global Struggle," 6.

34. Golding, "World Wide Wedge," 85.

35. Sarah Anderson and John Cavanagh, *The Top 200: The Rise of Global Corporate Power*, Institute for Policy Studies, 25 September 1996, 1.

36. Ibid.

37. Ibid.

38. Michael Dawson and John Bellamy Foster, "Virtual Capitalism: The Political Economy of the Information Highway," *Monthly Review*, July-August 1996, 43.

39. Ninety-one percent of the world does not have telephones according to the United Nations Development Program, *Human Development Report, 1996*, 167.

40. Golding, "World Wide Wedge," 82.

41. Ibid.

42. Ibid., 83.

43. Ibid.

44. Ibid.

45. McChesney, "The Global Struggle," 17.

46. Bill Gates, *The Road Ahead* (New York: Viking, 1995), 171.

8. How Cracked is the CIA-Contra Drug Connection?

1. See Patricia McRae and David J. Ackerman, "The Illegal Narcotics Trade (INT) as a TNC: Implications for the TNC/Government Interface," unpublished paper.

2. John F. Kerry, "Organized Crime Goes Global While the U.S. Stays Home," *Washington Post*, 11 May 1997, C4.

3. Juanita Darling, "Nicaragua's Coastal Epidemic: A Deadly Habit is Devastating Miskito Communities on Nation's Remote Eastern Shores," *Los Angeles Times*, 8 February 1997.

4. See articles by Gary Webb, *San Jose Mercury News*, 18-20 August 1996, at http://www.sjmercury.com/drugs.

5. "CIA Official Sees No Evidence of Crack Role," *New York Times*, 24 October 1994.

6. Bush was a former CIA director and under his watch a whole range of similar CIA drug-trafficking operations occurred. See Jonathan Marshall, *Drug Wars: Corruption, Counterinsurgency, and Covert Operations in the Third World* (Forestville, CA: Cohen and Cohen Publishers, 1991), 41, 46.

7. See Geri Smith, "Mexico's Drug Problems are also NAFTA's," *Business Week,* 10 March 1997.

8. Gary Webb, "America's 'Crack' Plague Has Roots in Nicaragua War," *San Jose Mercury News,* 18 August 1996.

9. Blandon sold automatic weapons and sophisticated communications equipment to Ross and his partner. He even tried to sell them a grenade launcher. See Gary Webb, "Testimony Links U.S. to Drugs-Guns Trade," *San Jose Mercury News*, 19 August 1996.

10. Webb, "America's 'Crack' Plague."

11. Douglas Farah, "Drug Dealer Depicted as Contra Fund-Raiser," *Washington Post*, 6 October 1996.

12. Ibid.

13. Doyle McManus, "Examining Charges of CIA Role in Crack Sales," *Los Angeles Times*, 12 October 1996.

14. Gary Webb, "Shadowy Origins of 'Crack' Epidemic," *San Jose Mercury News,* 19 August 1996.

15. Ibid.

16. Ibid.

17. McManus, "CIA Role in Crack Sales."

18. Brian Freemantle, *The Fix* (New York: Tom Doherty Associates, 1985), 32.

19. Henrik Kruger, *The Great Heroin Coup* (Boston: South End Press, 1980), 14, 31.

20. Alfred W. McCoy, *The Politics of Heroin: CIA Complicity in the Global Drug Trade* (New York: Lawrence Hill and Co., 1991), 18.

21. Kruger, *The Great Heroin Coup*, 89.

22. McCoy, *The Politics of Heroin*, 25.

23. Ibid., 19.

24. Ibid.

25. Ibid., 437.

26. Ibid., 438.

27. Ibid., 439.

28. Ibid., 478.

29. Jonathan Marshall, "Drugs and U.S. Foreign Policy," *Dealing With Drugs,* (Pacific Research Institute, 1987) , 166.

30. McCoy, *The Politics of Heroin*, 483.

31. U.S. Senate Subcommittee on Terrorism, Narcotics, and International Operations of the Committee on Foreign Relations, , *Drugs, Law Enforcement, and Foreign Policy,* December 1988, 36.

32. Ibid.

33. Ibid.

34. David E. Early, "MN Series Stirs National Debate," *San Jose Mercury News,* 6 October 1995.

35. Ibid.

36. Michael Tonry, "Race and the War on Drugs," *University of Chicago Legal Forum,* (1994): 144.

37. Omnibus Anti-Drug Abuse Act of 1988, Public Law No. 100-690.

38. Bureau of Justice Statistics, Department of Justice, "Drugs, Crime, and the Justice System," national report, December 1992, 24.

39. U.S. Sentencing Commission, monitoring data files, 1 April-1 July 1992. This was a representative sampling of all drug cases for FY 1992.

40. See "C.I.A., Crack, the Media," *The Nation,* 2 June 1997.

41. Jesse Katz, "Deposed King of Crack; Now Free after 5 Years in Prison, This Master Marketer was Key to the Drug's Spread in L.A.," *Los Angeles Times,* 20 December 1994.

42. Ibid.

43. Walter Pincus, "A Long History of Drug Allegations," *Washington Post,* 4 October 1996.

44. Geneva Overholser, "The CIA, Drugs, and the Press," *Washington Post,* 10 November 1996

45. See Michael A. Fletcher, "Conspiracy Theories Can Often Ring True," *Washington Post,* 4 October 1996.

46. Letter from Representative Maxine Waters to Attorney General Janet Reno, 30 August 1996.

47. See letter from Senator Barbara Boxer to CIA Director John Deutch, 29 August 1996, and letter from Senator Dianne Feinstein to Attorney General Janet Reno, 30 August 1996.

48. Peter Kornbluh, "CIA, Contras, and Crack," *JaxFax,* 10 October 1996.

49. Natalie Hopkinson, "Law Students Protest CIA-Crack Scandal," *The Hilltop,* 4 October 1996, 1.

50. Early, "MN Series Stirs Debate."

51. Ibid.

52. "CIA Official Sees No Evidence of Crack Role," *New York Times,* 24 October 1994.

53. Jerry Ceppos, "To readers of our 'Dark Alliance' series," *San Jose Mercury News,* 11 May 1997.

54. Ibid.

55. Ibid.

56. Ibid.

57. See Georg Hodel, "Hung Out to Dry: 'Dark Alliance' Series Dies," http://www.delve.com/confl.html.

9. The Souls of White Folk

1. Kimberlé Williams Crenshaw, "Color-blind Dreams and Racial Nightmares: Reconfiguring Racism in the Post-Civil Rights Era," in *Birth of a Nation 'hood,* eds. Toni Morrison and Claudia Brodsky Lacour (New York: Pantheon, 1997), 110.

2. See Richard J. Herrnstein and Charles Murray, *The Bell Curve: Intelligence and Class Structure in American Life* (New York: The Free Press, 1994); Dinesh D'Souza, *The End of Racism* (New York: The Free Press, 1995).

3. Richard Morin, "A Distorted Image of Minorities: Poll Suggests That What Whites Think They See May Affect Beliefs," *Washington Post,* 8 October 1995.

4. Ibid.

5. Haya El Nasser, "Poll: Whites Increasingly Accept Blacks," *USA Today,* 11 June 1997.

6. Ibid.

7. "Resources on Eugenics and Racist IQ Theories," *RaceFile,* May-June 1996, 34. See *Wall Street Journal,* 13 December 1996, for a long list of scholars who advocate racist theories regarding intelligence and genetics.

8. Ibid.

9. Patricia J. Williams, "Apologia Qua Amnesia," *The Nation,* 14 July 1997, 10.

10. See Martin Luther King, Jr., "Letter from a Birmingham Jail," in *A Testament of Hope,* 289-302.

11. Ibid.

12. See President Bill Clinton, University of California at San Diego commencement speech, 14 June 1997.

13. Crenshaw, "Color-blind Dreams," 105

14. Clinton, UC-San Diego commencement speech.

15. Randall Kennedy, "Where Do We Go from Here?" *Washington Post,* 15 June 1997.

16. Clinton, UC San Diego commencement speech.

17. Senator Bill Bradley speech in Los Angeles, "Race Relations in America, 11 January 1996.

18. Ibid.

19. Ibid.

20. Ibid.

10. Old Stories from the New South

1. Anne Eckman, "AFDC on the Block," *Southern Exposure,* Fall 1996, 8.

2. Sarah Anderson and Karen Harris, "After NAFTA," *Southern Exposure,* Fall 1996, 13.

3. John Zippert, "Not One More Acre," *Christian Social Action,* October 1994, 36.

4. Ibid.

5. Ibid. 37.

6. Ibid.

7. Michael A. Fletcher, "Black Farmers Allege Racism at USDA," *Washington Post,* 11 December 1996.

8. See Mark Hosenball, "Arkansas Gothic," *The New Republic,* 3 August 1992, 14-6; and James Risen and Edwin Chen, "Clinton's Ties to Controversial Medical Examiner Questioned," *Los Angeles Times,* 19 May 1992.

9. Geraldine Wilson, "Sticks and Stones and Racial Slurs Do Hurt: The Word Nigger is What's Not Allowed," in *Children, Race and Racism* (New York: Racism and Sexism Resource Center for Education, 1980), 16.

10. Marilyn Kern-Foxworth, *Aunt Jemima, Uncle Ben, and Rastus: Blacks in Advertising, Yesterday, Today, and Tomorrow* (Westport, CT: Praeger Publishers, 1994), 30.

11. Richard Merelman, *Representing Black Culture: Racial Conflict and Cultural Politics in the United States* (New York: Routledge, 1995), 3.

12. "Kentucky Faces Tradition of Offensive Road Names," *New York Times,* 11 November 1996.

13. "Church Fires Still Worry Task Force," *USA Today,* 17 January 1997.

14. See Center for Democratic Renewal "Black Church Burnings, Fire Bombings, Vandalism: January 1990–April 1996."

15. "Church Fires Still Worry Task Force," *USA Today,* 17 January 1997.

16. "Evangelicals Urged to Speak against Burning of Churches," *San Francisco Chronicle,* 18 June 1996.

17. "Confederate Group Inducts First Black," *Washington Post,* 20 January 1997.

18. Phillip Rawls, "Alabama Candidate Argues Slavery is Justified," *Buffalo News,* 10 May 1996.

19. "Retiring Old Virginny," *Washington Post,* 1 February 1997.

20. "In Fact…," *The Nation,* 27 May 1996, 7.

11. Of Louis Farrakhan and Others

1. Louis R. Harlan, *Booker T. Washington: The Making of a Black Leader, 1856-1901* (New York: Oxford University Press, 1972), 218.

2. See W.E.B Du Bois, *The Souls of Black Folk* (New York: Penguin, 1989).

3. See John Hope Franklin, *From Slavery to Freedom: A History of Negro Americans* (New York: Alfred Knopf, 1974).

4. Mattias Gardell, *In the Name of Elijah Muhammad: Louis Farrakhan and the Nation of Islam* (Durham, NC: Duke University Press, 1996), 142.

5. Ibid., 143.

6. Salim Muwakkil, "Why Did the Force of the Million Man March Stall."

7. Adolph Reed, Jr., "The Rise of Louis Farrakhan," *The Nation,* 21 January 1991, 56.

8. Ibid., 56.

9. See Wilson Jeremiah Moses, *The Golden Age of Black Nationalism, 1850-1925* (New York: Oxford University Press, 1978); and Raymond L. Hall, *Black Separatism in the United States* (Hanover, NH: University Press of New England, 1978).

10. See Allan Austin, *African Muslims in Antebellum America* (New York: Garland Publishing), 1997.

11. Ibid.

12. See C. Eric Lincoln, *The Black Muslims in America* (Trenton, NJ: Africa World Press), 1994.

13. Henry Louis Gates, "The Charmer," *The New Yorker,* 29 April and 6 May 1996, 125.

14. Michael Eric Dyson, *Race Rules: Navigating the Color Line* (Reading, MA: Addison-Wesley, 1996), 165.

15. Gardell, *In the Name of Elijah*, 82.

16. Ibid., 369.

17. Ibid., 100.

18. Ibid., 101.

19. Ibid., 123.

20. Ellen Hume, "Race Rhetoric Puts Farrakhan in Spotlight in Jesse Jackson Camp," *The Wall Street Journal*, 26 April 1984.

21. Gardell, *In the Name of Elijah*, 318.

22. Armstrong is a black conservative who made this comment about Louis Farrakhan's self-help message. Robert Novak, "Standing Behind Words on Farrakhan," *Buffalo News*, 27 March 1997.

23. Robert Novak, "Farrakhan is Knocking on GOP's Door," *Buffalo News*, 7 March 1997.

24. Ibid.

25. Ibid.

26. Manning Marable, "Toward a New Dialogue about Race,", http://www.tbwt.com /views/manning/default.htm.

27. "Day of Resistance against Neo-Nazis," *New Solidarity,* 5 March 1985.

28. "LaRouchians Feint to the 'Left,'" *The Monitor,* March 1991, 14.

29. Benjamin F. Chavis, "LaRouche Invades Black Community," *New York Voice,* 2 August 1986, 1.

30. Manning Marable, "The Million Man March: One Year Later, Part Two," http://www.columbia.edu/cu/iraas/million2.html.

31. Steven A. Holmes, "Farrakhan's Angry World Tour Brings Harsh Criticism at Home," *New York Times,* 22 February 1996.

32. Ibid.

33. Gregory Kane and Gilbert Lewthwaite, "Horror in Village Haunted by Slavery," *Baltimore Sun,* 17 June 1996; and Gregory Kane and Gibert Lewthwaithe, "Brothers Down Here...Are in Darkness," *Baltimore Sun,* 17 June 1996.

12. Beyond Patriachy and Conservative Nationalism

1. See Henry Louis Gates, *Colored People: A Memoir* (New York: Knopf, 1994), and Clifton L. Taubert, *Once Upon a Time When We Were Colored* (Tulsa, OK: Council Oak Books, 1989).

2. Adolph Reed, Jr., "Dangerous Dreams: Black Boomers Wax Nostalgic for the Days of Jim Crow," *Village Voice,* 16 April 1996, 27.

3. E. Frances White, "Africa on My Mind: Gender, Counterdiscourse, and African American Nationalism," in *Words of Fire: An Anthology of African-American Feminist Thought,* ed. Beverly Guy-Sheftall.(New York: New Press, 1995), 511.

4. See Nikol G. Alexander, "Selling Black: Black Public Intellectuals and the Commercialization of Black and Black Feminist Studies (Or, Race, Class, and Gender Go to Market) unpublished paper; and Nikol G. Alexander, "A World Without Feminism?: Reading Gender In(to) Nationalist Politics, " unpublished paper.

5. The Wellington Group, at one point, had worked in partnership with the Nation of Islam in POWER, one of the NOI's businesses. This author was one of the co-ordinators of the Howard/Wellington survey.

6. Martin Kilson, "The Interaction of the Black Mainstream Leadership and the Farrakhan Extremists," in *MultiAmerica: Essays on Cultural Wars and Cultural Peace,* ed. Ishmael Reed (New York: Viking Press, 1997), 245.

7. Maulana Karenga, "The Million Man March/Day of Absence Mission Statement," *The Black Scholar,* Fall 1995, 3.

8. Adolph Reed, Jr, "Whatever the March May Mean, Farrakhan is Not the Answer," *Ledger-Enquirer,* 29 October 1995.

9. Julianne Malveaux, "Not a 'He Thing' But a 'We Thing,'" *CommonQuest,* Spring 1996, 30.

10. Pauline Terrelonge, "Feminist Consciousness and Black Women," in *Words of Fire,* ed. Beverly Guy-Sheftall (New York: New Press, 1995), 496–8 .

11. Donald Muhammad, "The Role of the Black Woman in the Million Man March," *News Dimension,* 11 August 1995, 7.

12. Michel Marriott, "Black Women are Split over All-Male March on Washington," *New York Times,* 14 October 1995.

13. Kalamu Ya Salaam, "A Million is Just a Beginning," in *Million Man March/Day of Atonement: A Commemorative Anthology: Speeches, Commentary, Photography, Poetry, Illustrations, Documents,* ed. Haki Madhubuti and Maulana Karenga (Chicago: Third World Press, 1995), 110.

14. Ibid.

15. Keith Boykin, Dennis Holmes, and Steve Walker, "The Million Man March: What about Us?," position statement, National Black Gay and Lesbian Leadershi-Forum, 24 September 1995.

16. Ibid.

17. Ibid.

18. See Cornel West, *Race Matters* (Boston: Beacon Press, 1994); and Cornel West, "Nihilism in Black America," *Dissent,* Spring 1991.

19. Peniel E. Joseph, "'Black' Reconstructed: White Supremacy in Post-Civil Rights America, *The Black Scholar,* Fall 1995, 55.

20. Stephen Steinberg, *Turning Back: The Retreat from Racial Justice in American Thought and Policy* (Boston: Beacon Press, 1995), 130.

21 Michael Eric Dyson, "Redeeming Black Manhood," *CommonQuest,* Spring 1996, 30.

22. Ibid.

23. Ibid., 31.

24. Barbara Ransby, "Sexism in the March," *The Miami Herald,* 12 October 1995.

25. Malveaux, "Not a 'He Thing' but a 'We Thing,'" 30.

26. Ibid., 29

27. Ibid., 29.

28. Mary Frances Berry, "I Have Not Endorsed the March," *Washington Post,* 10 October 1995.

29. Robin D.G. Kelley, "The Million Man March: Beyond Self-help," *WeSpeak!,* Winter 1995, 12.

30. Major R. Owens, "Statement of Congressman Major R. Owens on the October 16th Million Man March," press statement, 16 October 1995, 1–2.

31. Marriott, "Black Women are Split."

32. Ibid.

33. Herb Boyd, "Farrakhan: 'This is Time of Doom,'" *Amsterdam News,* 19 October 1996, 1.

34. See Jehron Hunter, "Ben Chavis Fumbles First Interview as Muslim Minister," *News Dimension,* 21 February 1997, 4.

35. See Ron Daniels, "Vantage Point: Million Man March, NAALS Fail to Fulfill Expectations," http://www.tbwt.com/view/rd/index.html.

36. Martin Luther King, Jr., "Where Do We Go From Here: Chaos or Community?" in *A Testament of Hope: The Essential Writings and Speeches of Martin Luther King, Jr.,* ed. James M. Washington (New York: HarperCollins, 1986), 617. 37. Ibid., 621.

38. Ibid., 630.

39. Anne McClintock, "The Angel of Progress: Pitfalls of the Term 'Post-Colonialism,'" *Social Text,* No. 31-2 (1992), 91–2.

Selected Bibliography

Alexander, Nikol G., "Selling Black: Black Public Intellectuals and the Commercialization of Black and Black Feminist Studies (Or, Race, Class, and Gender Go to Market)," unpublished paper.

_____, "A World Without Feminism?: Reading Gender In(to) Nationalist Politics," unpublished paper.

Anderson, Sarah and John Cavanagh, *The Top 200: The Rise of Global Corporate Power,* Institute for Policy Studies paper, September 25, 1996.

Asante, Molefi, *The Afrocentric Idea* (Philadelphia: Temple University Press, 1987).

Austin, Allan, *African Muslims in Antebellum America* (New York: Garland Publishing, 1997).

Baldwin, James, "If Black English Isn't A Language, Then Tell Me What Is?," in James Baldwin, *The Price of the Ticket: Collected Nonfiction, 1948-1985* (New York: St. Martin's/Marek, 1985).

Barber, Benjamin R., *Jihad vs. McWorld: How the Planet is Both Falling Apart and Coming Together and What This Means for Democracy* (Toronto: Times Books, 1995).

Barlett, Donald L. and James B. Steele, *America: Who Stole the Dream* (Kansas City, MO: Andrews and McNeel, 1996).

Barnet, Richard and John Cavanagh, *Global Dreams: Imperial Corporations and the New World Order* (New York: Simon & Schuster, 1994).

Brecher, Jeremy and Tim Costello, *Global Village or Global Pillage?: Economic Reconstruction from the Bottom Up* (Boston: South End Press, 1994).

Burnett, Robert, *Global Jukebox: The International Music Industry* (New York: Routledge, 1996).

California Senate Office of Research, "Taking a Look at Affirmative Action," report, January 19, 1995.

Carnoy, Martin, *Faded Dreams: The Politics and Economics of Race in America* (New York: University of Cambridge Press, 1994).

Crenshaw, Kimberlé Williams, "Color-blind Dreams and Racial Nightmares: Reconfiguring Racism in the Post-Civil Rights Era," in Toni Morrison and Claudia Brodsky Lacour, eds., *Birth of a Nation 'hood* (New York: Pantheon, 1997).

Danaher, Kevin, ed., *Corporations Are Gonna Get Your Mama: Globalization and Downsizing of the American Dream* (Monroe, ME: Common Courage Press, 1996).

Dillard, J.L., *Black English: Its History and Usage in the United States* (New York: Vintage, 1973).

D'Souza, Dinesh, *The End of Racism* (New York: The Free Press, 1995).

Du Bois, W.E.B., *The Souls of Black Folk* (New York: Penguin, 1989).

DuCille, Anne, *Skin Trade* (Cambridge: Harvard University Press, 1996).

Dyson, Michael Eric, *Race Rules: Navigating the Color Line* (Reading, MA: Addison-Wesley Publishers, 1996).

Edwards, Harry, *The Revolt of the Black Athlete* (New York: Free Press, 1969).

Freemantle, Brian, *The Fix* (New York: Tom Doherty Associates, 1985).

Gardell, Mattias, *In the Name of Elijah Muhammad: Louis Farrakhan and the Nation of Islam* (Durham, NC: Duke University Press, 1996).

Gates, Bill, *The Road Ahead* (New York: Viking, 1995).

Gates, Henry Louis, *Colored People: A Memoir* (New York: Knopf, 1994).

General Accounting Office, "Displacement Rate, Unemployment Spells, and Reemployment Wages by Race," Washington, D.C., September 1994.

Giddens, Anthony, *The Consequences of Modernity* (Stanford: Stanford University Press, 1990).

Graham, Julie, "Multinational Corporations and the Internationalization of Production: An Industry Perspective," in G. Epstein, J. Graham, and J. Newbhard, eds., *Creating a New World Economy* (Philadelphia: Temple University Press).

Greider, William, *One World, Ready or Not: The Manic Logic of Global Capitalism* (New York: Simon & Schuster, 1997).

Grossman, Lawrence, *The Electronic Republic* (New York: Viking, 1995).

Guy-Sheftall, Beverly, ed., *Words of Fire: An Anthology of African-American Feminist Thought* (New York: The New Press, 1995).

Harlan, Louis R., *Booker T. Washington: The Making of a Black Leader, 1856-1901* (New York: Oxford University Press, 1972).

Harrison, Bennett, *Lean and Mean: The Changing Landscape of Corporate Power in the Age of Flexibility* (New York: Basic Books, 1994).

Henry, Lester, *NAFTA and GATT: World Trade Policy Impacts on African Americans* (New York: Du Bois Bunche Center for Public Policy, 1995).

Herrnstein, Richard J. and Charles Murray, *The Bell Curve: Intelligence and Class Structure in American Life* (New York: The Free Press, 1994).

Higginbotham, A. Leon, Jr., Aderson Bellegarde Francois, and Linda Y. Yuch, "The O.J. Simpson Trial: Who Was Improperly 'Playing the Race Card'?" in Toni Morrison and Claudia Brodsky Lacour, eds., *Birth of a Nation 'hood* (New York: Pantheon, 1997).

Hoberman, John, *Darwin's Athletes: How Sport Has Damaged Black America and Preserved the Myth of Race* (Boston: Houghton Mifflin Company, 1997).

Hoover, Gary, Alta Campbell, and Patrick J. Spain, eds., *Hoover's Handbook of American Business, 1994* (Austin, TX: The Reference Press, 1993).

International Labor Organization, "Employment in the World, 1996/1997," report, United Nations, 1997.

Johnson, Leola and David Roediger, "'Hertz, Don't It?': Becoming Colorless and Staying Black in the Crossover of O.J. Simpson," in Toni Morrison and Claudia Brodsky Lacour, eds., *Birth of a Nation 'hood* (New York: Pantheon, 1997).

Jones, Charles, ed., *The Black Panther Party Reconsidered* (Baltimore: Black Classic Press, 1997).

Kamel, Rachel, *The Global Factory: Analysis and Action for a New Economic Era* (Philadelphia: American Friends Service Committee, 1990).

Kern-Foxworth, Marilyn, *Aunt Jemima, Uncle Ben, and Rastus: Blacks in Advertising, Yesterday, Today, and Tomorrow* (Westport, CT: Praeger Publishers, 1994).

King, Martin Luther, Jr. in James M. Washington, ed., *A Testament of Hope: The Essential Writings of Martin Luther King, Jr.* (New York: HarperCollins, 1986).

Korten, David C., *When Corporations Rule the World* (West Hartford, CT: Kumarian Press, 1995).

Kruger, Henrik, *The Great Heroin Coup* (Boston: South End Press, 1980).

The Labor Institute, *Corporate Power and the American Dream* (New York: The Labor Institute, 1994).

Labov, William, *Language in the Inner City: Studies in the Black English Vernacular* (Philadelphia: University of Pennsylvania Press, 1972).

Lee, Thea M. "The Likely Impact of NAFTA on Women and Minorities," testimony before the Employment, Housing and Aviation Subcommittee of the U.S. House Committee on Government Operations, U.S. House of Representatives, November 10, 1993.

Lemelle, Sidney and Robin D.G. Kelley, *Imagining Home: Class, Culture, and Nationalism in the African Diaspora* (New York: Verso, 1994).

Lincoln, C. Eric, *The Black Muslims in America* (Trenton, NJ: Africa World Press, 1994.).

Mander, Jerry and Edward Goldsmith, eds., *The Case Against Globalization: And for a Turn Toward the Local* (San Francisco: Sierra Club Books, 1996).

Marshall, Jonathan, "Drugs & U.S. Foreign Policy," *Dealing With Drugs*, Pacific Research Institute, 1987.

_____, *Drug Wars: Corruption, Counterinsurgency and Covert Operations in the Third World* (Forestville, CA: Cohan and Cohen Publishers, 1991).

McCoy, Alfred W., *The Politics of Heroin: CIA Complicity in the Global Drug Trade* (New York: Lawrence Hill and Co., 1991).

McLean, Polly E., "Mass Communications, Popular Culture, and Racism," in Benjamin P. Bowser, ed., *Racism and Anti-Racism in World Perspectve* (Thousand Oaks, CA: Sage Publications, 1995).

McRae, Patricia and David J. Ackerman, "The Illegal Narcotics Trade (INT) as a TNC: Implications for the TNC/Government Interface," paper presented at the 1993 American Political Science Association, Washington, D.C.

Merelman, Richard, *Representing Black Culture: Racial Conflict and Cultural Politics in the United States* (New York: Routledge, 1995).

Owens, Major R., "Statement of Congressman Major R. Owens on the October 16th Million Man March," press statement, October 16, 1995.

Reich, Robert B., *The Work of Nations: Preparing Ourselves for 21st Century Capitalism* (New York: Vintage Books, 1992).

Rifkin, Jeremy, *The End of Work: The Decline of the Global Labor Force and the Dawn of the Post-Market Era* (New York: Putnam Books, 1995).

Rosenman, Samuel I., *The Public Papers and Addresses of Franklin D. Roosevelt* (New York: Harper & Row, 1950).

Smith, Robert C., *Racism in the Post-Civil Rights Era: Now You See It, Now You Don't* (Albany, NY: State University of New York, 1995).

Stoller, Paul, ed., *Black American English: Its Background and Its Usage in the Schools and Literature* (New York: Dell, 1975).

Strasser, J.B. and Laurie Becklund, *Swoosh: The Unauthorized Story of Nike and the Men Who Played There* (New York: HarperBusiness, 1993).

Taulbert, Clifton, *Once Upon a Time When We Were Colored* (Tulsa, OK: Council Oak Books, 1989).

Terrelonge, Pauline, "Feminist Consciousness and Black Women," in Beverly Guy-Sheftall, ed., *Words of Fire: An Anthology of African-American Feminist Thought* (New York: The New Press, 1995).

Thurow, Lester C., *The Future of Capitalism: How Today's Economic Forces Shape Tomorrow's World* (New York: William Morrow and Company, 1996).

U.S. Census Bureau, "Black-Owned Businesses Up 46 Percent Over Five Years, Census Bureau Survey Shows," press release, December 12, 1995.

_____, "New York Metro Area Leads List for Black-Owned Firms, Los Angeles Tops in Women-Owned Businesses, Census Bureau Reports," press release, March 16, 1996.

_____, "Number of Minority-Owned Businesses and Revenues Increase Substantially Between 1987 and 1992, Census Bureau Reports, press release, November 18, 1996.

U.S. Department of Justice, Office of Justice Programs,"Correctional Populations in the United States, 1994," *Bureau of Justice Statistics Executive Summary.*

U.S. Senate Subcommittee on Terrorism, Narcotics, and International Operations of the Committee on Foreign Relations, "Drugs, Law Enforcement, and Foreign Policy," December 1988.

United Nations Development Program, *Human Development Report 1992* (New York: United Nations, 1992).

Van Deburg, William L., *New Day in Babylon: The Black Power Movement and American Culture, 1965-1975* (Chicago: University of Chicago Press, 1993).

West, Cornel, *Race Matters* (Boston, MA: Beacon Press, 1993).

Wiggins, David K., "Critical Events Affecting Racism in Athletics," in Dana Brooks and Ronald Althouse, eds., *Racism in College Athletics: The African American Athlete's Experience* (Morgantown, WV: Fitness Information Technology, Inc., 1993).

Wilhelm, Sidney, *Who Needs the Negro?* (Cambridge, MA: Schenkman, 1970).

Williams, Patricia J., "Disorder in the House: The New World Order and the Socioeconomic Status of Women," in Stanlie M. James and Abena P.A. Busia, eds., *Theorizing Black Feminisms: The Visionary Pragmatism of Black Women* (New York: Routledge, 1993).

Williams, Robert L., ed., *Ebonics: The True Language of Black Folks* (St. Louis: Institute of Black Studies, 1975).

Wilson, Geraldine, "Sticks and Stones and Racial Slurs Do Hurt: The Word Nigger Is What's Not Allowed," in *Children, Race and Racism* (New York: Racism and Sexism Resource Center for Education, 1980).

Wilson, William Julius, *When Work Disappears: The World of the New Urban Poor* (New York: Alfred A. Knopf, 1996).

Index

About South End Press

South End Press is a nonprofit, collectively run book publisher with over 200 titles in print. Since our founding in 1977, we have tried to meet the needs of readers who are exploring, or are already committed to, the politics of radical social change. Our goal is to publish books that encourage critical thinking and constructive action on the key political, cultural, social, economic, and ecological issues shaping life in the United States and in the world. In this way, we hope to give expression to a wide diversity of democratic social movements and to provide an alternative to the products of corporate publishing.

Through the Institute for Social and Cultural Change, South End Press works with other political media projects—*Z Magazine*; Speakout, a speakers' bureau; Alternative Radio; and the Publishers Support Project—to expand access to information and critical analysis. If you would like a free catalog of South End Press books, please write to us at: South End Press, 116 Saint Botolph Street, Boston, MA 02115. Visit our website at http://www.lbbs.org.

Related Titles

African Americans at the Crossroads
By Clarence Lusane

Pipe Dream Blues
By Clarence Lusane

Chaos or Community
By Holly Sklar

Black Liberation in Conservative America
By Manning Marable

Faith
Words

LARGE
PRINT

Closer to GOD

to

Each Day

365 Devotions for Everyday Living

JOYCE MEYER

Faith
Words

LARGE PRINT

Unless otherwise noted, Scriptures are taken from *The Amplified Bible* (AMP). *The Amplified Bible*, copyright © 1965, 1987 by The Zondervan Corporation. *The Amplified New* copyright © 1954, 1958, 1987 by The Lockman Foundation. Used by permission.

Scripture quotations marked (KJV) are taken from the King James Version of the Bible.

Scripture quotations marked (NASB) are taken from *The New American Standard Bible*®, copyright © 1960, 1962, 1963, 1968, 1972, 1975, 1977, 1995 by The Lockman Foundation. Used by permission.

Scripture quotations marked (NIV) are taken from the *Holy Bible: New International Version*®, copyright © 1973, 1978, 1984 by International Bible Society. Used by permission of Zondervan Publishing House. All rights reserved.

Scripture quotations marked (NKJV) are taken from the *New King James Version*. Copyright © 1979, 1980, 1982 by Thomas Nelson, Inc., Publishers.

Scripture quotations marked (NLT) are taken from the *Holy Bible*, New Living Translation, copyright © 1996. Used by permission of Tyndale House Publishers, Inc., Wheaton, Illinois 60189. All rights reserved.

FaithWords
Hachette Book Group
1290 Avenue of the Americas
New York, New York 10104

www.faithwords.com

Printed in the United States of America

RRD-C

First Edition: October 2015

10 9 8 7 6 5 4 3 2 1

FaithWords is a division of Hachette Book Group, Inc.
The FaithWords name and logo are trademarks of Hachette Book Group, Inc.

The Hachette Speakers Bureau provides a wide range of authors for speaking events. To find out more, go to www.hachettespeakersbureau.com or call (866) 376-6591.

The publisher is not responsible for websites (or their content) that are not owned by the publisher.

Library of Congress Cataloging-in-Publication Data

Meyer, Joyce, 1943–
    Closer to God each day : 365 devotions for everyday living / Joyce Meyer.
        pages cm
    ISBN 978-1-4555-1736-7 (hardcover)—ISBN 978-1-4555-3629-0 (hardcover large print)—
ISBN 978-1-4789-6035-5 (audio cd)—ISBN 978-1-4789-0832-6 (audio playaway)—
ISBN 978-1-4789-6036-2 (audio download)—ISBN 978-1-4555-1735-0 (ebook)
1.   Devotional calendars.   I. Title.
    BV4811.M443 2015
    242'.2—dc23

2015028605

Come close to God and He will come close to you.
JAMES 4:8

Introduction

As I read through the Word of God, one of the most encouraging things I see is that God desires to be in a close relationship with His people. From the very first chapters in the Garden of Eden to the last pages of Revelation, we see God reaching out to His people in order that we might live in intimate fellowship with Him.

Too many people today think of God as distant, uncaring, and out-of-reach. At best, they assume He is uninterested in them; at worst, they fear He is angry with them. But this isn't the God we see in Scripture. The

Bible shows us that God is present in our circumstances. God spoke to Moses. He strengthened David. He provided for Ruth. He chose Mary. He walked with the disciples. He wept over Jerusalem. He forgave the thief on the cross. He gave Peter a second chance. He sent the Holy Spirit.

God isn't removed from your daily life. He sees what you're going through, and He wants to help you every step of the way.

That's why I've written this daily devotional. My desire is that each day you will be encouraged and strengthened by the truths, promises, and scriptures on each page. No matter what situation you are facing, I pray that each and every day you will be reminded that God loves you, He has a great plan for your life, and He is closer than you think.

—*Joyce Meyer*

Closer
to GOD
Each Day

Simple, Believing Prayer

And when you pray, do not heap up phrases (multiply words, repeating the same ones over and over) as the Gentiles do, for they think they will be heard for their much speaking.

MATTHEW 6:7

I was dissatisfied with my prayer life for many years. I was committed to praying every morning, but I always felt something was missing. I finally asked God what was wrong, and He responded in my heart by saying, "Joyce, you don't feel that your prayers are good enough." I wasn't enjoying prayer because I had no confidence that my prayers were acceptable.

Too often we get caught up in our own works concerning prayer. Sometimes we try to pray so long, loud, or fancy that we lose sight of the fact that prayer is really

just conversation with God. The length or loudness or eloquence of our prayer is not the issue. The only important elements to prayer are the sincerity of our hearts and a confidence that God hears and will answer us.

We can be confident that even if we simply say, "God help me," He hears and will answer. We can depend on God to be faithful to do what we have asked Him to do as long as our request is in accordance with His will.

———

Simple, believing prayer comes straight out of the heart and goes straight to the heart of God.

I Will Not Quit

I have strength for all things in Christ Who empowers me [I am ready for anything and equal to anything through Him Who infuses inner strength into me; I am self-sufficient in Christ's sufficiency].   PHILIPPIANS 4:13

So often, someone will come to me for advice and prayer, and when I tell them what the Word of God says, or what I think the Holy Spirit is saying, their response is, "I know that's right; God has been showing me the same thing. But, Joyce, it's just too hard." This is one of the most commonly expressed excuses I hear from people.

When I initially started reading in the Word of God about how I could become more like Jesus, and then compared it to where I was, I also said, "I want to do things Your way, God, but it is so hard."

God graciously showed me this is a lie the enemy tries to inject into our minds to get us to give up. But God's commandments are never too difficult for us to follow if we do them through Christ's strength.

Walking in obedience to God is not too hard because He has given us His Spirit to work in us powerfully and to help us in all He has asked of us (John 14:16). He is in us and with us all the time to enable us to do what we cannot do, and to do with ease what would be hard without Him!

Things get hard when we try to do them independently without leaning on and relying on God's grace.

Expect to Receive

*And therefore the Lord [earnestly] waits
[expecting, looking, and longing] to be
gracious to you; and therefore He lifts
Himself up, that He may have mercy on
you and show loving-kindness to you.
For the Lord is a God of justice. Blessed
(happy, fortunate, to be envied) are all
those who [earnestly] wait for Him,
who expect and look and long for Him
[for His victory, His favor, His love,
His peace, His joy, and His matchless,
unbroken companionship]!*

ISAIAH 30:18

I want you to get this firmly into your
heart: You can think about what you think
about! So many people's problems are rooted
in thinking patterns that end up producing the problems they experience. Remember that your actions are the direct result

of your thoughts. And although the enemy offers wrong thinking to everyone, you don't need to accept his offer.

Isaiah 30:18 has become one of my favorite scriptures. If you will meditate on it, it will begin to bring you great hope... and great power. In it, God is saying that He is looking for someone to be gracious (good) to, but it cannot be someone with a sour attitude and a negative mind. It must be someone who is expecting for God to be good to him or her.

The more you change your mind for the better, the more your life will also change for the better. When you begin to see God's plan for you in your thinking, you will begin to walk in it.

The mind is the leader or forerunner of all attitudes and actions. You can always expect good things from God!

By Your Fruit

Even so, every healthy (sound) tree bears good fruit [worthy of admiration], but the sickly (decaying, worthless) tree bears bad (worthless) fruit.   MATTHEW 7:17

The fruit in our lives (our behavior) comes from somewhere. A person who is angry is that way for a reason. His reaction is the bad fruit of a bad tree with bad roots. It is important for us to take a close and honest look at our fruit as well as our roots.

In my own life, there was a lot of bad fruit. I experienced regular bouts of depression, negativity, self-pity, a quick temper, and the chip-on-the-shoulder syndrome. I was harsh, rigid, legalistic, and judgmental. I held grudges and was fearful.

I worked hard at trying to correct it. Yet it seemed that no matter what kind of bad behavior I tried to get rid of, two or

three others popped up somewhere else like weeds. I was not getting to the hidden root of the problem, and it would not die.

If this scenario sounds familiar to you, it may be that you have unresolved issues in your life that need to be searched out and removed so that everything can be made fresh and new. Don't run away. If God can change me, He certainly can change you.

———

Rotten fruit comes from rotten roots; good fruit comes from good roots.

Receive God's Love

... God's love has been poured out in our hearts through the Holy Spirit Who has been given to us. ROMANS 5:5

The Bible teaches us that the love of God has been poured out in our hearts by the Holy Spirit Who has been given to us. That simply means that when the Lord, in the person of the Holy Spirit, comes to dwell in our heart because of our faith in His Son Jesus Christ, He brings love with Him, because God is love (1 John 4:8).

It's important to ask what we are doing with the love of God that has been freely given to us. Are we rejecting it because we don't think we are valuable enough to be loved? Do we believe God is like other people who have rejected and hurt us? Or are we receiving His love by faith, believing

that He is greater than our failures and weaknesses?

With God's help, we can love ourselves—not in a selfish, self-centered way that produces a lifestyle of self-indulgence, but in a balanced, godly way, a way that simply affirms God's creation as essentially good and right.

God's plan is this: for us to receive His love, love ourselves in a godly way, generously love Him in return, and then love all the people who come into our lives.

———

When God reaches out to love us, He is attempting to start a cycle that will bless not only us but also many others.

God Is for You

What then shall we say to [all] this? If God is for us, who [can be] against us? [Who can be our foe, if God is on our side?]   ROMANS 8:31

God is a big God; nothing is impossible with Him. We have nothing to fear from our enemies because none of them are as great as our God.

God is for us; He is on our side. The devil has one position—he is against us. But God is over us, under us, through us, for us, and He surrounds us. Of whom, then, should we be afraid?

So like Mount Zion, we should never be moved because God is all around us. And if that wasn't enough, I saved the best until last: He is in us, and He said that He will never leave us or forsake us.

Salvation is our most awesome blessing

from God, and we have been given the Helper, the Holy Spirit Himself, to empower us to be like Jesus. God has blessings and spiritual power in abundance for us. He is powerful and mighty and able to do what we can never do on our own.

God desires that we let the Holy Spirit flow through us in power to show people His love and to help people with His gifts. It all centers in Him.

God chooses the weak and foolish things of this world, on purpose, so that people may look at them and say, "It has to be God!"

Putting Your Trust in the Right Place

*Some trust in and boast of chariots and
some of horses, but we will trust in and
boast of the name of the Lord our God.*

PSALM 20:7

There are many facets of faith. The most
brilliant facet, however, is trust! Trust is
something we have, and we decide what to
do with it. We decide in whom or in what
to put our trust.

Where have you placed your trust? Is
your trust in your job, employer, bank
account, or friends? Perhaps your trust is
in yourself, your past record of successes,
education, natural talents, or possessions.
All of these are temporal, subject to change.
Only the Lord changes not. He alone is the
Rock that cannot be moved.

As children of God, we can have the
assurance that God will deliver us in current

troubles, just as He delivered us in the past. We can then take our trust and put it in the right place, which is in God alone.

Trust is not upset, because it has entered into God's rest. Trust is not confused, because it has no need to lean on its own understanding. Trust does not give up or panic. Trust believes that God is good and that He works all things out for good!

———————

Choose to place your trust in God. It pays marvelous dividends.

The Power of Being Positive

For as he thinks in his heart, so is he.
PROVERBS 23:7

Many years ago, I was an extremely negative person. My whole philosophy was this: "If you don't expect anything good to happen, then you won't be disappointed when it doesn't." So many devastating things had happened to me over the years, I was afraid to believe anything good might happen to me. Since my thoughts were all negative, so was my mouth; therefore, so was my life.

Perhaps you're like I was. You're avoiding hope to protect yourself from being hurt. This type of behavior sets up a negative lifestyle. Everything becomes negative because your thoughts are negative.

When I really began to study the Word and to trust God to restore me, one of the first things I realized was that the

negativism had to go. And the longer I serve God, the more I realize the tremendous power in being positive in my thoughts and words.

Our actions are a direct result of our thoughts. A negative mind will result in a negative life. But if we renew our mind according to God's Word, we will, as Romans 12:2 promises, prove in our experience "the good and acceptable and perfect will of God."

It is a life-changing exercise to line up our thoughts with God's thoughts.

How to Pray without Ceasing

Pray at all times (on every occasion, in every season) in the Spirit, with all [manner of] prayer and entreaty. To that end keep alert and watch with strong purpose and perseverance, interceding in behalf of all the saints (God's consecrated people).

EPHESIANS 6:18

Most believers are pretty familiar with the King James Version of 1 Thessalonians 5:17. It says, "Pray without ceasing."

I used to wonder, *Lord, how can I ever get to the place that I am able to pray without ceasing?* To me the phrase "without ceasing" meant nonstop, without ever quitting. I couldn't see how that was possible.

Now I have a better understanding of what Paul was saying. He meant that prayer should be like breathing, something we do

continually but often unconsciously. Our physical bodies require breathing. Likewise, our spiritual life is designed to be nurtured and sustained by continual prayer.

The problem is that because of legalistic, religious thinking we have the mistaken idea that if we don't keep up a certain schedule of prayer we are missing the mark. If we become too "religious" about prayer, thinking we must do it for a certain amount of time because that is how someone else does it, we will bring condemnation on ourselves. The important lesson about prayer is not the posture or the time or place, but learning to pray your way through the day. Pray in faith, at all times, in every place.

It is the Holy Spirit Who will lead you into a life of consistent prayer.

Tell Yourself the Truth

Behold, You desire truth in the inner being; make me therefore to know wisdom in my inmost heart.

PSALM 51:6

God wants us to face the truth in our inmost being, then perhaps confess it in an appropriate manner to the right person. And sometimes we're the ones who need to hear the truth the most.

When people come to me for help in this area, I often tell them, "Go and look at yourself in the mirror and confess the problem to yourself." Being honest with yourself sets you free!

If, for instance, your problem is that your parents did not love you as a child and you are resentful and bitter, face the facts as a reality once and for all. Look at yourself in the mirror and say, "My parents did not

love me, and perhaps they never will. But God loves me, and that is enough!"

You don't have to be one of those people who spends their life trying to get something they'll never have. If you have let the fact that you were unloved ruin your life thus far, don't let it claim the rest of your life. You can do what David did. Confess to yourself: "Although my father and my mother have forsaken me, yet the Lord will take me up [adopt me as His child]" (Psalm 27:10).

Whatever the problem may be that is bothering you, face it, consider confessing it to a trusted confidant, then admit it to yourself in your inmost being.

————

Admitting the truth causes the past to lose its grip on us.

Step Out and Take a Chance

But Jesus looked at them and said, With men this is impossible, but all things are possible with God.   MATTHEW 19:26

Many people I meet want to start at point A in their Christian life, blink their eyes twice, and be at point Z. Many of them are frustrated about not knowing what their gifts are or what God has called them to do with their life. Some of them are so afraid of failing and making mistakes that it keeps them from stepping out.

We all have undeveloped potential, but we will never see it manifested until we believe that we can do whatever God says we can do in His Word. Unless we step out in faith, believing that with God nothing is impossible, He cannot do the work in us that He wants to do to develop our potential. It takes our cooperation and

willingness through faith, determination, obedience, and hard work to develop what He has put in us.

Nobody can be determined for us, but we can be determined for ourselves. If we are not determined, the devil will steal from us everything we have. I encourage you to give your potential some form by doing something with it. You will never find what you are capable of doing if you never try anything. Don't be afraid to step out into what you believe God is leading you to do. When you step out, you will find you are capable of great things.

———

Be bold, be brave, and be all you can be!

Overcoming a Poor Self-Image

God said, Let Us [Father, Son, and Holy Spirit] make mankind in Our image, after Our likeness...

GENESIS 1:26

Second Samuel nine tells the story of Mephibosheth, the grandson of King Saul and the son of Jonathan. Crippled as a youth, Mephibosheth had a poor self-image. Instead of seeing himself as the rightful heir to his father's and grandfather's legacy, he saw himself as someone who would be rejected.

When David sent for Mephibosheth, he fell down before the king and displayed fear. David told him not to fear, that he intended to show Mephibosheth kindness because of David's covenant with Jonathan. Mephibosheth's initial response is an

important example of the kind of poor self-image we all need to overcome.

A poor self-image causes us to operate in fear instead of faith. We look at what is wrong with us instead of what is right with Jesus. He has taken our wrongs and given us His righteousness (2 Corinthians 5:21). We can joyfully walk in the reality of that truth.

I love the end of the story. David blessed Mephibosheth for Jonathan's sake. He gave him servants and land and provided for all of his needs. God will bless us for Jesus' sake!

We can all relate Mephibosheth's lameness to our own weaknesses. We may also fellowship and eat with our King Jesus—despite our faults and weaknesses.

We have a covenant with God, sealed and ratified in the blood of Jesus Christ.

Winning the Warfare Within

*For we are not wrestling with flesh
and blood [contending only with
physical opponents], but against...
this present darkness, against the spirit
forces of wickedness in the heavenly
(supernatural) sphere.*

EPHESIANS 6:12

Satan wars against us and one of his tactics is to make us feel bad about ourselves. He reminds us of all our failures and weaknesses, but we need to remember that God knows all about us and He loves us anyway.

We fight many battles, but probably the greatest battle we fight is the one with ourselves. We may struggle with feeling that we should have accomplished more in life than we have; we may feel we've failed in many ways. We can't change anything by being frustrated and struggling within.

Only God can change us as we trust in Him. He will fight our battles and win. Our part is to believe, cooperate with Him, and follow the leading of the Holy Spirit.

It is difficult to get to the place where we can be honest with ourselves about our sins and failures, our inabilities and fallibilities, and yet still know that we are seen as being right with God because of what Jesus did for us when He died for us and rose from the dead. If you are at war within yourself, knowing you are the righteousness of God in Christ is a tremendous key to tapping into peace and spiritual power.

———————

We can be changed as we worship and behold God—not as we look at ourselves, adding up our many flaws.

Enjoying the Journey

But Martha [overly occupied and too busy] was distracted with much serving; and she came up to Him and said, Lord, is it nothing to You that my sister has left me to serve alone?... LUKE 10:40

I believe that life should be a celebration. Far too many believers don't even enjoy life, let alone celebrate it. Many people truly love Jesus Christ and are on their way to heaven, but very few are enjoying the trip. For many years I was one of those people... I was like Martha!

Martha was busy doing what I used to do, running around trying to make everything perfect in order to impress God and everyone else. I complicated my relationship with the Lord because I had a legalistic approach to righteousness. I only felt good about myself when I was accomplishing

something. And I resented people like Mary, who enjoyed themselves. I thought they should be working like I was working.

My problem was that I was all Martha and no Mary. I loved Jesus, but I had not learned about the simple life He desired me to live. The answer, I discovered, was rooted in faith, discovering what it means to sit at the feet of Jesus, listen to His words, and trust God with all my heart and soul.

If you want to enjoy life, learn to live in balance. Work, worship, play, and rest. All work, with nothing else, produces a person who lives a complicated, complex, joyless life.

Authority Through Prayer

I will give you the keys of the kingdom of heaven; and whatever you bind (declare to be improper and unlawful) on earth must be what is already bound in heaven; and whatever you loose (declare lawful) on earth must be what is already loosed in heaven.   MATTHEW 16:19

Since we are not only physical creatures but spiritual beings as well, we are able to stand in the physical realm and affect the spiritual realm. This is a very definite privilege and advantage. We can go into the spiritual realm through prayer and bring about action that will cause change in a situation. "God is a Spirit..." (John 4:24), and every answer we need to every situation is with Him.

Jesus told Peter that He would give him the keys to the kingdom of heaven. All keys

unlock doors, and I believe those keys (at least in part) can represent various types of prayer. Jesus went on to teach Peter about the power of binding and loosing, which operates on the same spiritual principle.

The power of binding and loosing is exercised in prayer. When you and I pray about deliverance from some bondage in our lives or in the life of another, we are, in effect, binding that problem and loosing an answer. The act of prayer binds evil and looses good.

Jesus has given us the power and authority to use the keys of the kingdom to bring to pass the will of God on earth.

All Things Work Together for Good

We are assured and know that [God being a partner in their labor] all things work together and are [fitting into a plan] for good to and for those who love God and are called according to [His] design and purpose.   ROMANS 8:28

The apostle Paul does not say that all things are good, but he does say that all things *work together for good.*

Let's say you get in your car, and it won't start. There are two ways you can look at the situation. You can say, "I knew it! It never fails. My plans always flop." Or you can say, "Well, it looks as though I can't leave right now. I'll go later when the car is fixed. In the meantime, I believe this change in plans is going to work out for my good. There is probably some reason I need

to be at home today, so I'm going to enjoy my time here."

Paul also tells us in Romans 12:16 to "readily adjust yourself to [people, things]." The idea is that we must learn to become the kind of person who plans things but who doesn't get upset if that plan doesn't work out.

The choice is ours. Any time we don't get what we want, our feelings will rise up and try to get us into self-pity and a negative attitude. Or we can adjust to the situation and go ahead and enjoy what God has for us no matter what happens.

——————

The pathway to freedom from negativity begins when we face the problem and believe God will work good out of it.

Freedom from Self-Pity

There was a certain man there who had suffered with a deep-seated and lingering disorder for thirty-eight years.

When Jesus noticed him lying there [helpless], knowing that he had already been a long time in that condition, He said to him, Do you want to become well? [Are you really in earnest about getting well?]   JOHN 5:5–6

For many, many years, "Why me, God?" was the cry of my heart, and it filled my thoughts and affected my attitude daily. I lived in the wilderness of self-pity, and it was a problem for me, my family, and the plan of God for my life. I felt as though I was due something for the way I had been mistreated as a child, but I was looking to people to pay me back when I should have been looking to God.

When Jesus met the man who had been lying by the pool of Bethesda for thirty-eight years waiting for a miracle, He asked if he was serious about getting well. Many people would like a miracle, but like the man in our story, they are not willing to give up their blame and self-pity.

God wants to give us beauty for ashes, but we must be willing to let go of the ashes! That means giving up the self-pity, blame, and bitter attitudes. This day can be a new beginning for anyone who is willing to forget the past and truly follow Jesus!

———————

We can be pitiful or powerful, but we can't be both. Choose to give up self-pity to be free.

God's Way Is Not Too Hard

When Pharaoh let the people go, God led them not by way of the land of the Philistines, although that was nearer; for God said, Lest the people change their purpose when they see war and return to Egypt.

EXODUS 13:17

God led the Children of Israel on a longer, harder route in the wilderness because He knew they were not ready for the battles they would face in order to possess the Promised Land. He needed to do a work in their lives first, teaching them Who He was and that they could not depend on themselves.

You can be assured that anywhere God leads you, He is able to keep you. He never allows more to come against us than we can bear. We do not have to live in a constant

struggle if we learn to lean on Him continually for the strength we need.

If you know God has asked you to do something, don't back down because it gets hard. When things get hard, spend more time with Him, lean more on Him, and receive more grace from Him (Hebrews 4:16). Grace is the power of God coming to you at no cost, to do through you what you cannot do by yourself.

God knows that the easy way is not always the best way for us. That's why it is so important that we don't lose heart, grow weary, and faint.

Satan knows that if he can defeat us in our mind, he can defeat us in our experience.

The Root of Rejection

May Christ through your faith [actually] dwell (settle down, abide, make His permanent home) in your hearts! May you be rooted deep in love and founded securely on love.

EPHESIANS 3:17

Rejection starts as a seed that is planted in our lives through different things that happen to us. God loves and accepts us, but the devil steals that truth from us by making us think we're rejected so we feel rejected and unloved. When this happens, it affects every area of our lives. It becomes a tree with many branches that all bear bad fruit.

Whatever you are rooted in will determine the fruit in your life—good or bad. If you are rooted in rejection, abuse, shame, guilt, or a poor self-image—if you are rooted in thinking, *Something is wrong*

with me!—your "tree" will bear depression, negativism, a lack of confidence, anger, hostility, a controlling spirit, judgmental-ism, hatred, and self-pity. If you are rooted in Jesus and in His love, then you can relax and know you are loved and valuable. You can know that God sees you as *right* through your faith in Jesus.

All the areas of your life that are out of order can be reconciled through Jesus and the work that He has done on the cross. It happened to me, and God can do it for you.

Here is the good news—you can be delivered from the power of rejection!

Change Is a Good Thing

But we all, with unveiled face,
beholding as in a mirror the glory of the
Lord, are being transformed into the
same image from glory to glory, just as by
the Spirit of the Lord.

2 CORINTHIANS 3:18 NKJV

I want to grow and see change, and I am sure you do also. I want to see changes in my behavior. I want to see regular progress. For example, I want more stability; I want to walk in a greater measure of love and all the other fruit of the Spirit. I want to be kind and good to others, even if I don't feel good or am not having a particularly good day. Even when things are coming against me and things aren't working out the way I'd like, I still want to display the character of Jesus Christ.

Through the power of the Holy Spirit

within us, we are able to be joyful, nice, and kind, even when things are not going our way. We are able to stay calm when everything around us seems topsy-turvy, when everything seems to be conspiring against us to cause us to lose our patience and get angry and upset.

The key for me has been to finally learn that God changes me through His grace, not through my struggles to change myself. I suffered many years of wrestling with myself before I discovered God's power to change me within—little by little.

———————

This is how God changes us: He reveals something to us and then waits until we decide to trust Him with it before He works His character into that area of our lives.

Only Jesus

In [this] freedom Christ has made us
free [and completely liberated us]; stand
fast then, and do not be hampered and
held ensnared and submit again to a
yoke of slavery [which you have once
put off].   GALATIANS 5:1

Jesus came to this world and paid for our sins, taking our punishment upon Himself. He became our substitute, paid the debt we owed, at no cost to us. He did all this freely because of His great love, grace, and mercy.

Jesus inherited all the Father has to give and tells us that we are joint heirs with Him by virtue of our faith. He has provided the way for our complete victory both here and hereafter. He has conquered, and we get the reward without paying the price. We are more than conquerors.

How much simpler could it be? The Gospel is wonderfully uncomplicated.

Complication is the work of Satan. He hates simplicity because he knows the power and the joy that our faith brings. Whenever your relationship with God becomes complex, return to the simplicity of believing like a little child. Jesus said, "only believe" and you will see the glory of God (John 11:40).

Return to and celebrate the simplicity of your faith in Jesus alone.

———————

Believing is so much simpler than not believing.

A New Day

Therefore if any person is [ingrafted] in Christ (the Messiah) he is a new creation (a new creature altogether); the old [previous moral and spiritual condition] has passed away. Behold, the fresh and new has come!

2 CORINTHIANS 5:17

As "a new creation," you don't have to allow the old things that happened to you to keep affecting your new life in Christ. You are a new creature with a new life in Christ. You can have your mind renewed according to the Word of God. Good things are going to happen to you!

Begin to think positively about your life. That doesn't mean that you can get anything you want by just thinking about it. God has a perfect plan for each of us, and we can't control Him with our thoughts

and words. But it's important for us to think and speak in agreement with His will and plan for us.

If you don't have any idea what God's will is for you at this point, you can begin by thinking, *Well, I don't know God's plan, but I know He loves me. Whatever He does will be good, and I'll be blessed.*

God has begun a good work in you and He will bring it to completion (Philippians 1:6). So even when you feel discouraged because you are not making progress quickly, always remember that God is working in you and He will never leave you or forsake you.

Jesus will set you free to enjoy the good things in life. Trust God to renew your mind with His Word!

The Habit of Prayer

Now Peter and John were going up to the temple at the hour of prayer...

ACTS 3:1

Many people feel vaguely guilty about their prayer life because they compare themselves to others. God is a creative God and wants each person to have his or her own individual prayer life. Your prayer life doesn't have to be just like anyone else's.

Yes, there are proven principles of prayer that you can follow. As we see in Acts 3:1, the early disciples set aside certain hours of the day when they would go to a designated place to pray. That is good self-discipline, but that should be the start of learning to pray and not the finish. We can discipline ourselves to establish a prayer schedule that is individually suited to us, but we can also learn to pray without ceasing. That means

to pray at all times, in all places, with all kinds of prayer. I like to say, "Pray your way through the day." Let prayer become like breathing, something you do with ease and without effort.

We never have to "wait" to pray. Each time you see a need or think of anything you need help with, pray right away! Prayer is talking to God, and since He is everywhere, we can talk to Him all the time.

———————

God wants prayer to be a daily, regular part of our lives.

Accepting the Person God Made You to Be

*. . . [Do not merely desire peaceful relations with God, with your fellowmen, **and with yourself**, but pursue, go after them!]*
1 PETER 3:11 (EMPHASIS ADDED)

During my years of ministry, I have discovered that a lot of people really don't like themselves. They reject themselves! This is a much bigger problem than we think. It is certainly not God's will for His children to be against themselves. Rather, it is a part of Satan's attempt to make us miserable and prevent us from loving others.

If we don't get along with ourselves, we won't get along with other people. When we reject ourselves, it may seem to us that others reject us as well. Relationships are a vital part of our lives. How we feel about

ourselves is a determining factor in our success in life and in relationships. We need to be totally confident in Christ!

Our self-image is the inner picture we carry of ourselves. If what we see is not healthy, not true to the Scripture, we will suffer from fear, insecurity, and various misconceptions about ourselves.

God loves us and He wants us to accept His love. And because of His love, we can love ourselves in a healthy, balanced way. We are God's children—people who are loved, accepted, and by His grace improving daily!

———

Jesus came to bring restoration to our lives. One of the things He came to restore is a healthy, balanced self-image.

Hang Tough

And let us not lose heart and grow
weary and faint in acting nobly and
doing right, for in due time and at the
appointed season we shall reap, if we do
not loosen and relax our courage and
faint.   GALATIANS 6:9

In Galatians 6:9, "losing heart" and "fainting" refer to giving up in the mind. The Holy Spirit tells us not to give up in our mind, because if we hold on, we will eventually reap good things.

Think about Jesus. Immediately after being baptized and filled with the Holy Spirit, He was led into the wilderness to be tested and tried by the devil. He did not complain and become discouraged and depressed. He did not think or speak negatively. He did not become confused trying to figure out why this had to happen. He

went through each test victoriously (Luke 4:1–13).

Can you imagine Jesus traveling around the country, talking with His disciples about how hard everything was? Can you picture Him discussing how difficult the Cross was going to be...or how He dreaded the things ahead...or how frustrating it was to have no roof over His head, no bed to sleep in at night?

Jesus drew strength from His heavenly Father and came out in victory. We have His Spirit dwelling in us and the strength available to make it through whatever we are facing.

———————

We can handle our situations the same way Jesus did—by being mentally prepared through "victory thinking" rather than "give-up thinking."

Be Positive

. . . But we have the mind of Christ (the Messiah) and do hold the thoughts (feelings and purposes) of His heart.
1 CORINTHIANS 2:16

Ever since I started keeping my mind in a positive pattern, I can't stand the feeling of being negative. I've seen so many good changes in my life since I've been delivered from a negative mind that now I'm opposed to anything negative.

Here's what I suggest if you've struggled with staying positive: Ask the Holy Spirit to convict you each time you start to get negative. This is part of His work. John 16:7–8 teaches us that the Holy Spirit will convict us of sin and convince us of righteousness. When the conviction comes, ask God to help you. Don't think you can handle this yourself. Lean on Him.

Being positive does not mean that we don't face reality. The Bible says to do all the crisis demands and then stand firmly in your place (Ephesians 6:13). Our place is "in Christ," and in Him we can always be hopeful and positive because nothing is too hard for Him. Jesus was always positive and full of faith. We have His mind in us, and with His help, we can do the same things.

———

Think like God thinks, so you can be the person He wants you to be and have all that He wants you to have.

Childlike Trust

*... Whoever will humble himself
therefore and become like this little child
[trusting, lowly, loving, forgiving] is
greatest in the kingdom of heaven.*

MATTHEW 18:4

Children believe what they are told. Some
people say children are gullible, but children are not gullible; they are trusting. It is
a child's nature to trust unless he has experienced something that teaches him otherwise. And another thing we all know about
children is that they can literally enjoy just
about anything. They can even turn work
into a game!

Our heavenly Father desires for us to
come to Him as children. He wants us to
know that we are His precious little ones
and to put our complete faith in Him to
care for us. He wants us to take His hand

and lean on Him, continually asking for His help. Everything that God calls us to do, He will help us do. He is ready, waiting, and more than willing. We can come humbly as little children—sincere, unpretentious, honest, open—knowing that without Him, we can do nothing.

As God's children, we were never intended to live in bondage of any kind. We can experience glorious freedom and liberty—freedom to enjoy all that God has given us in Christ. He has given us life, and our goal should be to enjoy it.

————

Seek to become and remain child-like with all the simplicity of a child. It will enhance the quality of your life in the most amazing way.

The Beauty of Dependence

I am the Vine; you are the branches.
Whoever lives in Me and I in him bears
much (abundant) fruit. However, apart
from Me [cut off from vital union with
Me] you can do nothing.

JOHN 15:5

I was a very independent person, and God began speaking John 15:5 to me early in my walk with Him. When we come into God's power, we get to experience complete dependence upon Him. Faith involves us leaning entirely on God, trusting His power, wisdom, and goodness.

We are to lean on, rely on, and entirely depend on Him, taking all the weight off of ourselves and putting it all on Him. Without God's help, we can't change anything in our lives. We can't change ourselves, our spouse, our family, our friends, or our

circumstances. Truly, apart from Him we cannot do anything.

We forfeit peace and joy when we fail to let God be God. We try to figure out things we have no business even touching with our minds. Nothing is too hard or too wonderful for God, but many things are too hard for us. With the help and leading of the Holy Spirit, we can grow to the place where we rest in the truth that we know the One Who knows all the answers, even when we don't . . . and we can trust Him!

———

It is so liberating to say, "Lord, I don't know what to do, and even if I did, I couldn't do it. But my eyes are on You. I am going to wait and watch You work it all out."

Prayer Produces Peace

Do not be anxious about anything,
but in every situation, by prayer and
petition, with thanksgiving, present your
requests to God. And the peace of God,
which transcends all understanding,
will guard your hearts and your minds
in Christ Jesus.

PHILIPPIANS 4:6–7 NIV

In this passage, the apostle Paul does not say, "Pray and worry." Instead, he is saying "Pray and don't worry." Why are we to pray and not worry? Because prayer is an important way we *cast our care* upon the Lord. Prayer is what opens the door for God to work in our lives and the lives of other people.

When the devil tries to give us something to worry about, we can turn and give that care to God. If we pray about

something and then keep on worrying about it, we are mixing a positive and a negative. The two cancel each other out so that we end up right back where we started—at zero.

Prayer is a positive force; worry is a negative force. The Lord has shown me the reason many people operate at zero power spiritually is that they cancel out their positive prayer power by giving in to the negative power of worry.

As long as we are worrying, we are not trusting God. It is only by trusting, by having faith and confidence in the Lord, that we are able to enter into His rest and enjoy the peace that transcends all understanding.

———

You can make a decision now to cast all your cares on the Lord and begin to trust Him to take care of you.

God Has a Plan

For I know the thoughts and plans that I have for you, says the Lord, thoughts and plans for welfare and peace and not for evil, to give you hope in your final outcome.   JEREMIAH 29:11

If you have a poor self-image, it has already adversely affected your past, but you can be healed and not allow the past to repeat itself. I encourage you to let go of what lies behind, including any negative ways you have felt about yourself, and press on toward the things God has in store for you.

God has a good plan and a purpose for each of us and a specific way and perfect time to bring it to pass, but not all of us experience it. Many times we live far below the standard that God intends for us to enjoy.

For years I did not exercise my rights

and privileges as a child of God. Although I was a Christian and believed I would go to heaven when I died, I did not know that anything could be done about my past, present, or future. I had a poor self-image, and it affected my day-to-day living, as well as my outlook for the future.

Today, you can accept God's love for you and make His love the basis for your love and acceptance of yourself. Receive His affirmation, knowing that you are changing and becoming all that He desires you to be. Then start enjoying yourself—where you are—on your way to full spiritual maturity.

Let God be God in your life. Put Him in the driver's seat. He knows what He is doing.

When You Feel Stressed

And the peace of God, which transcends all understanding, will guard your hearts and your minds in Christ Jesus.

PHILIPPIANS 4:7 NIV

Years ago, I went to a doctor because I was constantly sick. He told me the symptoms were the result of being under stress. I wasn't getting enough sleep, and I was eating improperly, and pushing myself too hard.

Stress is a normal part of everyone's life. God has created us to withstand a certain amount of pressure and tension. The problem comes when we push beyond our limitations and ignore the warnings our body gives us when it hurts or is exhausted.

I urge you to take good care of yourself, because if you wear out the body you have, you cannot go to a store and buy a new

one. Many of the things we do that give us stress overload are things we could change if we would. Be honest with yourself about why you are doing some of the things you do and let God help you prune off the ones that are wearing you out and bearing no good fruit.

Peace is meant to be the normal condition for every believer in Jesus Christ. He is the Prince of Peace, and in Jesus we find our own inheritance of peace. It is a gift from the Holy Spirit, which He gives as we live in obedience to His Word.

The peace Jesus gives operates in good times and bad. His peace operates in the middle of a storm.

What Do You Think of Yourself?

There we saw the Nephilim [or giants], the sons of Anak, who come from the giants; and we were in our own sight as grasshoppers, and so we were in their sight.   NUMBERS 13:33

We read in Numbers 13 of how Moses sent twelve men to scout out the Promised Land to see if it was good or bad. Ten of the men came back with what the Bible refers to as "an evil report" (Numbers 13:32). They told Moses, "*The land is good, but there are giants in it!*" They also referred to themselves as "grasshoppers," meaning they believed they were insignificant and incapable of defeating the enemy.

The fear they had of the giants prevented God's people from entering the land that He had promised to give them. It wasn't really the giants that defeated these

people; it was their poor self-image. They only saw the giants; they failed to see God, and they failed to believe that with God, they could do anything they needed to do.

Joshua and Caleb were the only ones who had a proper attitude. Caleb said to Moses and the people, "*Let us go up at once and possess it; we are well able to conquer it*" (Numbers 13:30). They had the attitude that God wanted them to have. They believed that with God, all things were possible.

God had a glorious future planned for all of the Israelites, just as He does for us, but only the ones with a proper attitude toward God and themselves will live in it and enjoy it.

————————

God does not have a bad attitude toward you; don't have one toward yourself!

Set Your Mind and Keep It Set

And set your minds and keep them set on what is above (the higher things), not on the things that are on the earth.

COLOSSIANS 3:2

We can have right and wrong mind-sets. The right ones benefit us, and the wrong ones hurt us and hinder our progress. With God's help we can set our minds in the right direction.

Some people see life negatively because they have experienced unhappy circumstances all their lives and can't imagine anything better. Then there are some people who see everything as negative simply because their personality leans in that direction. Whatever its cause, a negative outlook leaves a person miserable and unlikely to grow spiritually. To enjoy God's good plan

for us, we need to be in agreement with Him, and He definitely is not negative!

With God's help and your hard work and determination, you can break negative mind-sets and old habits that are trying to keep you far from God. The devil doesn't want you to break through because he knows that if you do, you will enjoy your life and be a blessing to others. Your life will change, which will cause many other lives to change. If you set your mind in the right direction, it is going to bring you closer to God and allow you to fulfill your God-ordained destiny.

———

Expect good things to happen to you and through you!

Prayer Produces Rest

Come to Me, all you who labor and are heavy-laden and overburdened, and I will cause you to rest. [I will ease and relieve and refresh your souls.]

MATTHEW 11:28

If we are not at rest, we are not truly believing, because the fruit of believing is rest.

For many years of my life I would claim, "Oh, I'm believing God; I'm trusting the Lord." But I was not doing either of those things, because I was anxious, worried, irritable, and on edge most of the time.

Just as we can be involved in outward activity, we can be involved in inward activity. God wants us not only to enter into His rest in our body, He also wants us to enter into His rest in our soul.

To me, finding rest, relief, ease, refreshment, recreation, and blessed quiet for my

soul means finding freedom from wrong mental activity. It means not having to live in the torment of reasoning, always trying to come up with an answer I don't have. I don't have to worry; instead, I can remain in a place of quiet peace and rest through prayer.

If we are truly believing God and trusting the Lord, we have entered into His rest. We have prayed and cast our care upon Him and are now abiding in the perfect peace of His daily presence.

————

You can speak His Word to your anxious mind just as Jesus spoke to the storm and said, "Peace, be still."

Believe

*Jesus replied, This is the work (service)
that God asks of you: that you believe...*
                    JOHN 6:29

Little children usually automatically believe
what their parents tell them, and that is
how God wants us to be with Him. He
wants us to believe what He says in His
Word! Christians are often referred to as
"believers," and believers should believe!

Are you a believing believer, or a doubtful believer? Simple childlike faith produces a lot of good fruit. For example, joy
and peace are found in believing (Romans
15:13). Doubt, reasoning, worry, and fear
produce all kinds of misery, but it all can be
avoided by making a decision to believe the
Word of God. Believe that something good
is going to happen to you. Believe that
when you repent, your sins are completely

forgiven. Believe that God wants to meet all of your needs, that He loves you and is always willing to help you.

When we believe, then we can enter the rest of God and really enjoy each day of our lives. We can take life one day at a time and trust that our future is secure in God.

———

If you are going to doubt anything, doubt your doubts!

You Are Loved

And we know (understand, recognize, are conscious of, by observation and by experience) and believe (adhere to and put faith in and rely on) the love God cherishes for us. God is love, and he who dwells and continues in love dwells and continues in God, and God dwells and continues in him.   1 JOHN 4:16

We are created by God for love. Loving and being loved are what make life worth living. It gives life purpose and meaning. But if we have allowed sin and unforgiveness and the past to separate us from God's love, it will leave us love-starved and unhappy.

Many people cannot maintain healthy, lasting relationships because either they don't know how to receive love or they place an unbalanced demand on others to give them what only God can give. The

resulting frustration can often lead to the ruin of marriages and the suffocation of friendships.

The Bible teaches us that God loves perfectly or unconditionally. His perfect love for us is not based on our perfection. God loves us because He wants to! God is love (1 John 4:8). Love is Who He is. God always loves; all you have to do is receive that love and live with confidence each day knowing that His love gives our lives purpose and meaning.

———

A revelation of God's perfect love for you can change your life and your walk with Him.

Waiting on God

Wait and hope for and expect the Lord; be brave and of good courage and let your heart be stout and enduring. Yes, wait for and hope for and expect the Lord.   PSALM 27:14

When we "wait" on God, we are not being lazy or passive, but we are actually being very active spiritually. We may not be "doing" anything, but we are trusting God to do what needs to be done. In effect, we are saying, "Lord, I will not try to do this in my own strength. I will wait on You to deliver me. And I'm going to enjoy my life while I wait for You."

Satan wants us to be frustrated from trying to solve our own problems. He hates our joy. He wants to see anything but joy, because the joy of the Lord is our

strength (Nehemiah 8:10). Worry robs us of strength, but joy energizes us.

We are tempted to think we are not doing our part if we don't worry or try to figure out an answer to our problems, but this will prevent our deliverance rather than aid it. It is not irresponsible to enjoy life while we wait on God and expect Him to do what we don't know how to do!

———————

Do not fear because the battle is not yours, but the Lord's.

Having a Ready Mind

These were more noble than those in Thessalonica, in that they received the word with all readiness of mind, and searched the scriptures daily, whether those things were so.

ACTS 17:11 KJV

The Bible says that we are to have a ready mind. That means we can have minds that are open to the will of God for us, whatever His will may be.

I once spoke with a young lady who experienced the sorrow of a broken engagement. She wanted the relationship to continue and was thinking, hoping, and believing that her former fiancé would feel the same way.

I advised her to have a "ready mind" in case it didn't work out that way. She asked, "Well, isn't that being negative?"

No, it isn't. Negativism would say, "My

life is over. No one will ever want me. I'll be miserable forever."

Having a positive mind says, "I'm really sad this happened, but I'm going to trust God. I'm going to ask and believe for our relationship to be restored; but more than anything, I want God's perfect will. If it doesn't turn out the way I want, I'll survive, because Jesus lives in me. It may be hard, but I trust the Lord. I believe that in the end, everything will work out for the best."

———————

Practice being positive in every situation that arises. God has promised to bring good out of whatever is taking place in your life at the moment.

Combating Fear with Prayer

So we take comfort and are encouraged and confidently and boldly say, The Lord is my Helper; I will not be seized with alarm [I will not fear or dread or be terrified]. What can man do to me?

HEBREWS 13:6

Fear attacks everyone. It is the enemy's way of trying to prevent us from enjoying the life Jesus died to give us. If we give in to fear and if we give voice to it, we open the door for the enemy and close the door to God.

But rather than give in to fear, we can learn to boldly confess that God is our Helper, our Refuge, and our Stronghold.

The Bible teaches us to watch and pray. Matthew 26:41 says: "All of you must keep awake (give strict attention, be cautious and active) and watch and pray, that you

may not come into temptation. The spirit indeed is willing, but the flesh is weak."

The major reference in this passage is to watching ourselves and the attacks that the enemy launches against our minds and our emotions. When these attacks are detected, we can pray immediately. It is when we pray that power is released in our lives—not when we think about praying later.

I encourage you to watch and pray about everything. I believe you will find this decision to be one that will produce more joy and peace for your everyday living.

In order to live in real victory, it is important that we dedicate ourselves to prayer.

Rest for the Weary

Do you not know that your body is the temple (the very sanctuary) of the Holy Spirit Who lives within you, Whom you have received [as a Gift] from God?
1 CORINTHIANS 6:19

The first key to overcoming stress is to recognize or admit we are experiencing it, and look for the source of it. There was a time in my life when I was constantly having headaches, backaches, stomachaches, neck aches, and all the other symptoms of stress, but I found it very difficult to admit I was pushing too hard physically, mentally, emotionally, and spiritually. I wanted to do all of the things I was doing and wasn't willing to ask God what He wanted me to do. I was afraid that He would lead me to give up something I wasn't ready to give up yet.

Although the Lord gives power to the

faint and weary, if you are worn-out from continually exceeding your physical limitations, you will have stress. Our bodies are the sanctuary (home) of God, and we are in disobedience when we push ourselves past God-ordained limitations and live in continual stress. We all have limits and we need to recognize what they are and eliminate excess stress from our lives.

If you wear out your body, you can't go to a department store and purchase another one, so take care of the one you have!

————

Getting regular rest is one of the wisest things you can do.

It's Your Choice

For we are God's [own] handiwork (His workmanship), recreated in Christ Jesus, [born anew] that we may do those good works which God predestined (planned beforehand) for us [taking paths which He prepared ahead of time], that we should walk in them [living the good life which He prearranged and made ready for us to live].   EPHESIANS 2:10

God has given you a wonderful gift: *free will*. God is offering you the opportunity to accept yourself as He created you to be, but you have a free will and can refuse to do so if you choose. To accept something means to view it as usual, proper, or right.

People who reject themselves do so because they cannot see themselves as proper or right. They only see their flaws and weaknesses, not their beauty and strength. This

is an unbalanced attitude often instilled by authority figures in the past who focused on what was weak and wrong rather than what was strong and right.

In Amos 3:3, we read, *"Do two walk together except they make an appointment and have agreed?"* You can walk with God—you can be close to Him—when you decide to agree with Him. He says He loves you and accepts you; therefore, if you agree with Him, you no longer have to dislike or reject yourself.

When God created you, He created something wonderful.

Keep On Keeping On

Therefore, since Christ suffered in his body, arm yourselves also with the same attitude, because whoever suffers in the body is done with sin. As a result, they do not live the rest of their earthly lives for evil human desires, but rather for the will of God.   1 PETER 4:1–2 NIV

Peter's beautiful passage teaches us a secret concerning how to make it through difficult times and situations. Here is my rendition of these verses:

"Think about everything Jesus went through and how He endured suffering in order to do God's will, and it will help you make it through your difficulties. Arm yourselves for battle; prepare yourselves for it by thinking as Jesus did... 'I will patiently suffer rather than fail to please God.' For if you suffer, having the mind of

Christ toward it, you will no longer be living just to please yourself, doing whatever is easy and running from all that is hard. But you will be able to live for what God wills and not by your feelings and carnal thoughts."

There are difficulties that we go through in life, but we also experience the joy of victory. Trials and tests will come, and God uses them to develop the potential He has put in you. Your part is to decide that you are never going to quit, no matter what, until you see the promises of God revealed in your life. There is one kind of person the devil can never defeat—one who is not a quitter.

_____

Keep on keeping on, and you'll get there.

Prayer Produces Patience and Hope

Moreover [let us also be full of joy now!] let us exult and triumph in our troubles and rejoice in our sufferings, knowing that pressure and affliction and hardship produce patient and unswerving endurance. And endurance (fortitude) develops maturity of character (approved faith and tried integrity). And character [of this sort] produces [the habit of] joyful and confident hope of eternal salvation.

ROMANS 5:3–4

It is easy to say, "Don't worry." But to actually do that requires experience with the faithfulness of God. When we trust God and then see and experience His faithfulness in our lives, it gives us great confidence to live without worry, fear, and anxiety.

That's why it is so important to continue

to have faith and trust in God in the very midst of trials and tribulations. With God's help, we can steadfastly resist the temptation to give up and quit when the going gets rough. God uses those hard, trying times to build in us patience, endurance, and character that will eventually produce the habit of joyful and confident hope.

Always remember that when you are in a battle, you are gaining valuable experience that will benefit you in the future. You will more easily trust God when difficulty comes, and you will be able to testify to others regarding the goodness and faithfulness of God. If you are in a battle right now, you can let it defeat you or make you stronger! Make the right decision and let it help bring you into a deeper level of spiritual maturity.

———

We serve a God Who is so marvelous that He can work out things for our good that Satan intends for harm.

Faith and Grace

For by grace you have been saved
through faith, and that not of yourselves;
it is the gift of God, not of works, lest
anyone should boast.

EPHESIANS 2:8–9 NKJV

It is wonderful to realize that salvation comes by the free grace of God and can be easily received through simple child-like faith. Thankfully, we don't have to work for our salvation because Jesus has already done all the work. We receive by faith alone! I believe the same way that we receive forgiveness of our sins and eternal life (salvation) is the same way that we should live out our daily lives. We should mix our faith with everything we do.

Faith is the leaning of the entire human personality on God in absolute trust and confidence in His power, wisdom, and

goodness. When we go through life leaning on Him in absolutely everything, He will always guide us and give us the strength and ability to do whatever we need to do. The good news is that you never have to try to do things on your own! God has sent the Holy Spirit Who is your helper, so ask for and receive the help you need today and every day, and relax in God's love, mercy, and grace.

———————

Trade all your fears, anxieties, and worries for simple faith and enjoy your day!

Forgiving Others

*And become useful and helpful and
kind to one another, tenderhearted
(compassionate, understanding, loving-
hearted), forgiving one another [readily
and freely], as God in Christ forgave
you.*   EPHESIANS 4:32

I once heard that medical studies indicate
75 percent of physical sickness is caused by
emotional problems. And one of the greatest emotional problems people experience is
guilt. They are refusing to relax and enjoy
life because, after all, they feel they don't
deserve to have a good time. So they live in
a perpetual strain of regret and remorse.
This kind of stress often makes people sick.

Two of the things that cause us to get all
knotted up inside are meditating on all the
negative things done to us by others, and
the sinful and wrong things we have done.

We have a hard time getting over what others have done to us, and we find it difficult to forget the mistakes we have made.

In my own life I had a choice to remain bitter, full of hatred and self-pity, resenting the people who had hurt me, or I could choose to follow God's path of forgiveness. This is the same choice you have today. I pray that you will forgive others and receive God's forgiveness for yourself. You will be healthier and happier if you do!

———————

God's way is forgiveness.

Take Your Position

And Jehoshaphat bowed his head with his face to the ground, and all Judah and the inhabitants of Jerusalem fell down before the Lord, worshiping Him.
2 CHRONICLES 20:18

In 2 Chronicles 20:18, the king and the people of Judah bowed with their faces to the ground and worshipped when they heard the Lord's instruction. The position of worshipping God was helping them prepare for battle. If you are in a battle right now, I strongly urge you to trade all worry for worship. Kneeling in reverence before God, or other types of worship, is a battle position and a key to spiritual power.

To "praise" God has been defined as to ascribe to Him the glory due to His name. It is to talk about and sing out about the goodness, grace, and greatness of God. To

"worship" has been defined as to give reverence to and to serve. Broadly, it may be regarded as the direct acknowledgment of God, of His nature, attributes, ways, and claims, whether by expressing your heart in praise and thanksgiving or by deed done in such an acknowledgment.

With God's help, we can learn to fight His way, not the world's way. Our battle position is one of worship, and this is a position that brings us closer to God. We fight every battle with a heart of praise and worship, believing that God will work in our life and circumstances.

———

As we worship the Lord, we release the emotional or mental burden that is weighing us down. It is swallowed up in the awesomeness of God.

The Power of Hope

[For Abraham, human reason for] hope being gone, hoped in faith that he should become the father of many nations, as he had been promised...

No unbelief or distrust made him waver (doubtingly question) concerning the promise of God, but he grew strong and was empowered by faith as he gave praise and glory to God.

ROMANS 4:18–20

In our ministry we want to help more people every year, and we believe God wants us to grow. But we also realize that if God has a different plan, and if we end our year with no growth, we cannot let that situation control our joy.

We believe *for* many things, but beyond them all, we believe *in* Someone. That Someone is Jesus. We don't always know

what is going to happen. We just know it will always work out for our good!

It is reported that Abraham, after sizing up his situation (he didn't ignore the facts), considered the utter impotence of his own body and the barrenness of Sarah's womb. Although all human reason for hope was gone, he hoped in faith. *Abraham was very positive about a very negative situation!*

Hebrews 6:19 tells us that hope is the anchor of the soul. Hope is the force that keeps us steady in a time of trial. Don't ever stop hoping. Don't be afraid to hope. No one can promise that you'll never be disappointed. But you can always have hope and be positive.

Have hopeful expectation every day of your life.

Prudence

I, Wisdom [from God], make prudence my dwelling, and I find out knowledge and discretion.   PROVERBS 8:12

A word you don't hear very much teaching about is "prudence." In the Scriptures "prudence" or "prudent" means being good stewards of the gifts God has given us to use. Those gifts include abilities, time, energy, strength, and health as well as material possessions. They include our bodies as well as our minds and spirits.

God has given each of us different gifts and grace according to how He wants us to use them. One person may be gifted to sing and does so in their local area, while another person's singing ability is known in most of the world. The Bible tells us to use our gifts according to the grace given to us (Romans 12:6).

Each of us would be wise to know how much we are able to handle, to be able to recognize when we are reaching "full capacity" or "overload." Instead of pushing ourselves into overload to please others, satisfy our own desires, or reach our personal goals, we can learn to listen to the Lord and obey Him. If we follow the Lord's leading, we will enjoy blessed lives.

We all experience stress and at times we feel the effects of it, but we should learn to manage it well. Ask God to show you areas in your life that could be changed to help you eliminate excess stress better.

God is good, and He wants you to enjoy a peaceful life.

Self-Acceptance

*For whom the Lord loves He corrects,
even as a father corrects the son in whom
he delights.*   PROVERBS 3:12

Perhaps you have been struggling with accepting yourself. You see the areas in yourself where change is necessary. You desire to be like Jesus. Yet it is very difficult for you to think or say, "I accept myself." You feel that to do so would be to accept all that is wrong with you, but that is not the case. We can accept and embrace ourselves as God's unique creation, and still not like everything we do.

God will change us, but we cannot even begin the process of change until this issue of self-acceptance is settled in our individual lives. When we truly believe that God loves us unconditionally just as we are, then we will have a closeness to Him, and we

will be willing to receive His correction, which is necessary for true change.

Change requires corrections—people who do not know they are loved have a very difficult time receiving correction. Correction is merely God giving us divine direction for our lives. He is guiding us to better things, but if we are insecure we will always feel condemned by correction instead of joyfully embracing it.

God does not approve of all of our actions, but He does love and approve of us as His beloved children.

———————

Be patient with yourself. Keep pressing on and believe that you are changing every day.

Run Your Race

Wherefore seeing we also are compassed about with so great a cloud of witnesses, let us lay aside every weight, and the sin which doth so easily beset us, and let us run with patience the race that is set before us.   HEBREWS 12:1 KJV

If we are going to run our race in life, if we want to fulfill our destiny and do God's will, it is important that we lay aside every weight and sin and run the race with patience. In the days this verse was written, runners conditioned their bodies for a race just as we do today. But at the time of the race, they stripped off their clothing except for a loincloth, so that when they ran there would be nothing to hinder them. They also oiled their bodies with fine oils.

In our Christian life, we are called to remove anything that hinders us from

running the race that God has set before us. It is essential to be well oiled, or anointed, with the Holy Spirit (often symbolized by oil) if we are going to win our race.

The devil has many ways to entangle us and prevent us from living in obedience to God's Word, developing an intimate relationship with Him. There are many distractions and requirements on our time. But with God's guidance, we can strip away the things that will hinder us. Keep your eyes on your goal and learn to say "no" to things that distract you and keep you from fulfilling your full potential.

———

Be determined that nothing is going to hinder you from fulfilling God's plan and purpose for your life.

The Power of Agreement

All of these with their minds in full agreement devoted themselves steadfastly to prayer. ACTS 1:14

Whenever believers are united in prayer, there is great power present. Jesus Himself said, "For wherever two or three are gathered (drawn together as My followers) in (into) My name, there I AM in the midst of them" (Matthew 18:20).

Throughout the book of Acts, we read that the people of God came together "with one accord" (Acts 2:1, 46; 4:24; 5:12; 15:25 KJV). And it was their united faith, their corporate agreement, and love that made their prayers so effective. They saw God move in mighty ways to confirm the truth of His Word as they gave testimony to their faith.

Living in agreement doesn't necessarily

mean that we feel the exact same way about everything, but it does mean that we are committed to walking in love. We can respect someone's opinion even if we don't share it! Dave and I don't share the same opinions about many things, but we do live in peace and harmony and it gives us power in prayer.

In Philippians 2:2 we are told by the apostle Paul, "Fill up and complete my joy by living in harmony and being of the same mind and one in purpose..."

Prayer is a wonderful privilege, and one that we should exercise often. But in order to have good results, we should also strive to remove all disharmony and disunity from our lives.

————

Being in agreement is often more important than being right!

Courage and Obedience

After these things, the word of the Lord came to Abram in a vision, saying, Fear not, Abram, I am your Shield, your abundant compensation, and your reward shall be exceedingly great.

GENESIS 15:1

In Genesis 12:1, God gave Abram a tall order. In so many words He said, "Pack up and leave everyone you know and everything you are comfortable with and go to a place I will show you."

If Abram had bowed his knee to doubt and uncertainty, the rest of the story would never have come to pass. He would never have experienced God as his Shield, his great compensation, and he would never have received his exceedingly great reward.

In the same way, if Joshua had not overcome his fear and been obedient to God's

command to lead His people into the Promised Land, neither he nor they would ever have enjoyed all that God had planned and prepared for them.

There is power in God's Word to equip us to stop bowing our knee in fearful uncertainty. We can do what God wants us to do, even if we have to do it afraid. When we're intimidated by an obstacle, we can say: "Lord, strengthen me. This is what You have told me to do, and with Your help I am going to do it, because it is Your revealed will for me. I am determined that my life is not going to be ruled by fear but by Your Word."

———

God doesn't always deliver us "from" things; often He walks us "through" them.

The Purpose of Faith

... Be vigilant and cautious at all times; for that enemy of yours, the devil, roams around like a lion roaring [in fierce hunger], seeking someone to seize upon and devour.

Withstand him; be firm in faith [against his onset—rooted, established, strong, immovable, and determined]...

1 PETER 5:8–9

Oftentimes we make the mistake of trying to use faith to get to the place where there is total freedom from trouble. But the purpose of faith is not always to keep us from having trouble; it is often to carry us through trouble. If we never had any trouble, we wouldn't need any faith.

The temptation exists to run away from our problems, but the Lord says that we are to go through them. The good news is that

He has promised that we will never have to go through them alone. He will always be there to help us in every way. He has said to us, "Fear not, for I am with you" (Isaiah 41:10).

In our daily experience, we can learn to stand our ground and effectively resist the devil. Learning to be stable in hard times is one of the best ways to get close to God and to press through any difficulty we may face. God is with you to help you, so don't give up!

———————

The devil will give up when he sees that you are not going to give in.

Receive Your Forgiveness

I, even I, am He Who blots out and cancels your transgressions, for My own sake, and I will not remember your sins.
ISAIAH 43:25

No matter what your problem or how bad you feel about yourself as a result of it, take this truth into your heart: God loves you. Jesus Christ gave His life that you might be forgiven, and He has given you a new life. God has given you a new family and new friends to love and accept and appreciate and support you. You are going to make it because of the One Who lives inside you and cares for you.

Repent of whatever sin it is that stands between you and Him and receive forgiveness. No matter what you may have done, say, "Lord, I did it, and it is a marvel to me to realize that You love me unconditionally,

and that You forgive me. You have put my sins as far away from me as the east is from the west, and You remember them no more!" (Psalm 103:12.)

Once you have repented of your sins and received God's forgiveness, if you continue to drag them up to Him every time you go to Him in prayer, you are reminding Him of something He has not only *forgiven* but also actually *forgotten*.

———

From this moment, stop punishing yourself for something that no longer exists.

How Long, Lord?

But those who wait for the Lord [who expect, look for, and hope in Him] shall change and renew their strength and power; they shall lift their wings and mount up [close to God] as eagles [mount up to the sun]; they shall run and not be weary, they shall walk and not faint or become tired.

ISAIAH 40:31

Waiting on God does not mean that we do nothing, while expecting God to do everything for us. To me it means that I wait, expecting God to give me direction if there is something He wants me to do, while also trusting Him to do what only He can do. Often as I have waited on God and put my trust in Him, He has shown me things that need to be adjusted in my behavior or attitude. You see, God doesn't merely want

to change our circumstances, but He also wants to change us.

As we spend quiet time with God, He reveals things to us, and we are refreshed in His presence. Closeness and intimacy with God is one of our greatest privileges as His children. The more time we spend with Him, the more we are transformed into His image. Study God's Word and receive it as a personal letter from Him to you. It will both comfort and correct you. Wait on God with a trusting, expectant heart, and look forward to all the good things He has planned for you.

———————

God will change you little by little each day, as you trust Him.

A Glad Heart

All the days of the desponding and afflicted are made evil [by anxious thoughts and forebodings], but he who has a glad heart has a continual feast [regardless of circumstances].

PROVERBS 15:15

An "evil foreboding" is a vague, threatening feeling that something bad is going to happen. There was a point when I realized that I had actually carried these feelings with me most of my life. In fact, I had been made miserable by evil thoughts and forebodings.

Perhaps you have these feelings as well. You have circumstances that are very difficult, but even when you don't you are still miserable because your thoughts are poisoning your outlook and robbing you of the ability to enjoy life and see good days.

Proverbs 15:15 promises you that these feelings need not remain. Faith's attitude is one of leaning on God, trusting and being confident in Him—it is joyful feasting on the expectancy of good. Rather than dreading something by anticipating that it will make you miserable, you can have faith that God will give you the power to enjoy it.

Your joy, peace, righteousness, and power are on the inside of you through the presence of the Holy Spirit. Don't let worry and anxiety rule in your life any longer. Expect God's help, blessing, and power in all that you do.

With the proper attitude, you can be energized to do mundane, everyday tasks with great joy.

Victory over Stress

... Now we serve not under [obedience to] the old code of written regulations, but [under obedience to the promptings] of the Spirit in newness [of life].

ROMANS 7:6

There are times in life when we have to deal with stress, but we can be on *top* of it, not *under* it. Through the Holy Spirit's guidance and power, we can handle our work and responsibilities with ease instead of stress. As we follow the promptings of the Spirit we will know how to handle each situation we encounter.

All of us have situations that come our way that we don't like. But with the power of God, we can go through those circumstances while also avoiding stress. The more we lean on, and trust in, God, the easier life is. Every situation in life is not

"easy," but we can handle them with what I call "Holy Spirit Ease." In other words, God empowers us to do whatever we need to do through Him. He energizes us and helps us.

God will guide us, but we need to trust Him enough to follow His directions. He never gives us any advice that is not for our benefit and progress in life. God is leading you into a place of victory and triumph, not into a place of defeat. As you follow His lead, I believe you will experience less stress than ever before. He may prompt you not to do something you want to do, or to do something you don't want to do, but obedience to His leadership keeps us from taking wrong roads in life and wasting time and energy!

Simply obeying the promptings of the Holy Spirit will often relieve stress quickly.

How Can I Change?

Do not be conformed to this world (this age), [fashioned after and adapted to its external, superficial customs], but be transformed (changed) by the [entire] renewal of your mind . . .

ROMANS 12:2

Change does not come through struggle, human effort without God, frustration, self-hatred, self-rejection, guilt, worry, or works of the flesh. We are new creatures in Christ (2 Corinthians 5:17), and as such we all want to please God. We want to be what He wants us to be, and behave the way He wants us to behave, but in order for that to happen, we need to learn how to think like He thinks.

Change in your life comes as a result of having your mind renewed by the Word of God. As you agree with God and really

believe that what He says is true, it gradually begins to manifest itself in you. You begin to think differently, then you begin to talk differently, and finally you begin to act differently. This is a process that develops in stages, but while it is taking place you can still have the attitude, "I'm okay, and I'm on my way!"

Enjoy yourself while you are changing. Enjoy where you are on the way to where you are going. Enjoy the journey! Don't waste all of your "now time" trying to rush into the future. Relax. Let God be God. Stop being so hard on yourself. Change comes little by little, but in that process you're getting closer to Him each day.

We can come to Jesus just as we are. He takes us "as is" and makes us what we ought to be.

Be Patient

*But let endurance and steadfastness
and patience have full play and do
a thorough work, so that you may be
[people] perfectly and fully developed
[with no defects], lacking in nothing.*

JAMES 1:4

James teaches us that we can rejoice when
we find ourselves involved in difficult situations, knowing that God is trying our faith
to bring out patience. I have found that trials did eventually bring out patience in me,
but first they brought a lot of other junk to
the surface—such as pride, anger, rebellion,
self-pity, complaining, and many other
things. It seems that these ungodly traits,
with God's help, need to be faced and dealt
with because they hinder patience as well as
other good fruit like kindness, love, humility, and other things.

The Bible talks about purification, sanctification, and sacrifice. These are not popular words; nevertheless, these are things we go through in order to become like Jesus in our character. God's desire is to make us perfect, lacking in nothing. He wants us to ultimately be filled with the fruits of righteousness, which usually requires us to go through some difficulties that, although are unpleasant, do eventually help us mature.

I struggled with the difficulties in my life for a long time until I finally learned that God would work them out for good and use them to help me in many ways. He simply wants you and me to surrender and say, "I trust You, God. I believe when this difficulty is over, I will be a better person than I was before it began!"

No matter what you are going through, trust God that you are growing closer to Him each day!

God Changes People
Through Prayer

First of all, then, I admonish and urge that petitions, prayers, intercessions, and thanksgivings be offered on behalf of all men.   1 TIMOTHY 2:1

In Exodus 32, Moses interceded for the children of Israel so that the wrath of God would not destroy them. It's a stirring example that depicts how sincere prayer can change situations.

There are times when I find myself being led to pray for God to be merciful to a person, or to continue working with them and making the changes in them that are needed.

As Jesus told His disciples at Gethsemane, we can "watch and pray" (Matthew 26:41 KJV). We have the opportunity

to pray for one another, not judge and criticize each other. God allows us to discern people's needs in order to be part of the answer, not part of the problem. Remember we are not the potter. God is, and we certainly don't know how to "fix" people. We cannot change people, but we can pray and watch Him work.

When people are hurting, even from their own poor choices, they often are blinded to the truth. We can pray for their eyes to be opened and for them to truly see the truth so it will set them free. People who are hurting need God to intervene in their lives, but if they don't know how to call on Him, we can stand in the gap between them and God as intercessors and see breakthrough as we pray.

We can do the praying and let God do the work.

Faith and Contentment

. . . I have learned how to be content (satisfied to the point where I am not disturbed or disquieted) in whatever state I am.   PHILIPPIANS 4:11

The Bible teaches us to be content no matter what our circumstances may be (Hebrews 13:5). We don't have to be upset about anything, no matter what is happening. Instead, we can pray about it and tell God our need. While we are waiting for Him to move, we can be thankful for all that God has done for us already (Philippians 4:6).

I have discovered that the secret of being content is to ask God for what we want, knowing that if it is right, He will bring it to pass at the right time. And if it is not right, He will do something much better than what we asked for.

It is important that we learn to trust God completely if we ever intend to enjoy peaceful living. We have the opportunity to meditate on what God has done in our life instead of what we are still waiting on Him to do.

God loves you. He is a good God Who wants to be close to you. Be content knowing that His way is perfect, and He brings with Him a great reward for those who trust in Him (Hebrews 10:35).

———

God is working in secret, behind the scenes, even when it looks as though nothing will ever change.

Purchased by Jesus' Blood

In Him we have redemption (deliverance and salvation) through His blood, the remission (forgiveness) of our offenses (shortcomings and trespasses), in accordance with the riches and the generosity of His gracious favor.

EPHESIANS 1:7

Say aloud to yourself, "I was bought and cleansed from sin with a price; purchased with a preciousness; paid for and made God's own."

You are delivered from sin and all the "death" it brings with it. Worry, anxiety, and fear are forms of death. Strife, bitterness, resentment, and unforgiveness are forms of death. The blood of Jesus is the only antidote for death.

Jesus' blood is precious before the Father and should be precious to us. A precious

thing is something we protect, something we are careful with, and something we don't want to part with. The blood of Jesus is precious and it allows us to be close to our heavenly Father. His sacrifice lifted the veil between God and man, and now we have free access and an opportunity for closeness and intimacy with God (Hebrews 10:18–22).

The blood of Jesus cleanses us from sin and will continuously cleanse us (1 John 1:9). His blood is like a powerful cleansing agent. Just as our blood works to keep our bodies cleansed of all poison, the blood of Jesus continuously cleanses us from sin in all its forms and manifestations.

———————

Have faith in the power of Jesus' blood to keep you continually cleansed from sin in all its forms and manifestations.

The Words You Speak

Death and life are in the power of the tongue, and they who indulge in it shall eat the fruit of it [for death or life].

PROVERBS 18:21

The apostle Peter plainly tells us that enjoying life and seeing good days, and having a positive mind and mouth, are linked together. If we change our words, we can change our life!

Our mouth gives expression to what we think, feel, and want. Our minds tell us what to think, not necessarily what God thinks. Our wills tell us what we want, not what God wants. Our emotions tell us what we feel, not what God feels. As our soul is purified, it is trained to carry God's thoughts, desires, and feelings; then we will begin to speak life instead of death.

Your words, as reflections of your thoughts, have the power to bring blessing or destruction not only to your life but also to the lives of many others. In 1 Corinthians 2:16, the Word of God teaches us that we have the mind of Christ and that we hold the thoughts, feelings, and purposes of His heart. We don't manifest them all the time, but we are daily growing and being transformed into Christ's image. He that has begun a good work in us will complete it and bring it to its finish (Philippians 1:6). The closer we come to God, the quicker we will experience victory in our mind, mouth, moods, and bad attitudes.

No matter how far you have to go, I know you can change because I did. It took time and "heaping helpings" of the Holy Spirit, but it was worth it.

God Blesses Obedience

Now therefore, if you will obey My voice in truth and keep My covenant, then you shall be My own peculiar possession and treasure from among and above all peoples; for all the earth is Mine.

EXODUS 19:5

God's grace and power are available for us to use. God enables us or gives us an anointing of the Holy Spirit to do what *He* tells us to do. Sometimes after He has prompted us to go another direction, we still keep pressing on with our original plan. If we are doing something He has not approved, He is under no obligation to give us the energy to do it. We are functioning in our own strength rather than under the guidance of the Holy Spirit. Then we get so frustrated, stressed, or burned out, we

lose our self-control, simply by ignoring the promptings of the Spirit.

Many people are stressed and burned out from going their own way instead of God's way. They end up in stressful situations when they go a different direction from the one God prompted. Then they burn out in the midst of the disobedience and end up struggling to finish what they started outside of God's direction, all the while begging God to bless them.

Thankfully, God is merciful, and He helps us in the midst of our mistakes. But He is not going to give us strength and energy to disobey Him. We can avoid many stressful situations simply by obeying the Holy Spirit's promptings at all times.

———————

More obedience always equals less stress!

Healing for Damaged Emotions

The Spirit of the Lord God is upon me, because the Lord has anointed and qualified me to preach the Gospel of good tidings to the meek, the poor, and afflicted; He has sent me to bind up and heal the brokenhearted, to proclaim liberty to the [physical and spiritual] captives and the opening of the prison and of the eyes to those who are bound.

ISAIAH 61:1

Emotional healing is an important topic, because our inner life is much more important than our outer life. Romans 14:17 lets us know that the kingdom of God is not meat and drink (not outward things), but it is righteousness, peace, and joy in the Holy Spirit (inner things). Also, Luke 17:21 says the kingdom of God is within you.

Because of the abuse I suffered as a

child, I was an "emotional prisoner" for a long time, but God has healed and transformed me with His love. And He will do the same for you!

In Isaiah 61 the Lord said that He came to heal the brokenhearted. I believe that means those broken inside, those crushed and wounded inwardly. Jesus wants to lead you out of emotional devastation and into a place of health, wholeness, and closeness to God. Invite Him into every area of your heart and soul and let the healing work begin!

God will meet you wherever you are and help you get to where you need to be.

Wait on the Lord

*For you have need of steadfast patience
and endurance, so that you may perform
and fully accomplish the will of God,
and thus receive and carry away [and
enjoy to the full] what is promised.*

HEBREWS 10:36

There are multitudes of unhappy, unfulfilled
Christians in the world simply because they
are busy trying to make something happen,
instead of waiting patiently for God to bring
things to pass in His own time and His own
way. We are in a hurry, but God isn't.

Humility says, "God knows best, and
He will not be late!" Pride says, "I'm ready
now. I'll make things happen my own
way." A humble man waits patiently; he
actually has a "reverential fear" of moving
in the strength of his own flesh. Patience
is the ability to keep a good attitude while

waiting. But a proud man tries one thing after another, all to no avail. Pride is at the root of impatience.

Patience is a fruit of the Holy Spirit that manifests itself in a calm, positive attitude despite our life circumstances. Don't think you can solve all your problems or overcome difficulties on your own. As we humble ourselves under God's mighty hand, we begin to die to our own way and our own timing, and we become alive to God's will and way for us.

———————

It is only through patience and endurance in faith that we receive the promises of God.

You Are the Place of Prayer

For we are fellow workmen (joint promoters, laborers together) with and for God; you are God's garden and vineyard and field under cultivation, [you are] God's building.

1 CORINTHIANS 3:9

Under the Old Covenant, the temple was the house of God, the place of prayer for His people, the children of Israel. The temple had three compartments, one of which was the Holy of Holies, and it held the presence of God! Amazingly, now our renewed and sanctified spirit is the place where His presence dwells!

Under the New Covenant, the apostle Paul tells us that God's presence is now a mystery revealed, which is of Christ in us, "the Hope of glory" (Colossians 1:27). Because of the union you now have with

Christ, you can be close to God because you are God's living temple. You are indwelt by the Holy Spirit, a building still under construction, but nonetheless His house, His tabernacle. Paul goes to great length in encouraging us to live a holy life because we are the temple of God.

Whereas the children of Israel had to go to a specific place to offer their worship with detailed instructions, we have the incredible privilege of worshipping God anywhere and at any time. Therefore, we can be called a house of prayer.

We are always close to God because He dwells in us!

God Cares for You

Casting the whole of your care [all your anxieties, all your worries, all your concerns, once and for all] on Him, for He cares for you affectionately and cares about you watchfully.

1 PETER 5:7

Worry, anxiety, and care have no positive effect on our lives. They do not bring a solution to problems. They do not help us achieve good health, and they prevent our growth in the Word of God.

One of the ways that Satan steals the Word of God from our heart is through cares. The Bible says we are to cast our cares onto God, which is done by prayer. We cannot handle our own problems; we are not built for it. We are created by God to be dependent upon Him, to bring Him

our challenges, and to allow Him to help us with them.

It is not wise to take the cares of life upon ourselves. Keeping our cares is a manifestation of pride. It shows that we think we can solve our own problems and that we don't need the Lord.

We show our humility by leaning on God. Worry, anxiety, and care are not manifestations of leaning on God, but they state by their mere existence that we are attempting to take care of ourselves.

Pray about everything and worry about nothing. You will enjoy life much more.

———————

Worry is like rocking in a rocking chair: it keeps you busy and gets you nowhere!

Christlikeness

For those whom He foreknew [of whom He was aware and loved beforehand], He also destined from the beginning [foreordaining them] to be molded into the image of His Son [and share inwardly His likeness], that He might become the firstborn among many brethren.   ROMANS 8:29

The best goal a Christian can have is Christlikeness. Jesus is the express image of the Father, and we are called to follow in His footsteps. He came as the Pioneer of our faith to show us by example how we can live. We have the chance to behave with people the way Jesus did. Our goal is not to see how successful we can be in business or how famous we can be. It is not prosperity, popularity, or even building a big ministry,

but to be transformed into the image of Jesus Christ.

Spiritual maturity or Christlikeness cannot be obtained without "dying to self." That simply means saying *yes* to God and *no* to ourselves when our will and God's are in opposition. Jesus told His disciples that if they wanted to follow Him, they would need to take up their cross daily.

To follow Christ and become like Him, we choose to forget about what we want—our plans, having our own way—and instead trust Him to show us what His will is for us. His will always leads to deep joy and satisfaction.

———

You are God's Ambassador—represent Him well!

The Battle for the Mind

For we are not wrestling with flesh and blood [contending only with physical opponents], but against the despotisms, against the powers, against [the master spirits who are] the world rulers of this present darkness, against the spirit forces of wickedness in the heavenly (supernatural) sphere.

EPHESIANS 6:12

A careful study of Ephesians 6 informs us that we are in a war, and that our warfare is not with other human beings but with the wicked one. Our enemy, Satan, attempts to defeat us with lies and deceit, through well-laid plans and deliberate deception.

Jesus called the devil "the father of lies and of all that is false" (John 8:44). He lies to you and me. He tells us things about ourselves, about other people, and about

circumstances that are just not true. He usually does not, however, tell us the entire lie all at one time.

He begins by bombarding our mind with a cleverly devised pattern of little nagging thoughts, suspicions, doubts, fears, wonderings, reasonings, and theories. He moves slowly and cautiously. Remember, he has a strategy for his warfare.

Satan has studied us for a long time and knows what we like and what we don't like. He knows our insecurities, weaknesses, and fears. He knows what bothers us most and is willing to invest any amount of time it takes to defeat us. But we can outlast the enemy through the power of the Holy Spirit and through learning the truth of God's Word!

You are more than a conqueror through Christ Who loves you!

Be Still and Know God

Let be and be still, and know (recognize and understand) that I am God. I will be exalted among the nations! I will be exalted in the earth!

PSALM 46:10

Many people today run from one thing to the next. They are addicted to activity, and I used to be one of those people!

For a long time, I felt I had to find something to do all the time. I had to be involved and a part of whatever was going on. I thought I couldn't afford to miss any-thing because I didn't want anything to go on that I didn't know about. I couldn't be still. I had to be up doing something. I was not a human being—I was a human doing.

Thankfully, I discovered that if we will be still and not take matters into our own hands, we will see the amazing power of

God working in our lives. We are often stressed to the maximum degree simply because we keep trying to do things that only God can do. God wants to guide us, but to sense His direction we need to be still! Take time daily to listen. We have two ears and only one mouth, so God must have intended that we listen more than we talk.

When we have plans and ideas, we can submit them to God (acknowledge Him), and make sure we have peace as well as a plan!

God gives His highest and best to those whose trust is in Him. Be still and let Him show Himself strong in your life.

One Step at a Time

*... He Who began a good work in you
will continue until the day of Jesus
Christ... developing [that good work]
and perfecting and bringing it to full
completion in you.*

PHILIPPIANS 1:6

When I speak on the healing of emotional
wounds, I like to hold up several different-
colored shoestrings tied together in a knot.
I tell the audience, "This is you when you
first start the process of transformation
with God. You're all knotted up. Each
knot represents a different problem in your
life that has developed from the things
you have gone through. Untangling those
knots and straightening out those problems
may take a bit of time and effort, so don't
get discouraged if it doesn't happen all at
once."

If you want to receive healing and come into an area of wholeness, you must realize that healing is a process. Allow the Lord to deal with you and your problems in His way and in His time. Your part is to cooperate with Him in whatever area He chooses to start dealing with you first.

In our modern, instantaneous society, we expect everything to be quick and easy. The Lord never gets in a hurry, and He never quits. Sometimes it may seem that you are not making any progress. That's because the Lord is untying your knots one at a time. During the process, we are learning to trust God, and we are developing a close and intimate relationship with Him. God always finishes what He starts, and you will see freedom and victory in your life!

Don't give up!

Choosing to Persevere

That is why I would remind you to stir up (rekindle the embers of, fan the flame of, and keep burning) the [gracious] gift of God . . .

For God did not give us a spirit of timidity . . . but [He has given us a spirit] of power and of love and of calm and well-balanced mind . . .

2 TIMOTHY 1:6–7

On difficult days it is helpful to be reminded to persevere in order to fulfill the call of God on our lives. On those days when you feel like giving up, just remember that God has given you the power to hold on!

In the scripture for today we learn that Timothy was a young minister who simply felt like giving up. The fire that had once burned within him was beginning to grow

cold. The church in those days was experiencing a great deal of persecution, and Timothy had some fears. Perhaps he felt worn-out and that everything was crashing down upon him. He had reached a place where he needed to be encouraged to stir himself up in faith.

Paul was saying, "Timothy, you may feel like quitting, but I am reminding you of the call on your life. Remember the power of the Holy Spirit that changed your life. He gives you a spirit of power, love, discipline, and self-control." Paul encouraged Timothy to be stable.

If we have stability, we do what is right even when it is difficult and does not feel good. Be encouraged today that you can do whatever you need to do. In Christ, you've got what it takes!

———

Giving up is only an option for those who plan to fail in life.

How to Pray Effectively

[Yes] I will grant [I Myself will do for you] whatever you shall ask in My Name [as presenting all that I Am].

JOHN 14:14

I reached a point in my prayer life where I felt frustrated, so I began to seek God about it. I wanted the assurance that my prayers were being effective. I wanted to have confidence that when I prayed, power was released to work in the situation I had prayed about. I wanted those things, but to be honest, I didn't have that assurance or confidence.

Satan definitely wants to steal our confidence concerning prayer. Many people express the same frustrations that I felt. They pray, but all the while they're wondering if they are being effective. What is wrong? I believe that we mistakenly think

that we need to be perfect in order to have power in prayer, but we don't. That is why we have been given the name of Jesus in which to pray!

When we pray in Jesus' name, we are presenting to God the Father all that Jesus is, not what we are. Thankfully, I don't pray in Joyce's name; if I did I would never accomplish anything! The Holy Spirit helps us pray as we ought to, and the name of Jesus guarantees the answer! Be bold in prayer because you have the name above every other name and at the mention of that name, every knee must bow (Philippians 2:10).

Pray boldly, expecting results!

The Simplicity of Grace

But by the grace (the unmerited favor and blessing) of God I am what I am, and His grace toward me was not [found to be] for nothing (fruitless and without effect). In fact, I worked harder than all of them [the apostles], though it was not really I, but the grace (the unmerited favor and blessing) of God which was with me.

1 CORINTHIANS 15:10

There is nothing more powerful than the grace of God. Everything in the Bible— salvation, the infilling of the Holy Spirit, closeness to God, and all victory in our daily lives—is based upon it. Without grace, we are nothing, we have nothing, we can do nothing.

The grace of God is not complicated or confusing. In fact, it is so simple that

many of us miss its true meaning and end up making our lives incredibly complex. I know I did.

Reading God's Word, I constantly saw the need for change in my life. But I didn't know that the grace of God could bring about those changes. I didn't know how to allow the Holy Spirit to fill my life and cause those things to happen. So I tried to change myself and everything else in my life in my own strength. The results went beyond frustration and became emotionally destructive.

It was when I discovered the grace of God that I realized His power would enable me to do with ease what I could never do on my own. It changed my life, and it can change yours too.

———

Let everything you do in life be "by grace through faith," and you will live with peace and joy!

No More Guilt or Condemnation

Therefore, [there is] now no condemnation (no adjudging guilty of wrong) for those who are in Christ Jesus, who live [and] walk not after the dictates of the flesh, but after the dictates of the Spirit. ROMANS 8:1

One of the major problems for many believers is the recurrence of feeling guilty and condemned for past sins that they have received forgiveness for. Satan's great delight is to make us feel bad about ourselves, and one way to do that is by making us feel guilty. Even though it is a false guilt, if we accept it, we are affected adversely by it.

The Bible teaches that through the blood of Jesus, we have complete forgiveness and total freedom from condemnation. We don't need to add our guilt to His

sacrifice upon the cross. He is more than enough.

If the devil tries to bring that sin to your mind again in the form of guilt and condemnation, declare to him: "I was forgiven for that sin! It has been taken care of; therefore, I take no care for it." You will find that speaking aloud is often helpful to you because by doing so, you are declaring your stand on the Word of God. Declare to the enemy that Christ has set you free.

Don't just sit and listen to the devil's accusations and lies. Learn to talk back to him with the truth.

Supernatural Favor

For You, Lord, will bless the
[uncompromisingly] righteous [him who
is upright and in right standing with
You]; as with a shield You will surround
him with goodwill (pleasure and favor).

PSALM 5:12

When I first started ministering, I was scared. I was afraid of being rejected. In those days, for a woman to do what I was doing was even less popular than it is today when women preachers are more widely accepted. So I bent over backward to speak and behave the way I thought was expected of me.

The problem was that I was trying to have favor with people through my own works, and it didn't work. Trying to get favor on your own is not only hard work,

it is often pointless. The harder you try, the less people are attracted to you.

At the time, I knew nothing about supernatural favor. I didn't know that favor is a part of grace. In fact, in the English New Testament the words *grace* and *favor* are both translated from the same Greek word *charis*. So the grace of God is the favor of God. And the grace of God causes things to happen in our lives that need to happen. Grace is the power of God coming through our faith to do what we cannot do on our own. It is not by human power, or by human might, but by the Holy Spirit that we receive favor. It is by God's Spirit of grace that we find favor with God and with man.

———

Every day declare out loud that you believe you have favor with God and that He gives you favor with man! (Proverbs 3:4)

Tearing Down Strongholds

*For the weapons of our warfare are
not physical [weapons of flesh and
blood], but they are mighty before God
for the overthrow and destruction of
strongholds.*

2 CORINTHIANS 10:4

Through careful strategy and cunning deceit,
Satan attempts to set up "strongholds" in
our minds. A stronghold is an area in which
we are held in bondage (in prison) due to
a certain way of thinking. Strongholds are
lies that are believed.

The apostle Paul tells us that we have the
spiritual weapons we need in order to overcome Satan's strongholds. Using our weapons, we refute the enemy's lies, arguments,
theories, reasonings, and every other thing
that tries to exalt itself against the truth of
God's Word. We must take our thoughts

captive and refuse to indulge in the fleshly luxury of receiving and meditating on every thought that falls into our heads (2 Corinthians 10:5).

The primary weapon with which we do battle is the Word of God used in various ways—preached, taught, sung, confessed, meditated upon, written, and read. The knowledge of God's Word will renew our minds and teach us to think in a brand-new way. It will tear down old strongholds that have kept us in bondage!

No one will ever live a truly victorious life without being a sincere student of God's Word.

Jesus, Your Prince of Peace

*Peace I leave with you; My [own] peace
I now give and bequeath to you. Not
as the world gives do I give to you. Do
not let your hearts be troubled, neither
let them be afraid. [Stop allowing
yourselves to be agitated and disturbed;
and do not permit yourselves to be
fearful and intimidated and cowardly
and unsettled.]*   JOHN 14:27

When we are all stressed out, we usually
try to eliminate the things that are causing
our problems. But the source of stress is not
really our difficulties, circumstances, and
situations. Stress comes when we approach
problems with the world's perspective rather
than faith in Jesus Christ, the Prince of Peace.

It was Jesus' blood that bought our
peace. Peace is ours as a gift from Him,
but we need to be willing to change our

approach to life. We cannot have anxiety, frustration, bitterness, strife and offense, or rigid, legalistic attitudes and enjoy the peace of God.

Even though we will have disturbing issues to deal with, we can have Jesus' peace because He has overcome the world and deprived the world of its power to harm us (John 16:33). He left us with the power to "stop allowing" ourselves "to be agitated and disturbed"! Peace is available; all you have to do is choose it!

The Prince of Peace, Jesus, Who lives inside those who have received Him, knows and will reveal to us the specific actions for us to take in every situation to lead us into peace.

———————

It is absolutely amazing what we can accomplish in Christ if we live one day at a time in His peace.

Jesus and Emotions

For we do not have a High Priest Who is unable to understand and sympathize and have a shared feeling with our weaknesses and infirmities and liability to the assaults of temptation, but One Who has been tempted in every respect as we are, yet without sinning.

HEBREWS 4:15

According to the writer of Hebrews, Jesus experienced every emotion and suffered every feeling you and I do, yet without sinning. He did not sin because He did not give in to His wrong feelings. He knew the Word of God in every area of life because He spent years studying it before He began His ministry. You and I will never be able to say no to our feelings if we don't have a strong knowledge of God's Word.

When someone hurts me and I feel

angry or upset, I pray, "Jesus, I am so glad that You understand what I am feeling right now and that You don't condemn me for feeling this way. I don't want to give vent to my emotions. Help me to forgive those who have wronged me and not slight them, avoid them, or seek to pay them back for the harm they have done me."

No matter when or how temptation comes, God has enabled us to resist it. But we need to know His Word and lean on Him for help. We cannot do it in our own strength; it is His Word and Spirit that enable us to resist temptation! It is not wrong to feel tempted, but it is wrong if we give in to the temptation.

———————

Manage your emotions—don't let them manage you!

Stopping the Emotional Yo-Yo

But the fruit of the [Holy] Spirit... is love, joy (gladness), peace, patience (an even temper, forbearance), kindness, goodness (benevolence), faithfulness, gentleness (meekness, humility), self-control... GALATIANS 5:22–23

I remember the years when I was what I call a "yo-yo Christian." I was continually up and down emotionally. If my husband, Dave, did what I liked, I was happy. If he didn't do what I liked, I would get mad. I had not yet learned how to be led by the Holy Spirit and was letting my feelings control my behavior.

More than anything else, believers tell me how they feel. "I feel nobody loves me." "I feel my spouse doesn't treat me right." "I feel that I'll never be happy." "I feel... I don't feel..." and on and on it goes.

God wants us to realize that our emotions are never going to go away, so we must learn to manage them rather than let them manage us. We can choose to exercise self-control and not let our flesh rule us. Not one of us will, or even should, get everything we want. A spiritually mature believer can be peaceful and happy even when they don't get what they want. We can choose to tell ourselves that we are not going to be able to say everything we want to say, eat everything we want to eat, and always do what we feel like doing. Choose to let the Holy Spirit help you do what is right no matter how you feel!

———————

As Christians, instead of concentrating on how we feel, we can focus on what we know is true in the Word of God.

The Prayers of a Righteous Man

Elijah was a man with a nature like ours, and he prayed earnestly that it would not rain; and it did not rain on the land for three years and six months.

JAMES 5:17 NKJV

James tells us that the fervent prayer of a "righteous" man is powerful (James 5:16). This person has placed his faith in Jesus for salvation and the forgiveness of sins and is not under condemnation—one who has confidence in God and in the power of prayer. It does not mean a person without any imperfection in his life.

Elijah was a man of God who did not always behave perfectly, but he did not allow his imperfections to steal his confidence in God. Elijah had faith, but at times we also see fear in his life. He was obedient, but at times he was also disobedient. He

loved God and wanted to fulfill His will and calling upon his life. But sometimes he gave in to human weaknesses and tried to avoid the consequences.

In 1 Kings 18 we see him moving in tremendous power, calling down fire from heaven and slaying 450 prophets of Baal. Then immediately after that we see him fearfully running from Jezebel, becoming negative and depressed, and even wanting to die.

Like many of us, Elijah let his emotions get the upper hand sometimes. He was a human being just like us, and yet he prayed powerful prayers. His example should give us enough "scriptural power" to defeat condemnation when it rises up to tell us we cannot pray powerfully because of our weaknesses and faults.

———

Never underestimate the power of confident, effective, fervent prayer.

More and More Grace

But He gives us more and more grace (power of the Holy Spirit, to meet this evil tendency and all others fully). That is why He says, God sets Himself against the proud and haughty, but gives grace [continually] to the lowly (those who are humble enough to receive it).

JAMES 4:6

All human beings have evil tendencies, but James teaches us that God will give us more and more grace to meet these tendencies.

I spent much of my Christian life trying to overcome my own wrong motives and intentions. But all my trying just brought much frustration. I had to come to a place of humility and learn that God gives grace to the humble—not the proud. He gives help to those who are humble enough to ask for it.

We have our own ideas about what we can accomplish, but often we think more highly of ourselves than we ought. We should have a humble attitude, knowing that apart from God, we can do nothing.

If you are planning your own way, trying to make things happen in the strength of your own flesh, then you are frustrated. You probably have said, "No matter what I do, nothing seems to work!" Nothing will ever work until you learn to trust in God's grace.

Relax. Let God be God. Stop being so hard on yourself. Change is a process that brings you closer to Him little by little. You're on your way, so enjoy the trip.

If you desire to be free, be willing to exchange human effort for trusting in God.

Doorways of Pain

They who sow in tears shall reap in joy and singing.   PSALM 126:5

For many of us, forgiving someone who has hurt us is the most difficult part of emotional healing. It can even be the stumbling block that prevents it. Those who have been badly wounded by others know that it is much easier to say the word *forgive* than it is to do it.

First, let me say that it is not possible to have good emotional health while harboring bitterness, resentment, and unforgiveness toward someone. It's poison to your system. And it is impossible to get better if it's there.

When I finally allowed the Lord to begin to work in my life, He revealed to me I had been hiding behind "doorways of pain"—the painful events and situations of

my past. To pass back through the same, or similar, doorways and to be delivered and healed meant facing the issues, people, and truths I found so difficult, if not impossible, to face on my own.

Don't be afraid of the pain of healing. The temptation is to run away, but the Lord is close to you, and He wants to bring you through your problems. Going through is always better than running from a thing. Endure whatever you need to, knowing that there is joy on the other side.

———————

God does not bring hurts and wounds upon us. But if they are inflicted upon us, He is able to make miracles out of mistakes.

Different Kinds of Favor

And let the beauty and delightfulness and favor of the Lord our God be upon us; confirm and establish the work of our hands—yes, the work of our hands, confirm and establish it.

PSALM 90:17

There is a distinction between natural favor and supernatural favor. Natural favor can be earned, whereas supernatural favor can't.

If you work hard enough and long enough, you can get people to like and accept you most of the time. But that acceptance must be maintained the same way it was gained. Having to say and do all the right things all the time in order to stay in favor with people is a form of bondage.

If we will choose to follow God instead of people, He will grant us His favor. It is

a gift of His grace and cannot be earned. God doesn't want us to waste our time and energy trying to earn favor; He wants us to trust Him for it. When God gives us His favor, amazing things begin to take place. Doors of opportunity will open for you. You will end up with benefits and blessings that you have not earned or deserved.

We can pray daily for God's supernatural favor. It is a gift of God that comes by grace through our faith. Go ahead and ask, and keep on asking and you will receive!

When we know that everything we have and enjoy is a gift from God, a result of His supernatural favor upon us, then there is nothing left to do but say, "Thank You, Lord."

The Sword of the Spirit

And take the helmet of salvation and the sword that the Spirit wields, which is the Word of God.   EPHESIANS 6:17

The attacks of Satan against the church are more intense than ever before. So many people are experiencing tremendous attacks against their minds and enduring great attacks of fear.

A person who learns to abide in the Word of God and let the Word abide in him will have a two-edged sword with which to do battle. To abide means to remain, to continue in, or to dwell in. If you make God's Word a small part of your life, you will know only a partial truth and will experience only limited freedom. But those who *abide* in it will know the full truth and will experience complete freedom.

My life used to be a mess because I was

ignorant of the Word. For many years I was a Christian who loved God and was active in church work, but I had zero victory because I did not know the Word. Thankfully, I can now testify that the Word of God has caused me to be victorious and to recognize the attacks of Satan.

Learn the Word and allow the Holy Spirit to wield it by speaking, singing, or meditating on the portions of Scripture that you feel He is placing on your heart.

———————

If you keep your sword drawn, the enemy won't be so quick to approach you. Speak the Word!

Works Versus Grace

*Even when we were dead (slain) by
[our own] shortcomings and trespasses,
He made us alive together in fellowship
and in union with Christ; [He gave us
the very life of Christ Himself, the same
new life with which He quickened Him,
for] it is by grace (His favor and mercy
which you did not deserve) that you are
saved (delivered from judgment and
made partakers of Christ's salvation).*

EPHESIANS 2:5

We often get frustrated because we are trying to live by our own *works*, when our lives
were brought into being and designed by
God to be lived by *grace*. The more we try
to figure out what to do to solve our dilemmas, the more confused, upset, and frustrated we will become.

When you get into a frustrating situation, just stop and say, "O Lord, give me grace (Your power and ability)." Then believe that God has heard your prayer and is answering that prayer and working out the situation.

Faith is the channel through which you and I receive the grace of God. If we try to do things on our own, without being open to receive the grace of God, then no matter how much faith we think we have, we will still not receive what we are asking of God.

We can trust in and rely on the grace of God. He is close to us, He knows what we are facing in every situation of life, and He will work out things for the best if we will trust Him enough to allow Him to do so.

———

Remember, it is not by power or by might, but by the Spirit that we win the victory over our enemy.

No Pain, No Gain

...[The Lord] has sent me to comfort the brokenhearted and to proclaim that captives will be released and prisoners will be freed. He has sent me to tell those who mourn that the time of the Lord's favor has come... To all who mourn... he will give a crown of beauty for ashes, a joyous blessing instead of mourning, festive praise instead of despair....

ISAIAH 61:1–3 NLT

When moving to emotional wholeness, even with the Holy Spirit leading us, the pain of the healing process from emotional wounds can be more traumatic than experiencing physical pain. Because I experienced so much emotional pain early in my life, I grew weary of hurting. I was attempting to find healing by following the leadership of

the Holy Spirit, yet I could not understand why the process had to be so painful.

The Lord revealed to me that I had been hiding behind many "doorways of pain." I was deep in bondage, taking refuge behind false personalities, pretenses, and facades. I began to understand that when people are led out of bondage into freedom, they must pass back through similar doorways of pain to get on the other side of those doors. They pass through the emotional responses to their initial pain as the Lord leads them to face issues, people, and truths that are difficult. The good news is that we don't have to face them on our own. He is always near to you, and He will bring you to a place of healing if you will let Him.

———

Thank God, He heals the brokenhearted, opens prison doors, and sets the captives free! You don't have to live in the pain of your past!

God Is Unchanging

Jesus Christ (the Messiah) is [always] the same, yesterday, today, [yes] and forever (to the ages).   HEBREWS 13:8

What is the main thing that we love so much about Jesus? There are many answers to that question, of course, such as the fact that He died for us on the cross so we wouldn't have to be punished for our sins; then He rose again on the third day. But in our daily relationship with Him, one of the things we appreciate the most about Him is the fact that we can count on His unchanging nature. He can change anything else that needs to be changed, but He Himself always remains the same.

That is the kind of person we can aspire to be, but it will never happen if we cannot control our emotions. Being emotionally mature means making decisions based on

the leading of the Holy Spirit, not on our feelings. But it doesn't come naturally.

Our emotions will never go away, but we can learn to manage them. God is able to bring us into balance. It doesn't mean we become emotionless or dull. God gave us emotions so we could enjoy life. But it does mean we take control in the strength and power of the Holy Spirit as we're led by Him.

———

God does not want us to change every time our circumstances change. He wants us to always be the same, just as He is.

Short and Simple

And when you pray, do not keep on babbling like pagans, for they think they will be heard because of their many words. Do not be like them, for your Father knows what you need before you ask him.   MATTHEW 6:7–8 NIV

I believe if I can keep my request very simple and not confuse the issue by trying to come up with too many words, my prayer actually seems to be more clear and powerful.

We can choose to spend our energy releasing our faith, not repeating phrases over and over that only serve to make the prayer long and involved.

I remember a time when it was difficult for me to keep my prayers short and simple. I began to realize that my problem in praying was that I didn't have faith that my

prayer would get through if it was short, simple, and to the point. I had fallen into the same trap that many people do—"the-longer-the-better" mentality. I'm not advocating that we should only pray for short periods of time, but I am suggesting that each prayer be simple, direct, to the point, and filled with faith.

Now as I follow God's direction to keep it simple and make my request without repeating myself over and over, I experience a much greater release of my faith. And I know that God has heard me and will answer.

————

If your prayers are complicated, simplify them. Remember, you are heard because of your faith, not your amount of speaking!

Quick to Forgive

And become useful and helpful and kind to one another, tenderhearted... forgiving one another [readily and freely], as God in Christ forgave you.

EPHESIANS 4:32

The Bible teaches us to forgive "readily and freely." That is God's standard for us, no matter how we feel about it. We are to be quick to forgive.

According to 1 Peter 5:5, we can clothe ourselves with the character of Jesus Christ, meaning that we can choose to be long-suffering, patient, not easily offended, slow to anger, quick to forgive, and filled with mercy. My definition of "mercy" is to look beyond what is done to me that hurts and discover the reason why it was done. Many times people do things even they don't understand themselves, but there is always

a reason why people behave as they do. Perhaps they are hurting and in their own pain they don't even realize they are hurting someone else.

God forgives! We are to be merciful and forgiving, just as God in Christ forgives us our wrongdoing. He not only sees what we do that is wrong, but He understands why we did it, and is merciful and long-suffering. The choice to forgive others is ours. God will not force anyone to do it. Even if you don't understand it, believe that God's way is the best. It works. He can take what Satan meant to destroy you and turn it for your good.

We are to forgive in order to keep Satan from getting the advantage over us.

Get Plugged In

I am the Vine; you are the branches.
Whoever lives in Me and I in him bears
much (abundant) fruit...

JOHN 15:5

In our Christian walk, many times we end up with a lot of principles, formulas, and methods, but no real power. That may be true for teachings on faith, prayer, praise, meditation, Bible study, confession, spiritual warfare, and all the other precepts we have been hearing about and engaging in. They are all good, and we need to know about them, but they alone cannot solve our problems.

It's important to remember that, as good as these disciplines are, they are only channels to receiving from the Lord. They are of no help unless we are plugged in to the divine power source.

We get plugged in through a personal relationship with God, which requires time. We will never have any real lasting victory in our Christian life without spending time in personal, private fellowship with the Lord. He has an individual plan for you. If you ask Him, He will come into your heart and commune with you. He will teach and guide you in the way you should go.

Learn to respond quickly to the promptings of the Holy Spirit for an intimate relationship with God. Come apart with Him privately, and you will be rewarded in abundance.

It is only in the presence of the Lord that we receive the power of the Lord.

Closer to God in Prayer

Watch and pray so that you will not fall into temptation. The spirit is willing, but the flesh is weak.

MATTHEW 26:41 NIV

Prayer is a spiritual weapon God has given us to wage warfare. Prayer is relationship with the Godhead. It is coming and asking for help or talking to God about something that bothers us. Prayer interrupts Satan's plan for evil!

If you want to have an effective prayer life, develop a good personal relationship with the Father. Know that He loves you, that He is full of mercy, that He will help you. Get to know Jesus. He is your Friend. He died for you. Get to know the Holy Spirit. He is with you all the time as your Helper. Let Him help you.

All kinds of prayer are to be used in

our walk with God. There is the prayer of agreement between two people and also the united prayer of a group of people. There are prayers of thanksgiving, praise and worship, petition, intercession, commitment, and consecration.

Whatever kind of prayer you bring, learn to fill your prayers with the Word of God and offer them with the assurance that God keeps His Word.

We tend to put off praying, but I recommend that you pray right away any time you see or think of a need!

The Faith Attitude

But the Lord was with Joseph, and
showed him mercy and loving-kindness
and gave him favor in the sight of the
warden of the prison.

GENESIS 39:21

Although Joseph was being punished unfairly because he was jailed for something he didn't do, the Lord was still with him, giving him supernatural favor and taking care of him. He proved that a person is really not in too bad a shape, even if he ends up in prison, if God gives him favor.

No matter what happens to us in life, we can have favor with God and with other people (Luke 2:52). But like so many good things in life, just because something is available to us does not mean that we will partake of it. The Lord makes many things available to us that we never

receive and enjoy because we never activate our faith.

For example, if we go to a job interview confessing fear and failure, we will almost be assured not to get the job. On the other hand, even if we apply for a job that we know we aren't fully qualified for, we can still go in confidence, believing that God will give us favor in every situation that is His will.

God doesn't want us to be afraid of the hardships we face in life. He is in control, and He will work all things out for our good if we love and trust Him.

———

Joseph maintained a good attitude in a bad situation. He had a "faith attitude," and God gave him favor.

God Is Able

Now unto him that is able to do exceeding abundantly above all that we ask or think, according to the power that worketh in us.   EPHESIANS 3:20 KJV

Ephesians 3:20 is a powerful scripture that tells us that our God is able—able to do far above and beyond anything that you and I can ever dare to hope, ask, or even think. We can pray, do the asking in faith and trust. But it is God Who does the work, not us. How does He do it? *According to [or by] the power [or grace of God] that worketh in us.* Whatever you and I receive from the Lord is directly related to the amount of grace we learn to receive.

I was putting unbelievable stress on myself trying to change. I was under tremendous condemnation because every message I heard seemed to be telling me to

change; yet I couldn't change no matter how hard I tried. I was in terrible torment because I saw all the things about me that needed to be changed, but I was powerless to bring about those changes.

The closer you get to the Lord, the more you see that He has to be your Source in all things. He is the only One who can bring about changes in your life. Learn to say, "God, I cannot do anything without You, but You can do all things through me!"

———

God promises to strengthen us in our weaknesses if we trust Him and turn to Him. God's grace will be sufficient to meet our needs.

Walking Free

For God did not send the Son into the world in order to judge (to reject, to condemn, to pass sentence on) the world, but that the world might find salvation and be made safe and sound through Him.   JOHN 3:17

One of the biggest tools the enemy uses to try to make us feel bad is condemnation, which certainly can be a cause of discouragement. According to the Word of God, we who are in Christ Jesus are no longer condemned, no longer judged guilty or wrong. Yet so often we judge and condemn ourselves.

Until I learned and understood the Word of God, I lived a large part of my life feeling guilty. If someone asked me what I felt guilty about, I could not answer. All I knew was that there was a vague

feeling of guilt that followed me around all the time.

From that experience, God gave me a real revelation about walking free from guilt and condemnation. He showed me that you and I must not only receive forgiveness from Him, we must also forgive ourselves. We must stop beating ourselves over the head for something that He has forgiven and forgotten (Jeremiah 31:34; Acts 10:15).

I believe it is nearly impossible to get discouraged if the mind is kept under strict control. That is why we are told in Isaiah 26:3 that God will guard and keep us in perfect and constant peace—if we will keep our mind stayed on Him.

———

God has new things on the horizon of your life, but you will never see them if you live in and relive the past.

Do You Want to Get Well?

There was a certain man there who had suffered with a deep-seated and lingering disorder for thirty-eight years. When Jesus noticed him lying there [helpless], knowing that he had already been a long time in that condition, He said to him, Do you want to become well? [Are you really in earnest about getting well?] JOHN 5:5–6

Isn't this an amazing question for Jesus to ask this poor man who had been sick for thirty-eight long years: "Do you really want to become well?" That is the Lord's question to each of us as well.

Do you know there are people who don't really want to get well? They only want to talk about their problem. We should all ask ourselves if we truly want to get well, or if our problem has become our identity.

Sometimes people get addicted to having a problem. It becomes their identity, their life. It defines everything they think and say and do. All their being is centered around that particular problem.

If you have a "deep-seated and lingering disorder," the Lord wants you to know that it does not have to be the focal point of your entire existence. He wants you to trust Him and cooperate with Him as He leads you to victory over that problem one step at a time.

Whatever our problem may be, God has promised to meet our need and to repay us for our past hurts. Facing truth is the key to unlocking prison doors that may have held us in bondage.

God yearns to see you become all that He has planned for you to be.

God Is Always Good

Every good gift and every perfect (free, large, full) gift is from above; it comes down from the Father of all [that gives] light, in [the shining of] Whom there can be no variation [rising or setting] or shadow cast by His turning [as in an eclipse].   JAMES 1:17

James tells us that God is good, period. He is not good sometimes; He is always good.

Isn't it wonderful to have a God Who is always the same? With God there is no turning, no variation. We can depend on Him to be faithful all the time, to be merciful and forgiving all the time, to only do us good as long as we live.

If we are having a hard time, if we feel like giving up, God is still good. He is not the Author of our problems. If something bad happens to us, God is still good. He

doesn't do good things for us because we are good and we deserve them; He does good things for us because He is good and He loves us. We can depend on God's goodness in our lives!

———————

The key to happiness and fulfillment is not in changing our situation or circumstances, but in trusting God to be God in our life.

How Many Times Should I Pray?

Keep on asking and it will be given you; keep on seeking and you will find; keep on knocking [reverently] and [the door] will be opened to you. For everyone who keeps on asking receives; and he who keeps on seeking finds; and to him who keeps on knocking, [the door] will be opened.   MATTHEW 7:7–8

I don't believe we can make any strict rules on the subject of how often to pray about the same thing. But I do think there are some guidelines that may apply to help us have even more confidence in the power of prayer.

If my children need something, I want them to trust me to do what they have asked me to do. I wouldn't mind, and might even like it, if they occasionally said, "Boy, Mom, I'm sure looking forward to

those new shoes." That statement would declare to me that they believed I was going to do what I promised. They would actually be reminding me of my promise, but in a way that would not question my integrity.

I believe sometimes when we ask God the same thing over and over, it is a sign of doubt and unbelief, not of faith and persistence.

When I ask the Lord for something in prayer and that request comes to my mind later, I talk to Him about it again. But when I do, I refrain from asking Him the same thing as if I think He didn't hear me the first time. I thank the Lord that He is working on the situation I prayed about previously and expect Him to do what is best.

Faithful, persistent prayer builds even more faith and confidence in us as we continue to pray.

Grace Is Not for Sale

Through Him also we have [our] access (entrance, introduction) by faith into this grace (state of God's favor) in which we [firmly and safely] stand. And let us rejoice and exult in our hope of experiencing and enjoying the glory of God.   ROMANS 5:2

The devil wants you and me to think that we can buy the grace (favor) of God with our works. But God's grace is not for sale, because by its very definition—*unmerited favor*—it is a gift.

Grace cannot be earned by prayer, good works, reading the Bible, confessing scriptures, or church attendance. It cannot even be bought by faith. The grace of God is receivable, but it is not "buyable."

Even when we do all the right things, it is important that our motives are pure.

When we are fellowshipping with the Lord, if our motive is to get something from Him, we have moved from grace to works. Let us not fall into the trap of thinking that we *deserve* anything good from the Lord. God's goodness is a gift and all we can do is thank Him and be filled with gratitude. Anything we do for God should be done because we love Him, and never to get anything from Him.

We can seek the Lord and fellowship with Him for no other reason than the fact that we love Him and want to be closer to Him each day.

———————

Salvation and every good thing from God is a gift and is received by faith alone, so that man cannot boast.

When You Feel Discouraged

*[What, what would have become of me]
had I not believed that I would see the
Lord's goodness in the land of the living!*
PSALM 27:13

We have all been disappointed at some time. It would be surprising if we went through the week without encountering some kind of disappointment. We are "appointed" (set in a certain direction) for something to happen a certain way, and when it doesn't happen that way, we become "dis-appointed."

Disappointment not dealt with turns into discouragement. If we stay discouraged very long, we are liable to become devastated, and devastation leaves us unable to handle anything.

Many devastated Christians live defeated lives because they have not learned how to handle disappointment. The devastation

they are experiencing most likely began with a minor disappointment that was not dealt with properly.

It is not God's will for us to live disappointed, devastated, or oppressed. When we become "disappointed," we can choose to become "re-appointed" to keep from becoming discouraged, then devastated.

When we learn to place our hope and confidence in Jesus the Rock (1 Corinthians 10:4) and resist the devil at his onset (1 Peter 5:8–9), we can live in the joy and peace of the Lord, free from discouragement.

Choose to aggressively withstand the devil so you can live in the fullness of life God has provided for you through His Son Jesus Christ.

High Praises of God

Let the saints be joyful in the glory and beauty [which God confers upon them]; let them sing for joy upon their beds. Let the high praises of God be in their throats and a two-edged sword in their hands.   PSALM 149:5–6

We should form a habit of thanking and praising God as soon as we wake up each morning. While we are still lying in bed, let's give thanks and fill our minds with Scripture.

Praise defeats the devil quicker than any other battle plan. Praise is an invisible garment that we put on and it protects us from defeat and negativity in our minds. But it must be genuine, heartfelt praise, not just lip service or a method being tried to see if it works. We praise God for the promises in His Word and for His goodness.

Worship is a battle position! As we worship God for Who He is and for His attributes, for His ability and might, we draw closer to Him and the enemy is defeated.

We can never be too thankful! Thank God all day long and remember the many things He has done for you.

———————

God never loses a battle. He has a definite battle plan, and when we follow Him, we will always win.

Under God's Control

. . . [The Lord] brings low and He lifts up.   1 SAMUEL 2:7

It is important to remember that the Lord can bring one person down and lift up another. One instance is in the life of Esther. God raised her up from obscurity to become the queen of the entire land. He gave her favor with everyone she met, including the king, because she had found favor with God.

Esther drew upon that favor to save herself and her people, the Jews, from being murdered by the evil Haman, who was out to destroy them. She may have been afraid to go to the king and ask him to intervene, because doing so could have cost her very life, but she did it because she trusted her life to God.

Whatever situation comes into your life,

even if you are being harassed, persecuted, or discriminated against, or someone is trying to take something from you that rightfully belongs to you—whether it is your job, your home, your reputation, or anything in life—believe God for supernatural favor. Despite how hopeless things may look, God can lift up and He can bring down. If your life is in His hands, believe that the light of the Lord shines upon you to give you favor.

Don't go through life being afraid; God loves you and will always help you!

Face the Truth

... If you abide in My word [hold fast to My teachings and live in accordance with them], you are truly My disciples. And you will know the Truth, and the Truth will set you free.   JOHN 8:31–32

Anyone who needs emotional healing and restoration from past hurts must learn to face truth. We cannot be set free while living in denial. If you are hurt, talk to God about it openly because He cares about everything that concerns you.

Many times people who have suffered abuse or some other tragedy in their lives try to act as though it never happened. Early traumatic experiences can cause us to be emotionally damaged and wounded later in life because we develop opinions and attitudes about ourselves based on what happened to us.

From my own experience, as well as my years of ministry to others, I have come to realize that we human beings are marvelously adept at building walls and hiding things in dark corners, pretending they never happened. We do this because it may seem easier. But avoiding issues will keep us in bondage; facing them with God's help will set us free.

It is so wonderful to be in relationship with Jesus, because we don't have to hide anything from Him. He already knows everything about us anyway. We can always come to Him and know we will be loved and accepted no matter what we have suffered or how we have reacted to it.

Even though it may be hard to face the truth, Jesus promises to be with us and set us free.

The Lord Is Our Rock

He is the Rock, His work is perfect, for all His ways are law and justice. A God of faithfulness without breach or deviation, just and right is He.

DEUTERONOMY 32:4

God always loves us unconditionally. He doesn't love us if we are good and then stop loving us if we are bad. He always loves us. He is always kind, always slow to anger, always full of grace and mercy, always ready to forgive.

God is a Rock, unchanging and without deviation. He is great and unfailing, faithful and just, perfect and right in all His doing. He will never leave us or forsake us.

What would happen in our lives and in the lives of those around us if we were more like God? What would happen if we were always loving, always slow to anger, always

filled with grace and mercy, always ready to forgive? What would happen if we, like our God, were always positive, peaceful, and generous? He is our Rock, but He is also our Example. We are to strive to be the way He is.

We can all grow spiritually and be changed into the image of Christ. God does not expect us to become perfect overnight, but He wants to help us to become more and more like Him day by day.

God helps us daily to become more and more like Him. Don't be discouraged by how far you have to go—rejoice that you are growing!

Believe God Hears You

And this is the confidence (the assurance, the privilege of boldness) which we have in Him: [we are sure] that if we ask anything (make any request) according to His will (in agreement with His own plan), He listens to and hears us.

And if (since) we [positively] know that He listens to us in whatever we ask, we also know [with settled and absolute knowledge] that we have [granted us as our present possessions] the requests made of Him.

1 JOHN 5:14–15

In John 11:41–42, just before Jesus called Lazarus forth from the tomb, He prayed: "Father, I thank You that You have heard Me." What a confident prayer!

Satan does not want you to have that kind of confidence. But I encourage you to

be confident when you pray. Make a decision that you are a believer, not a beggar. Go to the throne in Jesus' name—His name will get attention!

As human beings, we often enjoy knowing someone important and being able to mention their name, hoping it will give us favor and open doors. If that works for us as human beings, just think how well it must work in the heavenly realm—especially when we use the name that is above all other names—the blessed name of Jesus!

When we pray in Jesus' name, we are offering to God all that Jesus is. That can give us great confidence that God hears and answers our prayers.

———

Go to God in prayer—boldly. With confidence. In the name of Jesus.

Forgiving God

*Therefore I will not restrain my mouth;
I will speak in the anguish of my spirit, I
will complain in the bitterness of my soul
[O Lord]!*
JOB 7:11

Like Job, many people have problems with
blaming God for their troubles. They are
angry with God! Those who have never
experienced that feeling may not understand it. But those who have know what
it is to feel animosity toward God because
they blame Him for not providing them
with something important in their lives.
Things have not worked out the way they
had planned. They believe that God could
have changed things if He had wanted to,
but since He didn't, they feel disappointed
and blame Him for their situation.

If you are holding on to an attitude like
this, you must realize that it is impossible

to have close fellowship with someone you are mad at. God is the One Who can help you, so the only answer is to let go of anger. When you are disappointed with life, run *to* God, not away from Him.

Often we think if we just knew why certain things happened to us, we would be satisfied. I believe God tells us only what we really need to know, what we are prepared to handle, and what will not harm us but will, in fact, help us. With God's help, we can learn to let go and not try to figure out everything in life.

There must come a time when we stop living in the past and asking why. Instead, we can learn to let God turn our scars into stars.

The Divine Enabler

Behold, I am the Lord, the God of all flesh; is there anything too hard for Me?
JEREMIAH 32:27

Our God is able to do far above and beyond anything we can ever dare to hope, ask, or even think (Ephesians 3:20). When we pray in faith, it opens the door for God to work in our lives. Nothing is too hard for Him.

If you are struggling with changes that need to be made in your own personality, this word is especially for you. You can't change yourself. But thanks be to God, He can! He knows what is wrong with you, and He's ready and able to bring about the changes that you need if you just ask.

You and I don't have a problem that is too big for the grace of God. If our problem gets bigger, God's grace gets bigger. If

our problems multiply, the grace of God also multiplies so that we are able to handle them.

It isn't any harder for God to deliver us from three problems than it is for Him to deliver us from one or two. Our biggest problem is still small to Him. God is able to do anything, so ask in faith and relax and let Him work.

———————

God knew all of our faults when He accepted us, and He will never reject us because of them.

God Chooses the Unlikely

God selected (deliberately chose) what in the world is foolish to put the wise to shame, and what the world calls weak to put the strong to shame.

1 CORINTHIANS 1:27

When you feel discouraged, remember that God chose you for His very own purpose, however unlikely a candidate you feel that you are. By doing so, He has placed before you a wide open door to show you His boundless grace, mercy, and power to change your life.

When God uses any one of us, though we may all feel inadequate and unworthy, we realize that our source is not in ourselves but in Him alone: "[This is] because the foolish thing [that has its source in] God is wiser than men, and the weak thing [that

springs] from God is stronger than men" (1 Corinthians 1:25).

Each of us has a destiny, and there is absolutely no excuse not to fulfill it. We cannot use our weakness as an excuse, because God says that His strength is made perfect in weakness (2 Corinthians 12:9). We cannot use the past as an excuse, because God tells us through the apostle Paul that if any person is in Christ, he is a new creature; old things have passed away, and all things have become new (2 Corinthians 5:17).

Spend some time with yourself and take an inventory of how you feel about yourself. What is your image of yourself? Do you see yourself re-created in God's image, resurrected to a brand-new life that is just waiting for you to claim it?

Each of us can succeed at being everything God intends for us to be.

Never an Excuse

*The Lord will fight for you, and you
shall hold your peace and remain at rest.*
EXODUS 14:14

Sadly, many people do not always accept the truth that God reveals to them. It is painful to face our faults and deal with them. We tend to justify misbehavior. We allow our past and how we were raised to negatively affect the rest of our lives.

Our past may explain why we're suffering, but we don't have to use it as an excuse to stay in bondage.

Everyone is without excuse because Jesus always stands ready to fulfill His promise to set us free. He is close to us, and He will walk us across the finish line in any area if we are willing to go all the way through it with Him.

God doesn't abandon us and leave us

helpless. He promises us that He will not allow us to be tempted beyond what we can bear, but with every temptation He will also provide the way out, the escape (1 Corinthians 10:13).

You may have some major strongholds in your life that need to be broken. Let me encourage you by saying, "God is on your side." In the spiritual battle going on in your mind, God is fighting on your side.

_____

No matter how great the temptation before us, God has promised us everything we need to walk in victory.

Over and Above

Now God made Daniel to find favor, compassion, and loving-kindness...
DANIEL 1:9

The story of Daniel and the Hebrew children finding favor with the Babylonian king may be a familiar story, but we must not miss the lesson of how God's supernatural favor was with them after being taken far from their homes and families.

Because of their sins against the Lord, the nation of Judah was carried away into captivity in Babylon. There, some of the most promising of them, including Daniel and three of his friends, were chosen to become attendants to the Babylonian king. As part of their three-year period of training, these young men were to follow a diet of rich meat and wine provided from the king's table. However, Daniel and his

friends determined not to defile themselves with this diet and asked to be allowed to follow their own Hebrew diet.

They refused to compromise their convictions, and we are told that the Lord gave Daniel "favor, compassion, and loving-kindness" with their overseers. They had permission to follow their own diet as long as it didn't harm them. Of course, not only did it not harm them, it made them stronger and healthier and led them to be chosen as trusted counselors.

Always stand firm in your convictions and don't compromise. You will be rewarded in the end!

Obey the Word

But be doers of the Word [obey the message], and not merely listeners to it, betraying yourselves [into deception by reasoning contrary to the Truth].

JAMES 1:22

I recall a woman who attended one of my seminars. She desperately wanted to be free of the emotional wounds that had left her insecure and fearful, but nothing seemed to work for her. At the conclusion of the seminar, she told me that she now understood why she had never experienced any progress.

She said, "Joyce, I sat with a group of ladies who had a lot of the same problems that I did. Step by step God had been delivering them. As I listened, I heard them say, 'God led me to do this, and I did it. Then He led me to another thing, and I did it.'

I realized that God had also told me to do the same things. The only difference was they did what He said to do, and I didn't."

To live in a close relationship with God and to receive what He promises, we must obey the Word. We should become doers of the Word and not hearers only. Obeying the Word requires consistency and diligence. Let us be dedicated and committed to following God's lead.

———

God's way works! And there is no other way that does. Make a determined decision to obey His Word step-by-step, every day.

A Rock-Solid Foundation

[Jesus] said to them, But who do you [yourselves] say that I am? Simon Peter replied, You are the Christ, the Son of the living God.

MATTHEW 16:15–16

When Peter said that Jesus was the Christ, the Son of the living God, it was a statement of faith. In making this statement, Peter was displaying faith.

I don't think Peter just casually or nonchalantly made that statement. I think he did it with a surety and a certainty that impressed Jesus because He immediately turned to Peter and told him that he was blessed. Then He went on to say that it was upon this rock-solid foundation of faith that He would build His church.

Jesus was saying to Peter, "If you maintain this faith, it will be a rocklike substance in

your life upon which I will be able to build My kingdom in you, and through you. Your faith will be developed to the place that even the gates of hell will not be able to prevail against you."

There have been many times in my life when I have been discouraged and not known what to do, or felt that nothing was working and that everybody was against me. The words I have heard over and over again are, "Only believe."

———————

This promise was not just for Peter alone. Jesus is saying the same thing to you and me. Only believe!

Know God as Your Father

And He said to them, When you pray, say: Our Father Who is in heaven, hallowed be Your name . . .

LUKE 11:2

For many years I prayed the "Lord's Prayer," and I didn't really know God as my Father. I didn't have any kind of a close personal relationship with God. I was just repeating something I had learned.

If you want to be closer to the Lord and effective in your prayer life, it is important to know God as your Father. When the disciples asked Jesus to teach them to pray, He taught them what we call the "Lord's Prayer," which is a spiritual treasure house of principles for prayer. But foremost, Jesus started it by instructing them to say, "Our Father Who is in heaven, hallowed be Your name."

Jesus was showing them the privileged relationship He came to bring to every believer. He told them they could have a relationship with God as their Father if they expected to go to Him in prayer. Don't go to God as someone that you're afraid of, but develop a Father-child relationship with Him. That intimate relationship will give you liberty to ask Him for things you would not have asked for if you had a distant, stiff relationship with Him.

Our heavenly Father loves us and has His eye on us at all times. Learn to enjoy God!

———

When you pray, remember you have a loving Father Who is listening.

Decide to Go On

And as for you, brethren, do not become weary or lose heart in doing right [but continue in well-doing without weakening].

2 THESSALONIANS 3:13

All of us must face and deal with disappointment at different times. No person alive has everything happen in life the way they want it to, in the way they expect.

When things don't prosper or succeed according to our plan, the first emotion we feel is disappointment. This is normal. There is nothing wrong with feeling disappointed. But we must know what to do with that feeling, or it will move into something more serious.

In the world we cannot live without experiencing disappointment, but in Jesus we can always be given re-appointment!

The apostle Paul stated that one important lesson he had learned in life was to let go of what lay behind and press toward all that lay ahead! (Philippians 3:13–14.)

When we get disappointed, then immediately get re-appointed, that's exactly what we're doing. We're letting go of the causes for the disappointment and pressing toward what God has for us. We get a new vision, plan, idea, a fresh outlook, a new mind-set, and we change our focus to that. *We decide to go on!*

———

Every day is a brand-new start! We can let go of yesterday's disappointments and give God a chance to do something wonderful for us today!

His Grace Is Sufficient

For sin shall not [any longer] exert dominion over you, since now you are not under Law [as slaves], but under grace [as subjects of God's favor and mercy].   ROMANS 6:14

The grace of God is greater than our sin or any other problem that we may have. You might be feeling guilty and tempted to shrink from God's presence, but He wants you to run *to* Him, not away from Him.

We have all sinned and come short of God's perfection, but God has provided the solution to our dilemma through Jesus. He ransomed us from all the misery of sin and offers us His grace that is received by simple faith.

We all have many challenges, struggles, and temptations in life, but God is always available to help us. No problem is too big

for Him. You might have what seems to be a mountain of problems, but God has a mountain of grace that is bigger. Even when we don't deserve God's help, it is still available if we will ask in childlike faith and believe!

————————

God never leads us where He cannot keep us. His grace is always sufficient for us—in any and every circumstance of life.

A Work in Progress

... The Word of God ... is effectually at work in you who believe [exercising its superhuman power in those who adhere to and trust in and rely on it].

1 THESSALONIANS 2:13

I encourage you to say every day, *"God is working in me right now—He is changing me!"* Speak out of your mouth what the Word says, not what you feel. When we talk only about how we feel, it is difficult for the Word of God to work in us effectively.

As we step out to be all we can be in Christ, we will make some mistakes— everyone does. But it takes the pressure off of us when we realize that God is only expecting us to do the best we can. He is not expecting us to be perfect. If we were perfect, we would not need a Savior. I believe God will always leave a certain number

of defects in us, just so we will know how much we need Jesus every single day.

I am not a perfect preacher. There are times when I say things the wrong way, times when I believe I have heard from God and find out I was hearing from myself. There are many times when I fall short of perfection. I don't have perfect faith, a perfect attitude, perfect thoughts, and perfect ways.

Jesus knew that would happen to all of us. That is why He stands in the gap between God's perfection and our imperfection. He continually intercedes for us because we continually need it (Hebrews 7:25).

We do not have to believe that God accepts us only if we perform perfectly. We can believe the truth that He accepts us "in the Beloved" (Ephesians 1:6).

You Have the Power

Behold! I have given you authority and power to trample upon serpents and scorpions, and [physical and mental strength and ability] over all the power that the enemy [possesses]; and nothing shall in any way harm you.

LUKE 10:19

Far too many believers are fainthearted, weak in determination, and diseased with an "I can't" attitude. They are plagued with a lack of spiritual power.

You and I don't have to beg God to give us power. We just need to realize and accept that we have been given power and then walk in what is already ours. We can develop and maintain a "power consciousness"—an aggressive, power-packed attitude.

God has given us spiritual power for

spiritual warfare. Spiritual power is released when our faith is firm. When we walk in faith in God, we can approach every situation with an enemy-conquering attitude.

An attitude of confidence will exude from us when we know who we are in Christ, how close He wants to be to us, and the power that the Bible says is ours through faith.

Do you desire to be a powerful believer? Try approaching every situation in your life with a simple, childlike faith—believing that God is good, that He has a good plan for your life, and that He is working in your situation.

———————

You have the power and authority of the name of Jesus. Walk in the strength of His conquering name!

Favored of the Lord

And Jesus increased in wisdom (in broad and full understanding) and in stature and years, and in favor with God and man.   LUKE 2:52

From childhood, Jesus walked in the supernatural favor of God and men. In fact, once He began His public ministry, He was so popular that He could hardly find time to get alone to pray and fellowship with His heavenly Father. Even those who did not believe in Him recognized that He enjoyed the favor of God. When the Pharisees sent guards to arrest Jesus, they went back saying, "Never has a man talked as this Man talks!" (John 7:46). Right up until the very end of His life, even on the cross, that special favor and power were recognized (Luke 23:47–48).

That is the way we need to see ourselves:

as the favored of the Lord. He doesn't see us as weak, helpless, sinful creatures. He sees us robed in righteousness, shod with the shoes of peace, adorned with the full armor of God, and wielding the sword of the Spirit, which is the Word of the Lord (Ephesians 6:13–17). That is how we ought to see ourselves.

Our children have favor with us, and anytime we can, we help them. Just think of how much more this must be true for us as God's children. No matter how we may appear to ourselves or to others, we must never forget that God can cause the light of His favor to shine upon us—just as He did for Jesus!

―――――――

See yourself as God does and get excited about your inheritance in Him.

Grace to Be His Ambassadors

So we are Christ's ambassadors, God making His appeal as it were through us. We [as Christ's personal representatives] beg you for His sake to lay hold of the divine favor [now offered you] and be reconciled to God.

2 CORINTHIANS 5:20

One time while I was reading about a famous minister and his great faith, I was deeply impressed by all the wonderful things he did in his ministry. I thought, *Lord, I know I'm called, but I could never do anything like that.* Just that quickly, I sensed the Lord speak to my heart, "Why not? Aren't you as big a mess as anybody else?"

You see, we often have it backward. We think God is looking for people who "have it all together." But that is not true. The Word of God says that God in His grace and favor

chooses the weak and foolish things of the world in order to confound the wise (1 Corinthians 1:27). He is looking for those who will humble themselves and allow Him to work His will through them.

If you will be careful not to get prideful, the Lord can use you just as mightily as any of the other great men and women of God. He doesn't choose us because we are able, but simply because we are available. That too is part of God's grace and favor that He pours out upon us when He chooses us to be Christ's personal ambassadors.

God wants you to have a dream for your life. And He wants you to walk it out by His grace as you put your faith in Him.

Be a Fighter

Fight the good fight of the faith; lay hold of the eternal life to which you were summoned and [for which] you confessed the good confession [of faith] before many witnesses.

1 TIMOTHY 6:12

Just as the apostle Paul said that he had fought the good fight of faith (2 Timothy 4:7), so he instructed his young disciple Timothy to fight the good fight of faith. That means that we should trust God at all times and never give up!

One part of fighting the good fight of faith is being able to recognize the enemy. As long as we are passive, Satan will torment us. Nothing is going to change about our situation if all we do is just sit and wish things were different. We can choose to take action. Too often we don't move

against the enemy when he comes against us with discouragement or fear or doubt or guilt. We listen to his lies, but we should tell him to get lost!

You and I don't have to be punching bags for the devil; instead, we can be fighters. We can stand firm in faith and know that God is good and that good things are going to happen to us.

God is faithful, and we will see His blessing manifested in our lives if we don't give up. Stand firm! Fight! Lift up your shield of faith! God is on your side and it is impossible for you to lose your battles if you follow Him.

Come against Satan when he is trying to get a foothold, and he will never get a stronghold.

God's Work in Your Life

And all of us, as with unveiled face, [because we] continued to behold [in the Word of God] as in a mirror the glory of the Lord, are constantly being transfigured into His very own image in ever increasing splendor and from one degree of glory to another; [for this comes] from the Lord [Who is] the Spirit.   2 CORINTHIANS 3:18

God changes us from one degree of glory to another, but don't forget to enjoy the glory you are in right now while you are headed for the next one. Don't compare yourself with other people, or examine what God is doing for you compared to what He is doing for them. Each of us is an individual, and God deals with us differently, according to what He knows we need.

You may not notice changes on a daily

basis, but I want to stir your faith up so you will believe that God is at work, just as He said He would be. Remember, we see *after* we believe, not *before*. We struggle with ourselves because of all that we are not, when we could be praising and worshipping God for all that we are. As we worship Him for Who He is, we see things released into our lives that we could have never made happen ourselves.

As we worship God, we are released from frustration. We enter God's rest and begin to enjoy life more than ever. The flaws that we have begin to vanish and God's character is released in our lives.

———————

We release God to work in our lives as we release our faith in Him.

No More Pretending

For we are God's [own] handiwork (His workmanship), recreated in Christ Jesus, [born anew] that we may do those good works which God predestined (planned beforehand) for us [taking paths which He prepared ahead of time], that we should walk in them [living the good life which He prearranged and made ready for us to live]. EPHESIANS 2:10

For many years I was miserable and unhappy. Yet, like so many people, I pretended that everything was fine. We human beings pretend for the benefit of others, not wanting them to know about our misery, but we also pretend for ourselves so that we do not have to face and deal with difficult issues.

Perhaps this describes you. Maybe you know what it's like to be one person on the inside and another on the outside. In my

life, I pretended to be confident, and in some ways I was. Still, I had very low self-esteem, and my so-called confidence was not really based on who I was in Christ. It was based on the approval of others, on my appearance and accomplishments, and on other external factors. Strip away the superficial exterior, and I was scared stiff.

The day came for me when I realized I had to face the truth and stop pretending. When we truly open our hearts and let God work in our lives, we can stop pretending to be something we are not. We can be happy and free, enjoying the person God made each of us to be.

————

We are never truly free until we can live without pretense and be comfortable being who we are!

The Help of the Holy Spirit

For they that are after the flesh do mind the things of the flesh; but they that are after the Spirit the things of the Spirit.

ROMANS 8:5 KJV

Romans 8:5 teaches us that if we "mind" the flesh, we will walk in the flesh. But if we "mind" the things of the Spirit, we will walk in the Spirit. Our actions follow our thoughts!

Let me put it another way: If we think fleshly thoughts, wrong thoughts, and negative thoughts, we cannot walk in the Spirit. It seems as if renewed, godlike thinking is a vital necessity to a successful Christian life.

Your life may be in a state of chaos because of years of wrong thinking. If so, it is important for you to come to grips with the fact that *your life will not get straightened*

out until your mind does. You should consider this area one of *vital necessity.*

Ask God to help you learn to think thoughts that He would have you think. You cannot overcome any problem by determination alone. It is important to be determined, but determined in the Holy Spirit, not in the effort of your own flesh. The Holy Spirit is close to you. He is your Helper—seek His help. Lean on Him. You can make it with His help.

————

Give the Holy Spirit control of your life. He will lead you into the perfect will of God for you, which includes exceeding, abundant blessings, peace, and joy.

The Missing Link

And I will pour out upon the house of David and upon the inhabitants of Jerusalem the Spirit of grace or unmerited favor and supplication...

ZECHARIAH 12:10

The message of God's grace has been the single most important message that the Holy Spirit has ministered to me. My entire Christian experience was a struggle before I learned about the spiritual power of grace. To teach people faith and not teach them grace is, in my opinion, "the missing link" in many people's faith walk.

Grace is the power of the Holy Spirit that is available to do whatever needs to be done in our lives, and power to bring and sustain change. It is the ability of God that comes to us free for the asking. Through faith the grace of God is received. Faith

is not the price that buys the blessings of God, but it is the hand that receives them.

Just hearing the word *grace* is soothing to me. Always remember that when you feel frustrated, it is because you have entered into your own effort and need to get back into God's power. Grace leaves you strong and calm; works of the flesh render you weak and powerless, frustrated and frantic. Lean on God in all that you do today and every day, for apart from Him, you can do nothing (John 15:5).

————

Receive not only the grace that saves, but receive grace, grace, and more grace so you may live victoriously and glorify Jesus in your daily life.

Receive Forgiveness and Forget Your Sin

... For I will forgive their iniquity, and I will [seriously] remember their sin no more.   JEREMIAH 31:34

No matter what your problem or how bad you feel about yourself as a result of it, God loves you and He wants to be in close relationship with you. In Jesus Christ He has given you a new life. He will give you a new family of Christian friends to love and accept and appreciate and support you. You are going to enjoy a victorious life because of Jesus, the One Who lives on the inside of you and cares for you.

When you sin, you can repent and receive forgiveness. When God shows you any sin in your life, just agree with Him and be amazed by His goodness. God not

only forgives us, but He promises to forget our sin.

God's mercy is wonderful and as we receive His love, forgiveness, and mercy, we can also learn how to give it to people in our lives who hurt and disappoint us. If you are angry with anyone, I recommend that you extend the same mercy to that person that God has given you. The more you let love flow to you from God and through you to others, the happier you will be.

––––––

God's mercy is new every morning. Each day we can find a fresh place to begin.

From Faith to Faith

*For therein is the righteousness of God
revealed from faith to faith: as it is
written, The just shall live by faith.*
> ROMANS 1:17 KJV

It is always my goal to live from faith
to faith. A number of years ago the Lord
revealed to me, "Joyce, you often go from
faith to faith to doubt to unbelief, and then
back to faith to doubt to unbelief."

Sometimes we have too much mixture
in life. We are confident at times, and then
we are fearful at other times; we are positive
and then we are negative, or we have faith,
but then we have doubt. That mixture is
even evident in our speech, as we see in
James 3:10: "Out of the same mouth come
forth blessing and cursing. These things,
my brethren, ought not to be so."

I am sure that it sounds almost impossible to always have faith and to never doubt, but even though it is impossible with man, with God all things are possible. Let's trust God to help us go from faith to faith, and to be confident in Him at all times.

———

Let each thing that you do, be done by faith, trusting that God is with you and that He is ready to help you!

Be Bold

Let us then fearlessly and confidently and boldly draw near to the throne of grace (the throne of God's unmerited favor to us sinners), that we may receive mercy [for our failures] and find grace to help in good time for every need [appropriate help and well-timed help, coming just when we need it].

HEBREWS 4:16

When you and I pray, we are to approach God as believers, not as beggars. Remember, according to Hebrews 4:16, we can come boldly to the throne: not beggarly, but boldly; not belligerently, but boldly.

Be sure to keep the balance. Stay respectful, but be bold. Approach God with confidence. Believe He delights in your prayers and is ready to answer any request that is in accordance with His will.

As believers, we should know the Word of God, which is His will. The more we study God's Word, the more confident we become in our asking.

As you and I come boldly before the throne of God's grace, asking in faith according to His Word and in the name of His Son Jesus Christ, we can know that we have the petitions that we ask of Him. Not because we are perfect or worthy in ourselves, or because God owes us anything, but because He loves us and wants to give us what we need in life.

Jesus has purchased a glorious inheritance for us by the shedding of His blood. As joint-heirs with Him, we can pray boldly.

A Root of Bitterness

Exercise foresight and be on the watch to look [after one another], to see that no one falls back from and fails to secure God's grace (His unmerited favor and spiritual blessing), in order that no root of resentment (rancor, bitterness, or hatred) shoots forth and causes trouble and bitter torment...

HEBREWS 12:15

When we allow unforgiveness in our lives, we are filled with resentment and bitterness. *Bitterness* refers to something that is pungent or sharp to the taste.

We remember that when the children of Israel were about to be led out of Egypt, they were told by the Lord to prepare a Passover meal that included bitter herbs. Why? God wanted them to eat those bitter herbs as a reminder of the bitterness they

had experienced in bondage. Bitterness always goes hand in hand with bondage.

How does bitterness get started? It grows from a root, which *The King James Version* speaks of as a *root of bitterness*. A root of bitterness from the seed of unforgiveness always produces the fruit of bitterness.

Bitterness results from the offenses people commit against us that we don't let go of, the things we rehearse over and over until they have become blown way out of proportion. The longer we allow them to grow and fester, the more deeply rooted they become. Learn to be quick to repent because the sooner you do it, the easier it is!

A root of bitterness will infect our entire being—our attitude and behavior, our perspective, and our relationships, especially our relationship with God.

Let It Go

Do not be quick in spirit to be angry or vexed, for anger and vexation lodge in the bosom of fools. ECCLESIASTES 7:9

There are certain things in life in which you have a measure of control—you can control who you spend time with, what you eat, and when you go to bed, for example. But there are many other things you can't control, such as what others say about you or the flat tire you got while running errands. The way you respond to the things you can't control—no matter how big or how small—often determines your stress level and your quality of life and health.

I have two suggestions about dealing with things you can't control. First, if you can't control them, don't take responsibility for them. And second, I like to say, "Do your best, pray, and let God do the rest."

People who regularly get upset over things beyond their control suffer in many ways. People who let them go do much better. Letting go of certain things doesn't mean you don't care; it simply means you've accepted the fact that you can't do anything to change them at that time. The flat tire has already happened. Calmly repairing it or changing it makes sense; throwing a tantrum and kicking the tire do not. If we appropriately deal with each stressor when it happens, we won't end up exploding in frustration over the unavoidable bumps on the road of life.

God can even use an inconvenience or frustration for your good. He is right there with you, and He is in control. If you trust Him to work things out, you'll be able to ride the ups and downs of life with peace, joy, and strength.

Don't Lose Yourself

Whoever finds his [lower] life will lose it [the higher life], and whoever loses his [lower] life on My account will find it [the higher life].   MATTHEW 10:39

Life is like a maze sometimes, and it is easy to get lost. Everyone, it seems, expects something different from us. There is pressure coming at us from every direction to keep others happy and meet their needs.

When we attempt to become what others want us to be, in the process, we may lose ourselves. We may fail to discover what God's intention is for us because we are trying so hard to please everyone else and yet are not pleased ourselves.

For years I tried to be so many things that I wasn't, and I got myself totally confused. I had to get off the merry-go-round and ask myself: "Who am I living for? Why

am I doing all these things? Have I become a people-pleaser? Am I really in God's will for my life?"

Have you also lost yourself? Are you frustrated from trying to meet all the demands of other people while feeling unfulfilled yourself? If so, you can choose to take a stand and be determined to know your identity, your direction, and your calling—God's will for your life. You will find yourself by drawing close to God, finding His will for your life, and doing it.

————

If you give your heart to doing God's will, you'll find your true self.

Jesus Is Your Rock

For as many as are the promises of God, they all find their Yes [answer] in Him [Christ]. For this reason we also utter the Amen (so be it) to God through Him [in His Person and by His agency] to the glory of God.   2 CORINTHIANS 1:20

In several places in the Bible, for example in 1 Corinthians 10:4, Jesus is referred to as the Rock. The apostle Paul goes on to tell us in Colossians 2:7 that we are to be rooted and grounded in Jesus.

If we get our roots wrapped around Jesus Christ, we are in good shape. But if we get them wrapped around anything or anyone else, we are in trouble.

No person or thing is going to be as solid and dependable as Jesus. That's why it is important to point people to Jesus. Humans are always liable to failure. But

Jesus Christ isn't. Put your hope wholly and unchangeably in Him. Not in man, not in circumstances, not in anything or anyone else.

If you don't put your hope and faith in the Rock of your salvation, you are headed for disappointment, which leads to discouragement and devastation. We should have so much confidence in God's love for us that no matter what comes against us, we know deep inside that He is with us and He will never let us down.

———

We are bankrupt in our own ability apart from Christ. Without God, we are helpless; with Him nothing is impossible to us.

A Vital Necessity

Either make the tree sound (healthy and good), and its fruit sound (healthy and good), or make the tree rotten (diseased and bad), and its fruit rotten (diseased and bad); for the tree is known and recognized and judged by its fruit.

MATTHEW 12:33

For the believer, right thinking is something that is so important that one simply cannot live without it—like a heartbeat is vital or blood pressure is vital. There are things without which there is no life. Our life source, our source for right thinking, is regular, personal fellowship with God in prayer and in the Word.

The Bible says that a tree is known by its fruit. The same is true of our lives. Thoughts bear fruit. Think good thoughts, and the fruit in your life will be good.

Think bad thoughts, and the fruit in your life will be bad.

Actually, you can look at a person's attitude and know what kind of thinking is prevalent in his life. A sweet, kind person does not have mean, vindictive thoughts. By the same token, a truly evil person does not have good, loving thoughts.

As you go through your day today, I encourage you to think healthy, positive, godly thoughts and allow them to set the course for your life, because as a man thinks in his heart, so is he (Proverbs 23:7).

The more time you spend in the Word of God, the easier it is to reject wrong thoughts and choose right thoughts.

Special Favor

. . . How much more will your Father Who is in heaven [perfect as He is] give good and advantageous things to those who keep on asking Him!

MATTHEW 7:11

Each of us would like to be favored or featured. Is that pride? No, not if that position comes from God and not from mere personal ambitions or our own selfish efforts to call attention to ourselves.

To be totally honest, I find it delightful to watch God feature a person. It is fun to watch Him single out someone for special attention or preferential treatment. To see Him work powerfully in someone's life provokes genuine praise and thanksgiving.

It is always enjoyable to have favor with God. It just seems that it doesn't happen as often as we would like. Part of the problem

is us. There are so many things that God would love to do for us, but He cannot because we won't ask. One reason we won't ask is because we don't feel worthy. None of us are worthy in ourselves, but God will give us favor if we ask!

It is time we believe that God wants to bless us. He loves to give us His favor. As a redeemed, forgiven, loved child of God, get this down in your heart today: You are the apple of God's eye. He loves you!

————

Our heavenly Father wants His children to stand up and be everything for which His Son, Jesus, gave His life that they might become.

At All Times

I will bless the Lord at all times; His praise shall continually be in my mouth.
PSALM 34:1

Faith and trust in God is meant to be exercised more than once in a while or from time to time; we can live in faith at all times. With God's help we can learn to live from faith to faith, trusting the Lord when things are good, and when things are difficult. It is easy to trust God when things are good, but when things are challenging and we decide to trust God, then we really develop character.

Psalm 34:1 encourages us to bless the Lord at all times. There are several other scriptures that tell us things to do at all times—resist the devil at all times, believe God at all times, love others at all times—not just when it's convenient or it feels good.

Temptation is a frequent visitor in our lives and as long as we are here on earth, we will have to discipline our emotions, our moods, and our mouths, so that we remain stable and calm, and peaceful—whatever our situation or circumstances. That enables us to be in close fellowship with God and walk in the joy of His Spirit.

—————

Since you can choose your own thoughts, when doubt comes, you can learn to recognize it for what it is, say, "No, thank you," and keep on believing!

Led by the Holy Spirit to Pray

But you, beloved, build yourselves up [founded] on your most holy faith [make progress, rise like an edifice higher and higher], praying in the Holy Spirit.

JUDE 20

Just as Ephesians 6:18 tells us that we are to pray at all times with all manner of prayers, we are also told by Jude that our prayers are to be "in the Holy Spirit." The apostle Paul tells us in Romans 8:26 that when we don't know how to pray, the Holy Spirit knows how to pray in our weakness.

It is the Holy Spirit of God within us Who provokes us and leads us to pray. Rather than delaying, we can learn to yield to the leading of the Spirit as soon as we sense it. That is part of learning to pray all manner of prayers at all times, wherever we may be, and whatever we may be doing.

Our motto can be like the old spiritual song, "Every time I feel the Spirit moving in my heart, I will pray." If we know we can pray anytime and anywhere, we won't feel far from God, and we won't feel we have to wait until just the right moment or place to pray.

When we are being led by the Holy Spirit, we can know that our prayers are reaching the throne of God and will be answered.

———

Ask the Holy Spirit to get involved in everything you do. He is the Helper, and He is waiting for you to ask.

The Simplicity of Joy and Peace

[After all] the kingdom of God is not a matter of [getting the] food and drink [one likes], but instead it is righteousness (that state which makes a person acceptable to God) and [heart] peace and joy in the Holy Spirit.

ROMANS 14:17

Many years ago, I had this thought: *Life should never be this complicated.* Something was lurking inside, constantly draining the joy out of me. It began to dawn on me that I was doubting instead of believing. I was doubting God's call on my life, wondering if He would meet our needs, questioning my decisions and actions.

I had become negative instead of positive. I was doubting instead of believing.

Doubt complicates everything. It creeps in through the door of your heart, filling

your mind with reasoning that leads to negativity. It rotates around and around the circumstances or situations of your life, attempting to find answers for them.

The Word of God does not instruct us to search for our own answers. We are, however, instructed to trust God with all of our heart and soul (Proverbs 3:5). When we follow the simple guidelines the Lord has laid out for us, they will unerringly bring us closer to Him, causing us to live in joy and peace.

When doubt knocks at your door, answer with a believing heart, and you'll always maintain the victory.

Joy is never released through unbelief but is always present where there is belief.

Quitting Is Not an Option

Looking away [from all that will distract] to Jesus, Who is the Leader and the Source of our faith . . .

HEBREWS 12:2

It does not take any special talent to give up and lie down on the side of the road of life and say, "I quit." Anybody, whether they are a believer or not, can do that.

Quitting is a temptation we all face at one time or another, but when you get close to Jesus, or better yet, when He gets close to you, He begins to pump strength and energy and courage into you. And something wonderful begins to happen—He causes you to *want* to press forward!

I used to want to give up and quit. But now I get out of bed and start each day fresh and new. I begin my day by praying and reading the Bible and speaking the

Word, seeking after God. It's amazing what a difference it makes when you begin your day drawing closer to God.

When you feel the urge or the temptation to quit, don't give in. Look to Jesus and follow His example. He pressed forward even in the most difficult circumstances, and He will give you the strength to do the same. He is your Leader; He is the Source and the Finisher of your faith.

———

Let's make a decision today that, come what may, we are going to keep pressing on, looking to Jesus, no matter what.

Matters of the Heart

Keep thy heart with all diligence; for out of it are the issues of life.

PROVERBS 4:23 KJV

Our hearts represent our minds and the deepest parts of us. It is important that we serve God with a pure heart. A person can do the right thing, and yet not do it with a right heart. King Amaziah was such a man. We are told that he did all the right things, but his heart was not right; and therefore, God was not pleased (2 Chronicles 25:2).

Taking the time to truthfully examine our motives can be a painful exercise, but it is very valuable. Serving God wholeheartedly is what brings us closer to Him.

The Bible says that we are not to do good works to be seen of men, or pray in order to impress people. If we do what we

do unto the Lord, then our reward will come from Him.

Take the time to prayerfully look at all the things you do and ask God to reveal to you if any of your motives are impure. If they are, then you can make a change with God's help. Do what you do because you truly believe it is God's will for you and do it to glorify Him. When you do this, your intimacy and closeness with God will increase.

God is more concerned with *why* we do things, than what we do. People see our actions, but God sees our heart!

You Are Not a Failure

[God] disarmed the principalities and powers that were ranged against us and made a bold display and public example of them, in triumphing over them in Him and in it [the cross].

COLOSSIANS 2:15

People who have been abused, rejected, or abandoned usually lack confidence. Such individuals are shame-based and guilt-ridden and have a very poor self-image. The devil knows that and begins his assault on personal confidence whenever and wherever he can find an opening. His goal is to make people believe they are failures.

The devil knows that an individual without confidence will never step out to do the things they truly want to do. He does not want you to fulfill God's plan for your life. If he can make you believe that

you are incapable, then you won't even try to accomplish anything worthwhile. Even if you do make an effort, your fear of failure will seal your defeat, which, because of a lack of confidence, you probably expected from the beginning. This is often what is referred to as the "Failure Syndrome." People fail because of wrong beliefs, and they continue to have wrong beliefs because they fail. It is hard to know which came first, but they find themselves in a trap they cannot seem to get out of.

Jesus defeated Satan and triumphed over him on the cross, and His victory is our victory. You can defeat failure syndrome because you are more than a conqueror through Christ (Romans 8:37).

God's victory purchased on the cross is total and complete.

Keep on Walking

*And Peter answered Him, Lord, if it is
You, command me to come to You on
the water. He said, Come! So Peter got
out of the boat and walked on the water,
and he came toward Jesus.*

MATTHEW 14:28–29

When Peter stepped out of the boat at the
command of Jesus, he was doing something he had never done before. As long as
he remained in faith he was successful, but
when fear gripped his heart, he began to
sink!

Peter's mistake was that he became preoccupied with the storm. When he focused
on the circumstance around him, rather
than the Savior close to him, he lost his
faith and began to doubt.

Romans 4:18–21 tells us that Abraham
did not waver in his faith when faced with

difficult circumstances. He was aware of his situation, but unlike Peter, he was not preoccupied with it. It was this determined and focused faith that propelled Abraham forward.

I believe that you and I can learn from Peter's mistake and Abraham's example. We can be aware of our circumstances but not preoccupied with them. We can purposely keep our mind on Jesus, trusting in faith that He will provide the miracle we need.

_____

When the storms come in your life, keep your eyes on Jesus and be determined to walk with Him no matter how high the waves are.

Pray and Fear Not

For God did not give us a spirit of timidity (of cowardice, of craven and cringing and fawning fear), but [He has given us a spirit] of power and of love and of calm and well-balanced mind and discipline and self-control.

2 TIMOTHY 1:7

God wants us to pray about everything and fear nothing. We would find ourselves in a closer, deeper personal relationship with the Lord if we would pray more, worry less, and fear less. Timothy says that God has not given us a spirit of fear. So when we feel fear, it is not from God. It's from the devil. The devil will try to intimidate us with all kinds of fear, and we can become so preoccupied with how we feel that we forget to pray.

If Abraham or Joshua or David had

bowed their knee to fear when the task before them seemed overwhelming, they never would have experienced God as their abundant provision.

Talking to God and spending time in His Word gives you the power to resist fear when it comes. When you put the Word into your heart, it will come out when you need it. I believe we should confess God's Word out loud and fill our prayers with the Word of God. Satan may not be afraid of you, but he is afraid of God's Word spoken in faith from a believer's mouth.

Fear cannot be wished away, it must be confronted. Prayer and the Word of God are our two most powerful weapons, so let's use them!

——————

Put on the armor of God through prayer and stand against all the enemy's fiery darts of fear.

Bless, Not Curse

Bless those who persecute you [who are cruel in their attitude toward you]; bless and do not curse them.

ROMANS 12:14

God in His Word instructs us to *forgive* others and then to *bless* them. In Romans 12:14, the word *bless* means "to speak well of." It is extending mercy to people who do not necessarily deserve it. And we are to pray for them to be blessed. We are to ask God to bring truth and revelation to them about any changes that need to be made in their attitude and behavior, and to help them come to a place of repentance so they can be set free from their sins.

Revenge says, "You mistreated me, so I will mistreat you." Mercy says, "You mistreated me, so I'm going to forgive you, restore you, and treat you as if you never

hurt me." What a blessing to be able to give and receive mercy. Give mercy, and you will receive mercy.

Mercy is an attribute of God that is seen in how He deals with His people. Mercy comes near to us when we deserve to be cast out. Mercy is good to us when we deserve judgment. Mercy accepts and blesses us when we deserve to be totally rejected. Mercy understands our weaknesses and does not judge us.

When we really appreciate the mercy God has shown us, we will be quick to give that same mercy to other people.

The power of forgiveness will never work if we say we forgive but then turn around and curse the offender with our tongues or rehash the offense with others.

More Joy

A cheerful heart is good medicine, but a crushed spirit dries up the bones.

PROVERBS 17:22 NIV

My understanding of *joy* is that it covers a wide range of emotions, from calm delight to extreme hilarity. The hilarious times are fun, and we all need those moments of laughing until our sides hurt. We probably won't live our daily lives that way, but we need those times. Why else would God give us the ability to laugh?

As Christians, we can grow in our ability to enjoy life and be able to say, "I live my life in a state of calm delight." I think calm delight is a mixture of peace and joy.

Some of the Greek words relating to joy in the Bible mean *delight, gladness, exceeding joyful, exuberant joy, to exult, rejoice greatly...with exceeding joy.* I've also heard

it defined as *great pleasure or happiness, a source of pleasure or satisfaction, to fill with joy, or to enjoy.*

Whichever definition you prefer, the sad reality is that so few believers know the joy of the Lord. Don't let another day pass by without experiencing the kingdom of God at its center—righteousness, peace, and joy in the Holy Spirit (Romans 14:17).

————————

There is nothing as tragic as being alive and not enjoying life.

Meditate on the Things of God

... Whatever is true, whatever is worthy of reverence and is honorable and seemly, whatever is just, whatever is pure, whatever is lovely and lovable, whatever is kind and winsome and gracious, if there is any virtue and excellence, if there is anything worthy of praise, think on ... these things [fix your minds on them]. PHILIPPIANS 4:8

Did you know that your feelings are hooked up to your thinking? If you don't think that is true, just take about twenty minutes or so and think about nothing but your problems. I can assure you that by the end of that time your feelings, and maybe even your countenance, will have changed.

I got up one day thinking about a problem I had. Suddenly the Spirit of the Lord spoke to me. He said to me, "Joyce, are you

going to fellowship with your problem or with Me?"

When you get disappointed, don't sit around and feel sorry for yourself. As difficult as things may seem, we do have a choice. We can choose to be in close fellowship with our problems or to be in close fellowship with God. We can allow our thoughts to dwell on our problems until we become totally discouraged and devastated, or we can focus our attention on all the good things that have happened to us in our life—and on all the blessings that God still has in store for us in the days ahead.

———

Our thoughts are silent words that only the Lord and we hear, but those words affect our inner man, our health, our joy, and our attitude.

Be a Believing Believer

Therefore, as the Holy Spirit says: Today, if you will hear His voice, do not harden your hearts, as [happened] in the rebellion [of Israel] and their provocation and embitterment [of Me] in the day of testing in the wilderness.

HEBREWS 3:7–8

In Hebrews 3 we see two wrong conditions of the heart—a hard heart and an unbelieving heart. In the wilderness, a hard heart caused the Israelites to rebel. A person with a hard heart cannot believe God easily, which is a major problem because everything we receive from God comes through believing. To receive from Him, all we have to do is come to Him in simple, childlike faith and just believe.

We call ourselves believers, but the truth is, there are a lot of "unbelieving believers."

For a long time, I was one of them. I had been hurt so much during my childhood, I developed a hardness of heart that God had to break through in my life.

Even Moses got to the place in the wilderness where he was slow of heart to believe God. That's why it's important for us to stay sharp spiritually so we can be quick to believe and to walk in faith day by day. We can choose to be careful to go from faith to faith and not begin to mix in any doubt and unbelief. A believing heart is essential if we want to live in close relationship with God.

———

Jesus wants to restore your soul, including your emotions. Let Jesus into those areas of your life that no one else could ever reach. Ask Him to change you into a person who has the same kind of heart that He has.

Pursuing God

My whole being follows hard after You and clings closely to You; Your right hand upholds me.   PSALM 63:8

I remember the emptiness I felt years ago when I realized that I sometimes had temporary happiness but not deep, satisfying joy. My relationship with God was much like the Israelites', who could only see God from a distance while Moses talked with God face-to-face. I wanted a closer walk with God, but had no idea how to do it.

Perhaps you are experiencing what I went through. I lived by the law, doing the things my church taught, and expecting my routine of good works to bring the peace and joy and spiritual power the Scripture promises. Instead, I found myself deeply disheartened that nothing seemed to be working. It wasn't until I learned to stop

trying to "do" so much for God and just "be" in relationship with Him that I began to live with a peace and contentment from the Lord.

If you want the blessings and power of God, crave and pursue Him. Lay aside other things and go after Him. Do what David spoke about in Psalm 27:4: Commit yourself to one thing—the manifest presence of God.

The only thing that truly satisfies the longing within is to know God more intimately today than we did yesterday.

Confidence in God Alone

Some trust in and boast of chariots and some of horses, but we will trust in and boast of the name of the Lord our God.

PSALM 20:7

In order to succeed at anything, it is essential to have confidence, but first and foremost it must be confidence in God and His promises, not confidence in anything else. As believers, we can be confident in God's love, goodness, and mercy. This confidence assures us that our heavenly Father wants us to succeed.

God did not create us for failure. We may fail at some things on our way to success, but if we trust Him, He will take even our mistakes and work them out for our good (Romans 8:28).

Hebrews 3:6 tells us to "... hold fast and firm to the end our joyful and exultant

confidence and sense of triumph in our hope [in Christ]." It is important to realize that a mistake is not the end of things if we hold on to our confidence.

We all have a destiny, but just because we are destined to do something does not mean that it will automatically happen. I went through many things while God was developing me and my ministry. There were times I nearly lost my confidence concerning the call on my life. Each time I had to rely on the Lord and put my confidence in Him before I could go forward again. The same is true for you. When you're tempted to lose your confidence, draw closer to God and place your trust in Him.

Put your confidence in God alone, and He will cause you to truly succeed.

The Prayer of Thanksgiving

Thank [God] in everything [no matter what the circumstances may be, be thankful and give thanks], for this is the will of God for you [who are] in Christ Jesus [the Revealer and Mediator of that will].   1 THESSALONIANS 5:18

After instructing us to pray without ceasing in 1 Thessalonians 5:17, the apostle Paul spends verse 18 directing us to give thanks to God in everything, no matter what our circumstances may be, stating that this is the will of God for us.

Just as prayer is a lifestyle that brings us closer to God, thanksgiving is the same thing. Giving thanks to God isn't just something we do once a day as we sit down somewhere and try to think of all the good things He has done for us and merely say, "Thanks, Lord." It is not just something

we do at mealtime. That can be empty religion, something we do simply because we think God requires it.

True thanksgiving flows continually out of a heart that is full of gratitude and praise to God for Who He is as much as for what He does. It is not something that is done to meet a requirement, win favor, gain a victory, or qualify for a blessing.

The type of thanksgiving that God the Father desires is heartfelt and it flows from us regularly because we are continually seeing and recognizing how good God is to us at all times. Let us be thankful and say so!

Be thankful always, continually acknowledging, confessing, and glorifying His name in prayerful praise and worship.

Every Good Gift

For out of His fullness (abundance) we have all received [all had a share and we were all supplied with] one grace after another and spiritual blessing upon spiritual blessing and even favor upon favor and gift [heaped] upon gift.

JOHN 1:16

You and I can live in victory today because the Holy Spirit is empowering our lives and teaching us to pray. He helps us ask God for what we need rather than trying to make things happen on our own.

The Holy Spirit is the One Who brings every good gift into your life, everything you need. His multiple roles as Comforter, Counselor, Helper, Intercessor, Advocate, Strengthener, and Standby can be summarized by saying that His purpose is to get as

close to us as possible and cause our lives to work out for the glory of God.

God is interested in every detail of your life. He wants to help with everything in your life. He stands by us at all times waiting for the first available opportunity to enter in and give us the help and strength we need. Ask for help as often as you need it. We have not because we ask not (James 4:2), so ask and ask and ask. Keep on asking so that you may receive and your joy may be full (John 16:24).

———

God's part is to give us His grace and Spirit; our part is to ask for His help and offer ourselves to Him as vessels for Him to work through.

Forgiveness Versus Feelings

Be still and rest in the Lord; wait for Him and patiently lean yourself upon Him; fret not yourself because of him who prospers in his way, because of the man who brings wicked devices to pass. Cease from anger and forsake wrath; fret not yourself—it tends only to evildoing.   PSALM 37:7–8

Perhaps the greatest misconception about forgiveness is the idea that if a person's feelings have not changed, he has not forgiven. Many people have this false idea. They decide to forgive someone who has harmed them, but if they continue to have angry and hurt feelings, they feel like they have not fully forgiven that individual.

You can be obedient to the Lord and make sound biblical decisions and still go a long time without "feeling" any different

from the way you felt before you decided to forgive. This is where faith can carry you through. You have done your part and now you are waiting for God to do His. His part is to heal your emotions, to make you feel well and not wounded. You have the power to make the decision to forgive, but only God has the power to change your feelings toward the person who hurt you.

Healing takes time. So don't get impatient and discouraged if you don't "feel" everything right at once. God is in control, and He is doing a wonderful work in you and your life.

———

Make the decision to obey God, and trust Him to change your heart. Eventually, your feelings will follow and line up with your decisions.

Pass Your Tests

But, O Lord of hosts, Who judges rightly and justly, Who tests the heart and the mind . . . to You I have revealed and committed my cause [rolling it upon You]. JEREMIAH 11:20

All of our life is filled with challenges that test our resolve and determination and the quality of our character—tests that can strengthen us and bring us into deeper relationship with God. They help us truly know ourselves, and they are helpful in locating weak areas in our character.

How is something tested? Pressure is applied to see if it can perform in the proper way. God allows tests to come into our lives to reveal both our strengths and weaknesses, and our goal should always be to pass our tests, not avoid them. Tests always come before promotion! If you want promotion,

you will have to take and pass your tests from God.

The apostle James stated that tests bring out the things that are in us (James 1:2–4), and I have certainly found that to be true. They show us the areas where we have grown in God, and the areas in which we still need help. This is a good thing, because we cannot improve in any area if we don't know where our weaknesses are.

Character is truly revealed when pressure is applied.

Celebrate Life

There is nothing better for a man than that he should eat and drink and make himself enjoy good in his labor. Even this, I have seen, is from the hand of God.   ECCLESIASTES 2:24

It is possible to live life blandly—going through the motions of working, accomplishing, doing, but never truly enjoying life. This is true of people who have not learned to really embrace and love the life God has given them.

Enjoying life is a decision that is based on more than just enjoyable circumstances. It is an attitude of the heart, a decision to enjoy everything, because everything— even little, seemingly insignificant things— has a part in God's overall "big picture" for our lives.

Our joy is found in Jesus, and if we do

all that we do with and for Him, then we can truly enjoy it all. Even when we have problems that we are waiting for God to solve, we can still enjoy our lives. Doubt and unbelief are thieves of joy, but simple, childlike believing releases the joy that is resident in our spirit because the Holy Spirit lives there. Trust God at all times and enjoy His presence! Your life is a gift from Him, so celebrate it!

———————

You can choose to celebrate in God's joy and enjoy every day of your life with Him!

Catch the Foxes

Catch the foxes for us, the little foxes that are ruining the vineyards...
SONG OF SOLOMON 2:15 NASB

Little disappointments can create frustration, which in turn may lead to bigger problems that can produce a great deal of damage.

Besides the huge disappointments that occur when we fail to get the job promotion or house we wanted, we can become just as upset by minor annoyances. For example, suppose you are expecting someone to meet you for lunch and they arrive late. Or suppose you make a special trip to the mall to buy something at a discount, but it's sold out.

These kinds of frustrations are minor, but they can add up to cause a lot of grief. That's why we have to know how to handle them and keep them in perspective. Otherwise,

they can get out of hand and be blown out of proportion.

We would be wise to be on our guard against the little foxes that steal our peace.

With God's help, we can learn to do as Paul did in the book of Acts when the serpent attached itself to his hand—he simply shook it off (Acts 28:1–5)! If we practice dealing quickly with disappointments as they come, they will not pile up and become a mountain of devastation.

———

Victory is not the absence of problems; it is the presence of God's power.

Secret Prayer

But when you pray, go into your [most] private room, and, closing the door, pray to your Father, Who is in secret; and your Father, Who sees in secret, will reward you in the open.

MATTHEW 6:6

Although some prayers are public prayers or group prayers, most of our prayer life is made up of secret prayers made in the secret place.

"Secret prayer" means that we don't tell everyone we know about our personal experiences in prayer and how much we pray. We pray about the concerns and people God places on our heart, and we keep our prayers between us and Him unless we have a really good reason to do otherwise. We refuse to make a display of our prayers to impress others.

For prayer to be properly called "secret prayer," it must come from a humble heart as demonstrated in the prayer of the despised tax collector in Luke 18:10–14. He humbled himself, bowed his head, and quietly, with humility, asked God to forgive him. In response to his sincerity, a lifetime of sin was wiped away in a moment.

God has not given us a bunch of complicated, hard-to-follow guidelines for prayer. Talking with God is a simple and powerful way to draw closer to Him.

Build your relationship with God by spending time with Him on a daily basis.

A Proud Heart

... That is why He says, God sets Himself against the proud and haughty, but gives grace [continually] to the lowly (those who are humble enough to receive it).

JAMES 4:6

Has God ever had to deal with you about pride? Here are some ways you can tell if you have an issue with pride: If you have an opinion about everything, if you are judgmental, if you can't be corrected, if you rebel against authority, if you want to take all the credit for yourself, or if you say "I" too often. These are signs of pride.

It is hard to let God replace our pride with His humility, but it is vital. If we want to live in close relationship with God, we must come to Him with an attitude of humility. Pride relies on self, but humility

relies on God. It is only in the place of humility that God can bless us.

The humble get the help! If we humble ourselves under God's hand, He will exalt us in due time (James 4:10). Proud people think they deserve everything they want "now," but humility says, "My times are in Your hands, Lord."

Pride says "I can," but humility says, "Christ can through me."

True Satisfaction

But He replied, It has been written, Man shall not live and be upheld and sustained by bread alone, but by every word that comes forth from the mouth of God.   MATTHEW 4:4

I don't think there is anything better than just to be satisfied. To wake up in the morning and think, *Life is good; praise God, I'm satisfied*, and to go to bed at night still satisfied is truly living abundantly. On the other hand, I don't think there is anything much worse than living in a low-level state of dissatisfaction all the time.

Here is a spiritual reality check: No matter what you own, where you go, or what you do, nothing can give you true gratification besides the close, personal, intimate presence of God. Money, trips, vacations, clothes, new opportunities, new furniture

and new houses, and getting married and having children are all things that can give us a degree of happiness. But we will never be permanently, consistently satisfied if we seek things to own or do in order to quench the empty void inside us.

There are many unhappy believers who live unfulfilled lives because they are seeking the wrong thing! Don't miss out on a close, intimate relationship with God because you're seeking the gift instead of the Giver.

————

The things of the world cannot truly satisfy. Always look to God first and He will satisfy the desires of your heart.

God's Good Plan

Your eyes saw my unformed substance,
and in Your book all the days [of my life]
were written before ever they took shape,
when as yet there was none of them.

PSALM 139:16

God had a good plan laid out for each of us before we made our appearance on this planet. And His unique plan for each of us is not a plan of failure and every type of misery.

In John 10:10, Jesus said, "The thief comes only in order to steal and kill and destroy. I came that they may have and enjoy life, and have it in abundance." The devil comes to destroy the good thing God has in mind for us, and we need to steadfastly resist him.

God's good plan may have been disrupted in your life, but it is not too late!

God is reaching out to you right now and offering to restore to you anything the enemy has stolen, and to give you double blessing for your former trouble (Zechariah 9:12). Ask Him to do it, and watch Him work in your life.

God will do for you what you cannot do for yourself.

Determined to Love

Iron sharpens iron; so a man sharpens the countenance of his friend [to show rage or worthy purpose].   PROVERBS 27:17

We all have a few people in our lives who are like sandpaper to us. Some are like an entire package of sandpaper. Believe it or not, God places them in our lives to smooth off our rough edges. We are all like diamonds in the rough. We have something beautiful and valuable underneath the hard crusty surface of our flesh.

When God began to work spiritual maturity in me, He placed several people in my life who were very difficult for me to deal with. I thought they needed to change, but God wanted to use them to change me. We must learn to deal with all kinds of people and appreciate the ways in which they are different from us.

Dave can wait a long time for things and never get frustrated, but I want things to happen quickly. He is quiet and I talk a lot; he likes to play music in the morning and I like it quiet. I am sure you have people in your life who are very different than you are also. Instead of being irritated, or proudly thinking we are right and they are wrong, we should seek to accept them in love, just as Christ accepts us.

We can be determined to love and to get along with each other no matter how different our personalities or situations may be. Because when we love the people around us—even the most difficult people—we are opening ourselves up to learn something God may be trying to teach us.

Choose to walk in the love of Christ and let Him shape you through the other people He brings into your life.

Become a *Now* Person

... One thing I do [it is my one aspiration]: forgetting what lies behind and straining forward to what lies ahead, I press on toward the goal to win the [supreme and heavenly] prize to which God in Christ Jesus is calling us upward.   PHILIPPIANS 3:13–14

Regret over the past is a primary thief of joy and peace. Whether a mistake was made twenty years ago or twenty minutes ago, there is nothing you can do about it except repent, receive forgiveness, forget the past, and go on. If there is something you can do to undo the results of your mistakes, then by all means, do it. But the bottom line is that you still must let go of the past in order to grasp the future.

Like Paul, we are all pressing toward the mark of perfection, but none of us have

arrived. Even though he endured difficulty, I believe Paul enjoyed his life journey and ministry, and this "one aspiration" of his was part of the reason why. He had learned to forget his mistakes and refused to live in regret of the past.

Always remember that regret steals *now*! God has called us to be closer to Him in the *now*. When we cling to the past, we lay aside our faith and stop believing, then lose our peace and joy.

Let this be a day of decision for you—a day when you decide to no longer operate in regret. Become a now person. Live in the present. God has a plan for you now. Trust Him today.

───────────

God gives grace and joy and peace for today, but He does not give grace today for yesterday or tomorrow. Live life one day at a time.

Christ in You, the Hope of Glory

To whom God was pleased to make known how great for the Gentiles are the riches of the glory of this mystery, which is Christ within and among you, the Hope of [realizing the] glory.

COLOSSIANS 1:27

You and I can realize and experience the glory of God in our lives because of Christ in us. He is our hope of seeing better things.

The glory of God is His manifested excellence. As the children of God, we have an inheritance in Christ, a right to experience that manifested excellence. Satan furiously fights to deceive us. He wants us to believe we are incapable, unworthy, and disqualified from God's best. That is why many look at themselves and feel defeated.

But if you'll remember that because of Christ in you, you can experience the glory of

God—the manifested excellence of God— you'll live full of hope. You'll press on toward better things each day of your life. Look past what you can do and focus on what God can do through you.

Are you ready to believe for an outpouring of God's goodness and excellence in your life? God is looking for someone to be good to, so let it be you!

God's best for you is on its way, so get excited and expect good things!

Life Under the New Covenant

But as it now is, He [Christ] has acquired a [priestly] ministry which is as much superior and more excellent [than the old] as the covenant (the agreement) of which He is the Mediator (the Arbiter, Agent) is superior and more excellent, [because] it is enacted and rests upon more important (sublimer, higher, and nobler) promises.

HEBREWS 8:6

The Old Covenant was a covenant of works, based on doing everything ourselves—struggling, striving, and laboring to be acceptable to God. It leaves us trapped in the works of the flesh. That kind of covenant steals our joy and keeps us at a distance from God.

But the New Covenant is a covenant of grace, which is not based on what we can

do, but what Christ has already done for us. Therefore, we are justified by our faith, not our works. That is so wonderful because it takes the pressure off of us to perform. We can give up struggle and frustration, and allow God to work through us by the power of His Holy Spirit within us.

The bottom line is this: The Old Covenant brings us bondage; the New Covenant brings us liberty. That's why a relationship with God, made possible by the work of Christ Jesus, is better than anything else we may experience. It frees us to be who we were created to be and then do what we are supposed to do for God.

Life in the New Covenant is an awesome journey of living in the presence of God and enjoying victory through Christ.

More Than Conquerors

Yet amid all these things we are more than conquerors and gain a surpassing victory through Him Who loved us.

ROMANS 8:37

As believers we can live with a sense of triumph because Paul assures us that through Christ Jesus we are more than conquerors. Believing that truth gives us boldness for daily living.

Sometimes our confidence is shaken when trials come, especially if they are lengthy. But when we have an assurance of God's love for us, no matter what comes against us, we know deep inside that we are more than conquerors. If we are truly confident, we have no need to fear trouble or trying times, because we know they will pass.

Whenever a trial of any kind comes

against you, always remember: *This too shall pass!* Be confident that during the trial you will learn something that will help you in the future.

The closer we are to God, the more steps of faith we take, deciding to be confident in all things in Him. Confident people get the job done. They are fulfilled because they are succeeding at being themselves.

———

We will not succeed at being ourselves until our confidence is in God.

The Importance of Intercession

And I sought a man among them who should build up the wall and stand in the gap before Me for the land...

EZEKIEL 22:30

To intercede means to *stand in the gap* for someone else, to plead his case before the throne of God. If there is a breach in people's relationship with God for any reason, we have the privilege of placing ourselves in that breach and praying for them. We can intercede for them and expect to see them comforted and encouraged while they wait. We can also expect a timely breakthrough for them concerning their need being met.

I don't know what I would do if people did not intercede for me. I petition God to give me people to intercede for me and for the fulfillment of the ministry to which He

has called me. We need each other's prayers of intercession.

Praying for others is equivalent to sowing seed. We must sow seed if we are to reap a harvest (Galatians 6:7). Sowing seed into the lives of other people through intercession is one sure way to reap a harvest in our own life. Each time we pray for someone else, we are inviting God to not only work in that person's life but also in our own.

Intercession is one of the most important ways we carry on the ministry of Jesus Christ that He began in this earth.

We can release God's power in the lives of others by praying for them.

Do It Afraid

Now [in Haran] the Lord said to Abram, Go for yourself [for your own advantage] away from your country, from your relatives and your father's house, to the land that I will show you.

GENESIS 12:1

How would you feel if God told you to leave your home, your family, and everything familiar and comfortable to you and head out to who knows where? Would you be afraid? That is precisely the challenge Abram faced, and it frightened him. That's why God kept saying to him again and again, "Fear not."

Elisabeth Elliot, whose husband was killed along with four other missionaries in Ecuador, tells how her life was controlled completely by fear. Every time she started to step out, fear stopped her, until a friend

told her something that set her free. She said, "Why don't you do it afraid?" Elisabeth Elliot and Rachel Saint, sister of one of the murdered missionaries, went on to evangelize the Indian tribes, including the people who had killed their husband and brother.

If we wait to do something until we are not afraid, we will probably accomplish very little for God, for others, or even for ourselves. Both Abram and Joshua had to step out in faith and obedience to God to do what He had commanded them to do—even while they felt afraid. We can do the same!

Be determined that your life is not going to be ruled by fear but by God's Word.

Secure in Jesus

I am the Vine; you are the branches.
Whoever lives in Me and I in him bears
much (abundant) fruit. However, apart
from Me [cut off from vital union with
Me] you can do nothing.   JOHN 15:5

God wants us to be as totally dependent and reliant upon Him as a branch is on a vine. We would be unwise to put confidence in the flesh—ours or anybody else's.

How many times have you trusted in your own strength and failed miserably? How many times have other people let you down after you put your trust in them? How many times have you been disappointed when others rejected you or failed to do what you expected? God will allow us to be disappointed time after time until we learn to lean on Him and put our confidence in Him alone.

I am not suggesting that we shouldn't have any confidence in people, but we do need to realize they are imperfect and it is impossible for them to never let us down. Jesus, however, does not disappoint us! He is always with us, always for us, and is the only one we can put our total trust in.

———

Have great relationships with people, but don't give them the trust that belongs only to God!

A Prayer of Commitment

Commit your way to the Lord [roll and repose each care of your load on Him]; trust (lean on, rely on, and be confident) also in Him and He will bring it to pass.
                    PSALM 37:5

When we are tempted to worry or take on the care of some situation in life, we can pray a "prayer of commitment." God intervenes in our situations when we commit them to Him.

In my own life, I found that the more I tried to take care of things myself, the bigger mess my life became. I was quite independent and found it difficult to humble myself and admit that I needed help. However, when I finally submitted to God in these areas and found the joy of casting all my care on Him, I could not believe I had

lived so long under such huge amounts of pressure.

Commit to the Lord your children, your marriage, your personal relationships, and especially anything you may be tempted to be concerned about. Only God really knows what needs to be done, and He is the only One Who is qualified to do it. The more we sincerely commit ourselves to God, the closer we will be to Him and the happier we will be.

———————

A believer who can trust the Father when things do not seem to make sense is a mature believer.

From the Pit to the Palace

And Pharaoh said to Joseph, Forasmuch as [your] God has shown you all this, there is nobody as intelligent and discreet and understanding and wise as you are.

You shall have charge over my house, and all my people shall be governed according to your word... Only in matters of the throne will I be greater than you are.   GENESIS 41:39–40

A pit is a ditch, a trap, or a snare. It refers to destruction. Satan always wants to bring us into the pit.

Joseph was sold into slavery by his brothers. They actually threw him into a pit and intended to leave him there to die, but God had other plans. Joseph ended up being sold into slavery in Egypt, where he was thrown in prison for refusing to compromise his integrity. Yet everywhere Joseph went, God

gave him favor. Ultimately, Joseph was promoted to the palace, second in command to Pharaoh.

How did Joseph get from the pit to the palace? I believe it was by remaining positive, refusing to be bitter, and choosing to boldly trust God. Even though it looked like he was defeated on many occasions, he refused to give up on trusting God.

Joseph had a right attitude. He knew God was in control even when it looked like the circumstances of his life were spinning out of control. The same is true in your life. If you'll keep a positive attitude, knowing that God is in control, He can take you from the pit to the palace in ways you never imagined.

No matter where you started, you can have a great finish!

Refuse to Be Bitter

But Jesus said to him, Judas! Would you betray and deliver up the Son of Man with a kiss?   LUKE 22:48

Jesus bore our sins so we do not have to bear them. But there are other things He endured on His way to the cross that serve as an example for us, things that we will have to go through and ways we will have to follow in His footsteps. Jesus faced the betrayal of Judas at the worst moment of His life but did not let it hinder Him.

Betrayal is especially painful when we are hurt by someone we love, respect, and trust. We may become defensive and bitter in an effort to never be hurt again. But with God's help, betrayal is something we can recover from and not let hinder us, no matter how we feel.

In Matthew 24:10–13, Jesus warns us

that in the last days betrayals will increase. As believers, how we respond to disappointment in people is more important than what they did to us. If you are betrayed or wounded by someone you trusted, refuse to get bitter. Instead, follow the example of Jesus and forgive them. We can't choose what other people do, but we can choose to have a right response.

We must determine that with God's help, we can allow our pain to make us better, not bitter.

A Divine Attitude Adjustment

And be constantly renewed in the spirit of your mind [having a fresh mental and spiritual attitude].

EPHESIANS 4:23

God wants us to always maintain a good attitude for two reasons. First, it glorifies Him and encourages other people to remain positive when they have problems; and second, it allows Him to work in our lives, bringing help and deliverance from our struggles.

Always having a good attitude is difficult unless we receive God's grace to do so. Jesus said that apart from Him, we could do nothing (John 15:5), but through Him we can do all things (Philippians 4:13).

Don't wait until you are tempted to have a bad attitude, but pray daily that no matter what comes your way, you can endure

it with a good attitude. We will always be tempted, but we can pray not to give in to the temptation.

A good attitude is one of our greatest assets. It keeps us hopeful no matter what is happening in our lives.

———————

Ask God to fill your attitude with His Holy Spirit at all times!

Putting Others First

*For by the grace (unmerited favor of
God) given to me I warn everyone
among you not to estimate and think of
himself more highly than he ought [not
to have an exaggerated opinion of his
own importance]...*   ROMANS 12:3

Humility that is manifested in not thinking we are better than other people always
helps us treat people with respect and
kindness. In Matthew 7:12 Jesus gave us
instruction that affects the way we deal
with every person we come across over the
course of a day—friends, family, coworkers, and even those people who are unkind
to us.

Jesus said, "Whatever you desire that
others would do to and for you, even so do
also to and for them, for this (sums up) the
Law and the Prophets." It's a pretty simple

concept and a great way to live life. In order to experience God's best for our lives, we are to treat people the way we would like to be treated. We should look for the needs of others first and see what we can do to serve them.

Our lives are going to be less than God's best if we are consumed with "self." Self-centeredness keeps us from seeing the needs of others and causes us to miss the blessings that come when we serve. We don't have to totally forget about our own needs. But we can chase selfishness away by not *always* thinking about our needs first.

If you'll begin to treat the people around you with love, kindness, and respect, you'll be surprised at how much it will impact the way they treat you in return.

The Joy of Believing

Where there is no vision...the people perish...   PROVERBS 29:18

The book of Proverbs says that where there is no vision, people perish. A vision is something we see in our minds, "a mental sight" as one definition puts it. It may be something God puts in our hearts or it may be something we want to see happen and have prayerfully submitted to God. A vision for our lives involves the way we think about ourselves and our future.

I've noticed that some people are afraid to believe for something good. They think they may be setting themselves up for disappointment. They have not realized they will be constantly disappointed if they don't believe. I feel that if I believe for a lot and just get half of it, I am better off than I would be to believe for nothing and get

all of it. I want to encourage you to start believing for good things. Believe you can do whatever you need to do in life through Christ. When you believe, it stirs up faith in your heart, and faith pleases God, bringing you closer to Him.

Avoid having an "It will never happen" attitude. Let your faith soar. If you're not sure how to do that, start by taking an inventory of your thoughts. What have you been thinking and believing lately? An honest answer may help you understand why you have not been receiving what you have wanted to receive.

God has invited us to pray boldly, with confidence in His goodness to us, and I suggest you start today!

Change Is a Process

And so after waiting patiently, Abraham received what was promised.

HEBREWS 6:15 NIV

Change doesn't come easily. I'll never forget about the lady who approached me one day after I finished teaching. In exasperation, she put her hands on her hips and said, "I want my money back!" I was pretty surprised by her declaration, and I replied, "What do you mean you want your money back?" She said, "Joyce, I gave to your ministry and I've been doing this stuff you say to do for *two whole weeks* and nothing's changed!"

In hindsight, it's pretty comical, but in the moment I explained to this woman that's not the way it works. Change takes time. And patience is required to successfully work through the process of getting

the result you want. She left disgusted because she wanted an instant fix, and that is not what God offers us. When you were saved, you stepped onto a road that led you to a lifetime journey of change. And our lives are changed through God's Word (James 1:21–25).

In order to live in close, intimate fellowship with God, make the decision to be a lifetime follower and learner. Read the Word. Listen to teachings about the Word. There is nothing better than getting the Word of God into your heart . . . it's the most important part of the process.

———

The Bible says we inherit the promises of God through faith and patience (Hebrews 6:12), and faith comes by hearing God's Word (Romans 10:17).

Getting Untangled

No soldier when in service gets entangled in the enterprises of [civilian] life; his aim is to satisfy and please the one who enlisted him.   2 TIMOTHY 2:4

Do you ever find yourself not taking time to spend with God because you're so busy with other things? In 2 Timothy 2:4, Paul tells his protégé, Timothy, that a wise soldier avoids getting entangled in things that won't satisfy the person who enlisted him. In other words, a child of God who wants to please God keeps his priorities straight and refuses to do things that could distract him from what is really important.

In order to grow closer to God on a daily basis, you'll have to avoid some of the distractions and entanglements of the world. This may mean saying no to an opportunity you'd like to take but really don't have

time for. It could mean exercising good boundaries and not getting too wrapped up in other people's problems. It's important to help people, but there is a difference between godly involvement and entanglement. It may even mean being less focused on the stresses and cares that come up over the course of each day, because they certainly can distract us from God's will and purpose for our lives.

God loves you and wants to be in relationship with you. Don't let the entanglements of the world keep you from enjoying daily fellowship with Him.

Don't let the less important things crowd out what is most important in your life.

Good Things to Come

Then I said to you, Dread not, neither be afraid of them. The Lord your God Who goes before you, He will fight for you just as He did for you in Egypt before your eyes.

DEUTERONOMY 1:29–30

Do you look forward to every day with a spirit of joy and expectation of good things to come, or do you awake each morning in a state of dread? One might dread going to work, driving in traffic, cleaning the house, or dealing with difficult people. Dread is a subtle form of fear that the devil uses to steal our joy and prevent us from enjoying life. It prevents us from walking in the will of God and moving forward in the plans of God to receive His blessings.

Dread comes after us aggressively and cannot be defeated passively. Allowing negative

feelings and thoughts into your mind will steal your joy and peace. But you can trust God to help you with anything you need to do. And as He gives you grace, the thing you were dreading turns out not to be so bad after all. We can choose to believe that Jesus goes before us and makes a way for us. When a project seems difficult or unpleasant, don't start dreading it. If you are going to do it anyway, you might as well enjoy it!

As Christians, we can find joy even in unpleasant circumstances because the presence of God is with us. We can enjoy our life with Him in the midst of adverse and difficult conditions. Our joy comes from Who is inside us, not in what is around us.

If we set our minds to it, we can enjoy everything we do in life. Where God guides, He provides.

Avoid Comparisons

... When they measure themselves with themselves and compare themselves with one another, they are without understanding and behave unwisely.
2 CORINTHIANS 10:12

If you've dealt with insecurity in your life, an important key to overcoming that insecurity is this: *Never compare yourself with anyone else because it invites feelings of inferiority.*

I really want to encourage you to stop comparing yourself with other people about how you look, what position you occupy, or how long you pray. Comparison puts the focus on self and thwarts God's plan for your life.

In the same way, we would be wise to avoid comparing our trials to those of other people. You may be going through something

difficult, but don't look at somebody else and say, "Why is all this happening to me while you've got it so easy?"

Jesus revealed to Peter ahead of time some of the suffering he would go through. Peter immediately wanted to compare his suffering and his lot in life with somebody else's by saying, "What about this man?" Jesus answered by saying, "If I want him to stay (survive, live) until I come, what is that to you? [What concern is it of yours?] You follow Me!" (John 21:22).

That is His answer to us also. We are not called to compare, only to comply to His will for us.

God wants you to know that you are unique and He has an individualized, specialized plan for your life.

Starting with Prayer

Be unceasing in prayer [praying perseveringly].

1 THESSALONIANS 5:17

I have been walking with God most of my life, and I am still learning the importance of not doing anything without praying about it first. The Bible says we are to pray without ceasing. This doesn't mean we sit around all day, doing nothing except praying. It simply means that we include prayer in everything we do. I like to say, "Pray your way through the day."

Praying is probably the most important part of life preparation. It has been said that every failure happens because of a failure to pray! I suggest you don't do anything without first praying.

The Bible says that we should acknowledge God in all our ways and He will direct

our steps and make them sure (Proverbs 3:6). It's encouraging to know that we can call on God and He will provide daily guidance and strength.

You become closer to God when you go to Him in prayer all throughout the day. It allows you to fellowship with God and it opens the door for Him to work in your life, your situation, and the lives of your loved ones.

———————

God will enable you to do things that will frequently surprise you if you take Him as your partner in life. But it all begins with prayer.

Having a Willing Heart

And Nathan said to the king, Go, do all that is in your heart, for the Lord is with you.   2 SAMUEL 7:3

A willing heart is a heart that "wants to." If there is something we want to do strongly enough, somehow we will find a way to do it. With God's help and a willing heart, we can have a close relationship with Him, keep our house clean, save money, get out of debt, or reach any other goal in life we may have set for ourselves. Our victory or defeat has a lot to do with our "want to."

Many times we lay the blame for our failures on the devil, other people, the past, and on and on. But the bottom line may be that we just don't have enough of the right kind of "want to."

If you really want to be closer to God, I believe you will be. Your willing heart will

cause you to seek Him with a new passion. You'll choose to spend time each day in prayer and studying the Word. God will see your heart and draw close to you even as you are drawing close to Him.

———————

We don't always feel like doing what we want to do, but you don't have to make your decisions based on feelings.

What Is Grace?

... The [Holy] Spirit [Who imparts] grace (the unmerited favor and blessing of God).   HEBREWS 10:29

Grace is the power of the Holy Spirit available to you to do with ease what you cannot do by striving in your own strength. Grace is God's power coming into our lives, freely enabling us to do whatever we need to do. God's grace is always available, but we do need to receive it by faith and refuse to try to do things in our own strength without God.

The Holy Spirit ministers grace to us from God the Father. Grace is actually the Holy Spirit's power flowing out from the throne of God toward people to save them and enable them to live holy lives and accomplish the will of God.

We can rejoice and be full of peace,

joy, and contentment each day because of God's grace in our lives. It is His grace that allows us to live in close fellowship with Him. With the grace of God, life can be enjoyed with an ease that produces rest and contentment.

————

We are saved by grace through faith, and we should learn to live the same way!

Change Your Thinking About Fear

Fear not [there is nothing to fear], for I am with you; do not look around you in terror and be dismayed, for I am your God. I will strengthen and harden you to difficulties, yes, I will help you; yes, I will hold you up and retain you with My [victorious] right hand of rightness and justice.   ISAIAH 41:10

With God's help, you can move from cowering in fear to overcoming fear by changing the way you think. The Bible refers to this as renewing your mind (Romans 12:2). Simply put, we can learn to think differently. Experiences or people from your past may have taught you to fear, but the Word of God can teach you to push past that fear. You can learn to be bold, courageous, and confident.

Don't let the fear of something prevent

your success and joy in daily living. Fear has a large shadow, but fear itself is actually very small. Fear brings unnecessary torment in your life. When you feel afraid, you don't have to quit or turn back. God is with you, and because He is with you, you can feel the fear and do it anyway.

Instead of thinking you cannot do something when you are afraid, make up your mind that you will meet your goal and conquer the challenge before you. You may have thoughts of fear, but the Holy Spirit inside of you can change your thinking about fear. Fear seems like a monster, but it is one that will back down quickly when confronted with the truth from God's Word. Fear is like a school bully: It pushes everyone around until someone finally challenges it.

———

When we fear we will suffer, we already suffer the thing we fear.

Relationship, Not Rules

A new heart will I give you and a new spirit will I put within you, and I will take away the stony heart out of your flesh and give you a heart of flesh.

EZEKIEL 36:26

Many times when somebody is born again, the first things they are told are: "You need to change your hairstyle, or dress differently. You have a tattoo that needs to be covered up. You've got an earring in the wrong place." Their introduction to Christianity is a list of rules, things they must do, and things they must not do, according to what *people* think is right and wrong.

Sadly, too many times no one talks to them at all about their heart or their relationship with God. Instead it's about all these things they have to do if they want to be part of a particular religious organization.

Although God will lead us to make positive changes in our lives, He totally accepts us as we are, and we need to do the same for new Christians. Give them time, and God will lead them by giving them new desires.

Jesus died so we could have a deep, passionate, personal relationship with God. He didn't die to give us a list of rules. He gave us something much deeper and much better—He gave us access to God so that we could be in close personal relationship with our heavenly Father.

————————

The closer you get to God, the more He lovingly and graciously changes you from the inside out.

Waiting on the Lord

Our inner selves wait [earnestly] for the Lord; He is our Help and our Shield.
PSALM 33:20

In our instant and fast-paced society, the spiritual discipline of waiting on the Lord is often lacking. We want everything we want and we want it right now! But if we are always in such a hurry, we will miss out on the close fellowship with God that takes time to develop. God wants to speak to our hearts if only we will be patient to listen.

Elijah was a man who knew the secret of being patient. After slaying the prophets of Baal, Elijah learned a valuable lesson on waiting on God. The Lord told Elijah to go stand on a mountain and wait. A great wind came; then came a great earthquake and a great fire, but the Lord was in none of those. Consider what 1 Kings 19:12 says:

"After the fire [a sound of gentle stillness and] a still, small voice." The Lord spoke in a still, small voice, *after* the wind, the earthquake, and the fire. If Elijah had been impatient in prayer, he would not have heard the Lord's voice.

David also learned to wait in the house of the Lord and "to meditate, consider, and inquire in His temple" (Psalm 27:4). In order for us to pray effectively, we can choose to wait patiently and listen for His Word. Waiting and listening takes our focus off of us and places it on Him, Who is the answer to all our needs.

———————

It is often in silence when the power of God is moving the most mightily. Allow the Holy Spirit to teach you how to wait in His presence.

Keep Trusting God

But He knows the way that I take [He has concern for it, appreciates, and pays attention to it]. When He has tried me, I shall come forth as refined gold [pure and luminous].   JOB 23:10

There will always be situations in life where we will be required to trust God no matter what happens or whether we understand everything. This is why we often find ourselves saying to God, "What is going on in my life? What are You doing? What is happening? I don't understand." Sometimes the things happening in us seem to be taking us in the exact opposite direction of what we feel God has previously revealed to us.

This is when many people give up and go back to something that will be quicker and easier for them. If you are in a place

right now where nothing in your life makes any sense, keep trusting God. He is close to you. He hasn't abandoned you. He is going to see you through.

There is no such thing as trusting God without unanswered questions. As long as God is training us to trust, there are always going to be things in our life we just don't understand. When heaven is silent, continue doing the things you have learned and know to do, and keep trusting Him. God will make all the pieces in your life work together for His purpose.

———

Tomorrow's answers usually don't come until tomorrow.

Learn to Love Yourself

...I have loved you with an everlasting love; therefore with loving-kindness have I drawn you and continued My faithfulness to you.   JEREMIAH 31:3

Many people don't really like themselves. They are very self-critical; they reject themselves and may even hate themselves. The Bible teaches us not to be selfish and self-centered, but it never instructs us not to love ourselves in a balanced way. I always say, "Don't be in love with yourself, but love yourself." If you don't love yourself, you will be miserable because you are always with yourself. You are the one person you will never get away from, not even for one second of your life.

I once heard a young woman ask a pastor to pray for her because she hated herself. He looked at her and took a step backward

in dismay. He said very clearly, "Who do you think you are to hate yourself after God sent His only Son to suffer so horribly and die in your place? If God loved you that much, surely you can love yourself."

His statement opened her eyes to the mistake she was making, and she began her journey of learning to love and accept herself. I encourage you to do the same. Take a step of faith and say, "I love myself with the love of God. I accept myself."

As you begin to see yourself as God sees you, your entire attitude and disposition will change. You will become a more positive, confident person, and you will begin to enjoy your life so much more.

———

Because God loves you, you can love yourself.

Pray About Everything and Fear Nothing

Be strong and let your heart take courage, all you who wait for and hope for and expect the Lord!

PSALM 31:24

Some time ago I felt the Lord speaking these words to me: "Pray about everything and fear nothing." Over the next couple of weeks, He showed me different things about prayer versus fear. Many of them dealt with little areas in which fear would try to creep into my life and cause me problems. He showed me that in every case, no matter how great or important or how small or insignificant, the solution was to pray.

Sometimes we become afraid by focusing on our circumstances. The more we focus on the problem, the more fearful we

become. Instead, we can choose to keep our focus on God. He is able to handle anything that we may ever have to face in this life.

God has promised to strengthen us, to harden us to difficulties, to hold us up and retain us with His victorious right hand (Isaiah 41:10). He also commands us not to be afraid. But remember, He is not commanding us never to feel fear, but rather not to let it control us.

The Lord is saying to us today, "Fear not, I will help you." But we never experience the help of God until we place everything on the line, until we are obedient enough to step out in faith.

———

Don't back down when you feel fear. Trust the Lord and keep moving.

Good from Bad

As for you, you thought evil against me,
but God meant it for good, to bring
about that many people should be kept
alive, as they are this day.

GENESIS 50:20

God wants to restore your soul. The closer you get to Him, the more you experience His healing, strengthening, restoring power. He'll take you back to where your life got off track and make everything right from that moment forward.

Joseph is the classic biblical example of how God takes what was meant for evil against us and works it for our good. In that dramatic scene where Joseph is speaking in Genesis 50:20, he tells his brothers that the evil they meant to do to him (and it was truly evil), God had used for good to save them and their families

and hundreds of thousands of others in a time of famine.

In my own life, I cannot truthfully say I am glad I was abused. But through the power of forgiveness and yielding my pain to God, He has healed me and made me a better, stronger, more spiritually powerful and sensitive person. He has restored my soul and driven out the fear and insecurity. I can trust, love, forgive, and live with simplicity in my approach to life because God has restored my soul, and He can do the same thing for you.

If bad things have happened in your life, remember this: Only God can restore your situation. He can bring good from bad.

The Power of Joy and Peace

Be well balanced (temperate, sober of mind), be vigilant and cautious at all times; for that enemy of yours, the devil, roams around like a lion roaring [in fierce hunger], seeking someone to seize upon and devour.   1 PETER 5:8

When you find yourself in a troublesome situation, let your goal be to simply stay calm. Each time you begin to feel upset or frustrated, stop and ask yourself, "What is the enemy trying to do here?"

If the devil cannot drive you to be fearful and upset about a problem, he has no power over you. You stay in God's strength and power when you maintain a calm, peaceful, trusting attitude.

The Holy Spirit works in an atmosphere of joy and peace. He does not work in turmoil. In a time of trial, your strength is

found in drawing close to God and entering into His rest. All of these biblical words—*abide, still, rest, stand*, and *in Christ*—say basically the same thing: *Do not lose your joy and peace.*

In Christ, you are called to be an overcomer. You have the assurance of always triumphing in Him. If you take each problem as it comes, it will work out all right. Jesus is always with you in each situation. Just remember to trust Him for enough joy and peace for today.

———————

There is tremendous power in choosing to walk in peace and joy, regardless of the circumstances around you.

When You Feel Worried

*To grant [consolation and joy] to those
who mourn in Zion—to give them
an ornament (a garland or diadem)
of beauty instead of ashes, the oil of
joy instead of mourning, the garment
[expressive] of praise instead of a heavy,
burdened, and failing spirit . . . that He
may be glorified.*   ISAIAH 61:3

God wants to take care of us, but in order
to let Him, it is important that we choose to
stop worrying. Many people say they want
God to take care of them, but they spend
their days worrying or trying to figure out
all the answers instead of waiting for God's
direction. They are actually wallowing
around in their "ashes," but they still want
God to give them beauty. In order for God
to give us the beauty, we have to give Him
the "ashes."

We give God our cares by believing that He can and will take care of us. Hebrews 4:3 says, "For we who have believed (adhered to and trusted in and relied on God) do enter that rest..."

We enter into the Lord's rest through believing. Worry is the opposite of faith. Worry steals our peace, physically wears us out, and can even make us sick. If we are worrying, we are not trusting God, and we are not entering His rest.

What a great trade God has provided. You give Him ashes, and He gives you beauty. You give Him all your worries and concerns, and He gives you protection, stability, a place of refuge, and fullness of joy—the privilege of being cared for by Him.

Jesus did not worry, and you do not have to worry either.

Stirred to Action

And Moses called Bezalel and Aholiab and every able and wisehearted man in whose mind the Lord had put wisdom and ability, everyone whose heart stirred him up to come to do the work.

EXODUS 36:2

Something powerful happens in your life when your heart is stirred up for action. It doesn't do us any good to say, "Oh, I wish I felt that way." We can decide to do something about the way we feel by stirring up our own hearts to do what God has called us to do.

How do we stir up our faith? I have discovered that the Word of God coming out of my own mouth in the form of prayer, praise, preaching, or confessions is the best way that I can find to fan the fire. It stirs up the gift within, keeps my faith and my

hope active, and prevents my spirit from sinking within me.

Passivity, procrastination, and laziness are tools the enemy uses against God's people. A passive person waits to be moved by an outside force before taking action. But we can be motivated and led by the Holy Spirit within us, not by outside forces. The best way to guard against passivity is to do whatever is before you with all of your might.

———

Keep your God-given gift, that fire within you, stirred up.

The Spirit of Adoption

For [the Spirit which] you have now received [is] not a spirit of slavery to put you once more in bondage to fear, but you have received the Spirit of adoption [the Spirit producing sonship] in [the bliss of] which we cry, Abba (Father)! Father!   ROMANS 8:15

The apostle Paul teaches us that the Holy Spirit is the Spirit of adoption. The word *adoption* means that we are brought into the family of God, even though we were previously outsiders, unrelated to God in any way. We were sinners and separated from God, but God in His great mercy redeemed us, purchased us, and brought us close to Him once again through the blood of His own Son.

We understand adoption in the natural sense. We know that some children without parents are adopted by people who

purposely choose them and take them as their own. What an honor to be chosen on purpose by those who want to pour out their love on them.

This is exactly what God did for us as believers in Christ. Because of what Jesus did for us on the cross, we are now eternally part of His family, and His Spirit dwells in our spirit and cries out to the Father. God the Father decided before the foundation of the world was laid that anyone who loved Christ would be loved and accepted by Him as His child. He decided He would adopt all those who accepted Jesus as their Savior. We become heirs of God and joint heirs with His Son, Jesus Christ.

―――――――――

It is the knowledge of our family relationship to God that gives us boldness to go before His throne and let our requests be made known.

Seek the One Thing

One thing have I asked of the Lord, that will I seek, inquire for, and [insistently] require: that I may dwell in the house of the Lord [in His presence] all the days of my life, to behold and gaze upon the beauty [the sweet attractiveness and the delightful loveliness] of the Lord and to meditate, consider, and inquire in His temple.

PSALM 27:4

If you knew you could only ask for one thing, what would your request be? David said there was only one thing he sought after: to dwell in God's presence.

Being close to God is the number one priority we should have in life.

But we can get so distracted with the events of daily life that we neglect the most important thing—spending time with God,

knowing Him, appreciating Him, seeking His direction.

There are many empty people in the world who are trying to satisfy the voids in their lives with a new car, a promotion, a relationship, or some other thing. But their efforts to find complete fulfillment in those things never work, because each of us has a God-shaped hole inside, and nothing can fill it except God Himself.

I encourage you to seek God first and put the other things in your life *after* Him. If you will put Him first in everything you do, you will be blessed beyond measure.

God is the "One Thing" who can give you great joy, peace, satisfaction, and contentment.

Secure Enough to Be Different

The sun is glorious in one way, the moon is glorious in another way, and the stars are glorious in their own [distinctive] way; for one star differs from and surpasses another in its beauty and brilliance.   1 CORINTHIANS 15:41

We are all different. Like the sun, the moon, and the stars, God has created us to be different from one another, and He has done it on purpose. Each of us meets a need, and we are all part of God's overall plan. When we try to be just like someone else, we lose ourselves and stray from who God created us to be. God designed us to fit into His plan, not to feel pressured trying to fit into everyone else's plans.

Not only is it okay to be different, it is how you were created. We are all born with different temperaments, different physical

features, different fingerprints, different gifts and abilities. Our goal should be to find out what we individually are supposed to be, then succeed at being that. That is why Romans 12 teaches us to give ourselves to our gift. We are to find out what we are good at and then throw ourselves whole-heartedly into it.

You can be free to love and accept yourself and others around you without feeling pressure to compare or compete. Secure people who know God loves them and has a plan for them are not threatened by the abilities of others. They enjoy what other people can do, and they enjoy what they can do too.

———————

God gave you gifts and desires for you to use. Focus on your potential instead of your limitations.

Rejoicing Every Step of the Way

Rejoice in the Lord always [delight, gladden yourselves in Him]; again I say, Rejoice!   PHILIPPIANS 4:4

Paul felt rejoicing in the goodness of God was so important that he tells us twice in this verse from Philippians to rejoice. He urges in the following verses not to fret or have any anxiety about anything but to pray and give thanks to God in everything—not *after* everything is over.

If we wait until everything is perfect before rejoicing and giving thanks, we won't have much fun. Learning to enjoy life even in the midst of trying circumstances is one way we grow closer to God. Paul also writes that we "are constantly being transfigured into His very own image in ever increasing splendor and from one degree of glory to another" (2 Corinthians 3:18).

That means we can enjoy the glory we are experiencing at each level of our development, because each new day is another step toward the person God is shaping us to be.

When I first started my ministry, my happiness was dependent on my circumstances. Finally the Lord showed me the doorway to happiness. He gave me a breakthrough by teaching me that fullness of joy is found in His "presence"—not in His "presents" (Psalm 16:11).

———

True joy is discovered when we seek God's face.

Shake Off Rejection

He who hears and heeds you [disciples] hears and heeds Me; and he who slights and rejects you slights and rejects Me; and he who slights and rejects Me slights and rejects Him who sent Me.

LUKE 10:16

It is a fact of life that we will deal with rejection from time to time. David dealt with rejection. Paul dealt with rejection. Even Jesus was rejected. So when you suffer rejection for doing what God leads you to do—doing things that are different from what others around you are doing—don't despair; you are in good company.

When I first started preaching, I was insecure and took my share of criticism and rejection. There were times when I was very discouraged. Finally, the Lord spoke to me in my spirit and said: "I am the One

Who called you. Don't worry what people think. If you do, you are going to be worrying all your life because the devil will never stop finding people who think something unkind about you."

In Acts 28:1–5, when the apostle Paul was bitten by a snake, he simply shook off the snake and suffered no evil effects. That is what we can do with rejection. When we are close to God and find our identity in Him, rather than in other people's opinion of us, we can shake off whatever is trying to discourage us. Whatever you are dealing with today—fear, rejection, discouragement, disappointment, loneliness—shake it off and go on.

———————

Even when our rejection is from people who are close to us, we can be determined to keep pressing on toward fulfilling what God has called us to do.

God's Protection

*He who dwells in the secret place of
the Most High shall remain stable and
fixed under the shadow of the Almighty
[Whose power no foe can withstand].*

PSALM 91:1

God's presence is a secret place where we
can dwell in peace, feel safe, and enter
God's rest. This secret place is not a physical
location; it is a spiritual place where worry
vanishes and peace reigns. It is the place of
God's presence. When we spend time praying and seeking God and dwelling in His
presence, we are in the secret place.

When you and I *dwell in Christ* or
dwell in the secret place, we do not just visit
there occasionally, we take up permanent
residence in this place of refuge. It is the
place we run to when we are hurting, overwhelmed, or feeling faint. It is the place we

run to when we are being mistreated or persecuted, and when we are in great need. It is also the place where we offer thanksgiving and praise for the goodness of God in our lives. I like to say that God's presence is my first "go to" place when I have any kind of need.

It is important that we be firmly planted in God—to know the Source of our help in every situation and in every circumstance. With God's help, we can have our own secret place of peace and security by simply relying on God and trusting Him completely. We are never more than one thought away from God's presence!

God wants us to take refuge under the protective shadow of His wings. He wants us to run to Him.

A Blameless Heart

For the eyes of the Lord run to and fro throughout the whole earth to show Himself strong in behalf of those whose hearts are blameless toward Him...

2 CHRONICLES 16:9

What does it mean to have a blameless heart? It means you have a heartfelt desire to do right and to please God. A person who has a blameless heart truly loves God, though he himself may not be blameless or perfect in all of his ways. He may still have weaknesses. He may make mistakes or lose his temper. But when he does, he is quick to repent and receive God's forgiveness. If he has offended someone else, he will humble himself and apologize. Because his heart is right toward God, it is easy for the Holy Spirit to teach him.

When God searches for those to work

through, He doesn't look for somebody with a perfect performance. If any one of us could have perfect behavior, we would not need Jesus. We can, however, love God with a perfect heart, and when we do, He shows Himself strong on our behalf.

—————

The Lord strengthens those who have a right heart attitude toward Him.

He Won't Let You Sink

Now to Him Who is able to keep you without stumbling or slipping or falling, and to present [you] unblemished (blameless and faultless) before the presence of His glory in triumphant joy and exultation [with unspeakable, ecstatic delight]—   JUDE 24

Many children who are just learning to swim feel afraid in a swimming pool. Unless they are being carried by a parent or another trusted adult, they feel insecure because they realize the water is over their heads.

At various points in our lives, all of us fear we're getting "in over our heads" or we feel we are "out of our depth." The reality is that without God we're always in over our heads. There are difficulties and challenges all around us in life. Some are small and

inconvenient; others are large and intimidating. The car breaks down, a job is lost, a friend or family member dies, an argument occurs, a bad report comes from the doctor. When these things happen, it's easy to panic because we feel we're in over our heads.

But the truth is we've never really been in control when it comes to life's crucial elements. We've always been dependent on the grace of God to carry us through. God is never out of His depth. When we depend on Him, we can relax and be at peace, knowing He'll carry us through. He'll never let us go.

———

You are safe in your Father's arms. Even when you feel you're in over your head, He is holding you by His grace.

Let the "Umpire" Make the Call

And let the peace (soul harmony which comes) from Christ rule (act as umpire continually) in your hearts [deciding and settling with finality all questions that arise in your minds, in that peaceful state] to which as [members of Christ's] one body you were also called [to live]. And be thankful (appreciative), [giving praise to God always].   COLOSSIANS 3:15

In Colossians 3:15, Paul tells us that peace is much like an umpire—it makes the call in our lives, settling every issue that needs a decision.

That simply means that if you don't feel peace about a decision or an action, don't go through with it. Let the "umpire" make the call. Some people make a career decision they didn't really have peace about, and then they wonder why they are stressed-out

and unhappy in their jobs. A lot of people make expensive purchases even though they don't have peace about it, and then they continue to lose their peace every month when they have to make payments on those purchases.

But we can let the peace of Christ "rule (act as umpire continually)" in our hearts. The presence of peace will help us decide with confidence the questions that arise in our minds. If you spend time in prayer and in the Word of God regularly, you'll discover great insight and wisdom from the Lord. You won't have to wonder, *Should I or shouldn't I? Is this the right thing to do or is this a mistake?* As a child of God, living in close relationship with your heavenly Father, you will be able to follow the peace that He provides.

When you're not sure what to do, always follow peace!

To Live Like Christ

God said, Let Us [Father, Son, and Holy Spirit] make mankind in Our image, after Our likeness, and let them have complete authority over the fish of the sea, the birds of the air, the [tame] beasts, and over all of the earth, and over everything that creeps upon the earth.   GENESIS 1:26

In Genesis 1:26, when God said, "Let us... make mankind in Our image," this image does not refer to a physical likeness, but to character likeness. We were created to take on His nature, His character, as reflected in His Son, Jesus.

The greatest goal for every believer is Christlikeness. It is our highest calling in life. It's exciting to know that we can be so close in our relationship with the Lord that we begin to handle situations the way Jesus

would handle them and to treat people the way He would treat them. Our aim is to want to do things the way Jesus would do them.

Jesus is our example. In John 13:15, He told His disciples, after washing their feet as a servant, "For I have given you this as an example, so that you should do [in your turn] what I have done to you." Every day, and in every way, look to Jesus and follow the example He set in the Word of God for your daily life.

———

God will graciously keep working with each of us until we get to the place where we act the way Jesus would act in every situation in life.

Developing Your Potential

Do you not know that in a race all the runners compete, but [only] one receives the prize? So run [your race] that you may lay hold [of the prize] and make it yours.   1 CORINTHIANS 9:24

When we draw close to God, choosing to shed fear and self-doubt, we are able to develop our potential and succeed at being all God intended us to be. But we cannot develop our potential if we fear failure. We will be so afraid of failing or making mistakes that it will prevent us from stepping out.

I often see people who have great potential, and yet when opportunities and promotions are offered them, they quickly turn them down. In many cases, they are insecure and unaware of how much they could accomplish if they would only step out in faith, knowing God is with them.

When we are insecure, frequently we will stay with what is safe and familiar rather than taking a chance on stepping out and failing. We avoid accepting greater responsibility because we feel we aren't ready—but the truth is that none of us is ever ready. However, God is always ready, and when He begins to move in your life, you can know that He will equip you with what you need at the time you need it.

Humbly leaning on God leads to success. When our faith is in Christ rather than ourselves, we are free to develop our potential, because we are free from the fear of failure.

Keep Life Interesting

Whatever may be your task, work at it heartily (from the soul), as [something done] for the Lord and not for men.

COLOSSIANS 3:23

Life wasn't meant to be dull and boring. We are not created by God to merely do the same thing over and over until it has no meaning at all. God is creative. If you don't think so, just look around you. Many of the animals, bugs, plants, birds, trees, and other living things are unique, out of the ordinary, and totally amazing.

You were created to be unique, out of the ordinary and totally amazing too. That is why I think it is good to occasionally do something that seems outrageous to people and perhaps even to you. Do something that people won't expect. It will keep your life interesting and keep other people from

thinking they have you tucked away nicely in a little box of their own design.

One great woman who was seventy-six years of age said that her goal was to do at least one outrageous thing per week. Isn't that a great idea? If you purposefully do something out of the norm on a regular basis, this will keep you from getting stuck in a rut, bored and unenthused about your life.

What outrageous thing will you do today?

————

Refuse to be bored and just limp along through life. Be creative and add fun to whatever you do.

Praying Bold Prayers

Up to this time you have not asked a [single] thing in My Name ... but now ask and keep on asking and you will receive, so that your joy (gladness, delight) may be full and complete.

JOHN 16:24

The most effective prayers are bold prayers. They are prayed by believers who are specific and have the boldness to come before God and really ask for the things they need in life, unashamed to make their requests known.

One of the major things that keeps people from praying boldly is they look at what they have done wrong instead of what Jesus has done right. The Bible teaches us plainly that God "...made Christ [virtually] to be sin Who knew no sin, so that in and through Him we might become...

the righteousness of God" (2 Corinthians 5:21). Because we are righteous in Him, we can approach the throne of grace boldly with our needs (Hebrews 4:16).

John 16:23–24 tells us we can come boldly before the throne in Jesus' name. The name of Jesus is powerful. When we use Jesus' name in our prayers, it's not some formula or magic charm that we tack on to the end of everything we pray. When we go in the name of Jesus, we're saying, "Father, I come to You presenting today all that Jesus is—not what I am."

Don't be vague or timid—be bold! You'll be surprised at the answers you'll receive.

God is waiting to surprise you with amazing things—are you ready to receive them?

God Has a Fantastic Plan for Your Life

Surely or only goodness, mercy, and unfailing love shall follow me all the days of my life, and through the length of my days the house of the Lord [and His presence] shall be my dwelling place.

PSALM 23:6

Psalm 23 is a powerful chapter of the Bible that describes the condition God wants us to live in constantly. He wants us to be protected, guided, and comforted. He wants to set a table of blessings before us in the very face of our enemies. He wants to anoint us with the oil of joy instead of mourning. He wants our cup of blessings to overflow continually in thanksgiving and praise to Him for His goodness, mercy, and unfailing love toward us. And He wants us to live every day, every moment, secure in His presence.

All these "wants" are a part of God's good plan for each of us. Regardless of how far we may have fallen, He wants to restore us to a closeness with Him and to that right and perfect plan He has for our lives.

It would benefit every one of us if we would say to ourselves several times a day, "God has a fantastic plan for my life. I want all that He wants for me. I receive His love and His goodness in my life. I will walk and live in the presence of the Lord."

———

Remember that the most important thing in receiving God's blessings is not our great faith but His great faithfulness.

Being Consistently Confident

*For in the Gospel a righteousness which
God ascribes is revealed, both springing
from faith and leading to faith ... The
man who through faith is just and
upright shall live ... by faith.*

ROMANS 1:17

Confidence is rooted in faith in God. This is
why it is important that we choose to be consistently confident, not occasionally confident.

I had to learn to remain confident when
I was told by friends and family that a
woman should not be teaching the Word
of God. I knew God had called me to teach
His Word, but I was still affected by the
rejection of people. I had to grow in confidence to the place where people's opinions
and their acceptance or rejection did not
affect my confidence level. My confidence
had to be in God, not in people.

Romans 1:17 tells us that we can go from faith to faith. I spent many years going from faith to doubt to unbelief and then back to faith. Then I realized that when I lose my confidence, I leave a door open for the devil. If I allow him to steal my confidence, I suddenly have no faith to minister to people.

If you want to succeed, choose to be consistently confident. Be confident about your gifts and calling, your ability in Christ. Believe you hear from God and that you are led by the Holy Spirit. Be bold in the Lord. See yourself as a winner in Him.

Focusing on God's great love for you helps you have great confidence to do great things!

Overcoming

The wicked flee when no man pursues them, but the [uncompromisingly] righteous are bold as a lion.

PROVERBS 28:1

Fear robs many people of their faith. Fear of failure, fear of man, and fear of rejection are some of the strongest fears employed by Satan to hinder us from making progress.

But no matter what kind of fear the enemy sends against us, the important thing is to overcome it. When we are faced with fear, we must not give in to it. It is imperative to our victory that we determine, "With God's help, I will overcome."

The normal reaction to fear is flight. The enemy wants us to run; God wants us to stand still and see His deliverance. Because of fear, many people do not confront issues; they spend their lives running.

We must learn to stand our ground and face fear, secure in the knowledge that we are more than conquerors through Christ (Romans 8:37).

Fear of failure torments multitudes. We fear what people will think of us if we fail. If we step out and fail, some people may hear about it; but they quickly forget it if we forget it and go on. It is better to try something and fail than to try nothing and succeed.

_____

Approach life with boldness. The Spirit of the Lord is in you—so make up your mind not to fear.

The Power of a Renewed Heart

. . . For the Lord sees not as man sees; for man looks on the outward appearance, but the Lord looks on the heart.

1 SAMUEL 16:7

God is the God of hearts. He does not look only at the exterior of a person, or even the things a person does, and judge the individual by that criterion. Man judges the flesh, but God judges the heart.

It is possible to do good works and still have a wrong heart attitude. It is also possible to do some things wrong but still have a right heart on the inside. God is much more inclined to use a person with a good heart and a few problems than He is to use a person who seems to have it all together but who has a wicked heart.

It is very important that we get in touch with our inner life and our heart attitude,

the way we feel and think about things (what the Bible calls the hidden man of the heart), if we want to hear from God and live in close relationship with Him.

When God seeks to promote someone, He chooses a person after His own heart.

Looking Forward

And He Who is seated on the throne said, See! I make all things new. Also He said, Record this, for these sayings are faithful (accurate, incorruptible, and trustworthy) and true (genuine).

REVELATION 21:5

So many people live miserable lives because they are conflicted and feel burdened about the mistakes of their past. If you have been unhappy or discouraged because of the things that have happened in your past, I encourage you to change your thinking and set your focus in a whole new direction. Determine to be what God wants you to be, to have what God wants you to have, and to receive what Jesus died to give you.

Your new life in Christ means that you have been completely forgiven of all your sins. God has wiped your slate clean and

taken up residence in your heart. You can let the past go and begin to get excited about your future.

When you feel discouraged, say, "I am not going to live in bondage anymore. I cannot do anything about what I have done in the past, but I can do something about my future. I am going to enjoy my life and have what Jesus died for me to have. I am going to let go of the past and go on pursuing God from this day forth!"

Yesterday is history. Tomorrow is a mystery. Today is a gift from God.

When We Need Him the Most

Lean on, trust in, and be confident in the Lord with all your heart and mind and do not rely on your own insight or understanding. In all your ways know, recognize, and acknowledge Him, and He will direct and make straight and plain your paths.   PROVERBS 3:5–6

Many times we say that we trust God, but inside we still have deeply embedded fears that He won't really come through for us when we need Him the most. So we falsely assume that if we keep thinking about the problem and worrying about it enough, then somehow we can take care of it on our own—just in case God doesn't show up and do something according to our timetable.

The problem with this attitude is that it brings us closer to our problems, not

closer to God. However, when we choose to believe that God is in control and that He is going to handle whatever situation we are in, we move closer to God and our problems don't seem so worrisome after all.

Trusting God will keep you from reasoning and trying to figure out the things you don't have answers for yet. When you are faced with an overwhelming situation, don't listen to that nagging voice inside, asking, *What are you gonna do? What are you gonna do?* Just remind yourself, *I'm going to trust God, and He will show me what to do . . . if I need to do anything.*

Hold your peace, remain at rest, and God will fight for you.

God's Timing Is the Right Timing

Consider it wholly joyful, my brethren, whenever you are enveloped in or encounter trials of any sort or fall into various temptations. Be assured and understand that the trial and proving of your faith bring out endurance and steadfastness and patience. But let endurance and steadfastness and patience have full play and do a thorough work, so that you may be [people] perfectly and fully developed [with no defects], lacking in nothing.

JAMES 1:2–4

We don't usually see it while it's happening, but God is working out His perfect plan for our lives behind the scenes. Though we want results right now, character development takes time and patience.

The Bible says that patience does a

thorough work in our lives. When we wait on God, He makes us fully developed and complete, lacking nothing. I've discovered that patience is more than the ability to wait; it is the ability to keep a good attitude while waiting. This practical fruit of the Spirit comes from a close relationship with God—it manifests itself in a calm, positive attitude despite the circumstances.

"God's timing is usually not our timing. We are in a hurry, but God isn't. He takes time to do things right—He lays a solid foundation before He attempts to build a building. We are God's building under construction. He is the Master Builder, and He knows what He is doing.

When you are feeling impatient, remember that God's timing is always perfect!

Fullness of Joy

You will show me the path of life;
in Your presence is fullness of joy, at
Your right hand there are pleasures
forevermore.   PSALM 16:11

The presence of the Lord is always with us, but we do not always recognize it or take time to be conscious of it. I think this is why there seems to be a lack of joy in the lives of many believers. There are a lot of unhappy people who are spending their lives chasing things, when nothing can keep us satisfied except God Himself.

When people are not satisfied inwardly, they usually look for some outward object to satisfy their hunger. Often they end up in a fruitless search for that which cannot fill the emptiness within. We've heard it said, many people spend their lives climbing the ladder of success, only to find when

they reach the top that their ladder is leaning against the wrong building.

When we keep our priorities straight, we
discover that everything we really need in
life is found in the Lord. Seek to dwell in
His presence. In Him is the path of life, the
fullness of joy, and pleasures forevermore.

**The reason we can laugh and enjoy
life in spite of our current circumstances is because Jesus is our joy.**

Open-Book Tests

The Lord tests and proves the [unyieldingly] righteous....

PSALM 11:5

Sometimes teachers let students take open-book tests. They are allowed to have their textbook open while answering the questions. We are all going to go through tests. There are no exceptions—everybody is tested at different times in life. But they are all open-book tests; the answers are found in the Book. No matter what we are going through, God has provided the answers in His Word.

Drawing close to God through His Word during difficulty gives us strength and answers that we need. God often allows us to go through a difficult place because He is testing, stretching, and strengthening us. During such times Satan attacks us

in our minds, telling us lies such as, "God doesn't love you, and if He was going to help you, He would have already done it. You might as well give up on trusting God and develop your own plan of escape." This is a time to hold on, not to give up!

Life isn't always easy. There are going to be some days and seasons when we are faced with challenges. But if you choose to lean on the Lord in those times, you'll realize that you can still have joy even on trying days. Godly strength, wisdom and knowledge, spiritual maturity, and character are developed in us as we go through tests.

In order to grow in God and do what He has called you to do, choose to be faithful. His character will be revealed in your life over time.

Kingdom Living

[After all] the kingdom of God is not a matter of [getting the] food and drink [one likes], but instead it is righteousness (that state which makes a person acceptable to God) and [heart] peace and joy in the Holy Spirit.

ROMANS 14:17

God's kingdom is made up of things far greater and more beneficial than worldly possessions. God does bless us with material possessions, but the kingdom is much more than that: It is righteousness, peace, and joy in the Holy Spirit.

Righteousness is not the result of what we do, but rather what Jesus has done for us (1 Corinthians 1:30). He takes our sin and gives us His righteousness (2 Corinthians 5:21). When we accept this truth by faith

and receive it personally, we are free to live and enjoy the life Jesus died to give us.

Peace is so wonderful—it is definitely kingdom living. This is why we pursue peace, crave it, and go after it (Psalm 34:14; 1 Peter 3:11). The closer we get to God, the more we understand that Jesus is our peace (Ephesians 2:14). God's will for you and me is to enjoy His peace that goes beyond understanding (Philippians 4:7).

Joy can be anything from calm delight to extreme hilarity. Joy improves our countenance, our health, and the quality of our lives. It strengthens our witness to others and gives us a godly perspective on life (Nehemiah 8:10).

It is clear in the Word of God: Seek God and His kingdom, and He will take care of everything else (Matthew 6:33).

There is no better life than life in the kingdom of God.

When You Feel Insecure

May Christ through your faith [actually] dwell (settle down, abide, make His permanent home) in your hearts! May you be rooted deep in love and founded securely on love.

EPHESIANS 3:17

Many people have feelings of insecurity about themselves because they can't accept themselves for who they are. Are you tired of being under pressure, wearing masks, trying to be someone you aren't? Wouldn't you like the freedom just to be accepted as you are, without pressure to be someone you really don't know how to be?

With God's help, we can learn our value is not in what we do but in who we are in Him. He wants us to come to Him as we are and trust Him to help us be all that He wants us to be.

The devil's plan is to deceive us into basing our worth on our performance, and then keep us focused on all our faults and shortcomings. Satan wants us to have a low opinion of ourselves so we'll pull away from God, and be miserable and unreceptive to His blessings, because we don't think we deserve them.

It is so important to develop a positive sense of being valuable, and being secure in Christ. Make a decision to accept yourself because that is what Jesus has already done. He will never reject anyone who comes to Him. You are greatly loved and highly valued!

———

God knows your faults and He loves you anyway. Nothing will ever change His love for you.

A Tender Conscience

Therefore I always exercise and discipline myself [mortifying my body, deadening my carnal affections, bodily appetites, and worldly desires, endeavoring in all respects] to have a clear (unshaken, blameless) conscience, void of offense toward God and toward men.   ACTS 24:16

One way to live closer to God is to keep your heart tender. Having a tender conscience enables us to live closer to God. We become sensitive to His touch and we can easily discern when our behavior is right and wrong. Then we can promptly repent and be completely restored to wonderful, refreshing fellowship with God.

Don't waste your time making excuses for disobedience. When God shows you that you have done something wrong, just

say, "You're right, Lord, I'm wrong. I have no excuse, so please forgive me and help me not to do it again."

It is amazing how much that will help you maintain a tender conscience toward God. When we are tender toward God, it enables us to be tender in our dealings with people. The world is filled with bruised, wounded, and brokenhearted people who need kindness and a loving touch from God. Let God touch them through you.

When you have a tender heart toward God, you will hear His voice more clearly and obey His Word more readily.

His Grace Will Carry You Through

If you are censured and suffer abuse
[because you bear] the name of Christ,
blessed [are you—happy, fortunate, to
be envied, with life-joy, and satisfaction
in God's favor and salvation, regardless
of your outward condition], because
the Spirit of glory, the Spirit of God, is
resting upon you . . .   1 PETER 4:14

Have you ever suffered for being a Christian—been made fun of, left out, misunderstood, passed over for promotion or worse?

Some think it is awful when they are mistreated because they are Christians, but God sees it in an entirely different light. God never expects us to suffer for Him without His help. We can firmly believe that any time we are reproached or mistreated in any way because of our faith in Christ, God gives us an extra measure of

grace to counterbalance the attack. There is power to overcome!

When we recognize and depend on the presence of God in our lives, we can go through difficult circumstances and keep our peace and joy. Like Shadrach, Meshach, and Abednego in Daniel 3:21–27, we can go into the fiery furnace, or into problems and struggles, and come out without even the smell of smoke upon us.

If we remain stable, confidently trusting God in difficult times, we can be assured that God's glory will be our reward.

———

Welcome the presence of God in your life and get excited about seeing His grace empower you for whatever you may face.

A Bigger Plan

But Jesus looked at them and said, With men this is impossible, but all things are possible with God.   MATTHEW 19:26

It is important to ask God to give you dreams and visions for your life. We atrophy without something to reach for. God has created us to have goals. Ephesians 3:20 (KJV) tells us that God is "able to do exceeding abundantly above all that we ask or think." This is why, as Christians, we can think big thoughts, have big goals, and hope for big things.

Many times we look at a task and think there is no way we can do what needs to be done. This happens when we are looking at ourselves instead of looking at God, Who can do all things.

When the Lord called Joshua to take the place of Moses and lead the Israelites into

the Promised Land, He said to him, "As I was with Moses, so I will be with you; I will not fail you or forsake you" (Joshua 1:5).

If God promises to be with us—and He does—that is really all we need. His strength is made perfect in our weakness (2 Corinthians 12:9). Whatever weaknesses you have, God's strength is available to do things in your life bigger than you ever thought possible.

God is honored when you trust Him to do the big things that seem truly impossible.

No More Self-Doubt

David was greatly distressed, for the
men spoke of stoning him because the
souls of them all were bitterly grieved,
each man for his sons and daughters.
But David encouraged and strengthened
himself in the Lord his God.

1 SAMUEL 30:6

If we don't believe in ourselves—in the talents and abilities God has given us—who is going to? God believes in us, and it's a good thing too; otherwise, we might never make any progress. We cannot always wait for someone else to come along and encourage us to be all we can be.

When David and his men found themselves in a seemingly hopeless situation, which the men blamed on him, David encouraged and strengthened himself in the Lord. Later

on, that situation was totally turned around (1 Samuel 30:1–20).

When David was just a boy, everyone around him discouraged him concerning his ability to fight Goliath. They told him he was too young and too inexperienced, and he didn't have the right armor or the right weapons. But David was close to God and had confidence in Him. David believed that God would be strong on his behalf and give him the victory.

Self-doubt is absolutely tormenting, but we can rid ourselves of it. Like David, we can learn to know our God—about His love, His ways, and His Word—then ultimately we can trust that He will provide us with the strength we need.

The way to end the torment of self-doubt is to look to God and have faith in His mighty power.

The Power of Declaration

Death and life are in the power of the tongue, and they who indulge in it shall eat the fruit of it [for death or life].

PROVERBS 18:21

If we want to see our prayers answered, it is essential we learn to pray and then make positive, faith-filled declarations about our circumstances. Negative confessions and faith just don't mix.

Let's say a mother is praying for her son who's having trouble in school. So she prays the prayer of faith and believes God for a breakthrough. Then she goes to lunch with two neighbors and spends the next hour saying, "I'm tired of all these problems I'm having with my child. Things aren't ever going to get better. Why me?" This kind of negative confession works against your faith.

After you have prayed, make the decision to keep your conversation in agreement with your prayers. Declare the Word of God! Declare your faith! When the neighbors ask how your son is doing, say, "You know what? In the natural, things have not changed a whole lot, but I'm praying for him, and I have assurance in my heart that God is with him, doing a mighty work in his life."

When your faith, your thoughts, and your words all agree with God's promises, it's just a matter of time until you see positive change.

———

Pray and then let what you say be in agreement with what you have prayed and you will surely see amazing results.

An Atmosphere of Worship

Give to the Lord the glory due to His name; worship the Lord in the beauty of holiness or in holy array.

PSALM 29:2

When we worship God, we are recognizing Him for Who He is, all that He has done in our lives, and all that He has yet to do.

Worship is not about us—it is all about God. But even though worship is not about you, worship transforms you. By starting to worship God for the changes that He is already working in you, you find that those changes start manifesting more and more, and you experience new levels of God's glory. In other words, God is close to the worshipper, and He will pour out His goodness on those who choose to magnify Him.

There is a release that comes through

worship. Sometimes we need a mental or emotional release. As we worship the Lord, we release our emotional or mental burden that is weighing us down. It is swallowed up in the awesomeness and majesty of God.

I encourage you to begin to worship early in the morning. Worship while you are getting ready for your day, and when you are at work or out running errands. And worship God at the end of the day for all He has brought you through. You will be amazed to see how things begin to change at home and on the job when you keep God at the highest place in your life.

Worship creates an atmosphere where God can work.

You Are Never Alone

. . . And behold, I am with you all the days (perpetually, uniformly, and on every occasion), to the [very] close and consummation of the age. Amen (so let it be).   MATTHEW 28:20

God wants you to know that you are never alone. Satan will try to make you believe you are all alone, but that is a lie. He will try to deceive you by telling you that no one understands how you feel, but that is not true. In addition to God being with you, many believers know how you feel, what you are going through, and they understand what you may be experiencing.

When you are following God and making spiritual progress, Satan often brings affliction to discourage you and make you feel alone. I remember a time many years ago when God called me to do a new thing

and it required me to separate myself from many of the people and things that were dear to me. Very often we have to let go of old things and ways in order to take hold of the new that God has for us. I was often lonely while establishing my new life, but God was with me each step of the way.

If you are battling loneliness and pain, draw strength from God. Know that He is with you, and He will move you forward. He has the power to turn your mourning into joy and to comfort you in your sorrow. Trust God with all of your heart, and don't let Satan steal your destiny.

———

Hope in God's love and know that He is always with you.

Greatly Loved

This is love: not that we loved God, but that he loved us and sent his Son as an atoning sacrifice for our sins.

1 JOHN 4:10 NIV

Many of us believe that God loves the world, but we're not as certain about His love for us individually, or we may feel that God loves us when we are good, but not when we make mistakes and sin. God's love is based on Who He is, not on what we do. He never stops loving us, not even for one second of our lives!

God loves *you*! You are special to Him. He doesn't love you because you are a good person or do everything right. He loves you because He is love. Love is not something God does; it is Who He is.

God's love cannot be earned or deserved. It must be received by faith. He is the

everlasting God, and He does not get weary. Many of us think we have worn God out with our failures and mistakes, but you cannot do that. He may not always love everything you do, but He does love you. Love is His unfailing nature.

No matter how hard you seek the things of God, if you have not received the fact that God loves you, you are not going to get far.

Let God love you. Receive His love for you. Meditate on it. Let it strengthen you and draw you into close relationship with Him. Then look for opportunities to share that love with others.

———————

If you had been the only person on the earth, Jesus would have gone through all His suffering just for you.

Free from Anxiety

Therefore do not worry and be anxious, saying, What are we going to have to eat? or, What are we going to have to drink? or, What are we going to have to wear?... your heavenly Father knows well that you need them all.

MATTHEW 6:31–32

Worry fills us with fear and anxiety, causing us to think: "What if we don't have enough? How will I find another job? What if things don't work out?" In other words, "What are we going to do if God doesn't come through for us?"

Instead of proclaiming the promises of God when we feel unsure about something, we often speak about our worries and frustrations, which only amplifies them and makes our problems seem worse than what they are.

Worry and anxiety are what people experience when they don't know that they have a heavenly Father Who loves them unconditionally. But you and I do know we have a heavenly Father Who is close to us and has promised to provide everything we need. It is important for us to remember this and to act in faith, trusting God every day. Just because we are tempted to worry doesn't mean we have to do it!

Jesus assures you that your heavenly Father knows all your needs before you even ask Him. So why should you worry? Instead, thank God in advance for His provision in your life.

Seek first the kingdom of God and His righteousness; then all these other things we need will be added to us (Matthew 6:33).

A Steadfast Heart

My heart is fixed, O God, my heart is steadfast and confident! I will sing and make melody.   PSALM 57:7

In order to experience victory in our lives and achieve great things for God, it is crucial that we choose to be determined. The Bible says that Jesus "steadfastly and determinedly set His face to go to Jerusalem" (Luke 9:51), and we can do the same thing as we live for God. If we are going to accomplish anything worthwhile, it is important we "steadfastly and determinedly" set our face in that direction and not give up.

When you receive Christ as your Savior and Lord, Satan will oppose you at every turn. He wants you to give up! The devil is not going to roll out a red carpet for us just because we decide to receive Christ. But Jesus has already overcome the devil.

Satan is a defeated foe. His opposition is not strong enough to stop you if you are close to God, walking in His strength and will for your life.

Don't fall into the trap of thinking that everything in life should be easy for us. Ask for God's help, receive His grace, and be determined to do the will of God, to stay positive and happy, and to walk in the peace of God no matter what.

———

Press on with holy determination, and God's plan will be fulfilled in your life.

Keep Moving Forward

That is why I would remind you to stir up (rekindle the embers of, fan the flame of, and keep burning) the [gracious] gift of God, [the inner fire] that is in you by means of the laying on of my hands [with those of the elders at your ordination].   2 TIMOTHY 1:6

In our spiritual lives we are either aggressively going forward on purpose, or we are slipping backward. There is no such thing as stagnant Christianity. It is vital to keep pressing on. That is why Timothy was instructed to fan the flame and rekindle the zeal that once filled his heart. He had gotten weary, and the fire that once burned in him had become a dim flicker.

Evidently Timothy had taken a step backward, perhaps because of fear. It is certainly easy to understand why Timothy may have

lost his courage and confidence. It was a time of extreme persecution, and his mentor Paul was in jail. Yet Paul strongly encouraged Timothy to stir himself up, get back on track, remember the call on his life, resist fear, and remember that God had given him a spirit of power and love and of a sound mind.

Any time we let fear dominate us, we begin to slip backward. Fear prevents our progress and causes us to want to turn and run instead of aggressively moving forward. If you are unsure, uncertain, or even feeling afraid today, receive Paul's encouragement to Timothy. Stir up your faith, be on fire for God, and never forget that He is with you. With Him at your side, no matter how difficult things may look, you can do whatever you need to do through Him.

Never, Never, Never . . . Give Up!

What Is Holding You Back?

Therefore then, since we are surrounded by so great a cloud of witnesses [who have borne testimony to the Truth], let us strip off and throw aside every encumbrance... and let us run with patient endurance...

HEBREWS 12:1

When the writer of the book of Hebrews wrote that we can *strip off and throw aside every encumbrance*, he was thinking of the runners in his day who would literally strip off their clothes, down to a simple loincloth. They made sure nothing could entangle them and prevent them from running as fast as they possibly could. They were running to win!

An important part of drawing closer to God is taking an inventory of our life and casting aside anything that entangles us

or pulls us away from Him. Being in close relationship with Him requires us to get rid of the things that grieve Him and distract us, things keeping us from living out God's plan for our life.

We often need to take a look at our lives and cast aside things that are entangling us or pulling us away from God. It is impossible to grow spiritually without doing so. When God shows you something to cast aside, I encourage you to do it without hesitation. Don't argue with God or feel sorry for yourself. What He is asking you to do will benefit you in the end. Whether it's a destructive friendship, a harmful habit, being offended, or any other sin in your life, be bold enough to deal with it. Ask God to help you and then draw strength from Him and His Word.

Lay aside everything that hinders and run the race of holiness. The reward is God himself.

You Have Spiritual "Power of Attorney"

Nevertheless I tell you the truth. It is to your advantage that I go away; for if I do not go away, the Helper will not come to you; but if I depart, I will send Him to you.   JOHN 16:7 NKJV

Oh, how wonderful it would have been to have physically walked with Jesus. But He told His followers they would be better off when He went away, because then He would send His Spirit to dwell in every believer. He told them that even though they were sorrowful at the news of His departure, they would rejoice again just as a woman has sorrow during her labor but rejoices when the child is born.

Jesus knew they would change their minds when they saw the glory of His Spirit in them and the power available to

each of them through the privilege of using His name in prayer. He was literally giving to them—and has given to all those who believe in Him—His "power of attorney," the legal right to use His name. His name takes His place; His name represents Him.

Jesus has already been perfect for us. He has already pleased the Father for us; therefore, there is no pressure on us to feel that we must have a perfect record of right behavior before we can pray. When we come before the Father in Jesus' name, we can confess our sin, receive His forgiveness, and boldly make our requests known to Him.

When the name of Jesus is spoken by a believer in faith, all of heaven comes to attention.

Entering the Rest of God

Blessed (happy, fortunate, to be envied) are the undefiled (the upright, truly sincere, and blameless) in the way [of the revealed will of God], who walk (order their conduct and conversation) in the law of the Lord (the whole of God's revealed will).   PSALM 119:1

There is a divine freedom and ease that comes when you truly love the Word of God—when you hear it, receive it and *obey* it. Even in tough circumstances, your life will be free from misery and frustration. Your joy is full when you draw close to God through His Word, believing His promises for your life and obeying His commands.

The key to overcoming the difficulties you face in life is to believe the Word and obey whatever God puts in your heart to do. Standing on His Word delivers you

from struggling so that you rest in the promises of God. Hebrews 4:3 says: "For we who have believed (adhered to and trusted in and relied on God) do enter that rest."

If you feel defeated today—if you're overwhelmed by a problem—the best thing you can do is dedicate yourself to hearing, receiving, and obeying God's Word. That is where you will find words of life. As soon as you start believing the Word of God, your joy will return and you will be at ease again.

———

A life of rest in Him is where God wants you to be every day of your life.

Come as a Little Child

*And He called a little child to Himself
and put him in the midst of them,
And said, Truly I say to you, unless you
repent (change, turn about) and become
like little children [trusting, lowly,
loving, forgiving], you can never enter
the kingdom of heaven [at all].*

MATTHEW 18:2–3

One of the beautiful things about children
is that they are not complicated. They will
always let you know what they need, they'll
run into your arms when they are frightened, and they'll give you a big kiss, sometimes for no apparent reason. It is refreshing
to communicate with children, because they
don't try to hide their fears or their feelings.

I believe that's how God wants us to
be when we talk with Him. He is pleased
when we approach Him with childlike

simplicity and faith. Just as children are naturally inclined to trust their parents completely, we can also be pure and full of enthusiasm as we trust God. Share your whole heart with God, and remember: You can entrust everything in your life to Him and know that He cares.

The Lord is not looking for complicated relationships. He is looking for sincere hearts and childlike faith. You can let God know what you want (Philippians 4:6), and you can run to Him when you feel afraid (Psalm 91:1–7). God wants you to feel free to show your affection for Him and to share your heart openly with Him. The more you learn to come to God with a childlike faith, the closer you'll grow in your relationship with Him.

We do not want to be childish in our relationships with God; we want to be childlike.

Faithful in the Wilderness

*O God, You are my God, earnestly will
I seek You; my inner self thirsts for You,
my flesh longs and is faint for You, in a
dry and weary land where no water is.*

PSALM 63:1

Eventually, no matter how much we love
the Lord and no matter how close we get
to Him, all of us go through dry times...
times when few things minister to us or
water our soul. We go to church, but we
feel no different when we leave than we
did when we arrived. We experience times
when our prayers seem dry, and times when
we can't hear or feel anything from God.

I have gone through mountaintop times,
and I have gone through valley times. I have
had dry times in my prayer life and in my
praise and worship. There have been times
when I could hear from God so clearly, but

there have been other times when I have not heard anything at all.

When you go through a season like this, don't let it get you down. God is with you, whether you *feel* His presence or not. The mature believer doesn't let how he feels determine his relationship with God. You can simply choose to believe God is with you today. You can make the choice to love and worship God in faith. You can pray, believe He hears you, and trust that He is going to provide everything you need. When you make these choices, you will find a new peace in your walk with the Lord, and you will be stable in every season of life.

God loves you and He is right here with you—whether you feel it or not. Be faithful in the wilderness as well as on the mountaintop.

Love Is Patient

Love endures long and is patient...
1 CORINTHIANS 13:4

The world today is filled with impatient people. It seems that everyone is in a hurry. Stress levels are very high, and the pressure we live under often provokes impatience. Christians deal with the same pressures as everyone else, and we are often just as impatient as the world, but we shouldn't be.

The Bible teaches us that love is patient. The more we learn to receive God's love, love Him in return, and love those around us, the more patient we become. This patience helps us live in peace. We are not always in a hurry. We take the time to wait on God and to fellowship with Him. Out of His love, God is patient with us and we can be the same way with other people.

When your life is marked by love, not

only will you be patient with other people, you will be patient with yourself. When you make mistakes, instead of being angry with yourself over them, you'll repent and stay in peace. You'll understand that God is working to correct those things in your life, and you'll patiently trust Him to do His work.

Patience is a wonderful virtue that can be developed in your life, but the key is to draw closer to God through trusting Him each and every day. The closer you get to the Lord, the easier it will be to let go of the frustrations of the world. You'll find a new sense of calm and peaceful assurance because God is the center of your life.

When you learn to respond patiently in all kinds of trials, you will find yourself living a quality of life that is not just endured but enjoyed to the full.

Prime the Pump

. . . For the joy of the Lord is your strength and stronghold.

NEHEMIAH 8:10

When we are going through difficult times, we can take some action to release joy before we start slipping into despair. We can start to rejoice whether we feel like it or not. It is like priming a pump by repeatedly moving the handle up and down until the pump kicks in and the water begins to flow.

I remember my grandparents had an old-time pump. I can recall standing at the sink as a small child, moving the pump handle up and down and sometimes feeling as though it would never take hold and start to supply water. It actually felt as if it was connected to nothing, and I was just pumping air.

But if I didn't give up, moving the

handle up and down would soon become more difficult. That was the sign that water would start flowing shortly.

This is the way it is with joy. We have a well of water on the inside of our spirit. The pump handle to bring it up is the choices we make—smiling, singing, laughing, and so forth. At first the physical expressions may not seem to be doing any good. And after a while it even gets harder, but if we keep it up, soon we will get a "gusher" of joy.

———————

The joy of the Lord is your strength. You can choose to be strong by choosing to live in joy.

The Truth of God's Word

Though a host encamp against me, my heart shall not fear; though war arise against me, [even then] in this will I be confident.   PSALM 27:3

I have discovered that being confident in who God created us to be is a key to living the joy-filled, overcoming life Jesus died to give us.

The devil is constantly trying to introduce thoughts into our heads to make us lose our confidence. The mind is the battlefield, and the devil lies to us through wrong thinking. He tries to tell us we aren't good enough, we've made too many mistakes, God is angry with us—any thought that would make us doubt the love God has for us. If we meditate on those wrong thoughts, our confidence begins to fade.

The key to winning the battle of the

mind is to fight against the lies of the enemy with the truth of God's Word. You don't have to dwell on wrong thoughts; instead you can believe the promises of God and boldly declare those promises over your life.

I encourage you to confidently declare what the Word of God says about you, such as: "I am more than a conqueror through Jesus (Romans 8:37). I can do all things through Christ Who strengthens me (Philippians 4:13). I am triumphant in every situation because God always causes me to triumph (2 Corinthians 2:14)."

When the devil tries to lie to you, boldly declare the truth of God's Word over your life.

Staying Positive

[For being as he is] a man of two minds (hesitating, dubious, irresolute), [he is] unstable and unreliable and uncertain about everything [he thinks, feels, decides].
                                    JAMES 1:8

If we take our concerns to the Lord in prayer and then continue to worry about them, we are actually contradicting our faith. Prayer is a positive force, and worry is a negative force. If we add them together, we come up with zero. I don't know about you, but I don't want to have zero power, so with God's help, I choose not to mix prayer and worry.

Even though we want to live an effective, powerful life, many people operate with zero power because they are always mixing the positives and the negatives. They have a positive confession for a little

while, then a negative confession for a little while. They pray for a little while, then they worry for a little while. They trust for a little while, then they doubt for a little while. As a result, they just go back and forth, never really making any progress.

Let's not magnify the bad—let's magnify the good! Let's elevate the good things God is doing by talking about them, by being positive in our thoughts, in our attitudes, in our outlook, in our words, and in our actions.

Why not make a decision to stay positive by trusting God and refusing to worry?

Practice being positive in each situation that arises. Even if whatever is taking place at the moment is not so good, expect God to bring good out of it.

Molded into His Image

And I am convinced and sure of this very thing, that He Who began a good work in you will continue until the day of Jesus Christ [right up to the time of His return], developing [that good work] and perfecting and bringing it to full completion in you.

PHILIPPIANS 1:6

According to the Bible, God is the Potter, and we are the clay (Romans 9:20–21). When we first come to the Lord, we are like a hard lump of clay that is not very pliable or easy to work with. But God puts us on His potter's wheel and begins to refashion and remake us so that we can discover the wonderful plan He has for our lives.

Sometimes that process of molding is uncomfortable at first. The reason it hurts is because God has to peel away the things

in our lives that would keep us distant from Him. So out of His love for us, He keeps working and working on us, trimming away this bad attitude and that wrong mind-set, carefully reshaping us until gradually we are changed into the likeness of His Son Jesus.

Don't be discouraged with yourself because you have not yet arrived. The more God works in your life, the closer you are growing in relationship to Him. Enjoy your life each day, even as God is shaping you. Let the Potter do His work, and trust that He has your best interest at heart.

———————

You can always trust God that He has your best interest at heart, and all that He does in your life is for your benefit.

Drawing upon God's Strength

. . . Be strong in the Lord [be empowered through your union with Him]; draw your strength from Him [that strength which His boundless might provides].

EPHESIANS 6:10

An important secret to being successful in any task that is set before you is to draw on God's strength. Your strength will run out eventually, but God's strength never will.

Many times in my life I have been in situations not knowing what to do, but God always helped me and brought me through to a place of victory. Each time He met me with His strength that I desperately needed in order to be successful. You can expect God to do the same thing for you no matter what challenges you are facing right now. God is your strength!

In Ephesians 6:10, Paul assures us that

God will pour strength into our lives as we live in close relationship with Him. And the prophet Isaiah says that those who have learned the secret of waiting on the Lord "shall mount up with wings as eagles" (Isaiah 40:31 KJV). These scriptures, and others like them, show us that we are strengthened as we go to God for what we are lacking.

God has promised to never leave us or forsake us. He is with us each step of our journey and He gives us the strength we need when we need it.

God wants to do more than just give you strength—He wants to be your strength.

In Times of Crisis

And it shall be that whoever shall call upon the name of the Lord [invoking, adoring, and worshiping the Lord—Christ] shall be saved.   ACTS 2:21

Years ago, before seat belt laws, a friend of mine was driving with his young son through a busy intersection one day. The car door on the passenger side was not secured tightly, and he made a sharp turn. The car door flew open, and the little boy rolled out right into traffic! The last thing my friend saw was a set of car wheels just about on top of his son. All he knew to do was cry out, "Jesus!"

He stopped his car and ran to his son. To his amazement, his son was perfectly safe. But the man driving the car that had almost hit the child was hysterical.

"Don't be upset!" my friend said. "My

son is okay. Just thank God you were able to stop!"

"You don't understand!" the man responded. "I never touched my brakes!"

Although there was nothing the man could do, the name of Jesus prevailed and the boy's life was spared.

In times of crisis, call upon the name of Jesus. The more you and I see how faithful He is in times of need and crises—the more we witness the power of His name over situations and circumstances—the more our faith is developed, our trust grows, and the closer we will be to Him.

———

There is power in the name of Jesus for every crisis you will ever face.

Accepting Who You Are on the Way to Where You're Going

Fear not, for you shall not be ashamed; neither be confounded and depressed, for you shall not be put to shame. For you shall forget the shame of your youth, and you shall not [seriously] remember the reproach of your widowhood any more.

ISAIAH 54:4

It's important that we embrace and accept ourselves. Ask yourself if you like yourself. If you don't like yourself, you are going to have a hard time liking anyone else. If you're unhappy with yourself, you'll have trouble with others.

When we are in close relationship with the Lord, we can be relaxed and at ease, knowing that our acceptance is not based on our performance or perfect behavior, but on the work Christ has done for and in

us. It is based on our personal relationship with Jesus.

To like ourselves simply means we accept ourselves as God's creation. We don't need to like everything we do in order to like and accept ourselves. God loves us unconditionally, and even when we make mistakes we are no less His child.

I encourage you to look at yourself in the mirror every morning and say, "I like myself. I am a child of God and He loves me. I have gifts and talents. I am a special person—and I like and accept myself." If you do that and really believe it, it will work wonders in helping you accept the person God created you to be.

———

You can be at peace with your past, content with your present, and sure about your future, knowing they are in God's loving hands.

Father Knows Best

. . . Be transformed (changed) by the [entire] renewal of your mind [by its new ideals and its new attitude], so that you may prove [for yourselves] what is the good and acceptable and perfect will of God, even the thing which is good and acceptable and perfect [in His sight for you].   ROMANS 12:2

There will be times in our lives when God asks us to do something we don't understand or particularly agree with. When He does this, it is because He has something good in mind for us. His ways are higher than our ways, and His will is always best.

When God asks us to do something contrary to our will, we can remember the words of Jesus: ". . . Not My will, but [always] Yours be done" (Luke 22:42). These words aren't easy to pray, but they always pay huge

dividends in our lives. When we want something, we don't usually give it up easily. It takes a lot of trust and brokenness to bring us to the place where we are willing to say, like Jesus, *not my will, but always Yours be done.*

The bottom line is that God has a great plan for our life, but that plan requires that we follow Him unconditionally. He may ask you to give away things you don't want to part with. He may ask you to go places, do things, or deal with people that are difficult for you. He may ask you to be quiet in some situations and speak up in others. But whatever God asks of you, do it and take comfort in the knowledge that your obedience is bringing you closer to Him.

Make the choice to always put God's will ahead of your own.

Drop it, Leave It, and Let It Go

And whenever you stand praying, if you have anything against anyone, forgive him and let it drop (leave it, let it go), in order that your Father Who is in heaven may also forgive you your [own] failings and shortcomings and let them drop.

MARK 11:25

"Drop it, leave it, and let it go," is what the Bible says we are to do with offenses (Mark 11:25). It is important to forgive quickly. The quicker we do it, the easier it becomes. A weed that has deep roots is harder to pull out than one that has just sprung up.

Love forgives; it does not hold a grudge. It is not touchy, easily offended, nor is it fretful or resentful (1 Corinthians 13:5). Knowing this, we can look at our own lives and easily understand if we are walking in love. If you have anything against anyone,

make the choice right now to "drop it, leave it, and let it go."

We have many opportunities every day to get offended, and each time we have a choice to make. If we choose to live by our feelings, we will constantly be offended and upset. But if we choose to live in love, we will forgive people when they offend us and trust God to defend us, rather than feeling like we always have to defend ourselves.

God is love, and He forgives and forgets: "For I will forgive their iniquity, and their sin I will remember no more" (Jeremiah 31:34 NASB). And He is glad to do so. The closer we get to Him, the more we become like Him. With God's help, we can learn to live a life of love and forgiveness.

———————

When you decide to "drop it, leave it, and let it go," joy and contentment are the natural results.

A Merry Heart

A merry heart does good, like medicine,
But a broken spirit dries the bones.

PROVERBS 17:22 NKJV

God is life, and every good thing He created is part of that life. We can get so caught up in doing and accomplishing, in working and earning, that if we are not careful, we will come to the end of our life and suddenly wake up and realize that we never really lived. God desires for us to enjoy life and live it to the full, till it overflows.

We have a choice in life. We can grumble our way through our troubles, or we can draw closer to God in difficult times, going through any trouble we face with a merry heart. Either way, we will all deal with troubles from time to time, so why not take the joy of the Lord as our strength and be filled with energy and vitality?

In John 15, Jesus talks about abiding in Him. In verse 11, He says, "I have told you these things, that My joy and delight may be in you, and that your joy and gladness may be of full measure and complete and overflowing." Jesus made it possible for us to have merry hearts. With His help, no matter what you go through, you can put a smile on your face and enjoy every day of your life in Him.

———————

Don't spend your life waiting for things to change before you can become happy. Make the decision to be happy now.

Waiting Expectantly for God

Why are you cast down, O my inner self? And why should you moan over me and be disquieted within me? Hope in God and wait expectantly for Him, for I shall yet praise Him, my Help and my God.

PSALM 42:5

If you've ever felt discouraged, you're not alone. David did too. But David didn't allow discouragement to keep him down. When he felt that way, David put his hope in God and waited for Him, praising Him as his Help and his God. We can do the same thing if we choose to.

To overcome his downcast feelings and emotions, David put his focus on God, praising Him for His wonderful acts and great exploits. David chose to focus on God, not on his problems.

David knew that if he focused on the

negative, it would be easy to get depressed and lose hope. That is why he chose to regularly encourage and strengthen himself in the Lord (1 Samuel 30:6).

When we find ourselves in a discouraging situation, we can follow David's example and wait expectantly for the Lord, praising Him no matter what the circumstances look like around us. The closer we are to God, the easier it is to take refuge in Him. Instead of giving in to frustration and discouragement, we can put our trust in the Lord, and trust Him to deliver us.

The Lord makes a covering over us and defends us. He fights our battles for us when we praise Him (2 Chronicles 20:17, 20–21).

The Truest Tests of Character

*And endurance (fortitude) develops
maturity of character (approved faith
and tried integrity). And character [of
this sort] produces [the habit of] joyful
and confident hope of eternal salvation.*

ROMANS 5:4

Our character is most accurately revealed
by what we do when nobody is watching.
An important key to living in close, intimate relationship with God is being a person of strong character, because when you
realize that God is with you every minute of every day—you live to please Him
regardless of whether others are watching
or not.

Many people will do the right thing
when somebody—a leader, an employer, a
person with influence—is watching them,
but they take the easy way out when nobody

sees but God. As Christians, our thought process should be, "I am going to do the right thing simply because I want to please the Lord."

Character is also seen when we do the right thing to others even though the right thing is not yet happening to us. Jesus demonstrated this for us—when He was "reviled and insulted, He did not revile or offer insult in return" (1 Peter 2:23). We can follow the example of Jesus by treating somebody right who is not treating us right, by blessing someone who is not blessing us, by loving people who don't necessarily love us. These are the things that Jesus did, and if we want to be like Him, we will need to choose to do them.

———

Our character is seen in how much we choose to do the right thing even when we don't want to do it.

Everyday Gratitude

Enter into His gates with thanksgiving and a thank offering and into His courts with praise! Be thankful and say so to Him, bless and affectionately praise His name!   PSALM 100:4

Grateful people are a joy to be around. There are people who go through life grumbling, complaining, and ungrateful, but there are also those who go through life joyful, optimistic, and full of gratitude. I sure prefer to be around joyful, optimistic, and grateful people—don't you?

Not only does our grateful attitude make us more enjoyable to be around, but it shows new levels of spiritual maturity as we go deeper with God. The closer we get to God, the more aware we become of all He has done for us, and the more thankful we naturally become.

If someone is not grateful for the things God has already given them, why would they think that God is going to give them more? A thankful heart shows God that we are good stewards of what He has given us and that we can handle even more blessings with the right heart and attitude.

The next time you feel a sense of ingratitude, just stop and praise God for what He has already done in your life. Even if you feel you only have a little, praise God for the little you have. When you do, you may be surprised how He'll reward your thankful heart.

Look around you and find something to be thankful for—a relationship, a provision, a past victory, an answer to prayer. Nothing is too small to praise God for today!

Doers of the Word

But be doers of the Word [obey the message], and not merely listeners to it, betraying yourselves [into deception by reasoning contrary to the Truth].

JAMES 1:22

An important part of living in close relationship with God is learning to become *doers* of the Word and not hearers only. If we read and hear the Word, but neglect to follow the instructions it gives us, we are going to live far short of God's best for our lives.

It is the truth of God's Word—and that truth alone—that will set us free. In order for that truth to work in our lives, it is essential that we put it into practice. Obedience to His Word is what brings peace, joy, and a life that is blessed in many ways.

The bottom line is this: God is your

Helper. He is your Healer. He has a personalized plan for your life in His Word. The more you read, study, and obey His Word, the more you can learn what that plan is and then begin to walk it out one step at a time. Obeying the Word requires decisive consistency and determination—it is a daily process. The more you study God's Word, the more you learn to love it. Something wonderful happens when you discover the instructions and promises of God found in His Word. You'll always want to go back for more!

———

You will walk in victory if you make the decision to do what the Lord says.

No More Insecurity

*And they who know Your name [who
have experience and acquaintance
with Your mercy] will lean on and
confidently put their trust in You, for
You, Lord, have not forsaken those who
seek (inquire of and for) You [on the
authority of God's Word and the right of
their necessity].*   PSALM 9:10

Every one of us has experienced a measure of insecurity. At one time or another,
we all want to step out and do something,
but at the thought of it, insecurity freezes
us in our tracks. But this is not the plan of
God for our lives. He wants us to step out
in faith and confidence.

Insecurity tries to torment us into being
so doubtful and miserable we will be prevented from doing what God wants us to
do and receiving all God has for us.

We can live without insecurity by building our faith on what God has said in His Word. When we open our mouth and confess what the Lord says to us and about us, God's Word will give us the power to overcome fear, insecurity, and uncertainty.

If you find yourself trying to avoid confronting some issue in your life because of dread or insecurity, I encourage you to pray and ask God to do for you what He has promised in His Word—to go before you and pave the way.

———

Ask God to strengthen you in the inner man, that His might and power may fill you, and that you may not be overcome with the temptation to give in to fear.

The Key to Conquering Frustration

[Therefore, I do not treat God's gracious gift as something of minor importance and defeat its very purpose]; I do not set aside and invalidate and frustrate and nullify the grace (unmerited favor) of God...   GALATIANS 2:21

I know what frustration is like because I spent many years living a frustrated life. I knew who God was, but I knew very little of His grace and how to live in close relationship to Him. I have since learned that when I get frustrated, it's almost always because I am trying to make something happen in my own strength instead of waiting on the Lord to make it happen. If I am frustrated, it is a sign that I am acting independently instead of relying on Him and receiving His grace.

Are you frustrated? In your relationships? In your career? In your walk with

the Lord? Are you wrestling with an area of your personality that is causing you problems, or is there a specific habit in your life that you can't break?

Frustration comes from trying to do something you cannot do on your own. God is the only One Who can make things happen for you in your life. You will be frustrated if you try to do things without Him. But the minute you say, "Lord, I can't do this on my own, so I turn it over to You. I am willing to do anything You ask me to do, but I will need Your grace (power) in order to do it"—when you sincerely pray that prayer, you will begin to enjoy the rest of God.

———

Let go and trust God to do what only He can do. Let God be God in your life.

Peace in Any Circumstance

Casting the whole of your care [all your anxieties, all your worries, all your concerns, once and for all] on Him, for He cares for you affectionately and cares about you watchfully.   1 PETER 5:7

The peace that passes all understanding is a great thing to experience (Philippians 4:7). When, according to all the circumstances, you should be upset, in a panic, in turmoil, and worried yet you have peace, that is unexplainable. The world is starving for this kind of peace. You cannot buy it; it is not for sale. It is a free gift from God that comes out of a deep, abiding closeness to Him, and it leads to unspeakable joy.

Peace comes when you turn over your burden to the Lord—when you choose to cast your care on Him instead of keeping it for yourself. The sooner you do this

the better. Commit your problems to God the moment you have one. Don't even try to handle them on your own. The longer you wait, the harder it is to break free from worry and anxiety.

Because God has promised that He is always with us, we can have incredible peace and joy...even in the midst of tribulation. Only He can give us that. That is what it means to have a peace that passes all understanding.

———————

The believer who is experiencing God's peace through his relationship with Jesus can have peace even in the midst of life's toughest storms.

Believe

But without faith it is impossible to please and be satisfactory to Him. For whoever would come near to God must [necessarily] believe that God exists and that He is the rewarder of those who earnestly and diligently seek Him [out].

HEBREWS 11:6

A positive, believing heart is one of the heart attitudes that is absolutely vital in our relationship with God. That may sound funny, since we are called believers. It's easy to assume that all believers believe, but I've noticed there are many well-intentioned but "unbelieving believers." I slip into that state myself from time to time.

In Matthew 8:13, Jesus says that it shall be done for you as you have believed. Isn't that a powerful thought? It is amazing how much God will do in our lives if we

will simply believe He can...and He will. Believing is a choice we make, and anytime we stop believing we lose our peace and joy. Form a habit of getting up each new day saying over and over, "I believe, I believe, I believe. With God's help, I believe I can do whatever He sets before me."

When you are tempted to doubt, just remind yourself that you are a believer, and believers always believe! Believing pleases God and releases the fulfillment of His promises in your life.

———

When you lose your joy and peace, check your believing!

Letting Go of the Ashes

To grant [consolation and joy] to those who mourn in Zion—to give them an ornament (a garland or diadem) of beauty instead of ashes, the oil of joy instead of mourning, the garment [expressive] of praise instead of a heavy, burdened, and failing spirit...

ISAIAH 61:3

Part of any restoration process in our lives is that God gives us beauty for ashes. But for that to happen, we must be willing to give Him the ashes.

You may have been hurt in the past and kept the ashes of that hurt somewhere close at hand. Every once in a while, you may get them out and grieve over them once again. If so, I understand because there was a time in my life when I did the same thing.

But I want to encourage you to do what

I did and let go of these ashes, allowing the wind of the Holy Spirit to blow them away to where they cannot be found again. This is a new day. There is no more time left for grieving over the ashes of the past. Your future has no room in it for your past.

God has the same good plan for you that He had the moment you arrived on this planet. He has never changed His mind, and He never will. From the very moment the enemy hurt you, God has had your restoration in His heart. Know that you are valuable, unique, loved, and special in His eyes. It is time to go forward!

———————

Allow the Holy Spirit to blow away the ashes and replace those ashes with beauty.

Exceedingly, Abundantly Above and Beyond

Now to Him Who, by (in consequence of) the [action of His] power that is at work within us, is able to [carry out His purpose and] do superabundantly, far over and above all that we [dare] ask or think [infinitely beyond our highest prayers, desires, thoughts, hopes, or dreams].   EPHESIANS 3:20

Have you ever been praying about all the people who are hurting and had a strong desire to help them all? I know I certainly have. In times like this I feel that my desire is bigger than my ability, and it is—but it is not bigger than God's ability.

When the thing we are facing in our life looms so big in our eyes that our mind goes "tilt," we can remember to think with the mind of Christ. In the natural, many

things seem impossible. But God wants us to believe for great things, make big plans, and expect Him to do things so amazing it leaves us with our mouths hanging open in awe.

God does not usually call people who are capable; if He did, He would not get the glory. He frequently chooses those who, in the natural, feel as if they are completely in over their heads but who are ready to stand up on the inside and take bold steps of faith. They have learned the secret of staying close to God and trusting that His "superabundant" power will work within them.

***

When your desires seem overwhelmingly big, and you don't see the way to accomplish them, remember that even though you don't know the way, you know the Waymaker!

Hanging Tough

The Lord God is my Strength, my
personal bravery, and my invincible
army; He makes my feet like hinds' feet
and will make me to walk [not to stand
still in terror, but to walk] and make
[spiritual] progress upon my high places
[of trouble, suffering, or responsibility]!
HABAKKUK 3:19

The Old Testament prophet Habakkuk spoke of hard times, calling them "high places," and stating that God had given him *hinds' feet* to scale those high places.

A "hind" refers to a certain kind of deer that is an agile mountain climber. It can scale up what looks like a sheer cliff, leaping from ledge to ledge with great ease. This is God's will for us, that when hardship comes our way, we are not intimidated or frightened.

To be truly victorious, we can grow to the place where we are not afraid of hard times but are actually challenged by them. In Habakkuk 3:19, these "high places" are referred to as "trouble, suffering, or responsibility." This is because it is during these times that we grow.

If you look back over your life, you will see that most of your spiritual growth didn't occur during the easy times in life; you grow during difficulty. Then during the easy times that come, you are able to enjoy what you have gained during the hard times. Life is filled with a mixture of abasing and abounding (Philippians 4:12), and both are valuable and necessary.

God often does His deepest work in some of the most difficult circumstances.

Recounting God's Victories

David said, The Lord Who delivered me out of the paw of the lion and out of the paw of the bear, He will deliver me out of the hand of this Philistine. And Saul said to David, Go, and the Lord be with you!   1 SAMUEL 17:37

When David volunteered to go and fight Goliath, no one really encouraged him. Everyone, including the king, told him he was too young, too inexperienced, too small, and he didn't have the right armor. But David encouraged himself by recounting the victories God had given him in the past. Finally, Saul told him to go, but he still didn't believe David could win.

There will be many times in life when you are left with no one to encourage you, and during those times, you will need to rely on God alone. The enemy never ceases

trying to discourage us. He wants to prevent us from being faithful to do what God wants us to do. Today, I want to encourage you that with God, you can do anything you need to do.

When you have to wait a long time for something, or when it seems that everything and everybody is against you, instead of getting negative and downcast, say to God, "Lord, I will be faithful to You. I remember what You've done in my life in the past. I know You will deliver me again. I trust You to see me through." God is closer to you than you may realize, and He will never fail you.

———

God is your strength, and all things are possible with Him.

The Greatest Thing in the World

*Beloved, if God loved us so [very much],
we also ought to love one another.*

1 JOHN 4:11

Loving and being loved are what make life worth living. To love and be loved is the way God created us—it gives life purpose and meaning. Love is the greatest thing in the world.

It is also the most fiercely attacked area in our lives. The devil's goal is to separate us from God's love, and he will use anything he can to complicate our understanding of God's love or make it confusing. His primary means of deception is to get us to believe that God's love for us depends on our worthiness.

Here's how it worked in my life: Whenever I failed, I would stop allowing myself to receive God's love and start punishing

myself by feeling condemned and guilty. I lived this way for many years of my life, dutifully carrying my heavy sack of guilt on my back everywhere I went. I made mistakes regularly, and I felt guilty about each one. Then I would try to win God's favor with good works.

Thankfully, the day of freedom finally came for me. God graciously revealed to me, through the Holy Spirit, His love for me personally. That single revelation changed my entire life and walk with Him. The same can be true for you. When you realize God loves you unconditionally, everything changes. You are loved, not because of what you have done or haven't done, but because of who God is.

God's love for you is perfect and unconditional. When you fail, He keeps on loving you because His love is not based on you but on Him.

Focus on Potential, Not Limitations

Having gifts (faculties, talents, qualities) that differ according to the grace given us, let us use them...

ROMANS 12:6

Believing in the potential God has placed inside of you is an important part of building confidence and overcoming insecurity. When you focus on your potential rather than your weaknesses, you are giving God room to work, because you are trusting that He has a plan for your life.

Though people may say, "You can do anything you set your mind to do," you and I cannot really do *anything*...in our own strength. And we cannot do anything or everything that we see other people doing. But we can do everything God has called us to do. And we can be anything God says we can be.

Each of us is full of gifts and talents, potential and ability. If we really begin to cooperate with God, identifying our strengths and being content with what He has given us, we will realize our full potential. Gifts and talents are distributed by the Holy Spirit according to the grace that is on each person to handle them. If you are going to go higher in life, if you are going to make the most of what God has given you, learn to focus on your potential—what God has created you to be—not on your limitations.

If God has called you to do something, you will find yourself loving it despite any adversity you may face.

Seeing People as God Sees Them

Let each of you esteem and look upon and be concerned for not [merely] his own interests, but also each for the interests of others.

PHILIPPIANS 2:4

A big problem among believers today is selfishness and self-centeredness. If we're not careful, we can get so self-absorbed that we never know the real joy of forgetting about self and serving God by helping others. When we reach out to others, God reaches out to us and takes care of our needs. What we make happen for someone else, God will make happen for us.

It is easy to judge and criticize other people, but God wants us to love them instead. He wants us to show them the same mercy that He has shown to us. Mercy triumphs over judgment according to God's Word,

so let's get busy being a blessing and our joy will increase.

It is impossible to be selfish and happy at the same time. Joy only comes through reaching out to others with the love of God. The more self-absorbed we are, the more miserable we will be. I spent many years being unhappy simply because I wasn't doing anything for anyone else. I finally learned that God didn't create us for "in-reach" but for "out-reach." When you reach out, then God will reach in and meet all of your needs.

Ask God to show you who you can help and bless today.

Priorities

Depart from evil and do good; seek, inquire for, and crave peace and pursue (go after) it!   PSALM 34:14

Being at peace should always be a priority in our lives. In Psalm 34:14, David instructs us to pursue peace, to crave and go after it. That's how important peace is.

Frustration and stress are natural enemies of peace. Many times, to combat these peace destroyers, it is necessary for us to reorganize our priorities and let go of things that are not bearing fruit.

If you want to live in the peace of God, make the choice not to exceed your limits. While many of the things in your life are important, are they all absolutely necessary? Think about it for a moment. Start looking at your life, figure out the commitments that are not bearing any fruit, and

start pruning those things back. You are the one who set your schedule, and you are the only one who can change it.

It is so important not to overcommit yourself. Ask God for wisdom and follow His leading as to what you are to be involved in and where you are to use your energy. When you do, you will find that time with Him is always the priority—everything else is secondary. When you make God your number one priority, and when you seek His direction for how to spend your time and energy after that, you'll be amazed at the peace that will come into your life.

You can rest in the assurance that God is with you in all that you face. He doesn't just give you peace—He is your peace.

Begun by Faith, Finished by Faith

Are you so foolish and so senseless and so silly? Having begun [your new life spiritually] with the [Holy] Spirit, are you now reaching perfection [by dependence] on the flesh? GALATIANS 3:3

Paul asked the Galatians a question I think it is important we ask ourselves today: Having begun our new lives in Christ by dependence on the Spirit, are we now trying to live them in the flesh?

Just as we are saved by grace (God's unmerited favor) through faith, and not by works of the flesh (Ephesians 2:8–9), we draw close to God each day through faith. We can begin each day by saying, "Lord, today I depend on You once again. It's not about what I can do in my own strength; it's about what You call me to do in Your strength."

When we were saved, we were in no

condition to help ourselves. Only pride, or a lack of proper knowledge, could make us feel differently today—we are still in no condition to help ourselves. But thankfully, we are in perfect condition to depend on God to be everything we need. As long as we look to Him, trusting His perfect work in our lives, we can relax and really enjoy the life Jesus died to give us.

Living in the flesh—doing things in our own effort—leads to frustration. But living in the Spirit—obeying, trusting, and depending on God—brings joy unspeakable. The next time you feel frustrated you might stop and ask yourself what you are trying to do without leaning on God, and you will probably find the source of your frustration.

It is the power of the Holy Spirit that enables you to live your new life in Christ.

The Power of "I AM"

And God said to Moses, I Am Who I Am and What I Am, and I Will Be What I Will Be; and He said, You shall say this to the Israelites: I Am has sent me to you!
EXODUS 3:14

Jesus replied, I assure you, most solemnly I tell you, before Abraham was born, I AM.
JOHN 8:58

When God said to Moses—and when Jesus told His disciples—"I AM," He was saying something quite incredible. It is something that can change the way we live our daily lives if we will really believe it.

God is so great, there is no word that can adequately describe Him. How can we describe, with one name, Someone Who is indescribable? God is not just one thing—He is everything. That is why God was saying to Moses, *I AM can take care of anything*

*you encounter. Whatever you need, I AM it.
There is nothing I can't handle. I have everything covered, not only now, but for all time.
You can relax, because I AM. I AM with you
and I AM able to do whatever needs to be
done!*

The same is true for you today. Whatever you need, God is I AM. In Him, you
will find provision, joy, peace, healing, restoration, and strength. Even before you
know what you need, I AM knows, and He
is always there to provide every good thing.

**There is nothing to fear in life when
you know you have access to the
limitless goodness, grace, and power
of I AM.**

The Servant Test

Each of you should use whatever gift you have received to serve others, as faithful stewards of God's grace in its various forms. 1 PETER 4:10 NIV

The closer we get to God, the more opportunities He gives us to serve others. I say "opportunities" because that is the way we need to view serving others. Every time we serve others, it not only blesses them, but it also brings tremendous joy to our lives. Jesus gave us an example of being a servant by washing the feet of the disciples and then saying, "You should do [in your turn] what I have done to you" (John 13:15).

Some people fail to live as servants because they don't know who they are in Christ. They feel they must be doing something they consider "important" to find a sense of self-worth. They fail to understand

that their identity comes from who they are in Christ, not how prestigious their career or platform is. When you are secure in your place in Christ, and when you find your strength and confidence in God, you take great joy in helping others every chance you get.

The "servant test" is simply how we respond to the opportunities God gives us to be a blessing to others. It reveals whether we really and truly want to be like Jesus. God has blessed and made us a blessing! God's blessings are never meant to be consumed solely on ourselves, but always to be shared with those around us.

————————

Look for ways to serve others today, including those in your own home. This will be a great experience for you and for them.

Going over the Mountain

When you pass through the waters, I will be with you, and through the rivers, they will not overwhelm you. When you walk through the fire, you will not be burned or scorched, nor will the flame kindle upon you.   ISAIAH 43:2

When we know that God is with us, we know that we can overcome any difficulty with Him. We never have to avoid our problems. We can meet them head-on in the power and wisdom of God. Anything we hide or run from still has power over us.

Sometimes we go around and around the same mountain, and we end up like the Israelites in the wilderness who wandered around for forty years (Deuteronomy 2:1–3). But the closer we get to God, the more determined we are to face our mountains and confidently go all the way

through with God. That is the only path to victory. David didn't run from Goliath, he ran toward him in the name of the Lord.

I encourage you to refuse to give up no matter how difficult your circumstance may seem. Trust that God has a plan for your life, and pray that God will give you the strength to keep climbing no matter how high the mountain seems.

Most importantly, I encourage you to be determined to enjoy the journey. Enjoying life is an attitude of the heart, a decision to enjoy everything because God can use everything—even the seemingly difficult things—to bring about His perfect plan.

The power and presence of God in your life will lift you above the circumstances that others can't seem to overcome.

First Things First

But seek (aim at and strive after) first of all His kingdom and His righteousness (His way of doing and being right), and then all these things taken together will be given you besides.

MATTHEW 6:33

Too often we spend all of our time seeking God for possessions, for blessings, for answers to our problems, when all we really need to do is just seek God. The more we seek God because we simply want to be in relationship with Him, the more everything else in our lives falls into place.

In the early years of my ministry, I sought God about how I could get the ministry to grow. The result was that it stayed just the same as it was. It didn't grow as quickly as I had hoped, and sometimes it even went backward. What I didn't realize

at the time was that all I needed to do was to seek the kingdom of God, and He would add the growth.

The truth is that we don't have to beg God to give us anything. If what we want is His will, He will give us what is best for us at the right time. All we need to do is love God and seek Him first and want to do things His way. As we do, we will develop a closeness with God that is vital in order to properly handle success, or the material blessings of God.

Always seek the "presence" of God, and not the "presents" of God. He will give you many good things, but He does require first place in our lives. We are to have no other gods before Him!

———————

Seek God before anything else, abide in Him, and you will draw closer to Him than ever before.

Conscious of God's Love

And we know (understand, recognize, are conscious of, by observation and by experience) and believe (adhere to and put faith in and rely on) the love God cherishes for us. God is love, and he who dwells and continues in love dwells and continues in God, and God dwells and continues in him.   1 JOHN 4:16

In 1 John 4:16, the Bible instructs us to "understand, recognize" and be "conscious of" the love God has for us. To be in close, personal relationship with God is to be conscious of His love at all times and to be continually amazed at the fact that He shows His love for us even when we don't deserve it.

One way I would encourage you to do this is to keep a book of remembrance, a book in which you write down special

things the Lord does for you. When you begin observing and making note of God's goodness in this way, you will be surprised at how often God's love manifests in practical ways (big and small) in your life.

God's love can change your life if you will allow it. It contains the power to heal your emotional wounds. His love strengthens you to press on in difficult times, and it softens your heart, enabling you to show more love to others. Can you imagine anything better to be "conscious" and aware of than this great love?

Perhaps the best thing you can do today is simply observe God's love, recognize and celebrate it with thanksgiving.

Preparing for the Best

Rejoice in the Lord, O you [uncompromisingly] righteous [you upright in right standing with God]; for praise is becoming and appropriate for those who are upright [in heart].

PSALM 33:1

How we approach each new day and each new situation makes a huge difference. If we decide ahead of time that we won't be happy or peaceful unless we get exactly what we want, then we will rarely be at peace.

I have heard people say things like, "If it rains tomorrow I am *not* going to be happy," or "If I don't get the job, I am going to be *so* upset." When we think thoughts such as this, we are setting ourselves up to be unhappy and to lose our peace and joy before we even have a problem.

Instead of preparing to be upset, we can prepare to be at peace. We can think and speak things like, "I really hope the weather is nice tomorrow, and I hope I get this new job. But my joy comes from my relationship with Jesus, so I choose to be happy and have rest in my soul no matter what I come up against tomorrow. Whether it's rainy or sunny, whether I get the job or not, I choose the joy of the Lord!"

The way we approach our lives makes all the difference in the quality of life we can have. When we can't fix life, let's remember that we can fix our approach toward it.

———————

Make up your mind that you will be happy if you get your way today... and if you don't.

Free to Fly

The Spirit of the Lord God is upon me, because the Lord has anointed and qualified me to preach the Gospel of good tidings to the meek, the poor, and afflicted; He has sent me to bind up and heal the brokenhearted, to proclaim liberty to the [physical and spiritual] captives and the opening of the prison and of the eyes to those who are bound.

ISAIAH 61:1

Love offers people both roots and wings. It provides a sense of belonging (roots) and a sense of freedom (wings). Love does not try to control or manipulate others.

Jesus said that He was sent by God to proclaim liberty. As believers, that is what we are meant to do also—to free people to fulfill God's will for their lives, not to bring them under our control.

Have you ever seen parents push their children to do things they do not even want to do just to meet the frustrated desires of their parents? Have you ever seen a person who is clingy and emotionally smothering to a new friend, because he is afraid to lose that person? Both of these examples bind rather than set free.

That is not the way true love works. Love does not try to gain personal satisfaction at the expense of others. Love will always proclaim liberty. When we love God, and when we love others, we will excitedly allow the people in our lives to follow God's plan—not our plan—and see who they can be and what they can accomplish in Christ Jesus.

A caged bird cannot fly! Proclaim liberty. Set people free and see what they can do.

Finding the Courage to Be Unique

Not with eyeservice, as menpleasers; but as the servants of Christ, doing the will of God from the heart.

EPHESIANS 6:6 KJV

In order to be the person you are called to be in Christ, choosing to live confidently in close relationship with God, it is essential you have the courage to be uniquely you. That means being content in how God created you, choosing not to be like everyone else.

One of the easiest traps we can fall into is the trap of being a "manpleaser." But trying to please others ultimately leads to frustration. At first, when we begin changing our personality to please other people, we hear comments that make us feel good about ourselves. But this won't last. People's opinions are fickle and superficial. It is only God's opinion that counts.

You are worth something because God sent His only Son to die for you. You are worth something because God loves you, not because of what anybody else thinks about you or says about you.

I encourage you to embrace the things that make you unique. If your hair is a little different, if your personality is unique, if your talent is uncommon—whatever it is, thank God that He created you in a special way and choose to use your gifts and talents and personality for His glory.

It is only when you embrace the person God made you to be that you will really enjoy the life Jesus died to give you.

Living with Purpose

This is the [Lord's] purpose that is purposed upon the whole earth . . . For the Lord of hosts has purposed, and who can annul it? And His hand is stretched out, and who can turn it back?

ISAIAH 14:26–27

God is a God of purpose—He moves strategically, and He implements His perfect plan. As His children, God desires for us to be people of purpose. The closer we are to Him, the more purpose we will live with.

Jesus knew His purpose. He said that He came into the world that we might have life and that He might destroy the works of the devil (John 10:10; 1 John 3:8).

As far as our specific purpose, that varies from person to person and from one season of life to the next, but God has a

general purpose we can all choose to live in each day.

For example, we love others, not because we always feel like it, but because we purpose to love others. The same is true when we give, show mercy, display kindness, forgive, and so many other things. Love, joy, peace, patience, kindness, goodness, and all the other fruit of the Spirit are ours to enjoy and to release to others if we do it on purpose. We do these things, not because we always necessarily feel like it, but because it is what we are called to do.

Joy and peace don't happen by accident; they come when you choose to live your life on purpose.

The Word of God Sets You Free

... Welcome the Word which implanted and rooted [in your hearts] contains the power to save your souls. JAMES 1:21

The most powerful and effective tool to bring about real and lasting transformation in our lives is the Word of God. It is the Word of God that draws us and keeps us close to God.

The devil will always try to deceive you, telling you things about yourself and your situation that are contrary to God's Word. As long as we believe the lies, we remain frustrated, miserable, and powerless. But when God's Word of truth uncovers those lies, the truth sets us free.

Only the Word of God has this power, and only God can change us. The Word exposes wrong motives, wrong thoughts, and wrong words. Truth can set us free

from guilt, self-rejection, condemnation, self-hatred, the works of the flesh, and every lie that we have bought into and brought into our lives. God is out to set us free so that we can enjoy the life He has given us.

A sword in the sheath is of no value. It must be wielded and appropriately used. Well, the Word of God is the believer's sword, and we can learn by applying it daily, getting it down in our heart, and speaking it out our mouth. The believer who does this is full of power and can accomplish great things for the kingdom of God.

Studying the Word is the number one way to draw close to God.

God Is Never Late

And let us not be weary in well doing: for in due season we shall reap, if we faint not.   GALATIANS 6:9 KJV

Many people think that they are being patient just because they have had to wait for something. But patience is more than waiting. Patience is having a good, positive, joyful attitude in the waiting process. It is fruit of the Spirit that manifests itself in a believer who is submitted to God, regardless of their circumstances. The patient person will always stay calm and point us to the provision of our heavenly Father.

We often want God's plan in our lives to happen right now. But God's perfect work takes time and requires us to be patient. God is not working on our timetable. Though we are rushed and hurried, God never is. He takes time to do things

right—He works on His masterpiece with thought, care, and precision.

We are God's masterpiece (Ephesians 2:10 NLT). He is the Designer, and He is crafting something beautiful out of your life. God's timing seems to be His own little secret. The Bible promises us that He will never be late, but I have also discovered that He is usually not early. No matter what you do, you cannot rush God. So I encourage you to enjoy the wait.

————————

Enjoy where you are on the way to where you are going!

Can You Laugh at Yourself?

Then were our mouths filled with laughter, and our tongues with singing. Then they said among the nations, The Lord has done great things for them.

PSALM 126:2

One of the beautiful things about being a Christian is that it's not complicated—in fact, we are instructed to humble ourselves and become as little children. While the Lord wants us to grow up in our attitude, behavior, and acceptance of responsibility in Christ (Ephesians 4:15), at the same time He wants us to be childlike in our dependence upon Him and in our desire to be close to Him.

One characteristic of a child is that he has fun no matter what he does. He manages to find a way to have a good time. God desires for us to be the same way. We

can learn how to enjoy everything we do, and to enjoy Him at all times. We can and should love all aspects of life, the secular as well as the sacred. You can enjoy being in a Bible study with friends, and you can enjoy doing household chores.

It is healthy to learn to enjoy yourself and find humor in your everyday life. We can even learn to laugh at ourselves. As Art Linkletter used to say, "People are funny!" And that includes us.

———————

Laugh as often as you possibly can, because a merry heart does you much good.

Convincing God or Trusting God?

For who has known the mind of the Lord and who has understood His thoughts, or who has [ever] been His counselor?   ROMANS 11:34

Life would be so much easier if we would live in the realization that God is smarter than we are. No matter what you or I may think, God's way is always better than our way.

We are often tempted to think we know what is best, and then we throw all our energy into bringing it to pass. We experience a lot of disappointment, which hinders joy and enjoyment, due to deciding for ourselves that something has to be done a certain way or by a certain time. When we want something very strongly, we often try to convince God why it is important and why He should bring our will to pass,

instead of simply trusting that He knows what is best for our life.

As Romans 11:34 reminds us, God has no need of a counselor to tell Him what He should do for us. His will is perfect, and He has good plans for us to become all that He intends us to be. The prophet Jeremiah says, "For I know the thoughts and plans that I have for you, says the Lord, thoughts and plans for welfare and peace and not for evil, to give you hope in your final outcome" (Jeremiah 29:11).

When you face puzzling situations, I encourage you to pray, "Well, Lord, this may not make sense to me right now, but I trust You. I believe You love me, You are with me, and You are doing what is best for me."

———

God does not need your counsel in order to work; He just needs your faith.

A Truly Fervent Prayer

... The effective, fervent prayer of a
righteous man avails much.

JAMES 5:16 NKJV

If you've been a believer for any period of time, you've probably heard it taught that for prayer to be effective it must be fervent. However, if we misunderstand the word *fervent*, we may feel that we have to work up some strong emotion before we pray; otherwise, our prayers will not be effective.

I know there were many years when I believed this way, and perhaps you have been likewise misled. But praying fervently just means that our prayers must come from our heart and be sincere.

I remember enjoying prayer times when I could feel God's presence, and then wondering what was wrong during the times when I didn't feel anything. I learned after

a while that faith is not based on feelings or emotions but the knowledge of the heart.

At times I experience a great deal of emotion while I'm praying. But there are more times when I don't feel emotional. Prayer that brings us closer to God only happens when we pray in faith, regardless of what we *feel* at any particular moment.

———————

Trust that your earnest, heartfelt prayers are effective because your faith is in God, not in your own ability to pray passionately or eloquently.

God Understands You

No one understands [no one intelligently discerns or comprehends]; no one seeks out God.   ROMANS 3:11

Anyone who decides to follow God closely will have times of being misunderstood by people who have not made the same commitment. Faithless people do not understand faithful people!

There will always be those who won't quite know what to think of us when we are fully surrendered to God. People did not know what to think of Jesus either. Nobody really understood Him or the call on His life, not even His family.

When we don't say or do what other people are saying and doing because we have decided to follow God rather than the world, we may be misunderstood and rejected. It hurts when that happens, but

always remember that Jesus never rejects you, and that is what really matters.

Your obedience to God may mean that you won't fit into the regular regimen of what is going on around you. You may feel out of place at times, but in those moments remember that God will reward your faithfulness. He loves you, and when other people are asking, "What is wrong with you?" God will be saying, "There is nothing wrong with you. You are mine and I am proud of you."

———

Make up your mind to stand with God and do what He says, even if nobody understands or supports you. Jesus understands you, and He is enough.

Bridges Instead of Walls

For even to this were you called [it is inseparable from your vocation]. For Christ also suffered for you, leaving you [His personal] example, so that you should follow in His footsteps.

1 PETER 2:21

Instead of the walls that I used to build around my life, I have learned to build bridges. By the power of grace and God's forgiveness, all the difficult and unfair things that happened to me in life have been turned into highways over which others can pass to find the same liberty that I found.

God is no respecter of persons (Acts 10:34). What He has done for me, He will do for you too. As you draw closer to God on a daily basis, you can discover the same freedom that I have found, and you

can become a bridge for others to pass over, instead of a wall that shuts them out.

Jesus pioneered a pathway to God for us. He became a highway for us to pass over. He sacrificed Himself for us, and now that we are benefiting from His sacrifice, He is giving us a chance to sacrifice for others so they can reap the same benefits we enjoy.

Instead of shutting people out, I suggest that you ask God to allow you to see them as He sees them. Love them, forgive them, and point them to God so He can heal their wounds and fill them with His peace and joy.

There are people who are lost and need someone to go before them and show them the way. Why not be that person for them?

Is It Worth It?

. . . Therefore love truth and peace.
ZECHARIAH 8:19 NKJV

It is God's sincere desire for you to live a life full of peace. The closer you get to the Lord—the more you depend on Him—the more peace you will have.

No position or possession is worthwhile if you don't have peace. Money, status, popularity—it's all meaningless if you don't have peace. You simply cannot put a price on the value of peace.

Many people spend their lives trying to climb the ladder of success, but every time they go up one more rung, they lose more of their peace, joy, and time to spend with their family. Their whole life is consumed with the pressure and stress of trying to keep what they've gained. But we are never truly successful unless we have peace.

Some even work several jobs to acquire what the world dangles in front of them, saying, "You must have this to be truly happy." They get those "things," but they still don't have any peace.

Romans 14:17 tells us, "The kingdom of God is not meat and drink"—it is not things that money or status can secure—but it is "righteousness, and peace, and joy in the Holy Ghost" (KJV). The kingdom of God is found in knowing who we are in Christ and having "the peace of God, which surpasses all understanding" (Philippians 4:7 NKJV).

God wants you to have your needs met abundantly and be in a position to bless others. Never doubt that God wants to bless you, but don't seek to have anything if you cannot have it peacefully.

Love Shows Respect

Let all men know and perceive and recognize your unselfishness (your considerateness, your forbearing spirit.) The Lord is near [He is coming soon].

PHILIPPIANS 4:5

Love is a generous, selfless act. A selfish person expects everyone to be just the way he is and to like whatever he likes, but love respects the differences in other people.

Respecting individual rights is very important. If God had wanted us to all be alike, He would not have given each of us a different set of fingerprints. I think that one fact alone proves that we are created equal, but different. We all have fingerprints, but they are all different!

We all have different abilities, different likes and dislikes, different goals in life, different motivations, and the list goes on

and on. We look different, we come in all sizes and shapes, and each of us is unique.

Love respectfully frees others to be who they were created to be. Freedom is one of the greatest gifts we can give. It was what Jesus came to give us, and it is what love allows us to give to others.

God's love for us is unconditional, and we should learn to love others the same way. Be generous with mercy and always believe the best.

———————

Unconditional love unselfishly loves selfish people, generously gives to stingy people, and continually blesses unappreciative people.

No Matter Where You Go . . . You're There

. . . You shall love your neighbor as [you do] yourself.   MATTHEW 19:19

I believe one of the greatest problems people have today concerns the way they feel about themselves. Many people go through life carrying a poor self-image and a low opinion of themselves. Oftentimes, people have had these negative thoughts so long they don't even realize they have them.

What do you think of yourself? What kind of relationship do you have with yourself? I ask because no matter where you go, or what you do in this life, you are always going to have to deal with you. There is no escaping from you.

The Lord commanded us to love our neighbors as we love ourselves, but what happens if we don't love ourselves? We

cannot give away what we do not have. God loves us, and that gives us permission to receive His love and love ourselves in a balanced way. Many of us think we have worn God out with our failures and sins, but that is impossible to do. God never gives up on us! The closer we come to God in our daily lives, the more we realize how dearly we are loved, and the easier it is to begin to love ourselves.

Receive God's love for you. Meditate on it. Let it change and strengthen you. Then give it away.

The True Source of Confidence

*For we [Christians] are the true
circumcision, who worship God in
spirit and by the Spirit of God and
exult and glory and pride ourselves in
Jesus Christ, and put no confidence or
dependence [on what we are] in the flesh
and on outward privileges and physical
advantages and external appearances.*

PHILIPPIANS 3:3

The most important key to becoming spiritually stronger and more secure is to discover the true source of confidence.

In what do you place your confidence today? Is it your level of education, your social group, the amount of money you have, or the position you hold at work—or is it rooted in God? That question must be settled for every believer who desires to draw closer to God each day.

If we place all our confidence in our education, our looks, our position, our gifts, our talents, or in other people's opinions, we are going to end up disappointed and miserable due to being insecure. Our heavenly Father is saying to us, "Though people and things may eventually fail you, I never will. You can put your trust and confidence in Me."

I encourage you to come to the place where your confidence is not in the flesh or the things of this world, but in Christ Jesus. He is the only One Who will strengthen you, always stand by you, and never let you down.

Honestly evaluate what your confidence is in, and if it is anything other than God, repent (change your mind for the better), and be ready to do things differently.

The Wisdom in Waiting Quietly

But Mary was keeping within herself all these things (sayings), weighing and pondering them in her heart.

LUKE 2:19

There is great wisdom in learning to quietly ponder what you feel the Lord has spoken to you, especially when you're not sure exactly how it will work out.

You may feel that God has promised something for your children, spoken a new direction for your career, instructed you to make some changes in your character—whatever it is, if you'll trust God, wait patiently, and ponder what the Lord has spoken, He will show you exactly how to cooperate with His plan.

Mary had some pretty amazing things happen in her life. She was just a teenage girl who loved God when an angel of the

Lord appeared to her and told her she was going to be the mother of the Son of God. But whatever Mary may have thought or felt, she trusted God, saying, "May it be done to me according to your word" (Luke 1:38 NASB).

When God speaks something to us, many times we need to keep it to ourselves. If He tells us things we don't really understand, things that seem to make no sense, we can follow the example of Mary. We can do a little more pondering instead of running to others for advice. The doubt of others can ruin your faith. Sometimes the best thing you can do is quietly hold on to God's promise and ask Him to make it clearer to you in His perfect timing.

When God calls you to do something, He also gives you the faith to do it.

The Best Time You Can Spend

. . . Let everyone who is godly pray— pray to You in a time when You may be found; surely when the great waters [of trial] overflow, they shall not reach [the spirit in] him.   PSALM 32:6

It's simple: The more time you spend with God, the more you connect yourself to His power. David tells us that it is in the secret place of the presence of God that we are protected (Psalm 91:1). When we spend time in God's presence, in prayer, and in His Word, we are in the secret place. The secret place is a wonderful place of peace and rest!

It's powerful to think that the awesomeness of God's presence is available to us as believers. With this in mind, why in the world would we not want to spend time with God? Even Jesus would get up early

in the morning to be alone with God. He knew the value of being in the presence of God. We draw strength and wisdom merely from being with God!

The best thing to do is dedicate a portion of your time to spend with God. Try not to be legalistic about it, but do try to be as regular with it as you can. Talk to God about anything and everything that is on your heart—He is interested in everything that interests or concerns you. Sometimes you may want to listen to music and worship; other times you may just want to sit still and enjoy silence. Set aside time to be with God and let the Holy Spirit lead you in the amazing journey of becoming closer to God!

Spending time in the secret place of His presence changes you from what you are to what only He can make you.

Love, Trust, and Faith

For [if we are] in Christ Jesus, neither circumcision nor uncircumcision counts for anything, but only faith activated and energized and expressed and working through love.   GALATIANS 5:6

Instead of trying so hard to work up faith, we would be wise to spend that time and effort simply receiving God's love and loving Him in return. We are only going to be able to walk in faith based on what we believe about the Father's love.

Galatians 5:6 says that faith works by love. Faith will not work without love. This scripture is telling us that if we don't know how much God loves us, we have nothing to base our faith on.

Trusting God and walking in faith is leaning on Him and trusting Him for everything. You can only do that with someone when you

know you are loved unconditionally. God's love is His free gift to us, and we simply need to receive it, be thankful for it, and let it bring us closer to Him.

The Bible says, "We love Him, because He first loved us" (1 John 4:19). When you are assured of the fact that God loved you first, you are excited to love Him in return—you are excited to live your life completely for Him.

Nobody in all the world will ever love you as God loves you.

Faith becomes stronger and works more powerfully by letting God love you.

Dedicated for His Use

I appeal to you therefore, brethren, and beg of you in view of [all] the mercies of God, to make a decisive dedication of your bodies [presenting all your members and faculties] as a living sacrifice, holy (devoted, consecrated) and well pleasing to God, which is your reasonable (rational, intelligent) service and spiritual worship. ROMANS 12:1

In order for God to use us, we must dedicate our lives to Him. When we truly dedicate ourselves to the Lord, we relinquish the burden of trying to run our own lives.

Dedicating your life to God must be sincere. It is quite easy to sing along with everyone else a song such as "I Surrender All." We may even feel moved emotionally, but the real test is found in daily life when circumstances don't always go the way

we thought they would. Dedicating your spirit, soul, and body to the Lord is more than a song—it's a daily decision.

An important part of drawing close to God is having a heart dedicated to Him. When we choose to live in obedience to the Word of God, it pleases the Lord greatly. When you sincerely dedicate yourself to Him, you're drawn into a new and deeper level of relationship that increases your strength and adds excitement to every day of your life.

———

Dedicate every part of your life to God and let the Holy Spirit make you into a vessel fit for the Master's use.

Balancing Work and Rest

For God did not give us a spirit of timidity (of cowardice, of craven and cringing and fawning fear), but [He has given us a spirit] of power and of love and of calm and well-balanced mind and discipline and self-control.

2 TIMOTHY 1:7

We have all been given twenty-four hours in each day. It is important how we use that time—how we regulate the different areas of our lives to keep them in proper perspective. If we have too much work and not enough rest, we get out of balance. We become workaholics and end up weary and worn-out.

I get a lot of satisfaction out of accomplishments and work. I don't like a lot of wasted time or useless activities. But because of my nature, it is easy for me to get out of balance in the area of work. I have

to regularly determine that I will not only work but also rest. It must be a priority in order for me to be healthy and close to God.

But it is also possible to have too much rest and not enough work. Solomon says that through "...idleness of the hands the house leaks" (Ecclesiastes 10:18). In other words, people who don't work enough end up in trouble. Their finances, spiritual life, possessions, bodies, and everything else suffer because they don't do the work necessary to keep things in order.

Ask God to help you have a healthy and proper balance of work and rest. Take time to accomplish the tasks before you, but be sure to seize your opportunities to be at peace and enjoy rest. Both are important. Balance is the key!

Pray for God to show you how to bring balance to your life one step at a time!

Keep Your Heart Free

And forgive us our debts, as we also have forgiven (left, remitted, and let go of the debts, and have given up resentment against) our debtors.

MATTHEW 6:12

Jesus frequently spoke of the need to forgive others. If we are to live in close relationship with God, it is important that we are quick to forgive. The quicker we forgive, the easier it is to live in peace. It allows us to deal with the problem before it gets rooted in our emotions. Bitterness will be much more difficult to pull out if it has long, strong roots.

When we hold a grudge against someone, we're not hurting that person—we're only hurting ourselves. Harboring unforgiveness against other people does not change them, but it does change us. It

makes us sour, bitter, miserable, and difficult to be around. Think of it this way: When you think you are holding a grudge, it is actually the grudge that is holding you.

Unforgiveness is Satan's deceptive way of keeping us in bondage. He wants us to think we are getting even, that we are protecting ourselves from being hurt again, but none of that is true. Unforgiveness continues to hurt you and keeps you from drawing closer to God.

If someone has hurt you, I encourage you to ask God for grace to forgive that person against whom you are holding a grudge. Determine from this point on to keep your heart and life free from this negative, destructive emotion.

———

It is only possible to have good emotional health when you let go of all bitterness and unforgiveness.

When You Feel Discouraged

Be glad in the Lord and rejoice, you [uncompromisingly] righteous...shout for joy, all you upright in heart!

PSALM 32:11

People from all walks of life have bouts with discouragement and despair. There are many underlying causes for despair and a variety of treatments offered to deal with it. Some are effective, but many offer only a temporary solution. The good news is that Jesus can heal us and deliver us from discouragement. He can restore our lives to one of joy and peace.

If you are a believer in Jesus Christ, the joy of the Lord is already inside you. Even when you don't seem to *feel* joyful, you can tap into that joy and release it by faith. You can experience what is yours as a result of

your faith in Jesus Christ. *It is God's will for you to experience joy!*

I had problems with discouragement and despair myself a long time ago. But thank God, I learned I didn't have to allow negative feelings to rule me. I learned how to release the joy of the Lord in my life! When discouragement comes, don't accept and agree with it, but encourage yourself by looking at God's promises and letting them fill you with hope. No matter what you have gone through in life or are going through now, being discouraged won't change it. No matter what you have lost, you still have a lot left. Stop living in the past and ask God to show you the future He has planned for you!

When you are tempted to be discouraged, say "no" to the temptation and stay positive, expecting something good to happen to you!

Filled with the Holy Spirit

If you then, evil as you are, know how to give good gifts [gifts that are to their advantage] to your children, how much more will your heavenly Father give the Holy Spirit to those who ask and continue to ask Him!   LUKE 11:13

We all need to be continually filled with the Holy Spirit. As believers in Jesus, we have the Holy Spirit, but perhaps have not surrendered ourselves entirely to Him for His use. That was the case with me for many years until I reached a crisis point in my life where I was no longer willing to limp along day after day with no real victory.

I ask God to do "something," and I was open to whatever His plan was! I didn't even know what I needed, but God did. He is always faithful to meet us right where we are and help us get to where we need to be.

I needed to be filled with God's Spirit, and by His grace and mercy, I was. I still ask God regularly to fill me afresh with His presence and power and enable me to be all that He wants me to be. We need the power of the Holy Spirit in order to do God's will. Never depend on yourself, for apart from Him you can do nothing (John 15:5).

Ask for the fullness of God's Spirit daily and you will experience closeness with God that is wonderful. When the Holy Spirit comes upon you, then you receive power to be His witness. You will change in amazing ways as you trust God's power to enable and strengthen you.

———

Ask for and receive the Holy Spirit's power in your life.

Unconditional Love

And this command (charge, order, injunction) we have from Him: that he who loves God shall love his brother [believer] also.   1 JOHN 4:21

According to God's Word, He loved us before the world was formed, before we loved Him or believed in Him or had ever done anything either right or wrong. Isn't that amazing? God's love for us was, is, and always will be unending and unconditional.

Because God does not require us to earn His love, we can follow His example, not requiring others to earn ours. Love is not something we do and then don't do. We should not turn it on and off, depending on who we want to give it to and how they are treating us.

As believers in Jesus Christ, the love we can demonstrate to the world is the

unconditional *love of God* flowing through us to them. We cannot understand this God-kind of love with our minds. It far surpasses mere knowledge. It is a revelation that God gives to His children. It is something we feel as we draw closer to the Lord, and it is something we can't wait to share with those around us.

Unconditional love always believes the best of people. It sees what they can become if only someone will love them. That is what God did for us. He believed the best and saw that His unconditional love could conform us to the image of His Son.

———————

If you'll freely receive God's love, you'll be able to freely give that same love away.

A Sacrifice of Praise

Through Him, therefore, let us constantly and at all times offer up to God a sacrifice of praise, which is the fruit of lips that thankfully acknowledge and confess and glorify His name.

HEBREWS 13:15

Praise is an opportunity to dwell on, be thankful for, and recount the goodness of God in our lives. And praise is something we can do continually. We can praise Him for His mighty works, the wonders He has created, and even the works of grace He is yet to do in our lives. We can also praise Him for His daily provision.

A sacrifice of praise means doing it even when we don't feel like it. As believers, in the hard times as well as the good, we can praise God for His goodness, mercy, loving-kindness, grace, and long-suffering.

While we are waiting to see the fulfillment of our prayers, we can choose to continually acknowledge and confess and glorify His name.

It is not our responsibility to worry and fret or try to do God's part by taking into our own hands situations that should be left to Him alone. Instead, it is our responsibility to simply cast our care upon the Lord (1 Peter 5:7), trusting Him and praising Him for what He has done, is doing, and what we believe by faith He is going to do.

Even on days when it's not easy—when we don't necessarily see how everything is going to work out—we can offer a sacrifice of praise. This pleases the Lord and boosts our faith as we trust Him regardless of the circumstances around us.

———

May a sacrifice of praise continually be in our mouths for the marvelous works of grace He has done for us.

Free

. . . If anyone should sin, we have an Advocate (One Who will intercede for us) with the Father—[it is] Jesus Christ [the all] righteous [upright, just, Who conforms to the Father's will in every purpose, thought, and action].

And He [that same Jesus Himself] is the propitiation (the atoning sacrifice) for our sins . . .   1 JOHN 2:1–2

There was a time in my life when, if you asked me, "What was the last thing you did wrong?" I could have detailed the precise time I had done it and how long I had been paying for it by feeling guilty. I worried about every tiny error I made and desperately tried to keep myself from sinning. It was not until I came to comprehend God's forgiveness that I was free from the self-analysis that complicated my life to the extreme.

If you believe you must be perfect to be worthy of love and acceptance, then you will be frustrated in life because you will never be perfect as long as you are in an earthly body. The closer you draw to God, the more you realize that He loves you even in the midst of your imperfections. Out of love for God, we will naturally seek to please Him, but we can be assured that He understands our imperfections.

Don't condemn yourself. God sees your heart—in that your desire is to please Him in all things—but your performance will not perfectly match your heart's desire until you get to Heaven. You can improve all the time and keep pressing toward the mark of perfection, but you will always need the mercy and forgiveness of Jesus.

God's answer for our imperfection is forgiveness.

The Gift of Righteousness

. . . [Righteousness, standing acceptable to God] will be granted and credited to us also who believe in (trust in, adhere to, and rely on) God, Who raised Jesus our Lord from the dead.

ROMANS 4:24

One of the first revelations God gave me in the Word was on righteousness. By "revelation," I mean something you understand to the point that it becomes part of you. The knowledge isn't only in your mind, but it is in your heart. You are assured of a truth.

Righteousness is God's gift to us. It is "granted and credited" to us by virtue of our believing in what God did for us through His Son, Jesus Christ. Jesus, Who knew no sin, became sin so that we might be made the righteousness of God in Him (2 Corinthians 5:21).

Above all else, the devil does not want us to walk in the reality that we are in right standing with God. He wants us to feel insecure, ashamed, guilty, and condemned so that we shrink from God instead of enjoying closeness with Him.

Jesus wants us to know that we are right with God because of what He has done for us. He wants us to enjoy Him and enjoy living in relationship with Him. Receive the gift of God's forgiveness, mercy, and right standing today and embark on a journey of freedom and joy.

You can have a revelation of the gift of righteousness by meditating on God's Word and believing what it says about who you are in Christ.

A Living Message in Your Heart

This Book of the Law shall not depart out of your mouth, but you shall meditate on it day and night, that you may observe and do according to all that is written in it. For then you shall make your way prosperous, and then you shall deal wisely and have good success.

JOSHUA 1:8

The Word of God reveals His very thoughts written down on paper for our study and consideration. His Word is how He thinks about every situation and subject.

In order to be close to God, it is essential that you allow His Word to be a living message in your heart. This is accomplished by meditating on the Word of God, allowing His thoughts to become your thoughts. When you do this, you begin to develop the mind of Christ. I strongly encourage

you to love God's Word and let it be the guiding light in your life.

Joshua 1:8 tells us that we can put the Word into practice mentally in order to experience good success physically. Meditating on or pondering the Word of God has the power to affect every part of our lives. Proverbs 4:20–22 even tells us that the words of the Lord are a source of health and healing to our bodies.

Remember the principle of sowing and reaping. The greater the amount of time you and I personally put into thinking about and studying the Word, the more we will get out of it.

———

The Lord reveals His thoughts to those who are diligent about reading the Word.

Awesome Containers for Power

[The Servant of God says] The Lord God has given Me the tongue of a disciple and of one who is taught, that I should know how to speak a word in season to him who is weary...

ISAIAH 50:4

Words are awesome containers for power. God created the earth with His words (Hebrews 11:3). The Holy Spirit changes lives with words. Jesus said that His words are spirit and life (John 6:63).

The power of words can either be used to lift people up or tear them down—it just depends on how we choose to use that power on a daily basis. People are encouraged or defeated by the words we speak. God's desire is for us to display His love to people through our encouraging, positive, life-giving words. Speaking the right word

to a person at the right time can turn their whole life around.

The same is true in our own lives. When we speak the Word of God over our situation, things begin to change. Words are that powerful.

This is why knowing the Word of God is so important. We can study it, learn it, and then speak it out according to our situations. For instance, if you feel discouraged, don't say, "I'll never make it out of this situation." Instead, say, "Why are you so downcast, O my soul? Put your hope in God" (Psalm 42:5). You will be absolutely amazed at how your life will change when you change the way you talk.

———————

Make the decision that your words will encourage, edify, and build up your life and the lives of those around you.

Rejoice in Each Day

This is the day which the Lord has brought about; we will rejoice and be glad in it. PSALM 118:24

One of my greatest desires in ministry is to see people thoroughly enjoy the quality of life Jesus died to give us—not just to read about it or talk about it, but to walk in it and experience it as a daily reality.

Many people, myself included, are extremely goal oriented. We are so focused on tomorrow that we often fail to appreciate and enjoy today because we are always thinking ahead, looking to the next event, working to complete the next assignment, and seeing what we can check off of our to-do lists.

Our fast-paced, high-pressure society urges us to accomplish as much as we can as quickly as we can—so we can then

accomplish even more. Over the years, I have learned that the intense pursuit of one goal after another can cause us to miss out on some of the enjoyment life offers us. God does have purposes and plans He wants us to fulfill during the course of our earthly lives, but He also wants us to enjoy and make the most of every day we live. God frequently reminds me to live in the moment!

The closer you draw to God the more you will realize it is okay to actually slow down and enjoy your life in Him. God's desire is for you to experience His love, His peace, and His joy on a daily basis.

Today is the day God has given you; choose to rejoice and be glad in it.

Freely You Have Received, Freely Give

Then Peter came up to Him and said,
Lord, how many times may my brother
sin against me and I forgive him and let
it go? [As many as] up to seven times?

Jesus answered him, I tell you, not up to
seven times, but seventy times seven!

MATTHEW 18:21–22

I don't know about you, but I am glad that God does not put a limit on how many times He will forgive us. Regardless of how many times we fail and fall short, He continues to demonstrate His love for us by forgiving us and welcoming us back time and time again.

But isn't it amazing how we are willing to keep receiving forgiveness from God, yet how little we want to give forgiveness to

others? We freely accept mercy, yet it is surprising how rigid, legalistic, and merciless we can be toward others.

The bottom line is this: As people who have been forgiven much, it is important we learn to share that same forgiveness with others. We can't live in close relationship with God while we harbor bitterness, resentment, and unforgiveness toward another person. These are chains that will keep us spiritually bound up and far from God's best in our lives.

If there are people who have hurt you and you are finding it difficult to forgive them, just remember all the things God has forgiven you for. When you look at it that way, forgiveness becomes something much easier to give to others.

God's grace helps us do things easily that would otherwise be hard.

Experiencing the Love of God

In this the love of God was made manifest (displayed) where we are concerned: in that God sent His Son, the only begotten or unique [Son], into the world so that we might live through Him.   1 JOHN 4:9

For many people, if they were asked, "Are you lovable?"—they would truthfully think to themselves, *No, I'm really not.*

I know this is true because I thought I was unlovable before I came to understand the true nature of God's love and His reason for loving me. This improper understanding of my value as a child of God affected the way I treated others. I was impatient with people, legalistic and harsh, judgmental, rude, selfish, and unforgiving.

A breakthrough came in my life when God began to show me that I wasn't loving

others because I had never received His love for me. Yes, I had acknowledged the Bible teaching that God loved me, but I had not embraced it and received it as a reality in my heart.

The truth is it pleases God to love us. Once you realize that you are loved by God, not because of anything you have or haven't done, then you can quit trying to deserve His love or earn His love and simply receive it and enjoy it. This is an essential step to living in close relationship with the Father.

———————

Say out loud ten times every day, "GOD LOVES ME!"

Pray

Do not fret or have any anxiety about anything, but in every circumstance and in everything, by prayer and petition (definite requests), with thanksgiving, continue to make your wants known to God.   PHILIPPIANS 4:6

Far too many times we treat prayer as a last-ditch effort. The reasons vary—we try to fix a problem on our own, we assume God is too busy with other things, or we feel God is mad at us and won't listen to our prayers. But when we fail to pray the result is the same: We carry burdens we do not need to bear.

For many believers, life is much harder than it has to be because we do not realize how powerful prayer is. If we did, we would pray about everything, not as a last resort, but as a first response.

In James 5:13, the apostle James offers a simple, three-word solution to some of life's challenges: "He should pray." The message to us in this verse is that no matter what happens over the course of a day, we can go to God in prayer. There is a great benefit in this decision—the more you pray, the closer to God you will be.

Anytime you have a problem, make prayer your first response. If you have a need, don't hesitate to tell God what it is. When you are discouraged or feel like giving up, let God be the first person you talk to about how you are feeling. He loves you, and when you go to Him in prayer, you will be amazed at what a difference it will make in your life.

———

Whatever situation you find yourself in, make prayer your first response not your last resort.

Confident of God's Presence in Your Life

For in the Gospel a righteousness which God ascribes is revealed, both springing from faith and leading to faith [disclosed through the way of faith that arouses to more faith]. As it is written, The man who through faith is just and upright shall live and shall live by faith.

ROMANS 1:17

Years ago, as I was learning about confidence and trying to live a confident life, I still worried about making mistakes or "missing" God. I remember He spoke to my heart very clearly, saying, "Joyce, don't worry about it. If you miss Me, I'll find you." This reassurance helped me learn to live my life in confidence and trust rather than fear.

When I speak about faith, I often use

the word *confidence*, because faith really is an attitude of complete confidence in God. It is an assurance that brings us into the rest of God.

I believe the closer we draw to God, the more confident we will become. Not confident in ourselves, but confident of His goodness and presence in our lives. We can be confident when we pray, confident in our relationships, confident when we make decisions, and confident as we carry out our daily responsibilities.

Today, I encourage you to take a bold stance and say: "I will live with complete confidence in my relationship with God. I believe He will lead me. I believe I can make good decisions. I believe my prayers are powerful. I believe God loves me and has a good plan for my life."

You don't have to "feel" confident in order to "be" confident!

Taking the Pressure off Other People

First of all, then, I admonish and urge that petitions, prayers, intercessions, and thanksgivings be offered on behalf of all men.   1 TIMOTHY 2:1

Love and acceptance are universal needs people have. This includes the people in our lives. If we demand that people change to be more like us or to suit our liking, we are putting a tremendous strain on those relationships.

I remember the years I furiously tried to change my husband, Dave, and each of our children in different ways. Those were frustrating years, because no matter what I tried, it didn't work. My efforts to change the people I loved weren't helping matters. In fact, I often just made things worse.

As humans, all of us require space, or freedom, to be who we were created to be.

We want to be accepted as we are. We don't want people giving us the message, even subtly, that we must change in order to be approved or loved.

This doesn't mean we accept sin in other people and merely put up with it. It just means that *the way to change is prayer, not pressure.* If we love people and pray for them, God will work. For change to last, it must come from the inside out. Only God can cause that type of heart change.

———

Nagging is not an effective tool for change. Only prayer and God's love will do the job.

Taking Care of Yourself

Do you not know that your body is the temple (the very sanctuary) of the Holy Spirit Who lives within you, Whom you have received [as a Gift] from God? You are not your own, you were bought with a price [purchased with a preciousness and paid for, made His own]. So then, honor God and bring glory to Him in your body.

1 CORINTHIANS 6:19–20

God calls each of us to do something special in this life. But to do that, it is important we determine to take care of our body—the house He has given us to live in. To fulfill our God-given purpose, we can choose to find balance in what we eat and drink, get enough rest and exercise, and maintain a healthy lifestyle.

There is nothing worse than going

through life feeling bad all the time. As a person who struggled for years with nutritional choices and weight concerns, I know the feeling all too well. When we are unhealthy and out of balance, we just don't feel right. It's hard to do what God has called us to do when our bodies are sluggish because we haven't take care of them properly.

I believe it's actually a spiritual matter to know your body, what it needs, and what is really best for it. When you live in close relationship with God, your whole life is affected—spirit, soul, *and* body. I encourage you today to ask the Lord to help you determine to make healthy, wise choices that will benefit the body He has given you.

Ask God to help you follow the positive, healthy leading of the Holy Spirit and reject the negative, destructive promptings of the flesh.

What God Says About You

To the praise of the glory of his grace,
wherein he hath made us accepted in the
beloved.   EPHESIANS 1:6 KJV

It is not God's desire for us to feel frustrated and condemned in our lives. He wants us to realize that we are His children, and we are pleasing to Him.

There are plenty of voices trying to tell us who and what we aren't, but the closer we get to God, the more we hear Him telling us who we are—righteous in Christ, loved and well-pleasing to our heavenly Father.

The devil tells us we cannot possibly be acceptable to God because of our faults and sins, but God tells us that we are accepted in the beloved because of what His Son, Jesus, has already done for us.

If you have dealt or are dealing with any

guilt or condemnation today, remember that God never reminds us of how far we have fallen. He always reminds us of how far we can rise. He reminds us of how much we have overcome, how precious we are in His sight, and how much He loves us.

———————

The more you walk with God, the better you feel about the person He created you to be.

A Heart of Obedience

But thank God, though you were once slaves of sin, you have become obedient with all your heart to the standard of teaching in which you were instructed and to which you were committed.

ROMANS 6:17

Paul wrote that the believers in Rome were obedient with all their heart. This was important because it is possible to have halfhearted obedience—to be reluctantly obedient in behavior, but not be joyfully obedient with all your heart.

Obeying what God says is not just a matter of putting on a show, but a matter of having the right attitude. When you really want to please the Lord, you can't wait to follow His direction and instructions for your life.

I want to encourage you to come up

higher in your obedience. Be quick to obey, radical and joyful in your obedience. Don't be the kind of person God has to deal with for weeks just to get you to do the simplest little thing. Gladly do what God asks of you.

Obedience is more than a spiritual obligation—it is a spiritual opportunity! Your obedience to God will ultimately be rewarded. Obedience sows the seed necessary to bring another blessing into your life. You can never outgive God; He will always reward your seeds of obedience.

———

A heart of obedience results in the blessing of God on your life.

The Fruit in Your Life

A good (healthy) tree cannot bear bad (worthless) fruit, nor can a bad (diseased) tree bear excellent fruit [worthy of admiration].

MATTHEW 7:18

During my first few years of ministry, I spent a lot of my prayer time asking God for powerful and dynamic gifts that would help me be an effective minister. I focused on the gifts I needed, but I didn't give much thought to the fruit of the Spirit. I must admit I was more concerned about power than godly character.

Then one day the Lord impressed upon me, "Joyce, if you would have put even half as much energy and time into praying about and trying to develop the fruit of the Spirit as you have the gifts, you'd already have both."

As Christians, many of us pray that God will give us great spiritual power, but our first priority really should be developing the fruit of the Spirit—love, joy, peace, patience, kindness, goodness, faithfulness, gentleness, and self-control. The closer we get to God, the more fruit we will naturally produce.

We are known by our fruit, not by our gifts. When people see the fruit of God's Spirit in your life, they can see what God is doing in your heart. I encourage you today to ask God to cultivate the fruit of the Holy Spirit in your life on a daily basis. If you'll focus on the fruit, the power will follow.

———

People want to see if what you have is real before they listen to what you say.

How to Cultivate the Fruit of the Spirit

If we live by the [Holy] Spirit, let us also walk by the Spirit. [If by the Holy Spirit we have our life in God, let us go forward walking in line, our conduct controlled by the Spirit.]

GALATIANS 5:25

When the Holy Spirit lives inside us, we have everything He has. His fruit is in our spirit. The seed has been planted. The closer we are to God, the more we allow the seed of the fruit to grow up and mature in us by cultivating it.

We can cultivate all the fruit of the Spirit in a very practical way—by focusing on love and self-control, the first and last in the list. All of the fruit are based in love and actually are a form of love, but they are kept in place by self-control.

If you are concentrating on developing

the fruit of love, you won't become impatient or unkind with people. You will be good to them, supportive, and faithful. You'll determine to live your life in a way that blesses others, rather than looking out for your needs first. This is a result of love.

Self-control helps us to make those little choices throughout the day to respond with the fruit of the Spirit. As we respond with those little choices, we begin to form good, healthy, God-pleasing habits. If you continue to cultivate these habits, you will grow the fruit into an exceptional life in the Spirit.

———

When our fruit is "squeezed," and we get caught off guard, we discover how developed or undeveloped our fruit is.

Take Time to Listen

*In the morning You hear my voice,
O Lord; in the morning I prepare [a
prayer, a sacrifice] for You and watch
and wait [for You to speak to my heart].*

PSALM 5:3

In order to hear the voice of God, it is necessary to find times just to be still. This is an important part of living in close fellowship with God. It is how you recognize God's leading in your life. A busy, hurried, frantic, stressful lifestyle makes it very challenging to hear the Lord.

If you are hungry to perceive God's voice, find a place to get quiet before Him. Get alone with Him and tell Him that you need Him and want Him to teach you how to receive His guidance and direction. Ask Him to tell you what He has for your life and what He wants you to do that day.

And then I encourage you to do this: Take time to listen.

Even if you don't feel an immediate prompting in your spirit, God promises that if you seek Him, you *will* find Him (Jeremiah 29:13). You *will* get a word from God. He will lead you by an inner knowing, by common sense, by wisdom, or by peace. And each time, however He leads you, His leading will always line up with His Word.

I have found that God doesn't always speak to us right away or necessarily during our prayer time. He may end up speaking to you two days later while you are in the middle of doing something completely unrelated. Though it may not be in our timing, God will speak to us and let us know the way we should go.

———

Listening is a vital part of your daily time with God.

There Is Nothing Too Hard for God

Alas, Lord God! Behold, You have made the heavens and the earth by Your great power and by Your outstretched arm! There is nothing too hard or too wonderful for You.   JEREMIAH 32:17

In our own strength, there are many things that are impossible for us to accomplish. But with God—in His strength—all things are possible. There is nothing too hard for our God!

God desires for us to believe for great things. He wants our expectations and our plans in Him to be so great they leave us breathless. We can dream big when we are close to God, because there is nothing He can't do. James 4:2 tells us we have not because we ask not. We can (and should) be bold in our asking.

You may think, *Well, I don't have the*

gifts or talents to do great things in my life. The truth is God doesn't call the qualified; He qualifies those He calls. If you will simply be available, God will use your life in ways you could have never imagined.

Don't limit God in your life today. Take a bold step of faith and trust that He can do something bigger than you ever thought possible. His plan for your life is exceedingly and abundantly more than you could ask or think. So simply say, "Lord, I am open to whatever You have for my life. I trust that You will give me everything I need to accomplish the great plans You have for me. In Jesus' name!"

When you don't feel capable or qualified, lean on the Lord and receive His strength. He will give you what you need to accomplish more than you ever imagined.

The One Thing That Never Fails

Love bears up under anything and everything that comes, is ever ready to believe the best of every person, its hopes are fadeless under all circumstances, and it endures everything [without weakening]. Love never fails [never fades out or becomes obsolete or comes to an end]...

1 CORINTHIANS 13:7–8

The love of God bears up under anything that comes. It endures everything without weakening. It is determined not to give up no matter what. Even the hard-core individual who persists in being rebellious can be eventually melted by love. The Bible says, "...God's kindness is intended to lead you to repentance" (Romans 2:4 NIV). It is God's love—His goodness, His kindness—that can change a heart.

I understand it is hard to keep showing

love to someone who never seems to appreciate it or even respond to it. It is difficult to keep showing love to those individuals who take from us all we are willing to give, but who never give anything back. But we are not responsible for how others act, only how we act.

We have experienced the love of God by His mercy, and now He instructs us to show that same kind of love to the world. Our reward does not come from man, but from God. Even when our good deeds seem to go unnoticed, God notices and promises to reward us openly for them (Matthew 6:4). If you'll determine to demonstrate the love of God to all those around you, not only will they be blessed, but God will see to it that you are as well.

God is love, and love never quits on anyone.

Sometimes You Just Need to Take a Step

And Nathan said to the king, Go, do all that is in your heart, for the Lord is with you.   2 SAMUEL 7:3

Is there something you desire to do, but you have been waiting? Has God placed something on your heart, but you've been hesitant to take a step?

I believe God's timing is very important, and I certainly don't think we should rush into anything without praying about it and getting good godly counsel. However, I've noticed some people spend their lives stuck in "waiting mode." They're waiting when they could be taking a step in faith.

There is nothing more stressful than going through the motions each day only to get to the end of the day, week, month, or year and feel you are no closer to reaching

your dream or goal. God doesn't want you to live in that frustration. He wants you to seek His will, then take an action step. If you miss God—if you take a step in the wrong direction—God will get you back on course.

It's your heart attitude that matters. God is pleased when He sees that you are stepping out in faith, trying to please Him and accomplish His will for your life. So don't be afraid today. Take a step, and watch God begin to work in your life.

———

God will put the desire in your heart, and He will help you accomplish it. Your job is to simply use your faith to take a step toward that goal.

No Excuses

Be not afraid of them [their faces], for I am with you to deliver you, says the Lord. JEREMIAH 1:8

Whether it's a challenge, an obstacle, or an opportunity, when we know God is with us, we can face the things before us. Running away is not an option. Whatever you run from will always be waiting for you somewhere else. Our strength to conquer is found in staying close to God and pressing forward with Him.

Jeremiah was a very young man who was given a very big job. God told him that he had been called as a prophet to the nations. He was to be a mouthpiece for God. The thought of it frightened Jeremiah, and he began to make all kinds of excuses about why he could not do what God was asking.

Jeremiah was making the initial mistake

you and I often make—he was looking at himself and his own abilities. All Jeremiah needed to do was to look at God. He was also looking at people and wondering what they would think and do if he took the bold step God was encouraging him to take. God told Jeremiah to just remember that He was with him and that is all Jeremiah needed.

In the final verse of chapter one, the Lord told Jeremiah that the people would oppose him, but they would not prevail for one simple reason: "I am with you."

Whatever you're facing today, be encouraged. God is facing it with you.

———

When you take your eyes off your circumstances and put them on the Lord, you are sure to overcome.

Believe and Receive from God

For out of His fullness (abundance) we have all received [all had a share and we were all supplied with] one grace after another and spiritual blessing upon spiritual blessing and even favor upon favor and gift [heaped] upon gift.

JOHN 1:16

Again and again, the Bible speaks of receiving from God. He is always pouring out His favor and His blessing. In order to experience that favor and blessing—and in order to live in close fellowship with God—it is important that we choose to freely receive all that He offers us.

One of our biggest challenges is that we do not trust the word *free*. We quickly find out in the world's system that things really are not free. Even when we are told

they are free, there is usually a hidden cost somewhere.

But God's kingdom of grace and love is not like the world's. God's wondrous love is a gift He freely gives us. All we need to do is open our hearts, believe His Word, and receive it with thankfulness.

No matter what the situation around you looks like today, stand on the Word of God and trust that His goodness and grace are being poured out over your life. Believe it and receive it today.

———

The world's system says, "I'll believe it when I see it." God's kingdom says, "I'll believe it before I receive it."

The Power of Rejoicing

Rejoice in the Lord always [delight, gladden yourselves in Him]; again I say, Rejoice!   PHILIPPIANS 4:4

One of the best instructions God gives us in His Word is to be filled with joy and rejoice. What a great idea! This is a command that pleases God and brings direct and tangible physical, emotional, and spiritual benefit to us as we do it.

The apostle Paul, inspired by the Holy Spirit, told the Philippians twice to rejoice. Any time the Lord tells us twice to do something, we would be wise to pay careful attention to what He is saying.

Many times people see or hear the word *rejoice* and say, "That sounds nice, but how do I do that?" They would like to rejoice but don't know how! Paul and Silas, who had been beaten, thrown into prison, and

their feet put in stocks, rejoiced by simply singing praises to God. They chose to rejoice, despite their circumstances. They looked to the things they believed and not just to what they could see.

The same power that opened the doors and broke the shackles off Paul and Silas, and those imprisoned with them, is available to you today. No matter what you're dealing with, no matter what your coworkers say about you, no matter how much the kids are driving you crazy—take a moment right in the middle of the chaos to rejoice. It will make all the difference!

Rejoicing is not something that happens accidentally. It is a conscious decision that says, "I will praise God today, regardless of the circumstances around me."

The Mind of Christ

... We have the mind of Christ (the Messiah) and do hold the thoughts (feelings and purposes) of His heart.

1 CORINTHIANS 2:16

You and I have been given the mind of Christ—this is a promise straight from the Word of God. To begin to understand what that means, consider what Jesus' mind was like when He lived on the earth. He was confident in Who He was. He didn't let the negativity of others distract Him. He was fully aware that He was loved by God. And He was focused on accomplishing God's plan for His life.

Now take a moment to consider what thoughts occupy your mind. If you're distracted by the opinions of others, if you get upset easily, or if your mind is full of doubt and unbelief, you are not yet experiencing

all that God desires for your life. But things can change. God can renew your mind and bring you to a place of victory!

The renewal of the mind is a process that requires time, and it's a process that the enemy aggressively fights against. It is important we purposely choose right thinking. When we feel the battle for our mind is difficult, we can determine that, with God's help, we are going to purposely choose life-generating thoughts.

The renewing of the mind takes place little by little, so don't be discouraged if progress seems slow. Take a stand and say, "I will never give up! God is on my side. He loves me, and He is helping me!"

———

Our thoughts affect our inner man, our health, our joy, and our attitude.

A Simple Faith-Filled Prayer

Then you will call upon Me, and you will come and pray to Me, and I will hear and heed you.

JEREMIAH 29:12

Sometimes when we pray a simple prayer, simply presenting to God our need or the need of another person, we think that we should do or say more. But I have found that when I pray what the Holy Spirit has put on my heart, without adding to it out of my own flesh, the prayer is very simple and not necessarily exceedingly long.

When we take a moment to thank God for something or ask Him for something, our mind tells us, "Well, that's not long enough, or that is not eloquent enough. You should pray louder and harder if you really want God to hear you."

Many times we think we have to impress

God or other people with our prayers, and that's when we are robbed of the enjoyment that each simple prayer of faith is supposed to bring. When we live in close fellowship with God, we can say what is on our heart and believe that He has heard us, and that He will take care of it His way, in His timing.

Children are always good examples to follow when searching for simplicity. Listen to a child pray, and it will radically change your prayer life.

————

Keep prayer simple, and you'll enjoy it more.

Get Some Rest

Come to Me, all you who labor and are heavy-laden and overburdened, and I will cause you to rest. [I will ease and relieve and refresh your souls.]
MATTHEW 11:28

In 1 Kings 19, the prophet Elijah is terrified by the threats of Jezebel and is so discouraged he wants to die. Why in the world would Elijah, who on the previous day had triumphed over 450 prophets of Baal, suddenly allow himself to be so fearful and in such despair?

If you study the story closely, it's clear that he was totally worn out from pushing himself so hard for so long. Elijah's mind and body were completely exhausted, and his emotions had fallen apart. He was afraid, depressed, discouraged, and hopeless.

Nothing in life looks good to us when we are exhausted. It seems to us that nobody loves us, nobody helps us, nobody is concerned about us. We feel misused, misunderstood, and mistreated. Many times when we feel we have deep problems, our biggest problem is that we are exhausted.

The Lord knew that Elijah was worn-out. So he provided a good night's rest and a couple of good meals. It was such a simple answer to an extreme problem. Perhaps your answer is the same. Get some good, well-needed rest, and take in some healthy nutrition. They could be the most spiritual things you do today!

———

Strength, wisdom, and courage come from a place of rest.

God's Love Overcomes and Transforms

*So he got up and came to his [own]
father. But while he was still a long way
off, his father saw him and was moved
with pity and tenderness [for him]; and
he ran and embraced him and kissed
him [fervently].*   LUKE 15:20

Any person can be completely transformed
by regular, persistent doses of God's love. It
doesn't matter what they have done in life or
how good or bad we might consider them,
God's love can warm even the coldest heart.

Religion often gives people rules to
follow and laws to keep. It leads them to
believe they must earn God's love and favor
through good works. That is the exact
opposite of true biblical teaching.

God's Word says that "mercy triumphs
over judgment" (James 2:13 NKJV). It is the

goodness of God that leads men to repentance (Romans 2:4), not the keeping of laws and rules. Jesus came to give us something better than religion—He came to give us a close, personal love relationship with the Father through Him.

God's unconditional love does not allow people to remain the same; instead, it loves them while they are changing. Jesus said that He did not come for the well, but for the sick (Matthew 9:12). Much of our world today is sick, and there is no answer for what ails it except Jesus Christ and all that He stands for.

Unconditional love will overcome evil and transform lives.

Receiving Your Encouragement

... If I do not go away, the Comforter (Counselor, Helper, Advocate, Intercessor, Strengthener, Standby) will not come to you [into close fellowship with you]; but if I go away, I will send Him to you [to be in close fellowship with you].   JOHN 16:7

Do you sometimes find yourself wishing you had more encouragement, maybe from your family, friends, or coworkers? I think we all feel this way at one time or another. When you are feeling in need of encouragement and you don't seem to be getting that from other people, you can encourage yourself in the Lord (1 Samuel 30:6), and you can also receive encouragement from the Spirit of God.

Did you know that the Holy Spirit is called "The Encourager"? The Greek word

for "Holy Spirit" is *parakletos* and includes comfort, edification, and encouragement as part of its definition.

Jesus sent a Helper, a Strengthener, an Edifier, and an Encourager when He sent the Holy Spirit—and He sent Him to be in close fellowship with us. He lives inside of those who are believers in Jesus Christ.

If you're in need of encouragement, look to God first. He will never tell you that you're not going to make it. He will never tell you that your case is hopeless. Instead, He will encourage you that all things are possible in Him. He'll remind you that He loves you, He is with you, and He gives you the strength you need to do all He has called you to do.

———————

Open your heart to receive comfort, reassurance, and encouragement from the Holy Spirit today.

Letting Go of Past Mistakes

Therefore, [there is] now no condemnation (no adjudging guilty of wrong) for those who are in Christ Jesus, who live [and] walk not after the dictates of the flesh, but after the dictates of the Spirit.   ROMANS 8:1

It is so comforting to know that God's compassion and kindness are new every morning. Because of His great love, God has provided a way for your past to have zero power over you. You don't have to live in guilt and condemnation over your past failings; you can live with great hope for a bright future ahead.

God's part is to forgive us—our part is to receive His gracious gift of forgiveness, mercy, and a new beginning. Many people think, *How could God forgive me when I've done so many bad things?* But the truth is

that God is able to overcome and do far more than we could ever imagine that He could do for us (Ephesians 3:20).

When we ask God to forgive us, He is faithful and just to do it. He continuously cleanses us from all unrighteousness (1 John 1:9). We are said to be new creatures when we enter into a relationship with Christ (2 Corinthians 5:17). Old things pass away and we have an opportunity for a new beginning. We become new spiritual clay for God to work with. He arranges for each of us to have a fresh start—we simply must be willing to let go of the past and move forward with God.

Don't allow mistakes in your past to hold you back and threaten your future.

The Greatest Blessing

*But if anyone has this world's goods
(resources for sustaining life) and sees
his brother and fellow believer in need,
yet closes his heart of compassion against
him, how can the love of God live and
remain in him? Little children, let us
not love [merely] in theory or in speech
but in deed and in truth (in practice
and in sincerity).*

1 JOHN 3:17–18

The quickest way to be blessed is to decide
to be a blessing to others. When you choose
to have a generous heart that reaches out to
meet the needs of those around you, God
pours His provision into your life. A person
who is a river of blessing never runs dry.

Something deep in the heart of every
believer wants to help others. However,
selfishness can make us so aggressive about

our own desires that we become oblivious to the needs around us.

People are hurting everywhere. Some are poor; others are sick or lonely. Still others are emotionally wounded or have spiritual needs. A simple act of kindness to a hurting person can make that individual feel loved and valuable.

People can get caught in the trap of striving to have more and more. The struggle often produces little or no results. With God's help, we can strive to excel in giving to others. If we do so, we will find that God makes sure we have enough to meet our own needs plus plenty to give away.

There is no greater blessing than giving to others in need.

When You Feel Afraid

Fear not [there is nothing to fear], for I am with you; do not look around you in terror and be dismayed, for I am your God. I will strengthen and harden you to difficulties, yes, I will help you; yes, I will hold you up and retain you with My [victorious] right hand of rightness and justice.   ISAIAH 41:10

One of the benefits available to us as believers is the freedom from fear. If fear has had power over you in the past, you can be free of it. With God's help, you can learn how to overcome fear and begin to experience the abundant life God has planned for you.

Even when we do *feel* afraid, we don't have to give in to that feeling. We can go ahead and act on what God is calling us to do, because God will be with us to protect us and see us through. He will help us, go

before us to fight the battle on our behalf, and bring us through victoriously as we obey Him.

The message of "fear not for I am with you" is expressed all throughout the Bible. God does not want us to fear, because fear prevents us from moving forward and doing all He has planned for us. He loves us and wants to bless us, but fear tries to keep us from experiencing God's best.

The best attitude that a Christian can have toward fear is this: "Fear is not from God, and I will not let it control my life! I will confront fear. I won't give in to fear. When I feel afraid, I will keep moving forward because I know God is with me."

Jesus is your Deliverer. As you draw closer to Him, He will deliver you from fear.

Thinking Positive Thoughts

... Whatever is true, whatever is worthy of reverence and is honorable and seemly, whatever is just, whatever is pure, whatever is lovely and lovable, whatever is kind and winsome and gracious, if there is any virtue and excellence, if there is anything worthy of praise, think on and weigh and take account of these things [fix your minds on them].   PHILIPPIANS 4:8

If you want to improve your life, one of the first things you can do is improve your thoughts. There is tremendous power that comes when we choose to be positive people. God is positive, and in order to grow closer to Him, it is important to agree with Him (Amos 3:3) and think positively.

Having a positive mind-set and attitude does not mean you are not facing

reality or ignoring real problems. It simply means that you are agreeing with the Word of God and dwelling on God's promises rather than the negative, depressing things of the world.

Notice that throughout His life Jesus endured tremendous difficulties, including personal attacks, and yet He remained positive. He always had an uplifting comment, an encouraging word. He always gave hope to those He came near. We can follow that example today. When we choose a positive outlook, maintain positive expectations, and engage in positive conversations, we are following the example Jesus gave us, and we are drawing closer to our heavenly Father.

Your life will follow the direction of your thoughts.

A Life That Pleases God

Therefore, since these [great] promises are ours, beloved, let us cleanse ourselves from everything that contaminates and defiles body and spirit, and bring [our] consecration to completeness in the [reverential] fear of God.

2 CORINTHIANS 7:1

In order to live in close relationship with God, there are some decisions we have to make on a daily basis. There will be times we need to say no to some things to which we would rather say yes, and yes to some things to which we would rather say no. This requires wisdom and self-control, but thankfully, the Holy Spirit gives us both these things.

It is important to teach people to live holy lives because it is an important part of living in close relationship with God. It

doesn't mean we never make a mistake—it just means that our heart's desire is to live in a manner that pleases the Lord. This is accomplished by seeking to please God in our thoughts, conversations, companionship, music, entertainment, and so forth.

If our flesh desires to walk one way but God's Word teaches us to go another way, we can receive God's grace to obey what He is saying. The good news is that there is tremendous reward when we do.

When we choose to live our lives for God, rather than for self, we will experience righteousness, peace, and joy in the Holy Spirit. We will live in victory no matter what comes against us. That's a wonderful life—that is the abundant, overcoming, joy-filled life Jesus died to give us.

———

Invest in your future: Choose to live an uncompromised life for God.

Coming Boldly Before God

For we do not have a High Priest who cannot sympathize with our weaknesses, but was in all points tempted as we are, yet without sin. Let us therefore come boldly to the throne of grace, that we may obtain mercy and find grace to help in time of need.

HEBREWS 4:15–16 NKJV

Jesus understands our human frailty because He was tempted in every way that we are, yet without sinning. Therefore, because Jesus is our High Priest, interceding before the Father for us, we can come boldly to God's throne to receive grace.

God has already made provision for every human mistake, weakness, and failure. Salvation and continual forgiveness of our sins are gifts bestowed on us by God because of our acceptance of His Son, Jesus

Christ. In Him you can find forgiveness for every wrong thing you will ever do.

But the grace of God doesn't mean He doesn't deal with sin in our lives. Sin produces bondage and suffering. That is why God calls us to repent of our sin. Though God never condemns us, He does convict us of sin. He brings conviction so that we can repent, change our behavior, and find freedom in Christ.

Because of Jesus we can receive forgiveness, set aside sinful behaviors, and come boldly before God's throne of grace. All of these actions are essential components of living in close relationship with God.

——————

Even at our very best, we make mistakes. To live under condemnation will not help us live a holier life.

Don't Settle for Average

Now to Him Who, by (in consequence of) the [action of His] power that is at work within us, is able to [carry out His purpose and] do superabundantly, far over and above all that we [dare] ask or think [infinitely beyond our highest prayers, desires, thoughts, hopes, or dreams].

EPHESIANS 3:20

God loves to use common, ordinary, every-day people who have uncommon goals and visions.

That is what I am—just a common, ordinary person with a goal and vision that fuel my determination. But just because I am common and ordinary does not mean that I am content to be average. I don't like that word. I don't want to be average. I don't intend to be average. I don't serve

an average God; therefore, I don't believe I have to be average—and neither do you.

The Word of God demonstrates that anyone can be used mightily by God. The closer we draw to God, the more it is possible for us to do great and mighty things, things that amaze even us. If we believe that God can use us, and if we will be daring enough to have uncommon goals and visions, God will do powerful things in us and through us.

An "uncommon goal" is something that is nearly impossible without God—it is beyond all that we could dare to hope, ask, or think, according to His great power that is at work in us. This is what God will do in our lives if we will determine to not settle for average.

———

Be determined to stretch your faith for something great. We can choose to be common people with uncommon goals.

Adapt and Adjust

Love one another with brotherly affection [as members of one family], giving precedence and showing honor to one another.

ROMANS 12:10

Demonstrating the love of God is a daily exercise in giving preference to others. The natural reaction of our human flesh is not to prefer someone else above ourselves. We tend to look to our own needs first, but love requires us to adapt and adjust ourselves to the needs of others.

To allow someone else to go first, or to insist another person have the best of something, takes a mental adjustment on our part. We were planning to be first, or to have the best, but love adapts and adjusts— love chooses to be second instead. We were in a hurry to get where we wanted to go,

but love chooses to wait on someone else who seems to have a greater need.

The closer we are to God, the more we are actually rooted and grounded in love (Ephesians 3:17). Showing preference to someone else is a by-product of receiving God's love. The more we know we are loved, the more we want to share that love with others.

We have multiple opportunities to adapt and adjust almost every day. But if we are locked into our own plans, it will be difficult to do so. I encourage you to ask God to help you adapt and adjust with a joyful heart and a positive attitude. Ask Him to help you experience the joy and peace that come with loving others.

Only the love of God can change us from self-centered individuals into humble servants of God and others.

God Does Not Reject You

Although my father and my mother have forsaken me, yet the Lord will take me up [adopt me as His child].

PSALM 27:10

We were created for acceptance, not rejection. To be rejected is to be thrown away as having no value or as being unwanted, but God does the opposite. He draws you to Himself, and He considers you to be of extreme value. The fact that God sent Jesus to die for you demonstrates that you are loved and valued by God.

If you have struggled with self-image issues in your life, it may be due to a root of rejection. The emotional pain of rejection is one of the deepest kinds known. Especially if the rejection comes from someone we love or expect to love us, like parents or a spouse. Overcoming rejection is certainly

not easy, but we can overcome it through the love of Jesus Christ.

In Ephesians 3:18, Paul prayed for the church that they would know "the breadth and length and height and depth" of the love that God had for them. He said this experience far surpasses mere knowledge.

Watch for all the ways that God shows His love for you, and it will overcome the rejection you may have experienced from other people. Every time God gives you favor, He is showing you that He loves you. There are many ways He shows His love for you all the time. I encourage you to begin watching for those today.

————

A deep revelation of God's love for you will destroy any root of rejection.

Being God-Minded

You will guard him and keep him in perfect and constant peace whose mind [both its inclination and its character] is stayed on You, because he commits himself to You, leans on You, and hopes confidently in You.   ISAIAH 26:3

Jesus had a continual fellowship with His heavenly Father because He was focused on God. It is only possible to have full fellowship with someone when your mind is on that individual. This is a lesson we can learn as believers. In order to live in close relationship with God, it is important for us to live "God-minded."

It is tremendously uplifting to think on the goodness of God and all the marvelous works He has done. If you want to experience victory, take time to regularly meditate on God's unsurpassed greatness.

Giving thanks to God and being aware of His goodness are two sure ways to begin enjoying life.

Jesus said that the Holy Spirit would bring us into close fellowship with Him (John 16:7). If we choose to think about the Lord, it will bring Him to the forefront of our lives, and we will begin to enjoy a fellowship with Him that brings joy, peace, and victory to our everyday life.

God is always with us, but it is important that we think about Him and be aware of His presence.

Showing Mercy

Blessed (happy, to be envied, and spiritually prosperous—with life-joy and satisfaction in God's favor and salvation, regardless of their outward conditions) are the merciful, for they shall obtain mercy!   MATTHEW 5:7

Being merciful can be defined as giving goodness that is undeserved. Anyone can give people what they deserve. It takes someone who desires to be close to God to give goodness to people when they do *not* deserve it.

Revenge says, "You mistreated me, so I'm going to mistreat you." Mercy says, "You mistreated me, but I'm going to forgive you, restore you, and treat you as if you never hurt me." What a blessing to be able to give and receive mercy.

Mercy is an attribute of God's character

that is seen in how He deals with His people. Mercy is good to us when we deserve punishment. Mercy accepts and blesses us when we deserve to be totally rejected. Mercy understands our weaknesses and infirmities and does not judge and criticize us.

Do you ever need God or man to show you mercy? Of course, we all do on a regular basis. The best way to get mercy is to be busy giving it away. If you give judgment, you will receive judgment. If you give mercy, you will receive mercy. Remember, the Word of God teaches us that we reap what we sow. Be merciful! Be blessed!

———

Receive God's mercy and love. You cannot give away something you don't have.

Are You Willing to Be Trained?

For you see your calling, brethren, that not many wise according to the flesh, not many mighty, not many noble, are called. But God has chosen the foolish things of the world to put to shame the wise, and God has chosen the weak things of the world to put to shame the things which are mighty.

1 CORINTHIANS 1:26–27 NKJV

A quick look at the disciples Jesus chose shows us that God does not always choose those who seem to be qualified. It doesn't matter what gifts, talents, experiences you feel like you lack—God will provide all the teaching and training you need to do what He has called you to.

It is not always conventional, but God will prepare you in whatever way He chooses. Sometimes it is formal training,

but often it is not. God will use everything in your life to train you if you are willing to be trained. It's sad to say that many people have great callings on their lives, but they are too impatient to go through the preparation that is necessary to equip them for the job.

Esther had to have a year of preparation before she was allowed to go before the king. For twelve months, she patiently went through the purifying process, and God used her to save her people from wicked Haman's evil plot.

If you're feeling under-qualified for something you believe God is calling you to do, don't let that stop you. He will be your trainer. Learn what He is teaching you during this season, and be ready to step out when the opportunity arises.

God will equip you for the vision He has given you.

It's Not That Complicated

Truly I tell you, whoever says to this mountain, Be lifted up and thrown into the sea! and does not doubt at all in his heart but believes that what he says will take place, it will be done for him.

MARK 11:23

People think that life is complicated, but oftentimes we are the ones who make things more complicated than they need to be. Living for God really isn't that complicated at all.

Think about the simple, uncomplicated approach a child has to life. Children are going to have fun and enjoy themselves no matter what. They are joyful, carefree, and completely without concern. And children believe what they are told. It is their nature to trust completely and enjoy their life on a daily basis.

The closer we grow to God, the more childlike we can become. Of course, God wants us to be mature in our behavior, but He also desires for us to have an attitude of trust and dependence toward Him that is simple and childlike in nature. When God speaks to your heart or when you read something in the Bible, you can simply say, "I trust God and I believe it's true!" It's that simple.

If God says He will prosper me, I trust God and believe it's true! If God says He will heal me, I trust God and believe it's true! If God says He will help me forgive those who hurt me, I trust God and believe it's true. If God says He is with me and I'm never alone, I trust God and believe it's true!

The simplest thing you can do is decide to trust God and obey His Word in every area of your life.

Standing on What You Know to Be True

To you it was shown, that you might realize and have personal knowledge that the Lord is God; there is no other besides Him. DEUTERONOMY 4:35

A lack of knowledge causes fear, but confident and certain knowledge removes fear and brings strength and courage. Let me give you an example:

One night years ago I was lying in bed and heard strange noises coming from somewhere in the house. The longer I listened to it the more frightened I became. Finally shaking in fear, I journeyed out of the bedroom to see what it was. I had to laugh when I discovered it was ice cubes falling in the ice tray from the icemaker. For some reason, they were making a noise

they did not normally make. Because I had no knowledge of what was making that noise, I was needlessly afraid.

This is how people often feel in their lives. They don't know that God loves them, He is with them, and He has provided everything they need, so they are terrified by many things. When they hear of economic woes, they are fearful. When they hear that someone doesn't like them, they panic. When they hear a negative report on the evening news, they are terrified.

If you have the knowledge of Who God is *and* who you are in Christ, fear will have no place in your life. No matter what the situation looks like on the outside, you will have a peace in your heart, a confident assurance that fills every area of your life.

———

When the unfamiliar sounds of the world try to fill you with fear, be confident God is with you.

The Beginning, the Middle, and the End

Better is the end of a thing than the beginning of it, and the patient in spirit is better than the proud in spirit.

ECCLESIASTES 7:8

The most important thing is not necessarily how we start something. The beginning is important, but so is the middle, and so is the end. In fact, seeing something through is more important than just starting it, especially when it's something God has called us to do.

Some people get started with a bang, but they never finish. Others are slow starters, but they finish strong. Regardless of how we start, God wants us to stay faithful every step of the way—beginning, middle, and end. God's desire is for you to finish well.

God has a good plan for each of us. But it is a possibility, not a "positively." It won't "positively" happen if we don't cooperate with God. We have a part to play in seeing the plan come true. God won't do anything in our lives without our cooperation.

I challenge you to cooperate with God every single day of your life to develop your potential and see His plan come to pass. Every day you can learn something new. Every day you can grow. Every day you can be a bit further along than you were the day before. This is how you turn a great start into an even better finish.

Cooperate with God to develop your gifts, talents, and capabilities to their fullest extent. Be all you can be for the glory of God!

Living in the Now

Beloved, we are [even here and] now God's children; it is not yet disclosed (made clear) what we shall be [hereafter], but we know that when He comes and is manifested, we shall [as God's children] resemble and be like Him, for we shall see Him just as He [really] is. 1 JOHN 3:2

The choices we make today will determine whether we will enjoy the moment or waste it by worrying. Sometimes we end up missing the moment of today because we are too concerned about tomorrow. We are wise when we keep our mind focused on what God wants us to be doing now.

It's important to understand that God wants us to learn how to be *now* people. For example, 2 Corinthians 6:2 says, "Behold, now is the day of salvation" (KJV) and

Hebrews 4:7 says, "Today, if you would hear His voice and when you hear it, do not harden your hearts."

We will be more fruitful for the kingdom of God, and happier in our lives, if we will determine to live in the moment. Often we spend our mental time in the past or the future. When we don't really give ourselves to what we are doing at the moment, we become prone to worry and anxiety. However, if we will live in the now, we will find the Lord there with us. Regardless of what situations life brings our way, we will know that today—right now—is a part of God's plan, and He will bring us through it if we will trust in Him.

————

The time you have now is valuable. Don't waste your "now" worrying about tomorrow.

Finding the Wisdom in Balance

If any of you is deficient in wisdom, let him ask of the giving God [Who gives] to everyone liberally and ungrudgingly, without reproaching or faultfinding, and it will be given him. JAMES 1:5

If the tires on your vehicle get out of balance, you're in for a bumpy ride. I think the same thing can happen in our lives. If we get out of balance in one or more areas, what could be a smooth journey becomes bumpy and uncomfortable.

It's possible to go overboard and get out of balance in any area of life—even the best areas. A woman can damage her marriage by getting too focused on the children. If she spends every waking moment and all her energy doing for the kids but failing to pay attention to her husband's needs, her marriage will suffer.

Men (and many women too) get consumed in their careers. If a man spends all his time at work, neglecting his wife and his children, he may be a great provider, but he is lacking as a husband and a father. Balance is key.

This is true even in the small areas of life. Some people rarely talk, and some talk too much. Some people overplan, and some don't plan at all. Sometimes we think too highly of ourselves, and sometimes we think too lowly of ourselves. Even the littlest things can get out of balance.

Take an honest look at your life and see if there is any area where you are out of balance. Ask God for the wisdom to make the necessary correction so that you can live a balanced, healthy, joy-filled life.

When you ask God for wisdom, He gives it to you.

New Hope for Each Day

*It is because of the Lord's mercy
and loving-kindness that we are
not consumed, because His [tender]
compassions fail not. They are new every
morning; great and abundant is Your
stability and faithfulness.*

LAMENTATIONS 3:22–23

I like the way God has divided up the days and nights. No matter how difficult or challenging a specific day may be, the breaking of dawn brings new hope. God wants us to regularly put the past behind and find a place of "new beginnings."

Perhaps you have felt trapped in some sin or addiction, and although you have repented, you still feel guilty. If that is the case, be assured that sincere repentance brings a fresh, new start because of God's promise of forgiveness.

Only when you understand the great mercy of God and begin receiving it are you more inclined to give mercy to others. You may be hurting from an emotional wound. The way to put the past behind is to forgive the person who hurt you. You do yourself a favor when you forgive.

God has new plans on the horizon of your life, and you can begin to realize them by choosing to live in the present rather than the past. Thinking and talking about the past keeps you trapped in it. Let go of what happened yesterday, make the choice to receive God's love and forgiveness today, so that you can get excited about His plan for tomorrow.

———

God's mercy is new every morning.

The Importance of Treating Others Well

And do not grieve the Holy Spirit of God [do not offend or vex or sadden Him], by Whom you were sealed (marked, branded as God's own, secured) for the day of redemption . . .

EPHESIANS 4:30

I take a verse such as Ephesians 4:30 very seriously—I certainly do not want to "grieve the Holy Spirit" and I know you don't either. But how do we avoid doing it?

Reading the verses surrounding verse 30 makes it clear that one thing that grieves the Holy Spirit is when people mistreat one another. Consider that:

- In verse 29 we are encouraged to edify others with the words or our mouth.

- Verse 31 exhorts us not to be bitter, angry, or contentious and to beware of slander, spite, and ill will.
- In verse 32 we are told to be kind to one another, forgiving readily and freely.

When we realize it grieves the Holy Spirit when we are sharp or hateful with someone, or when we stay angry with someone, we will look to change.

I encourage you to ask God to help you see others the way He sees them. Ask Him to give you the kindness and patience you need to deal gently and lovingly with the people in your life, especially those who are unkind or difficult to be around. God will be pleased when He sees you have a heart attitude that wants to love and bless others.

One of the most important secrets to being happy is to walk in love.

More Than Enough

For if our heart condemns us, God is greater than our heart, and knows all things.   1 JOHN 3:20 NKJV

Guilt and condemnation are major problems for many believers. Satan's great delight is to make us feel bad about ourselves. He never tells us how far we have come, but rather, he constantly reminds us of how far we still have to go.

When the enemy attacks, you can say to him, "I'm not where I need to be, but thank God I'm not where I used to be. I'm okay, and I'm on my way."

Like David, we can learn to keep ourselves encouraged in the Lord (1 Samuel 30:6). None of us has arrived at the state of perfection and we cannot perfect ourselves. Sanctification is worked out in our lives

by the Holy Spirit as a process, so learn to enjoy the process.

The Bible teaches that we can have total forgiveness of our sins (total freedom from condemnation) through the blood of Jesus Christ. We don't need to add our guilt to His sacrifice. He is more than enough.

Jesus has already done everything that needs to be done—the work is finished. He has made a way for you to be forgiven. All you have to do is receive it. Complete forgiveness is completely free!

Don't let the devil fill your head with thoughts of unworthiness as a sinner. Begin to see yourself as the righteousness of God in Christ Jesus.

The Most Important Time of the Day

O God, You are my God, earnestly will
I seek You; my inner self thirsts for You,
my flesh longs and is faint for You, in a
dry and weary land where no water is.

PSALM 63:1

God loves it when you spend time with Him in fellowship and worship on a daily basis. It is this time with God that will change your outlook on life, give you the strength you need to overcome, and draw you closer to God.

It is often in our most private times with God that He does the deepest work in our hearts. It is the intimate time you spend with God, just loving Him and letting Him love you, that is going to cause you to grow up and see real spiritual transformation take place.

Life is busy, and there will always be

excuses not to spend time with God. There will always be errands to run, phone calls to make, messes to clean up, and so on and so forth. But if you will determine to put God first, seeking Him regardless of the distractions of the day, you will be greatly rewarded.

The more time you spend with God, the more confidence, peace, joy, strength, favor, and victory you will experience. He is the source of all these things. When you commit to spending time with Him, they will naturally flow into your life.

————————

There is nothing more important in your life than your personal relationship with Jesus Christ.

Being God-Loves-Me-Minded

Beloved, let us love one another, for love is (springs) from God; and he who loves [his fellowmen] is begotten (born) of God and is coming [progressively] to know and understand God [to perceive and recognize and get a better and clearer knowledge of Him].

1 JOHN 4:7

The more we meditate on God's unconditional love for us, the more we begin to really experience it. I urge you to practice being conscious and aware of God's love for you. Paul prayed in Ephesians 3 that the people would experience the love of God for themselves. That's the life God wants us to live—a life where we truly know and experience His never-ending, unconditional love.

I became conscious of God's love for me

through learning scriptures about His love. I meditated on them and confessed them out of my mouth. I did this over and over for months, and all the time the revelation of His unconditional love for me was becoming more and more of a reality for me. The same thing can happen for you. If you'll study God's Word, standing on every promise of the Father's love, you'll learn to live in the life-changing revelation that you are loved. Think of it like this: There is never one moment in your life when you are not loved.

———————

You are loved!

Led by the Spirit

*But I say, walk and live [habitually]
in the [Holy] Spirit [responsive to and
controlled and guided by the Spirit];
then you will certainly not gratify the
cravings and desires of the flesh (of
human nature without God).*

GALATIANS 5:16

It's interesting that in Galatians 5:16 Paul
did not say the cravings, or the desires of
the flesh, would no longer exist for the children of God. He said that we can choose
to be led by the Holy Spirit, and by making that choice, we would not give in to the
temptations that would try to separate us
from God.

There are many things that try to lead
us—other people, the devil, our own flesh
(our body, mind, will, or emotions). There
are many voices in the world that are

speaking to us, and often several at the same time.

In order to live in close relationship with God, it is imperative that we choose to be led by the Holy Spirit instead of those other voices. He alone knows the will of God and is sent to dwell in each of us, to aid us in being all God has designed us to be, and to have all God wants us to have.

Being led by the Spirit means He leads us by peace and by wisdom, as well as by the Word of God. He speaks in a still, small voice in our heart as we seek to live our lives for God. The more we follow His leading, the more we will be victorious in life.

I encourage you to begin each day by saying, "Holy Spirit, I will listen for Your leading today. Give me wisdom and peace so I can move in step with Your guidance."

Love Is Not Envious or Jealous

. . . Love never is envious nor boils over with jealousy.   1 CORINTHIANS 13:4

The Bible tells us that love is not envious or jealous, but jealousy is a little thing that can easily sneak into our lives if we are not careful. I have discovered the best way to get over envy or jealousy is to admit it. When you begin to feel jealous, be honest with God and ask Him to help you live free from it.

I must admit, like most people, I have dealt with jealousy at times in my life. There were days when I heard about a blessing that someone had received and I thought, *When will that happen for me?* But I've learned that when thoughts like that enter my mind, I need to immediately open my mouth and say, "I am happy for that person, and I refuse to be jealous and envious."

A mark of spiritual maturity—of living in close fellowship with God—is choosing to bless others and not be afraid they will get ahead of us. We can choose not to envy anyone else's appearance, possessions, education, social standing, marital status, gifts and talents, job, or anything else, because it will only hinder our own blessing.

———————

Be confident in the gifts and talents you have. God has given you everything you need to fulfill His call on your life.

You Can Be Honest with God

Then He was praying in a certain place; and when He stopped, one of His disciples said to Him, Lord, teach us to pray, [just] as John taught his disciples.

LUKE 11:1

A successful prayer life is not developed overnight nor can it be copied from someone else. God has a personal plan for each of us. We cannot always do what someone else is doing and expect it to work for us. Our prayer life is progressive—it progresses as we progress.

Often our prayers are too vague, meaning they are not clearly expressed. When we pray, we can be clear and honest with the Lord. The Bible teaches that we can pray boldly, expectantly, specifically. Your heavenly Father loves you, so you can come

fearlessly, confidently, and boldly to the throne of grace (Hebrews 4:16).

If you need help with your prayer life, be honest with God. Tell Him your needs. He will help you if you ask Him to do so. Like the disciples, simply ask, "Lord, teach me to pray."

An essential key to prayer is more confidence in the name of Jesus and less confidence in ourselves or anyone else to solve our problems. There is power in the name of Jesus.

Look How Far You've Come

So that [the genuineness] of your faith may be tested, [your faith] which is infinitely more precious than the perishable gold which is tested and purified by fire. [This proving of your faith is intended] to redound to [your] praise and glory and honor when Jesus Christ (the Messiah, the Anointed One) is revealed.   1 PETER 1:7

There are many tests that come our way every day. For example, our boss tells us to do something we don't want to do. Or we're going to pull into a parking space and someone zooms in and takes it. Or someone speaks rudely to us when we've done them a favor.

In 1 Peter 4:12, Peter tells us not to be amazed and bewildered by the tests that we have to endure because by them God

is testing our "quality," or our character. Peter knew the value of being tested in his own life. We all go through them, and we shouldn't be confused about why they come our way. Our hearts are being tested in order to prove our character.

Every time God gives us a test, we can tell how far we've come and how far we still have to go by how we react in that test. Attitudes of the heart that we didn't even know we had can come out when we are in tests and trials. This is a good thing because we can never get to where we need to be if we don't recognize where we are.

Everything that God permits in our lives is for our good, even if it doesn't feel good at the time.

Everyone Has Limitations

Moses' father-in-law said to him, The thing that you are doing is not good.

You will surely wear out both yourself and this people with you, for the thing is too heavy for you; you are not able to perform it all by yourself.

EXODUS 18:17–18

God used Moses' father-in-law to tell Moses that he was trying to do too much. This is a message God is still speaking to many in the body of Christ today. Sometimes we like to think we are invincible. We don't like anybody telling us that something is too much for us to handle, and we push on and on despite what we feel.

I was always the kind of person who thought I could do anything I set my mind to. I was thoroughly convinced I could accomplish the task before me. If someone

told me differently, it just made me determined to prove them wrong. I found out that if we have an attitude that we must do everything, no matter how tough the task is, we can hurt ourselves. It took some health problems to prove it to me. We cannot push ourselves beyond reasonable limits without eventually falling apart.

Here's the truth: God does not give us power for anything He does not tell us to do, but He always gives us the power and ability to do joyfully and peacefully all that He is leading us to do. God wants you to enjoy your life, and you cannot do that if you live under constant stress.

Are there any adjustments you need to make in order to be healthy, peaceful, and in balance?

Speaking Love to Others

Pleasant words are as a honeycomb,
sweet to the mind and healing to the
body.   PROVERBS 16:24

An important part of learning to really love other people is learning to love them with our words. The strength and encouragement we share with our words make a difference! People everywhere need someone to believe in them. They have been wounded by wrong words, but right words can bring healing in their lives.

It's easy to point out the flaws, weaknesses, and failures in those around us. This is a natural reaction, one that comes from our flesh. But these words don't bring life—they magnify all that is wrong with people and situations. But the Bible says in Romans 12:21 that we are to overcome evil with good.

The closer we are to God, the more we will learn to speak positive, encouraging words of life. God is positive, and as we walk with Him, we will learn to be in agreement with Him (Amos 3:3).

It is easy to find something wrong with everyone, but love overlooks the faults of others. First Peter 4:8 says it this way: "Above all things have intense and unfailing love for one another, for love covers a multitude of sins [forgives and disregards the offenses of others]."

Believing the best about people and speaking words that build them up is an important way of loving them.

Dealing with Disappointment

We are assured and know that [God being a partner in their labor] all things work together and are [fitting into a plan] for good to and for those who love God and are called according to [His] design and purpose.   ROMANS 8:28

There are many causes of disappointment, ranging from minor letdowns to major setbacks, and Satan wants to use the disappointments in our life to steal our joy. He wants to keep us discouraged so that we won't receive all that Jesus died to give us.

No matter what the causes of disappointment—physical, emotional, mental, or spiritual—as soon as we feel disappointment coming on, we can choose to resist it immediately and take whatever action the Lord leads us to take.

As soon as we start feeling disappointed

(especially if it is a recurring issue), it is important for us to say to ourselves, *I'm going to focus on the goodness of God in my life today. Whatever I may have lost is nothing compared to all I have gained in Christ.* When you have this attitude, it will keep those disappointments from turning to discouragement and even depression.

Jesus gave us the "garment of praise for the spirit of heaviness" (Isaiah 61:3 KJV). This is something we can choose to put on rather than sinking into despair when things don't go our way. Resisting the enemy and making a conscious, determined choice to joyfully praise God even in the tough times will allow you to overcome disappointments and be a powerful Christian each and every day.

When you're not sure what to do, stand on the Word of God and declare His promises over your life.

Always Choose Life

Now the mind of the flesh [which is sense and reason without the Holy Spirit] is death [death that comprises all the miseries arising from sin, both here and hereafter]. But the mind of the [Holy] Spirit is life and [soul] peace [both now and forever].   ROMANS 8:6

The best condition for our minds is—as Paul described in Philippians 4:8—pure, lovely and lovable, kind and winsome and gracious, thinking on those things that are virtuous and excellent. This is what it means to have the mind of Christ. I like to remind people that it is important that we think about what we're thinking about.

Many people falsely think that the source of their misery or trouble is something other than what it really is. They are blaming an outside condition when it is their

own inner thoughts that are causing them trouble. But if we'll choose to "watch over" our thoughts, we can begin to take every thought captive into the obedience to Jesus Christ (2 Corinthians 10:5).

A big part of drawing close to God is submitting our thoughts to Him. When we do this, the Holy Spirit is quick to remind us if our minds are beginning to take us in a negative direction. The decision then becomes ours—will we continue down that path or will we choose to think with the mind of Christ? One way of thinking leads to frustration, negativity, and despair, the other leads to life. Choose life today!

Your thoughts, your words, your attitudes, and your actions are all results of the daily choices you make.

A Discerning Heart

Lean on, trust in, and be confident in the Lord with all your heart and mind and do not rely on your own insight or understanding. In all your ways know, recognize, and acknowledge Him, and He will direct and make straight and plain your paths.   PROVERBS 3:5–6

People who tend to overthink things have a difficult time with faith. When we overthink something, worrying and obsessing about how we can fix a problem or create an opportunity, we are usually trusting in ourselves instead of God.

I used to be a class A, chief over-thinker. I had to have everything figured out. I had to have a plan all worked out in order to be happy. I was continually asking, "Why, God, why? When, God, when?" Then one day the Lord spoke to my heart and said,

"As long as you continue to live in reasoning, you will never have discernment."

Discernment starts in the heart and moves up and enlightens the mind. As long as my mind was so busy reasoning apart from the Holy Spirit and contrary to the truth in the Word of God, Jesus could not get through to me. He wants us to use our mind to reason, but He wants us to reason in a way that lines up with His Word and allows Him to be in control.

I have discovered that I can reason in my mind about an issue until it begins to confuse me, and when that happens, it is my signal to let it go and wait for God to reveal to me what only He can show me.

———

If we try to figure out why everything happens in life, we will not have peace of mind and heart.

Watch and Pray

All of you must keep awake (give strict attention, be cautious and active) and watch and pray, that you may not come into temptation. The spirit indeed is willing, but the flesh is weak.

MATTHEW 26:41

Fear is Satan's way of trying to prevent us from going forward so we cannot enjoy the life Jesus died to give us. And fear attacks everyone at some time. But fears are not realities. Fears are **F**alse **E**vidence **A**ppearing **R**eal.

Fear is a force that can weaken our lives if we give in to it, but God desires to strengthen us as we fellowship with Him in prayer. Faith is released through prayer, which makes tremendous power available for our lives.

The Bible teaches us to "watch and pray." With God's help, we can watch ourselves and the circumstances around us and be alert to the attacks the enemy launches against our minds and emotions. When these attacks are detected, we can go to God immediately in prayer. He is our strong tower, and when we are in Him there is nothing to fear.

The best way to resist the devil is to pray. Our honest, sincere prayers draw us closer to God. And the closer we are to God, the easier it is to dismiss fear.

———

Pray about everything and fear nothing. When fear knocks at the door, let faith answer.

Be Usable

I appeal to you therefore, brethren, and beg of you in view of [all] the mercies of God, to make a decisive dedication of your bodies [presenting all your members and faculties] as a living sacrifice, holy (devoted, consecrated) and well pleasing to God, which is your reasonable (rational, intelligent) service and spiritual worship. ROMANS 12:1

If you are a believer, your life has been consecrated to God, set apart for His use. You don't belong to yourself; you're a part of something bigger now. It is amazing to think that our lives are not our own; we have been bought with a price (1 Corinthians 6:20). We belong to God and our lives have a great purpose in Him!

As we get closer to God, we discover that we belong to Him, and that we are partners

with Him in life and we should make ourselves available daily for His use.

I spent many years praying for God to give me what I wanted. "God, if only You would give me this or that, then I'd be happy." But God showed me joy comes when I submit my plans to Him. Instead of asking Him to do what I wanted, I began to learn to ask what He wanted for my life.

God simply requires that we be available and usable. All of us can do that! We can submit our lives to God, trusting Him to work out His good plan for our future.

We may not get everything we want. But if we'll trust God, we'll realize that what He wants for our lives is greater than anything we could imagine.

Developing Trust

So trust in the Lord (commit yourself to Him, lean on Him, hope confidently in Him) forever; for the Lord God is an everlasting Rock [the Rock of Ages].

ISAIAH 26:4

How many times have we allowed trying situations that come our way to frustrate us and get us needlessly upset? How many years of our lives have we spent saying, "Oh, I'm believing God. I'm trusting God," when in reality, we are worrying, talking negatively, and trying to figure everything out on our own?

Sometimes we think we are trusting God just because we are saying the words, but inside we are anxious and panicky. It is good that we are taking the initial steps to trust God, but we must also realize we can still grow in trust. Trusting God is more

than just words—it's words, attitudes, and actions.

Trust and confidence are built up over a period of time. It usually takes some time to overcome an ingrained habit of worry, anxiety, or fear. That is why it is so important to "hang in there" with God. Don't quit and give up, because you gain experience and spiritual strength as you go through situations. Each time you become a little stronger than you were the last time. Sooner or later, if you don't give up, you will find yourself in a place of complete rest, peace, and trust in God.

———————

If you are in a time of trial, realize that worry is completely useless, and use the time to build your trust in God.

Do Your Best and Let God Do the Rest

Not that I am implying that I was in any personal want, for I have learned how to be content (satisfied to the point where I am not disturbed or disquieted) in whatever state I am.

PHILIPPIANS 4:11

We function best when we have a calm, well-balanced mind. When our mind is calm, it is without fear, worry, or torment. When our mind is well balanced, we are able to look the situation over and decide what to do or not to do about it.

Where many of us get in trouble is when we get out of balance. Either we move into a state of total passivity in which we do nothing, expecting God to do everything for us, or we become hyperactive, operating most of the time in the flesh. The closer we are to

God, the more well balanced we become. We are able to face any situation of life and say, "I will do what God leads me to do, but I trust Him to do the rest."

It is useless to keep trying things that are not working. Wait on God and be obedient to Him, and realize that His timing is perfect in your life. Even if God seems to be doing nothing about your situation, don't panic. As long as you are trusting God, He is working, and you will see the results in due time.

———————

Once we have done what God asks us to do, we can trust Him with the rest.

The Reward of Sharing Love

By this shall all [men] know that you are My disciples, if you love one another [if you keep on showing love among yourselves]. JOHN 13:35

One of the best ways to share Jesus with the world is to simply show love to others. Jesus Himself taught on love and walked in love, because that is what the world needs. The world needs to know that God is love and He loves each person unconditionally (1 John 4:8).

The Word of God teaches that God wants us to be committed to developing the character of Jesus Christ in our own lives and then go out as Christ's ambassadors to the world (2 Corinthians 5:20).

To be His ambassadors, it is crucial that we have our minds renewed to what love really is. Love is not merely a feeling we

have; it is a decision to treat people the way Jesus would treat them.

When we truly commit to walking in love, it usually causes a huge shift in our lifestyle. Many of our ways—our thoughts, our conversation, our habits—need to change. Love is tangible; it is evident to everyone who comes in contact with it.

Loving others does not come easily or without personal sacrifice. Each time we choose to love someone, it will cost us something—time, money, or effort. But the reward of loving others is far greater than the cost ever is.

———

Loving others does not depend on our feelings; it's a choice we make.

Understanding Your Forgiveness

*In Him we have redemption
(deliverance and salvation) through His
blood, the remission (forgiveness) of our
offenses (shortcomings and trespasses),
in accordance with the riches and the
generosity of His gracious favor.*

EPHESIANS 1:7

One of the biggest obstacles that keeps us
from celebrating the life that God has freely
bestowed upon us is our own sin consciousness. Sin is a problem for everyone, but it
does not have to be the complicating problem we tend to make it.

That we struggle with our sins is a huge
understatement. When we make a mistake,
display a weakness, or fail in any way, we
often doubt that God loves us, wonder if
He is angry with us, try to do all kinds of

good works to atone for our failure, and surrender our joy as a sacrifice for our error.

God desires to give us the gift of forgiveness. When we confess our sins to Him, He forgives us of our sins, puts them away from Him as far as the East is from the West, and remembers them no more (Psalm 103:12). But for us to benefit from that forgiveness, it is essential we receive it by faith.

When I was a new believer, each night I would beg God's forgiveness for my past sins. One evening as I knelt beside my bed, the Lord spoke to my heart, "I forgave you the first time you asked, but you have not received My gift because you have not forgiven yourself."

———————

Jesus bore your sins on the cross, and He offers forgiveness. You don't have to condemn yourself anymore.

Conscious of Your Righteousness

For our sake He made Christ [virtually] to be sin Who knew no sin, so that in and through Him we might become [endued with, viewed as being in, and examples of] the righteousness of God [what we ought to be, approved and acceptable and in right relationship with Him, by His goodness].

2 CORINTHIANS 5:21

Believers who are living in close fellowship with God are not going to think about how terrible they are. They will have righteousness-based thoughts that come through meditating regularly on who they are "in Christ."

Yet a large number of Christians are tormented by negative thoughts about how sinful they are, or how displeased God is with them because of their weaknesses and

failures. How much time is wasted living under guilt and condemnation?

I encourage you to think about how you have been made the righteousness of God in Christ Jesus. Remember: Thoughts turn into actions. If you want to enjoy the life Jesus died to give you, it is important to align your thinking with God's Word.

Every time a negative, condemning thought comes to your mind, remind yourself that God loves you, and that you have been made righteous in Christ.

———

You are changing for the better all the time. Every day you're growing spiritually. God has a glorious plan for your life.

God Hears and Understands

And this is the confidence (the assurance, the privilege of boldness) which we have in Him: [we are sure] that if we ask anything (make any request) according to His will (in agreement with His own plan), He listens to and hears us.

1 JOHN 5:14

Prayer is one of the things that reflects our closeness to God and our confidence in Him. If we pray about everything instead of worrying and trying to work it out ourselves, we say by our attitude and actions, "Lord, I trust You in this situation."

I believe many of us pray and then wonder if God heard. We wonder if we prayed properly or long enough. We wonder if we used the right phrases, enough Scripture, and so on. We cannot pray properly with doubt and unbelief. Prayer requires faith.

God has been encouraging me to realize that simple faith-filled prayer gets the job done. I don't have to repeat things over and over. I don't need to get fancy in my wording. I can just be me and know that He hears and understands me.

I encourage you to simply present your request and believe that God has heard you and will answer at the right time. Have confidence when you pray. Know that God hears and is delighted by simple, childlike prayer coming from a sincere heart.

———

Trust God to answer your prayers in His way and in His perfect timing.

Chosen by God

You have not chosen Me, but I have chosen you and I have appointed you [I have planted you], that you might go and bear fruit....   JOHN 15:16

When God chooses us for His divine plans and purposes, He uses different criteria than what the world uses. The world chooses people based upon their looks, their talent, education, or their accomplishments, but God doesn't do that. In fact, 1 Corinthians 1:26–29 tells us that God chooses what the world thinks is foolish to put the wise to shame, and what the world calls weak to put the strong to shame.

I am so glad to know God deliberately chooses us despite our weaknesses. When God got the idea for *Joyce Meyer Ministries*, He didn't look for the most qualified. He chose someone who loved Him, someone

who would work hard, and someone who was determined. I had no special talent, except I communicated well, but even then, my voice was a bit unusual. I am sure the world would have rejected me as unqualified, but thankfully God didn't.

What was true for my life is true for yours too. People may look at the exterior, but God looks at the heart. There may be others more qualified or talented, but His choice is not based on appearance, education, possessions, or even talents. It is based on your heart attitude. If you have a good heart toward God and an available attitude, God can do more through your life than you ever thought possible.

If we continue being faithful to God, we will eventually get where God wants us to be.

Refuse to Give Up

Also [Jesus] told them a parable to the effect that they ought always to pray and not to turn coward (faint, lose heart, and give up).   LUKE 18:1

Many people drift backward when things get difficult, but with God's help we can press forward no matter how tough things seem. It's not always easy, but it's always worth it. Victory is on the other side if we will keep pressing ahead.

Jesus told us in John 16:33: "In this world you will have trouble. But take heart! I have overcome the world" (NIV). Just because we go through a difficulty, we don't have to despair and give up. We can believe that Jesus has overcome every trouble, and we can "take heart." We weren't created to turn back in the face of trouble; we were created to be strong in the Lord and in His

mighty power. If we never had a challenge, we would not need faith.

There are numerous examples of people in the Bible who simply refused to give up. Zacchaeus could not be kept from Jesus, despite his shortcomings. The woman with the issue of blood pressed through the crowd and was rewarded for her determination. They reached their objectives because they boldly pressed ahead to receive all that God had for them.

When faced with an obstacle, instead of drifting back in fear, ask God to give you the strength and courage to go forward in Him.

————

When you feel like quitting, make the declaration: "I will not give up! God is with me, and He will help me move forward one step at a time!"

Letting Love Win the War

For though we walk (live) in the flesh, we are not carrying on our warfare according to the flesh and using mere human weapons. For the weapons of our warfare are not physical [weapons of flesh and blood], but they are mighty before God for the overthrow and destruction of strongholds.

2 CORINTHIANS 10:3–4

We are definitely in a war. The Bible teaches us that the weapons of our warfare are not carnal, natural weapons, but ones that are mighty through God for the pulling down of strongholds.

Part of growing closer to God is working with the Holy Spirit in pulling down the strongholds of selfishness, pride, and self-importance. Purposely taking the focus off of ourselves and doing something for

someone else while we are hurting is one of the most important things we can do to overcome evil.

When Jesus was on the cross in intense suffering, He took time to comfort the thief next to Him (Luke 23:39–43). When Stephen was being stoned, he prayed for those stoning him, asking God not to lay the sin to their charge (Acts 7:59–60).

If the church of Jesus Christ, His body here on earth, will wage war against selfishness and walk in love, the world will begin to take notice.

———

Walking in love is an important part of spiritual warfare.

From Glory to Glory

And all of us, as with unveiled face, [because we] continued to behold [in the Word of God] as in a mirror the glory of the Lord, are constantly being transfigured into His very own image in ever increasing splendor and from one degree of glory to another; [for this comes] from the Lord [Who is] the Spirit.   2 CORINTHIANS 3:18

How do you see yourself?

Are you able to honestly evaluate yourself and your behavior and not come under condemnation? Are you able to look honestly at how far you still have to go, but also at how far you have come?

In 2 Corinthians 3:18, Paul states that God changes us "from one degree of glory to another." In other words, the changes in us personally, as well as those in our

circumstances, take place in degrees. Where you are now is not where you will end up.

If you are born again, then you are somewhere on the path of the righteous. You may not be as far along as you would like to be, but thank God you are on the path. Enjoy the glory you are in right now and don't get jealous of where others may be, or condemned about where you are. Perhaps we won't pass into the next degree of glory until we have learned to enjoy the one we are in at the moment.

————————

Don't be too hard on yourself. God is changing you day by day and drawing you closer to Him.

Faith Is the Antidote

For God did not give us a spirit of timidity (of cowardice, of craven and cringing and fawning fear), but [He has given us a spirit] of power and of love and of calm and well-balanced mind and discipline and self-control.

2 TIMOTHY 1:7

If you're dealing with doubt, worry, anxiety, or fear in any area of your life today, faith is the antidote.

Think of it this way: If you or I ingested some kind of poison, we would need an antidote right away. The same is true when dealing with the toxic poisons of doubt, worry, anxiety, and fear. There must be an antidote received—and that antidote is faith.

When these joy-stealers come knocking at our door, we can answer with faith,

knowing that our faith in God defeats the enemy and will draw us closer to Him and allow us to rest and find safety in Him.

James 1:5–7 tells us that when we find ourselves in need of something, we can pray in faith, and God will answer without faultfinding. This is simple, but very important. Even if we have not been perfect in our ways, all we have to do is ask God with faith, and He will help us!

————————

Put your faith in the Lord. He has the power to deliver you and set your life in a whole new direction.

Believing the Best

... For out of the fullness (the overflow, the superabundance) of the heart the mouth speaks.   MATTHEW 12:34

The person who is close to God thinks positive, uplifting, edifying thoughts about other people as well as about himself and his own circumstances.

You exhort others with your words only after you have first had kind thoughts about that individual. Remember that whatever is in your heart will come out of your mouth (Mathew 12:34). Thoughts and words are containers or weapons for carrying creative or destructive power (Proverbs 18:21). This is why it is so important to do some "love thinking" on purpose.

I encourage you to send thoughts of love toward other people. Speak words of encouragement. Come alongside others

and urge them to press forward in their spiritual life. Speak words that make others feel better and that encourage and strengthen them.

Everyone has enough problems already. We don't need to add to their troubles by tearing them down. We can build up one another in love (1 Thessalonians 5:11). Love always believes the best of everyone (1 Corinthians 13:7).

We are living in obedience to the Word of God when our thoughts, actions, and attitudes line up with what it says.

Better Than Self-Confidence

I have strength for all things in Christ Who empowers me [I am ready for anything and equal to anything through Him Who infuses inner strength into me; I am self-sufficient in Christ's sufficiency].   PHILIPPIANS 4:13

Confidence is generally referred to as "self-confidence" because we all know that we need to feel good about ourselves if we are ever to accomplish anything in life. We have been taught that all people have a basic need to believe in themselves. However, that is not the complete truth.

More than believing in ourselves—we need to believe in Jesus in us. We can't really think highly of ourselves apart from Him. We can do amazing things, but only through Christ!

If we believe the false assumption of

"self-confidence," we will create many complicated problems. We will live in fear and insecurity, and we will settle for less than our full potential in Christ.

Don't be concerned about yourself, your weaknesses, or your strengths. Put your focus squarely on God. If you are weak, He can strengthen you. If you have any strength, it is because He gave it to you. Either way, focus on the Lord and place your confidence in Him.

We do not need self-confidence; we need God-confidence.

Two Powerful Words for Your Life

...Fear not; stand still (firm, confident, undismayed) and see the salvation of the Lord which He will work for you today...   EXODUS 14:13

Jesus said that the devil is a liar and the father of all lies (John 8:44). The truth is not in him. He tries to use falsehood to deceive God's people into fear so they will not be bold enough to be obedient to the Lord and reap the blessings He has in store for them.

Often the fear of something is worse than the thing itself. If we will be courageous and determined to do whatever it is we fear, we will discover it is not nearly as bad as we thought it would be.

Throughout the Word of God we find the Lord saying to His people, "Fear not." I believe the reason He did that was to

encourage them so they would not allow Satan to rob them of their blessing.

In the same way, because He knows we tend to be fearful, the Lord continues to exhort and encourage us to press through what lies before us to do His will. Why? Because He knows that great blessings await us.

The enemy wants to tell you that your current situation is evidence that your future will be a failure, but the Bible teaches us that no matter what our present circumstances, nothing is impossible with God (Mark 9:23).

———

There is victory in store for your life if you'll put these two words into practice: Fear not.

A Grateful Attitude

Enter into His gates with thanksgiving and a thank offering and into His courts with praise! Be thankful and say so to Him, bless and affectionately praise His name!   PSALM 100:4

A person flowing in the mind of Christ will find his thoughts filled with praise and thanksgiving. A powerful life cannot be lived without thanksgiving. The Bible instructs us over and over in the principle of thanksgiving. It is a life principle.

Many doors are opened to the enemy through complaining. Some people are physically ill and live weak, powerless lives due to this disease called complaining that attacks the thoughts and conversations of people.

We can offer thanksgiving at all times—in every situation, in all things—and by so

doing, enter into the victorious life Jesus died to give us. It may require a sacrifice of praise or thanksgiving, but a person who consciously takes the time to be grateful is always happier than someone who does not.

You can choose to be filled with gratitude not only toward God but also toward people. Expressing appreciation blesses the people around you, but it is also good for you because it releases joy in your life.

Offer thanksgiving to God, and as you do, you will find your heart filling with life and light.

Grace Versus Works

[Therefore, I do not treat God's gracious gift as something of minor importance and defeat its very purpose]; I do not set aside and invalidate and frustrate and nullify the grace (unmerited favor) of God. For if justification (righteousness, acquittal from guilt) comes through [observing the ritual of] the Law, then Christ (the Messiah) died groundlessly and to no purpose . . .

GALATIANS 2:21

It is curious that we come to God through Christ just as we are, relying on nothing but the blood of Jesus to cleanse us from our sins. Our hearts are full of gratitude because we know we don't deserve it. But from that moment on, for some reason, we tend to want to earn everything else He gives us.

We assume God won't bless us because we

think we don't deserve it. We didn't read the Bible enough, didn't pray enough, or lost our temper in traffic. We find a million ways to be disqualified from God's love. God never stops loving us, but we often stop receiving it.

Despite all our emphasis on faith, we try to live a life that was brought into being and designed by God to be lived by grace in our own strength, by works. It's no wonder we feel frustrated and confused—both are signs that we are out of grace and into works.

When you have a problem in your life that you do not know how to handle, what you need is not more figuring and reasoning, but more grace. If you can't find a solution to your problem, simply trust God to reveal it to you. You don't have to earn God's help or qualify for it—He wants to equip and empower you every single day through His grace.

———

Where works fail, grace always succeeds.

Comfortable and Confident in Prayer

Be unceasing in prayer [praying perseveringly].

1 THESSALONIANS 5:17

The closer we are in our relationship with God, the more confident we become in prayer. The truth is that God wants us to be so confident and comfortable in prayer that it becomes like breathing, an effortless action that we do every moment we are alive. We don't work and struggle at breathing, and neither will we in prayer if we understand its simplicity.

To pray without ceasing like Paul talks about in 1 Thessalonians 5:17 does not mean that we must be offering some kind of formal prayer every moment twenty-four hours a day. It means that all throughout the day we can be in a prayerful attitude.

As we encounter each situation or as things come to our minds that need attention, we can simply submit them to God in prayer. I often say, "Pray your way through the day."

Don't forget: It is not the length or loudness or eloquence of prayer that makes it powerful—prayer is made powerful by the sincerity of it and the faith behind it.

We can pray anywhere at anytime about anything. Our prayers can be verbal or silent, long or short, public or private—the most important thing is that we pray.

Closer to God Each Day

For this is My Father's will and His purpose, that everyone who sees the Son and believes in and cleaves to and trusts in and relies on Him should have eternal life, and I will raise him up [from the dead] at the last day.   JOHN 6:40

The life for a Christian was never meant to be all about following rules and meeting a list of requirements. Yes, God gives us directions and instructions for living, but these aren't meant to be religious duties; they are principles that will help us discover the joyful, abundant, overflowing life Jesus died to give us.

God desires for you to move past "religion" and live in a deep, close, intimate relationship with Him. This is what it means to be closer to God. He is not some distant deity who is legalistic, cold and out

of reach. God is your heavenly Father Who loves you unconditionally and without fail.

No matter what happened in your past, no matter how many times you've failed, no matter what disadvantages you think you may have, you can live in close relationship to God. He will forgive you. He will comfort you. He will walk with you. And He will never leave you or forsake you.

God loves you more than you could ever imagine. All you have to do is receive His love today.

———————

Living "closer to God each day" is simply a matter of receiving God's love and learning to love Him in return.

About the Author

Joyce Meyer is one of the world's leading practical Bible teachers. Her daily broadcast, *Enjoying Everyday Life*, airs on hundreds of television networks and radio stations worldwide.

Joyce has written more than 100 inspirational books. Her best sellers include *Power Thoughts*; *The Confident Woman*; *Look Great, Feel Great*; *Starting Your Day Right*; *Ending Your Day Right*; *Approval Addiction*; *How to Hear from God*; *Beauty for Ashes*; and *Battlefield of the Mind*.

Joyce travels extensively, holding conferences throughout the year and speaking to thousands around the world.

Other Books by Joyce Meyer

Devotionals

Love Out Loud
New Day, New You
The Power of Being Thankful
Power Thoughts Devotional
Starting Your Day Right*
Trusting God Day By Day

* Also available in Spanish

Joyce Meyer Ministries U.S. & Foreign Office Addresses

Joyce Meyer Ministries

P.O. Box 655
Fenton, MO 63026
USA
(636) 349-0303

Joyce Meyer Ministries—Canada

P.O. Box 7700
Vancouver, BC V6B 4E2
Canada
(800) 868-1002

Joyce Meyer Ministries—Australia

Locked Bag 77
Mansfield Delivery Centre
Queensland 4122
Australia
(07) 3349 1200

Joyce Meyer Ministries—England

P.O. Box 1549
Windsor SL4 1GT
United Kingdom
01753 831102

Joyce Meyer Ministries—South Africa

P.O. Box 5
Cape Town 8000
South Africa
(27) 21-701-1056